A NORTON CRITICAL EDITION

Thomas Middleton
and
Thomas Dekker
THE ROARING GIRL

AUTHORITATIVE TEXT
CONTEXTS
CRITICISM

Edited by

JENNIFER PANEK

UNIVERSITY OF OTTAWA

W. W. NORTON & COMPANY
New York • London

W. W. Norton & Company has been independent since its founding in 1923, when William Warder Norton and Mary D. Herter Norton first published lectures delivered at the People's Institute, the adult education division of New York City's Cooper Union. The firm soon expanded its program beyond the Institute, publishing books by celebrated academics from America and abroad. By mid-century, the two major pillars of Norton's publishing program—trade books and college texts—were firmly established. In the 1950s, the Norton family transferred control of the company to its employees, and today—with a staff of four hundred and a comparable number of trade, college, and professional titles published each year—W. W. Norton & Company stands as the largest and oldest publishing house owned wholly by its employees.

Manufacturing by the Courier Companies—Westford division.
Book design by Antonina Krass.
Production manager: Eric Pier-Hocking.

Library of Congress Cataloging-in-Publication Data
Middleton, Thomas, d. 1627.
    The roaring girl : authoritative text, contexts, criticism / Thomas Middleton and Thomas Dekker ; edited by Jennifer Panek. — 1st ed.
        p. cm. — (A Norton critical edition)
    Includes bibliographical references.
    ISBN 978-0-393-93277-5 (pbk.)
    1. Cutpurse, Moll, 1584?–1659—Drama. 2. Middleton, Thomas, d. 1627. Roaring girl. I. Dekker, Thomas, ca. 1572–1632. II. Panek, Jennifer. III. Title.
    PR2714.R6 2010
    822'.3—dc22

                                                                2010043291

W. W. Norton & Company, Inc., 500 Fifth Avenue
New York, NY 10110
wwnorton.com

W. W. Norton & Company Ltd., Castle House,
75/76 Wells Street, London W1T 3QT

1 2 3 4 5 6 7 8 9 0

The Editor

JENNIFER PANEK is Associate Professor of English at the University of Ottawa. She is the author of *Widows and Suitors in Early Modern English Comedy* (Cambridge UP, 2004) as well as articles and book chapters on early modern culture, gender, and sexuality.

W. W. NORTON & COMPANY, INC.
Also Publishes

ENGLISH RENAISSANCE DRAMA
edited by David Bevington et al.

THE NORTON ANTHOLOGY OF AFRICAN AMERICAN LITERATURE
edited by Henry Louis Gates Jr. and Nellie Y. McKay et al.

THE NORTON ANTHOLOGY OF AMERICAN LITERATURE
edited by Nina Baym et al.

THE NORTON ANTHOLOGY OF CHILDREN'S LITERATURE
edited by Jack Zipes et al.

THE NORTON ANTHOLOGY OF CONTEMPORARY FICTION
edited by R. V. Cassill and Joyce Carol Oates

THE NORTON ANTHOLOGY OF DRAMA
edited by J. Ellen Gainor, Stanton B. Garner Jr., and Martin Puchner

THE NORTON ANTHOLOGY OF ENGLISH LITERATURE
edited by M. H. Abrams and Stephen Greenblatt et al.

THE NORTON ANTHOLOGY OF LITERATURE BY WOMEN
edited by Sandra M. Gilbert and Susan Gubar

THE NORTON ANTHOLOGY OF MODERN AND CONTEMPORARY POETRY
edited by Jahan Ramazani, Richard Ellmann, and Robert O'Clair

THE NORTON ANTHOLOGY OF POETRY
edited by Margaret Ferguson, Mary Jo Salter, and Jon Stallworthy

THE NORTON ANTHOLOGY OF SHORT FICTION
edited by R. V. Cassill and Richard Bausch

THE NORTON ANTHOLOGY OF THEORY AND CRITICISM
edited by Vincent B. Leitch et al.

THE NORTON ANTHOLOGY OF WORLD LITERATURE
edited by Sarah Lawall et al.

THE NORTON FACSIMILE OF THE FIRST FOLIO OF SHAKESPEARE
prepared by Charlton Hinman

THE NORTON INTRODUCTION TO LITERATURE
edited by Alison Booth and Kelly J. Mays

THE NORTON READER
edited by Linda H. Peterson and John C. Brereton

THE NORTON SAMPLER
edited by Thomas Cooley

THE NORTON SHAKESPEARE, BASED ON THE OXFORD EDITION
edited by Stephen Greenblatt et al.

For a complete list of Norton Critical Editions, visit
www.wwnorton.com/college/English/nce_home.htm

Contents

Criticism

Introduction

The Roaring Girl herself, some few days hence,
Shall on this stage give larger recompence;
Which mirth that you may share in, herself does woo you,
And craves this sign: your hands to beckon her to you.

(Epilogue 35–40)

With these lines, Middleton and Dekker script a boy in women's clothing—the young actor who has played Moll Cutpurse for the duration of *The Roaring Girl*—to transform the conventional end-of-show applause of the audience at the Fortune playhouse into an invitation, beckoning the real-life Moll—a sometime thief and notorious cross-dresser named Mary Frith—to come and perform on that same stage. That Frith did so, "some few days hence" from the play's first performance in late April or early May of 1611, is witnessed by an entry in the Consistory Court of London's *Correction Book*, which records how she appeared "at ye Fortune in man's apparel and in her boots and with a sword by her side" and "sat there upon the stage in the public view of all the people . . . and played upon her lute and sang a song." With this act, Frith managed to offend the city's moral authorities in at least three ways at once: by defying the law which barred women from the public stage, by openly wearing the clothes and accoutrements of the opposite sex, and by entertaining her audience with "immodest and lascivious speeches," which apparently included a teasing invitation to follow her home and find out which sex she *really* was. A stint in Bridewell, London's workhouse-prison for petty offenders, did little to discourage her: later that year, she was strolling around St. Paul's Cathedral on Christmas day, "with her petticoat tucked up about her in the fashion of a man . . . to the disgrace of all womanhood."[1]

The Roaring Girl manages to pull off the unusual feat of being both a topical artifact of 1611 London, and a play which can engage modern readers and audiences in the most current questions of gender

---

1. Both incidents are described in the excerpt from the *Correction Book*, pp. 147–48 of this Norton Critical Edition.

identity and sexual politics. If scholars today have a tendency to see its protagonist through their own feminist or queer lenses, we might remember that even in her own time, Mary Frith the individual was overlaid with the myriad of meanings that playwrights, poets, legal authorities, moralists, and ordinary London citizens attached to the increasingly legendary figure of Moll Cutpurse. What we know about the real Mary Frith comes down to us mainly through court records: she was about fifteen when she first ran afoul of the law in 1600, arrested along with two other young women for stealing a man's purse in Clerkenwell; similar charges appear two years later, and more serious ones—breaking into a house to steal more than ten pounds worth of goods—in 1609.[2] By January of 1610, however, she was celebrating a "not guilty" verdict on the burglary charges, and had already begun to attain a certain amount of celebrity for her cross-dressing and other attention-getting exploits: that summer, the playwright John Day wrote "A Book called the Mad Pranks of Merry Moll of the Bankside, with her walks in Man's Apparel and to what Purpose." "To what Purpose," unfortunately, will never quite be known, as no copy of the book survives, but the "Mad" and "Merry" of its title suggest a light-hearted, even celebratory approach, certainly not a moralizing criminal exposé. Middleton and Dekker's *The Roaring Girl* and the Fortune performance described above followed soon after. For that 1611 Christmas jaunt "in the fashion of a man"—plus assorted charges of swearing, drunkenness, and associating with "Ruffianly swaggering and lewd company"—Frith found herself once again sentenced to Bridewell and also to public penance. To that solemn occasion, as John Chamberlain records (see his letter, p. 120), she arrived impressively drunk and upstaged the minister who was supposed to be preaching against her sins. That Frith challenged men to duels, as Moll does Laxton in 3.1 of *The Roaring Girl*, is borne out by Chamberlain's note that she "challenged the field of diverse gallants"; that she ran a quasi-legal trade in returning stolen goods to their owners—as Moll describes at 5.1.305–307—is confirmed by a 1621 lawsuit brought against her by one Margaret Dell, who allegedly pickpocketed a man during a sexual encounter and did not appreciate being brought to Frith's house for identification (see pp. 148–50). The last legal document to bear witness to Frith's life is her will, signed on June 6, 1659, and leaving most of her estate to Frances Edmonds, her niece (pp. 150–51).

There is one other document which might come as a surprise to readers who first encounter Moll in *The Roaring Girl*: in its records for March 23, 1614, the Parish Register of Saint Saviour's (also called

2. Gustav Ungerer, "Mary Frith, Alias Moll Cutpurse, in Life and Literature," *Shakespeare Studies* 28 (2000): 42–84, pp. 62–64.

St. Mary Overbury) in Southwark lists the marriage of Mary Frith to Lewknor Markham. Little is known about Markham, and even less about why Frith might have married him. What is known, though, is that the couple lived together only briefly, if at all: in 1624, when a hatmaker named Richard Pooke sued Frith over an allegedly unpaid hat bill, he reported that she was "married to one Markham who hath not lived with her this ten years or thereabouts." Pooke and his lawyer also claimed that Frith used her married status to evade lawsuits such as theirs, and it is indeed tempting to speculate that it was from the start a marriage of convenience, entered into for precisely some such economic motive.[3] There is little reason, though—other than how the Moll mythology plays to what we'd like to believe of a convention-defying female transvestite—to conclude that this was necessarily the case. With divorce unavailable, Mary and Lewknor would certainly not have been the only couple in early modern London living out a long separation after an ill-advised match went sour.

While Middleton and Dekker could not have foreseen Frith's marriage back in 1611, when their resolutely chaste and independent Moll announces that it will be doomsday before she submits to being a wife, its omission from a much later and even more substantial piece of Moll Cutpurse myth-making—her purported autobiography, published in 1662 under the title *The Life and Death of Mrs. Mary Frith, Commonly Called Moll Cutpurse*[4]—reminds us not to mistake textual representations of Moll for evidence of a real woman's life in early modern London. The line between fact and fabrication in the "autobiography" is difficult to draw, but much of it would seem to fall into the latter category: its Moll shares characteristics with an earlier virago of London folklore, Long Meg of Westminster (on whom, see Simon Sheperd, pp. 199–212); the *Oxford Dictionary of National Biography* aptly describes it as "a patchwork of legends and representations"; and its veracity is further complicated by the fact that its author or authors appropriated Frith for their own political ends, refashioning her into a royalist heroine who spent the civil war years in counterrevolutionary exploits.[5] In this Norton Critical Edition, I have included excerpts from *The Life and Death* which relate to Moll as she is portrayed in *The Roaring Girl*, focusing on her gender-bending and her role as an intermediary between London thieves and their victims, but they no more represent the historical individual than does the play's characterization. Authors shaped a Moll who served their purposes: for Middleton and Dekker, a

3. On Frith's marriage, see Mark Eccles, "Mary Frith, The Roaring Girl," *Notes and Queries* 32.1 (March 1985): 65–66; Ungerer 52–54.
4. The title "Mrs," an abbreviation of "mistress," was used in this period for unmarried women as well as married ones.
5. Melissa Mowry, "Thieves, Bawds, and Counterrevolutionary Fantasies," *Journal for Early Modern Cultural Studies* 5.1 (2005): 26–48.

delightfully eccentric heroine who defies her bad reputation by proving both chaste and honest; for Nathaniel Field in *Amends for Ladies*, a foul-mouthed bawd with a walk-on part as contrast to a virtuous wife; for the Restoration-era author of *The Life and Death*, a louche businesswoman who taunted the Puritans while pimping both men and women out of an innovative brothel; for the eighteenth- and nineteenth-century compilers of criminal biographies, all things sensational, from a hermaphrodite to a highway(wo)man. Moll even reappears in a twentieth-century novel, Ellen Galford's *Moll Cutpurse: Her True History* (1985), fashioned into a lesbian who enjoys a long-term love affair with an apothecary named Bridget.

With the growth of feminist criticism through the 1980s and 1990s, and on up to the present, Moll Cutpurse has come to serve important scholarly purposes as well. A search on *Roaring Girl* in the online *MLA Bibliography* charts the play's rise from obscurity—only eight brief articles between 1934 and 1977, almost all on textual or authorship issues—to the forefront of early modern gender studies, with thirty-four entries between 1983 and 2008. More than Shakespeare's cross-dressed girl heroines, like Rosalind in *As You Like It* or Viola in *Twelfth Night*, who pursue marital goals in the protection of male disguise, Moll—a grown woman who has no interest in passing as a man but combines male and female attire as she pleases, smokes a pipe, defends herself with a sword, and flatly refuses marriage—provides fertile ground for investigating our central questions about gender and sexuality in early modern English culture and in our own. *The Roaring Girl* has become a focal point for inquiry into cultural constructions and performances of gender; androgyny, hermaphroditism and monstrosity; cross-dressing as theatrical convention and as social transgression; early modern women's economic activities; homoeroticism and the extent to which modern notions of sexual orientation are relevant to early modern sexualities. Attending to both the play and the historical figure of Mary Frith, critics debate the extent to which *The Roaring Girl* unsettles the gendered norms of its period. Does it offer a radical alternative to conventional assumptions about women's nature and feminine social roles? Does Moll's status as "deviant" merely reaffirm the dominance of the beliefs and conventions she defies? Do Middleton and Dekker whitewash the genuinely transgressive Frith into a harmless eccentric who ultimately reinforces patriarchal order by championing heterosexual marriage, legitimate inheritance, and the power of aristocratic gentlemen over the criminal underclass? The best of such work, including the gender-based criticism reprinted in this Norton Critical Edition, recognizes that there are few straightforward answers to these questions.

The play itself seems to delight in ambiguities and contradictions in its portrayal of Moll's challenge to the gendered social order. The same Moll who gives an impassioned defense of women who succumb to men's advances out of economic necessity—"Distressed needlewomen and trade-fall'n wives. / Fish that needs must bite or themselves be bitten" (3.1.96–97)—can elsewhere be found speculating cynically about how many women in London would happily give up their chastity if only men were more skilled in the arts of seduction (2.1.326–335). Incisive criticism of a wife's subjection to her husband—"Marriage is but a chopping and changing, where a maiden loses one head and has a worse i'the'place" (2.2.44–46)—rubs shoulders with more equivocal remarks which seem at least to pay lip service to the prescribed domestic hierarchy. How, for instance, is one to read Moll's assertion that "a wife, you know, ought to be obedient, but I fear me I am too headstrong to obey; therefore I'll ne'er go about it" (2.2.39–40)? Does a statement like "I have the head now of myself, and am man enough for a woman" (2.2.43–44) support the assumption that women *do* require male "headship"—though the man-like Moll does not—or undermine it? Or try, for a moment, to unpack the gender implications of the following lines, part of Moll's assertion that she will never stoop to prostitution:

> Base is that mind that kneels unto her body,
> As if a husband stood in awe on's wife!
> My spirit shall be mistress of this house
> As long as I have time in't. (3.1.138–141)

Turn this statement one way, and it is a reaffirmation of the traditional misogynist dichotomy that aligns men/mind/reason against women/body/passion and justifies a husband's authority; turn it another, and the dichotomy falls to pieces.

Moreover, far from reflecting wholly modern concerns, the questions about gender, sex, and nature raised by a character described variously as "both man and woman" (2.1.217), "a creature . . . nature hath brought forth to mock the sex of woman" (1.2.128–129), and "a monster with two trinkets" (2.2.80–81) were already under debate in Elizabethan and Jacobean England. A recurrent fad for masculine clothing and accessories on women—doublets in place of bodices, broad-brimmed feathered hats, cropped hair, boots with spurs, decorative daggers—had been surfacing periodically in London since at least 1583, when the moralist Philip Stubbes denounced women who "have doublets and jerkins, as men have" (see pp. 118–19). By 1620, the fad had been enthusiastically adopted by enough women to provoke no less an authority than King James I himself to demand that it be denounced from the city's pulpits, and to threaten the husbands and parents who were evidently permitting, if not encouraging and financially enabling, their wives and daughters to wear what Stubbes describes as "such wanton and lewd attire that is incident only to men." Reading such denunciations should remind us of their largely unrecorded corollary: despite the grave threat to moral order that the authorities detected in women with doublets and daggers, a large proportion of the population, men included, evidently saw no harm at all in such fashions.

Pamphleteers cashed in on the controversy, and no doubt fanned its flames, by publishing a condemnatory tract titled *Hic Mulier; or the Man-Woman*, followed quickly by a response purporting to defend women's wearing of masculine fashions (and accusing men of effeminacy) titled *Haec Vir; or the Womanish Man*. (Substantial excerpts from both can be found on pp. 123–46.) Readers who come to these texts expecting tedious invective against sin are in for a surprise, for the terms of these debates are fascinating: the anti-cross-dressing moralists do indeed invoke the Old Testament curse upon those who wear the apparel of the opposite sex, but they also betray an anxiety that women who put on men's clothing manage somehow to change their very nature, becoming, if not men, then some kind of monstrous hybrid. Modern scholars who argue that the outward signifiers of masculinity and femininity—clothing, gestures, speech patterns—are constitutive of gender itself are anticipated in interesting ways by Stubbes's claim that "Our apparel was given as a sign distinctive, to discern between sex and sex, and therefore one to wear the apparel of another sex, is to participate with the same, and to adulterate the verity of his own kind" (p. 119) and by the slippage from accoutrements to essence in *Hic Mulier's* insistence that cross-dressed women are "man in body by attire, man in behaviour by rude complement, man in nature by aptness to anger" (p. 128). *Haec Vir*, for its part, mounts a vigorous and provocative argument that much of what we hold to be "natural" is in fact no more than social convention, contingent on time and place; even the pamphlet's ending, which finds the cross-dressed woman promising to return to her subordinate, feminine place as soon as men reclaim their masculinity, may not be as conservative a move as it seems. Who, after all, gets to decide just when men are manly enough?

While gender issues are never far from the surface in *The Roaring Girl*, recent criticism has begun to remind us that the play is not just "about" gender and cross-dressing, nor, for that matter, just about Moll Cutpurse. It is, after all, a *city* comedy, and Moll with her remarkable sartorial habits and insider knowledge of local lowlife is just one of a cast of urban characters with decidedly urban concerns who populate Middleton and Dekker's stage version of the city of London, circa 1611. William N. West's essay on underworld cant (2003) and Jonathan Gil Harris's essay on consumption (2004) in this Norton Critical Edition return to the idea of the city that drove the work of earlier critics like Alexander Leggatt (1973) and Theodore Leinwand (1986), with a closer focus on specific aspects of the culture of early modern London. Consumers and consumption—some of it exceed-ingly conspicuous—permeate the play from the beginning, when Mary Fitzallard poses as a seamstress delivering a box of custom-made collars, and Sir Alexander brags to his dinner guests about how much his furniture cost, co-opting the playhouse audience to stand in for his impressive portrait gallery. Act Two plunges us into the heart of con-sumer London, opening on a busy shopping street where gallants flaunt their indulgence in the imported luxury of tobacco, a married pair of shopkeepers bicker over an order of delicate linen underclothes to be made up for aristocratic customers, and a fastidiously fashion-able young man sets aside an entire hour to shop for just one perfect feather. Moll herself is in her element here, sharing a pipe with the gallants, shopping for a shag ruff, hiring a servant, instructing a tailor on how she'd like her new breeches sewn. As Harris argues, *The Roar-ing Girl* marks the period in early modern English culture when "con-sumption," previously denoting physical illness or loss, began to acquire its modern associations with economic well-being; moreover, the play itself participates in the production of consumer desire, entic-ingly displaying on stage the luxury goods that the audience might buy in the city outside (see pp. 304–15). Beneath this busy world of sup-pliers and consumers lies its shadow, a criminal underworld where—at least in the minds of contemporary writers—rogues mirror the hierarchies of the crafts and trades companies by categorizing them-selves according to specialty and communicating in their own profes-sional jargon. *The Roaring Girl*'s "canting scene" (5.1), often cut in modern productions, illustrates the fascination early modern London-ers had with this supposed language of the underworld; the essay by West (pp. 289–304) makes some of that fascination intelligible to the modern reader.

The canting scene is perhaps the easiest to assign to a specific author in this Middleton-Dekker collaboration: it is almost certainly Dekker's, given his earlier publication of rogue pamphlets like *The Bellman of London* (see pp. 111–17). Other scenes have been tenta-tively ascribed to one playwright or the other—for example, 1.1 and 1.2 to Dekker, all of Act Two to Middleton—based either on stylistic parallels to their known works, or on newer, less impressionistic methods of sub-stylistic analysis. On the whole, however, it seems safest to agree with Paul Mulholland, who after a careful review of the evidence concludes that "[f]ew scenes point conclusively to either dramatist as the main writer," with most suggesting the presence of both. Scenes may have been written collaboratively, or written by one and revised by the other.[6] The two playwrights had experience working together, having already collaborated twice, first on *The Magnificent*

---

6. Paul A. Mulholland, ed., *The Roaring Girl*. The Revels Plays. Manchester: Manchester University Press, 1987, 8–12.

Entertainment which welcomed James I to London in March 1604, and then, more extensively, on the comedy *The Honest Whore, Part One*, which played at the Fortune later the same year. More important than the question of exactly who wrote what is the simple fact that *The Roaring Girl* brought together two of the theatre's sharpest and most dedicated observers of London and its inhabitants. By 1611, Middleton was already known for his bawdy, ironic city comedies like *A Mad World, My Masters* (1605) and *Your Five Gallants* (1607); a couple of years later, in 1613, he would produce the first of his seven Lord Mayor's pageants, elaborate allegorical entertainments that wound their way through the city streets to celebrate a new mayor's installation. Dekker's most famous play, *The Shoemaker's Holiday* (1599), celebrated the career of Simon Eyre, a shoemaker who rose to become Lord Mayor of London and an icon of city folklore, while his steady output of prose pamphlets exposed the city's criminal underbelly. "Merry Moll of the Bankside" could have done far worse than to have these two playwrights immortalize her on the public stage.

Not that theatrical immortality was guaranteed. After the 1611 performance, there are no records to indicate that Middleton and Dekker's Moll appeared again on stage until the play was revived in 1951 by the Brattle Theatre Company of Cambridge, Massachusetts. Mulholland, examining performances of *The Roaring Girl* up to 1983, notes that the Brattle revival was staged as a Restoration-era farce, with extra songs added to cater to the talents of Nancy Walker, the musical-comedy actress who played Moll. Reviews seem to have been mixed: the *Harvard Crimson*, for instance, praises Walker for "extract[ing] a good deal of humor from her material," in particular a scene in which she "makes love to a cello with a savage determination that is generally both frightening and funny," but ultimately pronounces the play "too strained, too contrived to be truly entertaining today."[7] With only two productions—one of them a radio play—between 1951 and 1979, *The Roaring Girl* had to wait until directors and audiences discovered its modern entertainment value in its relevance to feminist concerns. A 1979 adaptation by Sue-Ellen Case at the University of California, Berkeley, saw the addition of scenes set in the dressing-room, where the all-female cast interrogated the male-authored script they had to perform in the "real" play. Performances by other university companies in 1980 and 1982 also foregrounded feminist issues, if less obtrusively, while the Royal Shakespeare Company's 1983 season alternated *The Roaring Girl* (directed by Barry Kyle and starring Helen Mirren) with Shakespeare's *The Taming of the Shrew* to highlight the plays' contrasting depic-

---

7. Stephen O. Saxe, "The Playgoer: At the Brattle," *Harvard Crimson* (May 4, 1951). theharvardcrimson.com/article/1951/5/4/the-playgoer-psince-the-brattle-theatre/

tions of early modern women. Reaction, once again, was mixed, with reviews divided between "those sympathetic to the play and the value of a revival, and those left cold by both play and production."[8]

After the RSC production, there were no major performances of *The Roaring Girl* until the turn of the millennium, when it resurfaced on both sides of the Atlantic at once: in 2000, Abigail Anderson directed the Steam Industry troupe at Finborough Theatre, London, while the Shenandoah Shakespeare Express (now the American Shakespeare Center) took it across North America as part of its 2000–2001 "Charm Your Tongue" tour. The overtly feminist revisions of the 1970s and 1980s were now largely a thing of the past: the Steam Industry billed its Moll as "a figurehead for all those who wish to break out of their social boundaries, female and male," and both troupes performed the play more or less as written, allowing it to stand on its own merits. While sticking closely to the original text was in keeping with the educational mandate of the Shenandoah Shakespeare Express, the text itself occasioned some grumbling among the Steam Industry's reviewers, one of whom called it "a fair old muddle," was bored by the canting scene, and faulted the director for "overestimat[ing] our relish for antiquated talk." Other reviews were more positive: while noting "enough subplots ... to confuse the most attentive of theatregoers," *What's On* praised the "uniformly brilliant cast" for ensuring that one had "no real trouble understanding the double-dealing shenanigans which unfold so delightfully."[9] Flanking these two "straight" productions, 1999 and 2004 saw a pair of wildly different adaptations, the first by Penny Penniston and Jeremy Wechsler for the Chicago troupe Shakespeare's Motley Crew, and the second by Alice Tuan at New York's Foundry Theatre. Tuan (who also directed) refashioned the original into a modern social satire on the infringement of free speech, with Moll as "an androgynous producer of semi-pornographic, left-wing theatrical events":[1] most reviews were not favorable. Penniston and Wechsler, by contrast, pared down Middleton and Dekker's meandering plot to a fast-paced and by all accounts hilarious comedy, directed by Wechsler, which earned a Joseph Jefferson nomination for Best Adaptation. Though the rewritten play conserved a mere quarter of the original dialogue and the barest bones of the plot—the Mary/Moll ruse, the Mrs. Gallipot/Laxton story, and Goshawk's (successful) seduction of a Bible-quoting

8. Mulholland 52. A fuller account of productions up to and including 1983 is found in Paul Mulholland, "Let her roar again: *The Roaring Girl* Revived," *Research Opportunities in Renaissance Drama* (1985): 15–27.
9. Both reviews of the Steam Industry production are in *Theatre Record* 20.23 (2000): 1491.
1. Mary Bly, review of *The Roaring Girle*, *Shakespeare Bulletin* 22.3 (Fall 2004): 86–88.

Mrs. Openwork—the *Shakespeare Bulletin* review approvingly declared "Middleton's story . . . not so much simplified as it is clarified and enhanced."[2]

Clarification and enhancement also happen to be what this volume received from the many people to whom I owe thanks. Above all, I am indebted to the play's previous editors: David Bevington, whose text of the play from *English Renaissance Drama: A Norton Anthology* is used for this Norton Critical Edition; Paul Mulholland for the Revels edition; Kathleen E. McLuskie and David Bevington (again) for the Revels Student edition; and Coppélia Kahn for the Oxford *Thomas Middleton: The Complete Works* (Gen. eds. Gary Taylor and John Lavagnino). I am grateful to Carol Bemis at W. W. Norton and Company for proposing the project and, along with Rivka Genesen, for patiently answering my queries throughout; I would also like to thank Peter McCullough and Amber Chow. Francesca Odell at the National Portrait Gallery in London was tremendously helpful, as were the librarians at the University of Toronto's Thomas Fisher Rare Book library. Penny Penniston and Jeremy Wechsler, contacted out of the blue about their decade-old production of *The Roaring Girl*, generously supplied me with their script, a packet of reviews, and stimulating e-mail discussion. Bonnie Hughes was an exemplary research assistant; Christina Luckyj, together with numerous friends and colleagues at the University of Ottawa, provided invaluable advice. Sincere thanks are also due to the University of Ottawa's Faculty of Arts for a publication grant to help defray the cost of permissions. Last and most unexpectedly, but certainly not least, I must thank two gentlemen of the Missouri Hunting Spaniel Club, Tim Baker and George K. Hobson, for illuminating one of early modern drama's most baffling stage directions: "*Spits in the dog's mouth.*"

2. Justin Shaltz, review of *The Roaring Girl*, *Shakespeare Bulletin* 18.2 (Spring 2000): 20–21.

The Text of
THE ROARING GIRL

Title page of *The Roaring Girle, or Moll Cut Purse* (1611).
Reproduced by permission of the Huntington Library, San Marino,
California.

The Roaring Girl

[The Epistle]

To the Comic Play Readers: Venery and Laughter

The fashion of playmaking I can properly compare to nothing so naturally as the alteration in apparel. For in the time of the great-crop doublet, your huge bombasted plays, quilted with mighty words to lean purposes, was only then in fashion; and as the doublet fell, neater inventions began to set up. Now in the time of spruceness, 5
our plays follow the niceness of our garments: single plots, quaint conceits, lecherous jests, dressed up in hanging sleeves; and those are fit for the times and the termers. Such a kind of light-color summer stuff, mingled with divers colors, you shall find this published comedy—good to keep you in an afternoon from dice, at home in 10
your chambers. And for venery, you shall find enough for sixpence, but well couched, an you mark it. For Venus, being a woman, passes through the play in doublet and breeches—a brave disguise and a safe one, if the statute untie not her codpiece point! The book I make no question but is fit for many of your companies, as well as 15
the person itself, and may be allowed both galley room at the playhouse and chamber room at your lodging. Worse things, I must needs confess, the world has taxed her for than has been written of her; but 'tis the excellency of a writer to leave things better than he finds 'em. Though some obscene fellow, that cares not what he 20
writes against others, yet keeps a mystical bawdy house himself, and

Title. *Venery*: sexual enjoyment.
3. *bombasted*: stuffed; full of showy rhetoric.
4. *doublet*: fitted jacket with padded stomach; *fell*: went out of style.
6. *niceness*: fastidiousness.
7. *conceits*: ideas.
8. *termers*: people who come to London to pursue lawsuits during the periods ("terms")
    when the courts are in session.
9. *stuff*: fabric; *divers*: various.
12. *well couched . . . mark it*: well concealed, if you pay attention.
13. *brave*: handsome; daring.
14. *if . . . codpiece point!*: if the law against indecency does not remove her male attire; the
    codpiece, a pouch covering the genitals, was fastened to the breeches with tags called
    "points."
18. *taxed*: accused her of.
21. *mystical bawdy house*: secret brothel.

entertains drunkards to make use of their pockets and vent his private
bottle ale at midnight—though such a one would have ripped up the
most nasty vice that ever hell belched forth and presented it to a
modest assembly, yet we rather wish in such discoveries, where rep-   25
utation lies bleeding, a slackness of truth than a fullness of slander.
Thomas Middleton

DRAMATIS PERSONAE

[The PROLOGUE]
SIR ALEXANDER Wengrave and NEATFOOT, his man[1]
SIR ADAM Appleton[2]
SIR DAVY Dapper
SIR BEAUTEOUS Ganymede[3]
[SIR THOMAS Long]
LORD NOLAND[4]
Young [SEBASTIAN] Wengrave [Sir Alexander's son]
JACK DAPPER [Sir Davy's son] and GULL,[5] his page
GOSHAWK[6]
GREENWIT[7]
LAXTON[8]

TILTYARD[9] [a feather-seller]
OPENWORK [a sempster][1]   } cives[3]
[Hippocrates] GALLIPOT[2] [an apothecary]
[MRS. TILTYARD]
[MRS. Rosamond OPENWORK] } uxores[4]

22–23. *vent . . . ale*: sell his illegally brewed beer.
  23. *ripped up*: exposed.
  25. *modest assembly*: respectable audience.
25–26. *where reputation . . . slander*: I.e., in revealing ("discovering") something that might
      hurt a person's reputation, it is better to go easy on the truth than to tell everything
      and risk slander.
   1. I.e., his servingman. A "neat's foot" is a cow's foot used as food; the name plays on
      this meaning and the idea of a neatly or daintily shod foot. Neatfoot's clothing may
      match his affectedly fancy language at the beginning of the play.
   2. Allusion to the Biblical account of original sin, in which Adam ate the apple offered
      by Eve.
   3. In Greek mythology, Ganymede was the beautiful young page-boy and lover of Zeus;
      in early modern England, the name had definite homoerotic connotations.
   4. Pun on "no land"; young aristocrats who sold their inherited lands to finance urban
      extravagances were common targets of satire on the early modern stage.
   5. A gullible person, a simpleton; *Jack Dapper*: inversion of "dapper jack," disparaging
      term for an excessively fashionable man.
   6. A large, short-winged hawk.
   7. Greenwit's wit is "green" in the sense of "inexperienced" or "immature."
   8. Pun on "lacks stone," referring to his lack of land, his lack of a testicle ("stone"), or both.
   9. A space for jousting tournaments, also called "tilts"; jousters adorned themselves
      with an abundance of ornamental feathers, making "Tiltyard" an appropriate name
      for a feather-seller.
   1. A tailor. *Openwork*: decorative needlework; also puns on "open work" in the sense
      of straightforward, honest dealings.
   2. Small earthenware pot for the ointments and medicines an "apothecary" would
      have made and sold. *Hippocrates*: ancient Greek physician considered the founder
      of medicine.
   3. citizens (Latin).
   4. wives (Latin).

[MRS. Prudence GALLIPOT]

MOLL [Cutpurse], the Roaring Girl[5]
[Ralph] TRAPDOOR
[TEARCAT][6]

SIR GUY Fitzallard
MARY Fitzallard, his daughter

CURTALAX, a sergeant,[7] and
HANGER, his yeoman[8]

Ministri[9] [including a SERVANT to Sir Alexander]
[A FELLOW with a long rapier
A PORTER
A TAILOR
A COACHMAN
Several CUTPURSES
Gentlemen]

[THE SCENE: London.]

Prologus

[*Enter the Prologue.*]

PROLOGUE   A play expected long makes the audience look
    For wonders, that each scene should be a book,
    Composed to all perfection; Each one comes
    And brings a play in's head with him; up he sums
    What he would of a roaring girl have writ;   5
    If that he finds not here, he mews at it.
    Only we entreat you think our scene
    Cannot speak high, the subject being but mean.
    A roaring girl (whose notes till now never were)
    Shall fill with laughter our vast theatre;   10
    That's all which I dare promise: Tragic passion
    And such grave stuff is this day out of fashion.

5. A "roaring boy" is a swaggering young urban thug who likes to drink and fight; the pro-
    logue describes what might be expected from the novel concept of a roaring *girl*. *Moll*:
    a name associated with prostitutes, but also the diminuitive of "Mary," a name with
    connotations of chastity; *cutpurse*: a thief who steals by slitting a money-bag ("purse")
    to remove its contents, but Moll's masculine behavior—particularly her treatment of
    "Laxton"—suggests that "purse" as "scrotum" may also be relevant.
6. To "tear a cat" is to give an over-the-top theatrical performance, to "chew the scenery."
7. An officer who arrests offenders; *curtalax*: cutlass.
8. A sergeant's assistant; *Hanger*: strap to attach a sword to a belt.
9. Servants (Latin).
3. *one*: audience member.
6. *mews*: makes derisive noises.
7–8. *our scene . . . mean*: our play won't have lofty speeches, as it's about ordinary people.
9. *whose notes . . . were*: who has never been heard (on stage) until now.

I see Attention sets wide ope her gates
Of hearing, and with covetous list'ning waits
To know what girl this roaring girl should be,   15
For of that tribe are many. One is she
That roars at midnight in deep tavern bowls,
That beats the watch, and constables controls;
Another roars i'th'daytime, swears, stabs, gives braves,
Yet sells her soul to the lust of fools and slaves.   20
Both these are suburb roarers. Then there's besides
A civil city roaring girl, whose pride,
Feasting, and riding, shakes her husband's state,
And leaves him roaring through an iron grate.
None of these roaring girls is ours: she flies   25
With wings more lofty. Thus her character lies.
Yet what need characters, when to give a guess
Is better than the person to express?
But would you know who 'tis? Would you hear her name?
She is called Mad Moll; her life our acts proclaim.   [*Exit.*] 30

[1.1]

*Enter Mary Fitzallard, disguised like a sempster, with a case for
bands, and Neatfoot, a servingman, with her, with a napkin on
his shoulder, and a trencher in his hand, as from table.*

NEATFOOT   The young gentleman, our young master,
Sir Alexander's son—is it into his ears, sweet damsel, emblem
of fragility, you desire to have a message transported, or to
be transcendent?
MARY   A private word or two, sir, nothing else.   5
NEATFOOT   You shall fructify in that which you come for; your
pleasure shall be satisfied to your full contentation. I will,
fairest tree of generation, watch when our young master is

14. *covetous*: eager.
18. *beats . . . controls*: beats the night watchman and overpowers policemen;
19. *braves*: defiant challenges.
20. *slaves*: rascals.
21. *suburb roarers*: brawlers from the areas outside the city limits, known for taverns and
    brothels.
23–24. *shakes . . . grate*: impoverishes her husband and leaves him calling out for charity in
    debtors' prison.
26. *character*: prose sketch describing a type of person.
27–28. *Yet . . . express*: What need do we have for character sketches, which are only useful
    when you need to guess at what a person is like?
30. *mad*: eccentric.
s.d. *disguised like . . . case for bands*: dressed as a seamstress, with a case for detachable
    shirt-collars; *trencher*: wooden plate.
 4. *transcendent*: delivered; Neatfoot tries to impress his listeners with grandiose, repet-
    itive language.
 6. *fructify*: be fruitful (with sexual innuendo, continued throughout the rest of the speech).
 7. *contentation*: contentment.
 8. *generation*: procreation.

erected, that is to say, up, and deliver him to this your most
white hand.   10

MARY   Thanks, sir.

NEATFOOT   And withal certify him that I have culled out for him,
now his belly is replenished, a daintier bit or modicum than any
lay upon his trencher at dinner. Hath he notion of your name,
I beseech your chastity?   15

MARY   One, sir, of whom he bespake falling-bands.

NEATFOOT   Falling-bands: it shall so be given him. If you please to
venture your modesty in the hall amongst a curl-pated company
of rude servingmen and take such as they can set before you, you
shall be most seriously and ingeniously welcome—   20

MARY   I have dined indeed already, sir.

NEATFOOT   Or will you vouchsafe to kiss the lip of a cup of rich
Orleans in the buttery amongst our waiting-women?

MARY   Not now, in truth, sir.

NEATFOOT   Our young master shall then have a feeling of your   25
being here presently. It shall so be given him.

MARY   I humbly thank you, sir.   *Exit Neatfoot.*
                              But that my bosom
Is full of bitter sorrows, I could smile
To see this formal ape play antic tricks;   30
But in my breast a poisoned arrow sticks,
And smiles cannot become me. Love woven slightly,
Such as thy false heart makes, wears out as lightly;
But love being truly bred i'th'soul, like mine,
Bleeds even to death at the least wound it takes   35
The more we quench this fire, the less it slakes.
Oh, me!

           Enter Sebastian Wengrave with Neatfoot.

SEBASTIAN   A sempster speak with me, say'st thou?

NEATFOOT   Yes, sir, she's there, viva voce, to deliver her auricular
confession.   40

SEBASTIAN [*to Mary*]   With me, sweetheart? What is't?

MARY   I have brought home your bands, sir.

9. *up*: up from the dinner table.
12–14. *I have . . . dinner*: Neatfoot imagines Mary as a tasty dessert he will present to Sebas-
    tian.
16. *bespake falling-bands*: ordered wide linen collars.
18. *curl-pated*: curly-haired.
22–23. *kiss . . . buttery*: graciously agree to drink a cup of French wine in the pantry.
25–26. *a feeling . . . presently*: a sense of your being here, immediately.
28. *But that*: except for the fact that.
30. *formal*: ceremonious.
32–33. *Love . . . lightly*: thinly woven love, like Sebastian's, wears out easily.
36. *slakes*: goes out.
39. *viva voce*: in person; literally "living voice" (Latin).
39–40. *auricular confession*: confession made privately to a priest.

SEBASTIAN   Bands?—Neatfoot!
NEATFOOT   Sir?
SEBASTIAN   Prithee look in, for all the gentlemen are   45
   upon rising.
NEATFOOT   Yes, sir. A most methodical attendance shall be given.
SEBASTIAN   And dost hear, if my father call for me, say I am busy
   with a sempster.
NEATFOOT   Yes, sir. He shall know it that you are busied with a   50
   needlewoman.
SEBASTIAN   In's ear, good Neatfoot.
NEATFOOT   It shall be so given him.   *Exit Neatfoot.*
SEBASTIAN   Bands? You're mistaken, sweetheart, I bespake none.
   When, where, I prithee, what bands? Let me see them.   55
MARY   Yes, sir, a bond fast sealed with solemn oaths,
   Subscribed unto (as I thought) with your soul,
   Delivered as your deed in sight of heaven.
   Is this bond canceled? Have you forgot me?
SEBASTIAN   Ha! Life of my life! Sir Guy Fitzallard's daughter!   60
   What has transformed my love to this strange shape?
   Stay: make all sure. [*He tests the doors.*] So: now speak and be
      brief,
   Because the wolf's at door that lies in wait
   To prey upon us both. Albeit mine eyes   65
   Are blessed by thine, yet this so strange disguise
   Holds me with fear and wonder.
MARY   Mine's a loathed sight.
   Why from it are you banished else so long?
SEBASTIAN   I must cut short my speech. In broken language,
   Thus much, sweet Moll: I must thy company shun;   70
   I court another Moll. My thoughts must run
   As a horse runs that's blind, round in a mill,
   Out every step, yet keeping one path still.
MARY   Umh! Must you shun my company? In one knot
   Have both our hands by th'hands of heaven been tied,   75
   Now to be broke? I thought me once your bride;
   Our fathers did agree on the time when.
   And must another bedfellow fill my room?

---

   45. *Prithee*: abbreviation of "I pray thee."
45–46. *Prithee . . . rising*: Please look into the dining room, as the gentlemen are about to
      get up from the table.
   59. *Is this bond canceled?*: "band" and "bond" could be used interchangeably to mean
      a) the tie uniting two persons (here, in betrothal) and b) the legal document, or "deed,"
      formalizing a covenant between two parties. Mary puns on both meanings.
   67. *Mine's a loathed sight*: You loathe the sight of me.
   70. *Moll*: diminutive of "Mary."
72–73. *As a horse . . . still*: blind horses, harnessed to spokes extending from a millshaft,
      walked in circles to power the mill.
   75. *Have both . . . tied*: Mary and Sebastian have entered a contract, witnessed by their
      fathers, to marry at a future date; such a contract, known as spousals *de futuro*,
      could be legally dissolved by mutual consent, but both Mary and Sebastian consider
      their vow binding in the eyes of God.

SEBASTIAN   Sweet maid, let's lose no time. 'Tis in heaven's book
 Set down that I must have thee; an oath we took   80
 To keep our vows. But when the knight your father
 Was from mine parted, storms began to sit
 Upon my covetous father's brow, which fell
 From them on me. He reckoned up what gold
 This marriage would draw from him, at which he swore,   85
 To lose so much blood could not grieve him more.
 He then dissuades me from thee, called thee not fair,
 And asked, "What is she but a beggar's heir?"
 He scorned thy dowry of five thousand marks.
 If such a sum of money could be found,   90
 And I would match with that, he'd not undo it,
 Provided his bags might add nothing to it,
 But vowed, if I took thee—nay, more, did swear it—
 Save birth from him I nothing should inherit.
MARY   What follows then? My shipwreck?
SEBASTIAN   Dearest, no.   95
 Though wildly in a labyrinth I go,
 My end is to meet thee. With a side wind
 Must I now sail, else I no haven can find,
 But both must sink forever. There's a wench
 Called Moll, Mad Moll, or Merry Moll—a creature   100
 So strange in quality, a whole city takes
 Note of her name and person. All that affection
 I owe to thee, on her, in counterfeit passion,
 I spend to mad my father. He believes
 I dote upon this roaring girl, and grieves   105
 As it becomes a father for a son
 That could be so bewitched. Yet I'll go on
 This crooked way, sigh still for her, feign dreams,
 In which I'll talk only of her. These streams
 Shall, I hope, force my father to consent   110
 That here I anchor, rather than be rent
 Upon a rock so dangerous. Art thou pleased,
 Because thou see'st we are waylaid, that I take
 A path that's safe, though it be far about?
MARY   My prayers with heaven guide thee!
SEBASTIAN   Then I will on.   115

---

  89. *marks*: a mark was 2/3 of a pound; Mary's dowry is in fact larger than average for
   women of her social status.
 91–94. *And I would . . . inherit*: Sebastian's father declares that he won't prevent his son
   from marrying a five-thousand-mark dowry as long as Sebastian doesn't expect any
   further money from him—and is prepared to be disinherited as well.
  95. *shipwreck*: ruin.
 97–98. *With a side . . . sail*: I must use indirect means.
 111–12. *That here I . . . dangerous*: i.e., that I anchor in the safe harbor of Mary, rather than
   be wrecked on the dangerous rock of Moll.
  113. *waylaid*: impeded.

My father is at hand; kiss and be gone.
Hours shall be watched for meetings. I must now,
As men for fear, to a strange idol bow.

MARY   Farewell!

SEBASTIAN   I'll guide thee forth. When next we meet,   120
A story of Moll shall make our mirth more sweet.   *Exeunt.*

[1.2]

*Enter Sir Alexander Wengrave, Sir Davy Dapper, Sir Adam
Appleton, Goshawk, Laxton, and gentlemen.*

OMNES   Thanks, good Sir Alexander, for our bounteous cheer.

SIR ALEXANDER   Fie, fie! In giving thanks you pay too dear.

SIR DAVY   When bounty spreads the table, faith, 'twere sin,
At going off, if thanks should not step in.

SIR ALEXANDER   No more of thanks, no more. Ay, marry, sir,   5
Th'inner room was too close. How do you like
This parlor, gentlemen?

OMNES   Oh, passing well.

SIR ADAM   What a sweet breath the air casts here, so cool!

GOSHAWK   I like the prospect best.

LAXTON   See how 'tis furnished.

SIR DAVY   A very fair sweet room.

SIR ALEXANDER   Sir Davy Dapper,   10
The furniture that doth adorn this room
Cost many a fair grey groat ere it came here;
But good things are most cheap when they're most dear.
Nay, when you look into my galleries,
How bravely they are trimmed up, you all shall swear   15
You're highly pleased to see what's set down there:
Stories of men and women, mixed together
Fair ones with foul, like sunshine in wet weather.

---

117. *Hours . . . meetings*: We'll find times to meet.
  3. *faith*: in faith (a mild oath).
  4. *At going off*: upon leaving the table.
  5. *marry*: by the Virgin Mary (a mild oath).
  6. *close*: stuffy.
  7. *passing*: surpassingly, extremely.
  9. *prospect*: view.
 11. *furniture*: decor, including pictures, hangings, etc., as well as "furniture" in the modern sense.
 12. *groat*: silver coin worth fourpence.
 13. *good things . . . dear*: i.e., top quality, expensive ("dear") things are the best value ("most cheap").
 14. *look . . . galleries*: Sir Alexander gestures towards the audience sitting in the theatre's galleries: the tightly-packed, expectant faces become his portrait gallery and, figuratively, his library of "new books" (l. 22). The stage itself is then described as an island floating on a "sea" made up of the moving heads of those standing in the pit (ll. 29–32).
 15. *How bravely . . . trimmed up*: How handsomely they are decorated.

Within one square a thousand heads are laid
So close that all of heads the room seems made;   20
As many faces there filled with blithe looks,
Show like the promising titles of new books
Writ merrily, the readers being their own eyes,
Which seem to move and to give plaudities;
And here and there, whilst with obsequious ears   25
Thronged heaps do listen, a cutpurse thrusts and leers
With hawk's eyes for his prey. I need not show him;
By a hanging villainous look yourselves may know him,
The face is drawn so rarely. Then, sir, below,
The very floor, as 'twere, waves to and fro,   30
And like a floating island seems to move
Upon a sea bound in with shores above.

Enter Sebastian and Master Greenwit.

OMNES   These sights are excellent.
SIR ALEXANDER   I'll show you all;
    Since we are met, make our parting comical.
SEBASTIAN   This gentleman, my friend, will take his leave, sir.   35
SIR ALEXANDER   Ha? Take his leave, Sebastian? Who?
SEBASTIAN   This gentleman.
SIR ALEXANDER [*to Greenwit*]   Your love, sir, has already given me
        some time,
    And if you please to trust my age with more,
    It shall pay double interest. Good sir, stay.
GREENWIT   I have been too bold.
SIR ALEXANDER   Not so, sir. A merry day   40
    'Mongst friends being spent is better than gold saved.—
    Some wine, some wine! Where be these knaves I keep?

Enter three or four servingmen and Neatfoot.

NEATFOOT   At your worshipful elbow, sir.
SIR ALEXANDER   You are
    Kissing my maids, drinking, or fast asleep.
NEATFOOT   Your Worship has given it us right.
SIR ALEXANDER   You varlets, stir!   45

19. *one square*: the Fortune was London's only square amphitheatre.
24. *plaudities*: applause.
28. *hanging*: gloomy; fit to be hanged.
29. *rarely*: skillfully.
34. *comical*: cheerful.
37. *love*: courtesy.
38–39. *if you please . . . interest*: if you'll indulge an old man by staying longer, I'll make it worth your while.
40. *I . . . bold*: I've already imposed on you too much.
42. *keep*: employ.
45. *given it us*: described us; *You varlets, stir*: Move it, you rascals!

Illustrations

Chairs, stools, and cushions.

> [*The servants fetch chairs and wine.*]
> Prithee, Sir Davy Dapper,

Make that chair thine.

SIR DAVY   Tis but an easy gift,
And yet I thank you for it, sir. I'll take it.

SIR ALEXANDER [*to servants*]   A chair for old Sir Adam Appleton.

NEATFOOT [*providing a chair*]   A backfriend to Your Worship.

SIR ADAM   Marry, good Neatfoot,   50
I thank thee for it. Backfriends sometimes are good.

SIR ALEXANDER   Pray make that stool your perch, good
Master Goshawk.

GOSHAWK   I stoop to your lure, sir.

SIR ALEXANDER   Son Sebastian,
Take Master Greenwit to you.

SEBASTIAN [*to Greenwit*]   Sit, dear friend.

SIR ALEXANDER   Nay, Master Laxton. [*To servants*] Furnish
Master Laxton   55
With what he wants: a stone.—A stool, I would say, a stool.

LAXTON   I had rather stand, sir.

SIR ALEXANDER   I know you had, good Master Laxton. So, so.

>   *Exeunt* [*Neatfoot and*] *servants*.

Now here's a mess of friends, and, gentlemen,
Because time's glass shall not be running long,   60
I'll quicken it with a pretty tale.

SIR DAVY   Good tales do well
In these bad days, where vice does so excel.

SIR ADAM   Begin, Sir Alexander.

SIR ALEXANDER   Last day I met
An agèd man upon whose head was scored
A debt of just so many years as these   65
Which I owe to my grave. The man you all know.

OMNES   His name, I pray you, sir?

SIR ALEXANDER   Nay, you shall pardon me.
But when he saw me, with a sigh that brake,

---

50. *backfriend*: chair with a backrest; a supportive friend or "backer"; a false friend. Sir Adam puns on the three meanings.

53. *I . . . lure*: I descend to take what you offer (Goshawk responds to Sir Alexander's joke about his "perch" by continuing the hawking metaphor: to "stoop to the lure" means "to fly down to take food").

56. *With . . . stone*: what he lacks: a testicle. "Stones" was the common word for testicles; Sir Alexander's slip of the tongue draws attention to "Laxton" as "lacks-stone."

57. *stand*: stand up; have an erection.

59. *mess*: group that shares (or has shared) a meal.

60. *time's glass*: hourglass.

63. *Last day*: yesterday.

65–66. *A debt . . . grave*: i.e., a man exactly my own age; Sir Alexander imagines the grave as a creditor to whom one owes a debt equivalent to one's years.

68. *brake*: broke.

Or seemed to break, his heartstrings, thus he spake:
"Oh my good knight," says he—and then his eyes   70
Were richer even by that which made them poor,
They had spent so many tears they had no more—
"Oh, sir," says he, "you know it, for you ha' seen
Blessings to rain upon mine house and me;
Fortune, who slaves men, was my slave; her wheel   75
Hath spun me golden threads, for, I thank heaven,
I ne'er had but one cause to curse my stars."
I asked him then what that one cause might be.

OMNES   So, sir.

SIR ALEXANDER   He paused, and—as we often see   80
A sea so much becalmed there can be found
No wrinkle on his brow, his waves being drowned
In their own rage; but when th'imperious winds
Use strange invisible tyranny to shake
Both heaven's and earth's foundation at their noise,   85
The seas, swelling with wrath to part that fray
Rise up and are more wild, more mad than they—
Even so this good old man was by my question
Stirred up to roughness. You might see his gall
Flow even in's eyes; then grew he fantastical.   90

SIR DAVY   Fantastical? Ha, ha!

SIR ALEXANDER   Yes, and talked oddly.

SIR ADAM   Pray, sir, proceed.
How did this old man end?

SIR ALEXANDER   Marry, sir, thus:
He left his wild fit to read o'er his cards;
Yet then, though age cast snow on all his hairs,   95
He joyed because, says he, "The god of gold
Has been to me no niggard; that disease
Of which all old men sicken, avarice,
Never infected me."

LAXTON [aside]   He means not himself, I'm sure.   100

SIR ALEXANDER   "For, like a lamp
Fed with continual oil, I spend and throw
My light to all that need it, yet have still
Enough to serve myself. Oh, but," quoth he,
"Though heaven's dew fall thus on this agèd tree,   105

---

75. *slaves*: enslaves. The Roman goddess Fortuna was depicted holding a wheel which she
turned at random, symbolizing the instability of human luck. Here, her wheel is con-
flated with the wheel the Fates use to spin the thread of human life.
82. *his*: its.
86. *fray*: battle.
89. *gall*: bile, associated with anger and bitterness.
90. *fantastical*: strange
94. *to . . . cards*: to consider the hand he'd been dealt (figuratively).

I have a son that's like a wedge doth cleave
My very heart root."
SIR DAVY   Had he such a son?
SEBASTIAN [aside]   Now I do smell a fox strongly.
SIR ALEXANDER   Let's see: no, Master Greenwit is not yet
    So mellow in years as he; but as like Sebastian,   110
    Just like my son Sebastian—such another.
SEBASTIAN [aside]   How finely like a fencer my father fetches
    his by-blows to hit me! But if I beat you not at your own
    weapon of subtlety—
SIR ALEXANDER   "This son," saith he, "that should be
    The column and main arch unto my house,   115
    The crutch unto my age, becomes a whirlwind
    Shaking the firm foundation."
SIR ADAM   'Tis some prodigal.
SEBASTIAN [aside]   Well shot, old Adam Bell!
SIR ALEXANDER   No city monster neither, no prodigal,
    But sparing, wary, civil, and—though wifeless—   120
    An excellent husband, and such a traveler,
    He has more tongues in his head than some have teeth.
SIR DAVY   I have but two in mine.
GOSHAWK   So sparing and so wary,
    What then could vex his father so?
SIR ALEXANDER   Oh, a woman.
SEBASTIAN [aside]   A flesh fly. That can vex any man.   125
SIR ALEXANDER   A scurvy woman,
    On whom the passionate old man swore he doted.
    "A creature," saith he, "nature hath brought forth
    To mock the sex of woman." It is a thing
    One knows not how to name; her birth began   130
    Ere she was all made 'Tis woman more than man,
    Man more than woman, and—which to none can hap—
    The sun gives her two shadows to one shape.

----

106. *like . . . cleave*: like a wedge that splits.
108. *Now . . . strongly*; i.e., I smell something fishy.
110. *mellow*: ripe.
113. *by-blows*: side-blows.
114. *subtlety*: craftiness.
117. *prodigal*: the parable of the Prodigal Son, who spent his inheritance in loose liv-
      ing, is told in Luke 15:11–32.
118. *Adam Bell*: a legendary archer and outlaw.
120. *sparing*: thrifty.
121. *husband*: manager (of money and goods).
122. *tongues*: languages.
125. *flesh fly*: fly that lays its eggs in dead flesh; figuratively, a prostitute who profits
      from men's "flesh."
126. *scurvy*: worthless.
127. *On . . . doted*: i.e., the angry old man swore his son was besotted with her.
130–131. *her birth . . . made*: she was born before she was fully formed; Sir Alexander
      implies Moll is a hermaphrodite, with indeterminate or perhaps double genitalia.
132. *hap*: happen.

Nay, more, let this strange thing walk, stand, or sit,
No blazing star draws more eyes after it.   135
SIR DAVY   A monster. 'Tis some monster.
SIR ALEXANDER   She's a varlet.
SEBASTIAN [*aside*]   Now is my cue to bristle.
SIR ALEXANDER   A naughty pack.
SEBASTIAN [*aloud*]   'Tis false!
SIR ALEXANDER   Ha, boy?
SEBASTIAN   'Tis false.
SIR ALEXANDER   What's false? I say she's naught.
SEBASTIAN   I say that tongue
That dares speak so, but yours, sticks in the throat   140
Of a rank villain. Set yourself aside—
SIR ALEXANDER   So, sir, what then?
SEBASTIAN   Any here else had lied.
    (*Aside*) I think I shall fit you.
SIR ALEXANDER   Lie?
SEBASTIAN   Yes.
SIR DAVY   Doth this concern him?
SIR ALEXANDER   Ah, sirrah boy,
Is your blood heated? Boils it? Are you stung?   145
I'll pierce you deeper yet.—Oh, my dear friends,
I am that wretched father, this that son
That sees his ruin, yet headlong on doth run.
SIR ADAM [*to Sebastian*]   Will you love such a poison?
SIR DAVY   Fie, fie!
SEBASTIAN   You're all mad.
SIR ALEXANDER   Thou'rt sick at heart, yet feel'st it not. Of all these, 150
What gentleman but thou, knowing his disease
Mortal, would shun the cure?—Oh, Master Greenwit,
Would you to such an idol bow?
GREENWIT   Not I, sir.
SIR ALEXANDER   Here's Master Laxton. Has he mind to a woman
As thou hast?
LAXTON   No, not I, sir.
SIR ALEXANDER   Sir, I know it.   155
LAXTON   Their good parts are so rare, their bad so common,
I will have naught to do with any woman.
SIR DAVY   'Tis well done, Master Laxton.

---

135. *blazing star*: meteor (considered a bad omen).
138. *naughty pack*: worthless hussy.
139. *naught*: bad, immoral; *that*: any.
142. *Any . . . lied*: If anyone else but you had said such things, I'd call him a liar (a serious insult to a man's honor).
143. *fit . . . you*: give you what you deserve.
144. *him*: i.e., Sebastian; *sirrah*: used to address inferiors.
152. *mortal*: deadly.
154. *mind to*: desire for.
157. *naught*: nothing; but "to be naught with" meant "to have sex with."

SIR ALEXANDER   Oh, thou cruel boy,
  Thou wouldst with lust an old man's life destroy.
  Because thou see'st I'm halfway in my grave,   160
  Thou shovel'st dust upon me. Would thou mightest have
  Thy wish, most wicked, most unnatural!
SIR DAVY   Why, sir, 'tis thought Sir Guy Fitzallard's daughter
  Shall wed your son Sebastian.
SIR ALEXANDER   Sir Davy Dapper,
  I have upon my knees wooed this fond boy   165
  To take that virtuous maiden.
SEBASTIAN   Hark you a word, sir.
  You on your knees have cursed that virtuous maiden,
  And me for loving her, yet do you now
  Thus baffle me to my face? Wear not your knees
  In such entreats! Give me Fitzallard's daughter.   170
SIR ALEXANDER   I'll give thee ratsbane rather!
SEBASTIAN   Well, then, you know
  What dish I mean to feed upon.
SIR ALEXANDER   Hark gentlemen,
  He swears to have this cutpurse drab to spite my gall.
OMNES   Master Sebastian!
SEBASTIAN   I am deaf to you all.
  I'm so bewitched, so bound to my desires,   175
  Tears, prayers, threats, nothing can quench out those fires
  That burn within me.   *Exit Sebastian.*
SIR ALEXANDER   Her blood shall quench it, then.
  [*To them*] Lose him not. Oh, dissuade him, gentlemen!
SIR DAVY   He shall be weaned, I warrant you.
SIR ALEXANDER   Before his eyes
  Lay down his shame, my grief, his miseries.   180
OMNES   No more, no more! Away!
                  Exeunt all but Sir Alexander.
SIR ALEXANDER   I wash a Negro,
  Losing both pains and cost. But take thy flight;
  I'll be most near thee when I'm least in sight.
  Wild buck, I'll hunt thee breathless; thou shalt run on,
  But I will turn thee when I'm not thought upon.   185

---

    165. *fond*: foolish.
    166. *Hark you a word*: listen to me for a moment. Lines 167 to 171 are probably a private
      exchange between Sebastian and his father, not overheard by the other characters.
    169. *baffle*: disgrace; cheat.
169–70. *Wear . . . entreats*: Don't wear out your knees begging me to take her.
    171. *ratsbane*: rat poison.
    173. *drab*: whore.
    178. *Lose him not*: Don't give up on him.
    181. *I wash a Negro*: "To wash an Ethiop white" was proverbial for "to attempt the
      impossible."

Enter Ralph Trapdoor [bowing and scraping].

Now, sirrah, what are you? Leave your ape's tricks and speak.

TRAPDOOR   A letter from my captain to Your Worship.

SIR ALEXANDER   Oh, oh, now I remember. 'Tis to prefer thee into
my service.

TRAPDOOR   To be a shifter under Your Worship's nose of a clean
trencher, when there's a good bit upon't.   190

SIR ALEXANDER   Troth, honest fellow. [*Aside*] Humh—ha—let
me see:
This knave shall be the ax to hew that down
At which I stumble. H'as a face that promiseth
Much of a villain. I will grind his wit,
And if the edge prove fine, make use of it.—   195
Come hither, sirrah. Canst thou be secret, ha?

TRAPDOOR   As two crafty attorneys plotting the undoing of their
clients.

SIR ALEXANDER   Didst never, as thou hast walked about this town,
hear of a wench called Moll, Mad, Merry Moll?   200

TRAPDOOR   Moll Cutpurse, sir.

SIR ALEXANDER   The same. Dost thou know her, then?

TRAPDOOR   As well as I know 'twill rain upon Simon and Jude's
day next. I will sift all the taverns i'th'city, and drink half-pots
with all the watermen o'th'Bankside, but if you will, sir, I'll   205
find her out.

SIR ALEXANDER   That task is easy; do't, then. Hold thy hand up.
[*Examining his hand*] What's this, is't burnt?

TRAPDOOR   No, sir, no, a little singed with making fireworks.

SIR ALEXANDER [*giving money*]   There's money. Spend it. That   210
being spent, fetch more.

TRAPDOOR   Oh, sir, that all the poor soldiers in England had
such a leader! For fetching, no water spaniel is like me.

SIR ALEXANDER   This wench we speak of strays so from her kind,

---

187. *my captain*: Trapdoor claims to be a discharged soldier, but 5.1.65–114 suggests
he's probably lying.
188. *prefer*: recommend.
189–90. *To be . . . upon't*: To give you a clean plate at the table when there's still a nice
morsel (for me to eat) left on the dirty one.
192–93. *ax . . . stumble*: I.e., he'll be the instrument to get rid of Moll.
194. *grind*: sharpen
203–04. *Simon and Jude's day*: October 28, the feast of the apostles St. Simon and St. Jude,
and the day before the Lord Mayor's pageant—an outdoor performance that had
to be postponed if it rained.
205. *watermen o'th'Bankside*: watermen rowed customers across the Thames; the
Bankside, on the southern shore, was known for its taverns.
207–08. *hand . . . burnt*: convicted felons who had claimed "benefit of clergy" (a legal loophole offering leniency to first-time offenders) were branded on the thumb to identify them in case of future offences.
214. *strays . . . kind*: is so unlike a natural woman.

Nature repents she made her. 'Tis a mermaid   215
Has tolled my son to shipwreck.
TRAPDOOR   I'll cut her comb for you.
SIR ALEXANDER   I'll tell out gold for thee then. Hunt her forth;
Cast out a line hung full of silver hooks
To catch her to thy company. Deep spendings   220
May draw her that's most chaste to a man's bosom.
TRAPDOOR   The jingling of golden bells, and a good fool with a
hobbyhorse, will draw all the whores i'th'town to dance in a
morris.
SIR ALEXANDER   Or rather, for that's best (they say sometimes she   225
goes in breeches), follow her as her man.
TRAPDOOR   And when her breeches are off, she shall follow me.
SIR ALEXANDER   Beat all thy brains to serve her.
TRAPDOOR   Zounds, sir, as country wenches beat cream till
butter comes.   230
SIR ALEXANDER   Play thou the subtle spider; weave fine nets
To ensnare her very life.
TRAPDOOR   Her life?
SIR ALEXANDER   Yes, suck
Her heart-blood if thou canst. Twist thou but cords
To catch her, I'll find law to hang her up.
TRAPDOOR   Spoke like a worshipful bencher.   235
SIR ALEXANDER   Trace all her steps; at this she-fox's den
Watch what lambs enter. Let me play the shepherd
To save their throats from bleeding, and cut hers.
TRAPDOOR   This is the goll shall do't.
SIR ALEXANDER   Be firm, and gain me
Ever thine own. This done, I entertain thee.   240
How is thy name?
TRAPDOOR   My name, sir, is Rafe Trapdoor, honest Rafe.
SIR ALEXANDER   Trapdoor, be like thy name, a dangerous step
For her to venture on; but unto me—
TRAPDOOR   As fast as your sole to your boot or shoe, sir.   245
SIR ALEXANDER   Hence, then. Be little seen here as thou canst.
I'll still be at thine elbow.
TRAPDOOR   The trapdoor's set.

215–16. *Tis . . . shipwreck*: Sir Alexander imagines the mermaid's song as a funeral bell,
          summoning Sebastian to his ruin.
   217. *cut her comb*: emasculate her; a cock's comb was cut when he was castrated.
   218. *tell*: count.
   221. *draw . . . bosom*: draw even the chastest woman into a man's arms.
   224. *morris*: a country dance, traditionally featuring a man with a horse-shaped frame-
          work—the "hobbyhorse"—fastened around his waist.
   226. *follow . . . man*: serve her as her manservant.
   229. *Zounds*: God's wounds (an oath).
   235. *worshipful bencher*: distinguished magistrate, who would be titled "your Worship."
   236. *Trace*: follow.
   239. *goll*: hand.
   240. *Ever thine own*: as your friend forever; *entertain thee*: employ you as my servant.

Moll, if you budge, you're gone. This me shall crown:
A roaring boy the roaring girl puts down.

SIR ALEXANDER   God-a-mercy. Lose no time.   *Exeunt.*

[2.1]

*The three shops open in a rank: the first a pothecary's shop, the
next a feather shop, the third a sempster's shop, Mistress
Gallipot in the first, Mistress Tiltyard in the next, Master
Openwork and his wife in the third. To them enters Laxton,
Goshawk, and Greenwit.*

MRS. OPENWORK   Gentlemen, what is't you lack? What is't you buy?
See fine bands and ruffs, fine lawns, fine cambrics.
What is't you lack, gentlemen, what is't you buy?

LAXTON   Yonder's the shop.

GOSHAWK   Is that she?   5

LAXTON   Peace!

GREENWIT   She that minces tobacco?

LAXTON   Ay. She's a gentlewoman born, I can tell you, though it be
her hard fortune now to shred Indian potherbs.

GOSHAWK   Oh, sir, 'tis many a good woman's fortune, when   10
her husband turns bankrupt, to begin with pipes and set up
again.

LAXTON   And indeed the raising of the woman is the lifting up of
the man's head at all times; if one flourish, t'other will
bud as fast, I warrant ye.   15

GOSHAWK   Come, thou'rt familiarly acquainted there, I grope that.

LAXTON   An you grope no better i'th'dark, you may chance lie
i'th'ditch when you're drunk.

GOSHAWK   Go, thou'rt a mystical lecher.

LAXTON   I will not deny but my credit may take up an ounce of   20
pure smoke.

---

249. *roaring boy*: see page 7 note 5 to Dramatis Personae.
250. *God-a-mercy*: thank you.
  2.1 *s.d. location rank*: row; *a pothecary's shop*: an apothecary was the equivalent of today's
        pharmacist, selling medicines and herbs, including tobacco; *sempster*: a sempster (the
        word could refer to either sex) sewed and mended clothes.
    1. *what . . . lack?*: shopkeeper's typical invitation to customers: "what can I do for you?"
    2. *fine . . . cambrics*: both lawns and cambrics are varieties of fine linen.
    5. *she*: i.e., Mrs. Gallipot.
    6. *Peace*: shush!
    9. *potherbs*: tobacco from the West Indies.
   11. *pipes*: pipes for smoking, but also suggests penises.
13–15. *raising . . . fast*: Laxton continues the sexual innuendo with "raising," "lifting up of
        the man's head," and "bud"; ostensibly, however, he is merely saying that when a
        wife does well financially, it lifts her husband up to the same economic level.
   16. *thou'rt familiarly . . . that*: you know all about that, I grasp (with pun on the sexual
        sense of "grope").
   17. *An*: if.
   19. *mystical lecher*: secret seducer.

GOSHAWK   May take up an ell of pure smock! Away, go. [*Aside*] 'Tis
the closest striker! Life, I think he commits venery forty foot
deep; no man's aware on't. I, like a palpable smockster, go to
work so openly with the tricks of art that I'm as apparently seen   25
as a naked boy in a vial; and were it not for a gift of treachery
that I have in me to betray my friend when he puts most trust in
me—mass, yonder he is too—and by his injury to make good
my access to her, I should appear as defective in courting as a
farmer's son the first day of his feather, that doth nothing at   30
court but woo the hangings and glass windows for a month
together and some broken waiting-woman forever after. I find
those imperfections in my venery that, were't not for flattery
and falsehood, I should want discourse and impudence; and he
that wants impudence among women is worthy to be kicked out   35
at bed's feet.—He shall not see me yet.

[He stands aside.]

GREENWIT [*at the tobacco shop*]   Troth, this is finely shred.
LAXTON   Oh, women are the best mincers.
MRS. GALLIPOT   'T had been a good phrase for a cook's wife, sir.
LAXTON   But 'twill serve generally, like the front of a new almanac;   40
as thus: calculated for the meridian of cooks' wives, but generally
for all Englishwomen.
MRS. GALLIPOT   Nay, you shall ha't, sir; I have filled it for you.

She puts it to the fire.

LAXTON   The pipe's in a good hand, and I wish mine always so.
GREENWIT   But not to be used i'that fashion!   45

---

22. *May . . . smock*: Goshawk's joke plays on a) the similarity in sound between "smoke"
    and "smock" (a woman's slip-like undergarment); b) the double meaning of "take
    up" as both "purchase" and "lift"; and c) the proverb "give him an inch and he'll take
    an ell." An ell was a linear measure equivalent to 45 inches; the modern version of
    the proverb replaces "ell" with "mile."
22–24. *Tis . . . on't*: He's the most secret seducer! By God's life (an oath), I think he has sex
    forty feet underground, so no-one's aware of it.
24. *smockster*: chaser of smocks (i.e., women).
25–26. *seen as . . . a vial*: I'm as obvious to be seen as a fetus in a specimen jar.
28. *mass . . . he is too*: by the mass (a mild oath), there's Openwork; Goshawk plans to
    seduce Mrs. Openwork.
30–32. *farmer's son . . . forever after*: i.e., the first time the farmer's son wears a fashionable
    feathered hat to court, where he spends a month practicing his wooing techniques
    to wall hangings and his own reflection in windows, only to end up with an already-
    deflowered maidservant.
34. *want*: lack.
38. *mincers*: plays on three meanings of "mince": to shred, to "mince words," and to
    walk daintily and affectedly.
40. *almanac*; book of astrological predictions calculated for a given place and year; Lax-
    ton parodies a typical almanac title, e.g., "calculated for the latitude and meridian
    of the honorable city of London, and may very well serve for all England."
43. *ha't*: have it (i.e., the pipe she has filled).
43. s.d. *puts . . . fire*: lights it.
44. *pipe's . . . always so*: Laxton begins more sexual innuendo on pipes as penises; Green-
    wit interjects that he wouldn't want his penis lit on fire, playing on the fact that "to
    be burnt" meant "to catch syphilis." Syphilis was called "the French disease," so
    Laxton's rejoinder suggests "I don't have syphilis."

LAXTON   Oh, pardon me, sir, I understand no French. [*To
   Goshawk*] I pray be covered. Jack, a pipe of rich smoke?
GOSHAWK   Rich smoke; that's sixpence a pipe, is't?
GREENWIT   To me, sweet lady.   [*The men smoke.*]
MRS. GALLIPOT [*aside to Laxton*]   Be not forgetful; respect my   50
   credit; seem strange. Art and wit makes a fool of suspicion;
   pray be wary.
LAXTON [*aside to her*]   Push, I warrant you.—Come, how is't,
   gallants?
GREENWIT   Pure and excellent.   55
LAXTON   I thought 'twas good, you were grown so silent. You are
   like those that love not to talk at victuals, though they make a
   worse noise i'the nose than a common fiddler's prentice, and
   discourse a whole supper with snuffling. [*Aside to
   Mrs. Gallipot*] I must speak a word with you anon.   60
MRS. GALLIPOT [*aside to him*]   Make your way wisely, then.
                    [*They stand aside and converse privately.*]
GOSHAWK [*to Greenwit*]   Oh, what else, sir? He's perfection itself,
   full of manners, but not an acre of ground belonging to 'em.
GREENWIT   Ay, and full of form. H'as ne'er a good stool in's
   chamber.   65
GOSHAWK   But above all, religious: he prayeth daily upon elder
   brothers.
GREENWIT   And valiant above measure: he's run three streets from
   a sergeant.
LAXTON   Pooh, pooh.   *He blows tobacco in their faces.* 70
GREENWIT [*and*] GOSHAWK   Oh, pooh, ho, ho!
                    [*They move away. Laxton and Mrs. Gallipot
                    resume their private conversation.*]
LAXTON   So, so.
MRS. GALLIPOT   What's the matter now, sir?
LAXTON   I protest I'm in extreme want of money. If you can
   supply me now with any means, you do me the greatest pleasure,   75
   next to the bounty of your love, as ever poor gentleman tasted.
MRS. GALLIPOT   What's the sum would pleasure ye, sir?
   Though you deserve nothing less at my hands.
LAXTON   Why, 'tis but for want of opportunity, thou know'st. [*Aside*]
   I put her off with opportunity still. By this light, I hate her, but 80
   for means to keep me in fashion with gallants; for what I take

47. *I . . . covered*: please put on your hat.
49. *To me*: give me a pipe.
50–51. *respect. . . strange*: respect my reputation; pretend you don't know me well.
53. *Push. . . you*: Pooh—of course I will.
57. *victuals*: meals.
60. *anon*: immediately.
63. *manners . . . belonging to 'em*: Laxton has manners (playing on "manors") but no land.
64. *form*: etiquette, formality; also, a low bench, cheaper than a stool.
66–67. *prayeth . . . brothers*: he prays with the Puritan brethren; he preys on rich heirs (eldest sons inherited the family's land).
69. *sergeant*: officer who arrests for debt.
78. *Though . . . hands*: Money from me is the last thing you deserve.

from her I spend upon other wenches, bear her in hand still. She
has wit enough to rob her husband, and I ways enough to
consume the money. [*To Goshawk and Greenwit, who are
coughing*] Why, how now? What, the chin-cough?   85

GOSHAWK   Thou hast the cowardliest trick to come before a man's
face and strangle him ere he be aware! I could find in my
heart to make a quarrel in earnest.

LAXTON   Pox, an thou dost, thou know'st I never use to fight with
my friends; thou'll but lose thy labor in't.   90

Enter Jack Dapper and his man Gull.

Jack Dapper!

GREENWIT   Monsieur Dapper, I dive down to your ankles.

JACK DAPPER   Save ye, gentlemen, all three, in a peculiar salute.

GOSHAWK   He were ill to make a lawyer; he dispatches three at once.

LAXTON [*receiving a purse from Mrs. Gallipot*]   So, well said.   95
But is this of the same tobacco, Mistress Gallipot?

MRS. GALLIPOT   The same you had at first, sir.

LAXTON   I wish it no better. This will serve to drink at my
chamber.

GOSHAWK   Shall we taste a pipe on't?   100

LAXTON   Not of this, by my troth, gentlemen. I have sworn before
you.

GOSHAWK   What, not Jack Dapper?

LAXTON   Pardon me, sweet Jack. I'm sorry I made such a rash oath,
but foolish oaths must stand. [*Dapper starts to move away.*]   105
Where art going, Jack?

JACK DAPPER   Faith, to buy one feather.

LAXTON   One feather? [*Aside*] The fool's peculiar still.

JACK DAPPER [*to his servant*]   Gull!

GULL   Master?   110

JACK DAPPER [*giving coin*]   Here's three halfpence for your
ordinary, boy. Meet me an hour hence in Paul's.
                    [*Dapper makes his way to the feather shop.*]

GULL [*to himself*]   How? Three single halfpence? Life, this will
scarce serve a man in sauce. A ha'p'orth of mustard, a

82. *bear . . . still*: keep stringing her along.
85. *chin-cough*: whooping-cough.
89. *an*: if; *never use to*: make it a habit not to.
90. *lose . . . in't*: waste your effort.
92. *dive . . . ankles*: bow deeply, with wordplay on "divedapper," a kind of waterfowl.
93. *save . . . salute*: God save ye (a greeting) . . . in a single (but also strange) salutation.
94. *He were . . . lawyer*: He'd make a bad lawyer; lawyers profited from drawing out their
    clients' suits, not efficiently dispatching them.
96. *same tobacco*: Laxton and Mrs.Gallipot pretend the purse contains tobacco, not money.
98. *drink*: smoke.
103. *What . . . Dapper?*: Doesn't Jack get to smoke some?
112. *ordinary*: fixed-price meal served in a tavern, or a tavern offering such a meal; *Paul's*:
    St. Paul's Cathedral, a fashionable meeting place.
114. *scarce . . . sauce*: this will barely pay for condiments; *ha'p'orth*: half-penny worth.

ha'p'orth of oil, and a ha'p'orth of vinegar; what's left then   115
for the pickle herring? This shows like small beer i'th'morning
after a great surfeit of wine o'ernight. He could spend his
three pound last night in a supper amongst girls and brave
bawdy-house boys. I thought his pockets cackled not for
nothing; these are the eggs of three pound. I'll go sup   120
'em up presently.   *Exit Gull.*

LAXTON [*aside, as he counts the money*]   Eight, nine, ten angels.
Good wench, i'faith, and one that loves darkness well; she
puts out a candle with the best tricks of any drugster's wife in
England. But that which mads her: I rail upon opportunity still,   125
and take no notice on't. The other night she would needs lead
me into a room with a candle in her hand to show me a naked
picture, where no sooner entered but the candle was sent of an
errand. Now I, not intending to understand her, but like
a puny at the inns of venery, called for another light innocently.   130
Thus reward I all her cunning with simple mistaking. I know she
cozens her husband to keep me and I'll keep her honest as long
as I can, to make the poor man some part of amends. An honest
mind of a whoremaster! [*To the gallants*] How think you
amongst you? What, a fresh pipe? Draw in a third man.   135
GOSHAWK   No, you're a hoarder; you engross by th'ounces.

At the feather shop now.

JACK DAPPER [*examining a feather*]   Pooh, I like it not.
MRS. TILTYARD   What feather is't you'd have, sir? These are most
worn and most in fashion amongst the beaver gallants,
the stone riders, the private stage's audience, the twelvepenny-   140
stool gentlemen, I can inform you, 'tis the general feather.

116–17.   *small beer . . . o'ernight*: weak beer in the morning after bingeing on wine the night
before.
119.   *bawdy-house*: brothel.
119–20.   *Pockets cackled . . . pound*: Gull imagines the three pounds jingling last night
in Dapper's pockets as cackling fowl; all that remains are the "eggs"—the three
half-pence—they left behind.
120–21.   *I'll gos up . . . presently*: I'll go eat them right away.
122.   *angels*: gold coins worth ten shillings.
125.   *I rail . . . still*: I keep complaining that we never have an opportunity (to have sex).
128–29.   *sent . . . errand*: put out.
130.   *puny . . . venery*: a sexually inexperienced youth; plays on "a puny at the Inns of
Court," which would be a first-year law student.
132.   *cozens . . . to keep me*: she defrauds her husband to financially support me; *honest*:
chaste.
133–34.   *honest . . . whoremaster!*: I have quite the virtuous mind, for a playboy!
136.   *engross*: monopolize (the tobacco).
139–41.   *beaver gallants . . . gentlemen*: fashionable young men in beaver-fur hats, riders of
stallions, patrons of the expensive indoor playhouses, and men who spend
twelvepence (12 times the basic admission fee to an outdoor playhouse) for a seat
on the stage, the best place to see and be seen.

JACK DAPPER   And therefore I mislike it. Tell me of general! Now
a continual Simon and Jude's rain beat all your feathers
as flat down as pancakes! Show me—a—spangled feather.
MRS. TILTYARD   Oh, to go a-feasting with! You'd have it for a   145
henchboy. You shall.

At the sempster's shop now.

OPENWORK [*to his wife*]   Mass, I had quite forgot. His Honor's
footman was here last night, wife. Ha' you done with my lord's
shirt?
MRS. OPENWORK   What's that to you, sir? I was this morning at His   150
Honor's lodging ere such a snail as you crept out of your shell.
OPENWORK   Oh, 'twas well done, good wife.
MRS. OPENWORK   I hold it better, sir, than if you had done't
yourself.
OPENWORK   Nay, so say I. But is the countess's smock almost   155
done, mouse?
MRS. OPENWORK   Here lies the cambric, sir, but wants, I fear me.
OPENWORK   I'll resolve you of that presently.
                                            [*He takes the work and retires.*]
MRS. OPENWORK   Heyday! Oh, audacious groom,
Dare you presume to noblewomen's linen?   160
Keep you your yard to measure shepherds' holland!
I must confine you, I see that.

At the tobacco shop now.

GOSHAWK [*as they smoke*]   What say you to this gear?
LAXTON   I dare the arrant'st critic in tobacco to lay one fault upon't.

Enter Moll in a frieze jerkin and a black safeguard.

GOSHAWK   Life, yonder's Moll!   165
LAXTON   Moll? Which Moll?
GOSHAWK   Honest Moll.
LAXTON   Prithee, let's call her.—Moll!

143. *Simon and Jude's rain*: see note to 1.2.204–205.
144. *spangled*: speckled, unless Dapper means something as outrageous as a feather
        covered in sequins.
146. *henchboy*: pageboy.
147. *His Honor's*: the nobleman's.
148–49. *my lord's shirt?*: a loose shirt worn under a doublet; like a woman's smock, a man's
        shirt was considered intimate apparel.
156. *mouse*: a term of endearment.
157. *wants*: lacks (finishing, or perhaps fabric).
159. *Heyday!*: an exclamation of surprise; *groom*: servant (an insult).
160. *linen*: undergarments.
161. *yard*: a measuring rod of 36 inches, but also the common word for penis; *holland*:
        coarse linen cloth.
163. *gear*: stuff.
164. *arrant'st*: most extreme.
164. **s.d.** *frieze jerkin . . . safeguard*: a man's woolen jacket and a woman's riding skirt (a
        safeguard was an overskirt to protect clothes from mud while on horseback).

ALL   Moll, Moll, psst, Moll!

MOLL   How now, what's the matter?   170

GOSHAWK   A pipe of good tobacco, Moll?

MOLL   I cannot stay.

GOSHAWK   Nay, Moll, pooh! Prithee hark, but one word, i'faith.

MOLL   Well, what is't?

GREENWIT   Prithee come hither, sirrah.   175

LAXTON [aside]   Heart, I would give but too much money to be
nibbling with that wench. Life, sh' has the spirit of four great
parishes, and a voice that will drown all the city! Methinks a
brave captain might get all his soldiers upon her, and ne'er be
beholding to a company of Mile End milksops, if he could come   180
on and come off quick enough. Such a Moll were a marrowbone
before an Italian; he would cry "bona-roba" till his ribs were
nothing but bone. I'll lay hard siege to her. Money is that aqua
fortis that eats into many a maidenhead. Where the walls are
flesh and blood, I'll ever pierce through with a golden auger.   185

GOSHAWK [offering tobacco]   Now, thy judgment, Moll. Is't not good?

MOLL   Yes, faith, 'tis very good tobacco. How do you sell an ounce?
Farewell. God buy you, Mistress Gallipot.

[She starts to go.]

GOSHAWK   Why, Moll, Moll!

MOLL   I cannot stay now, i'faith. I am going to buy a shag ruff.   190
The shop will be shut in presently.

[She heads for the other shops.]

GOSHAWK   'Tis the maddest, fantastical'st girl! I never knew so
much flesh and so much nimbleness put together.

LAXTON   She slips from one company to another like a fat eel
between a Dutchman's fingers. [Aside] I'll watch my time for her.   195

MRS. GALLIPOT   Some will not stick to say she's a man, and some,
both man and woman.

LAXTON   That were excellent. She might first cuckold the husband
and then make him do as much for the wife.

175. sirrah: "sirrah" addressed to a woman expresses friendly familiarity, not the
       addressee's social inferiority, as it does when addressed to a man; compare
       3.2.163; 4.2.10.
179. get: beget.
179–80. be beholding: never be obliged to choose soldiers from among the citizen militia
       that trains at Mile End (a field east of the city wall).
181. come on and come off: advance and retreat; mount and ejaculate; marrowbone:
       bone marrow is a gourmet delicacy and was thought to be an aphrodisiac.
182. "bona-roba": "good stuff"(Italian), said of loose women; Italians had a reputation
       for buggery.
183–84. aqua fortis: nitric acid, a strong corrosive.
184. maidenhead: hymen.
185. auger: tool for boring holes.
187. How: For how much.
188. God buy you: God be with you.
190. shag: velvet.
196. stick: hesitate.
198–99. first . . . wife. i.e., have sex with the wife, and then have sex with the husband.

The feather shop again.

MOLL [*as she approaches*]   Save you! How does Mistress Tiltyard?   200
JACK DAPPER   Moll!
MOLL   Jack Dapper!
JACK DAPPER   How dost, Moll?
MOLL   I'll tell thee by and by. I go but to th'next shop.
JACK DAPPER   Thou shalt find me here this hour about a feather.   205
MOLL   Nay, an a feather hold you in play a whole hour, a goose will
    last you all the days of your life.   [*She moves on.*]

The sempster shop.

Let me see a good shag ruff.
OPENWORK   Mistress Mary, that shalt thou, i'faith, and the best in
    the shop.   210
MRS. OPENWORK   How now, greetings? Love terms, with a pox,
    between you? Have I found out one of your haunts? I send you
    for hollands, and you're i'th' Low Countries, with a mischief. I'm
    served with good ware by th'shift that makes it lie dead so long
    upon my hands I were as good shut up shop, for when   215
    I open it I take nothing.
OPENWORK   Nay, an you fall a-ringing once, the devil cannot stop
    you. I'll out of the belfry as fast as I can.—Moll!
                [*He goes to join Goshawk and the others.*]
MRS. OPENWORK [*to Moll*]   Get you from my shop!
MOLL   I come to buy.   220
MRS. OPENWORK   I'll sell ye nothing. I warn ye my house and
    shop.
MOLL   You, Goody Openwork, you that prick out a poor living.
    And sews many a bawdy skin-coat together,
    Thou private pand'ress between shirt and smock,   225
    I wish thee for a minute but a man;
    Thou shouldst never use more shapes. But as th'art,

---

204. *by and by*: soon.
211. *with a pox*: an interjection of annoyance or disgust; the "pox" was syphilis.
214. *hollands . . . Countries*: I sent you for linen and you're attending to matters below
      the waist; the wordplay is on "holland" as both a fabric and a region, part of the
      "Low Countries" corresponding roughly to the modern Netherlands, Belgium,
      and Luxembourg.
213–16. *I'm served . . . nothing*: "ware" means both "merchandise" and "male genitals"; "by
      the shift" means "as makeshift, in a pinch." Using shopkeeper's terms, Mrs. Open-
      work complains that her husband only serves her with his "ware" on the rare occa-
      sions he is obliged to make do with his wife, and even then he can't get an erection
      ("lie dead . . . upon my hands"), to the point where she might as well give up having
      sex with him altogether.
217–18. *fall . . . you*: once you start ringing your bells—i.e., telling me off—even the devil can't
      make you be quiet.
221. *warn ye*: warn you to stay away from.
223. *Goody*: "Goodwife," title for a married woman of low social status.
224. *bawdy*: lewd.
225. *shirt and smock*: see note to 2.1.150.
227–28. *as th'art . . . revenge*: as you are (i.e., a woman), I'd feel sorry for you if I were to
      take revenge.

I pity my revenge. Now my spleen's up,
I would not mock it willingly. Ha! Be thankful.
Now I forgive thee.   230

MRS. OPENWORK   Marry, hang thee! I never asked forgiveness in
my life.

Enter a Fellow with a long rapier by his side.

MOLL [*to the Fellow, as she draws her sword*]   You, goodman
swine's face!

FELLOW   What, will you murder me?   235

MOLL   You remember, slave, how you abused me t'other night in a
tavern?

FELLOW   Not I, by this light.

MOLL   No, but by candlelight you did. You have tricks to save your
oaths, reservations, have you? And I have reserved somewhat for   240
you. [*She strikes him.*] As you like that, call for more. You know
the sign again.

FELLOW [*to himself*]   Pox on't, had I brought any company
along with me to have borne witness on't, twould ne'er have
grieved me; but to be struck and nobody by, 'tis my ill fortune   245
still. Why, tread upon a worm, they say 'twill turn tail but indeed
a gentleman should have more manners.

Exit Fellow.

LAXTON   Gallantly performed, i'faith, Moll, and manfully!
I love thee forever for't. Base rogue! Had he offered but the least
counterbuff, by this hand, I was prepared for him.   250

MOLL   You prepared for him? Why should you be prepared for
him? Was he any more than a man?

LAXTON   No, nor so much by a yard and a handful, London measure.

MOLL   Why do you speak this, then? Do you think I cannot ride a
stone horse unless one lead him by th'snaffle?   255

LAXTON   Yes, and sit him bravely; I know thou canst, Moll. 'Twas
but an honest mistake, through love, and I'll make amends
for't any way. Prithee, sweet plump Moll, when shall thou and I
go out o'town together?

MOLL   Whither? To Tyburn, prithee?   260

---

228.   *spleen*: anger.
229.   *mock it*: disappoint my anger (i.e., by preventing it from beating you up).
233.   *goodman*: title for a man of low social status, the counterpart of "Goody" (see
       2.1.223).
236.   *abused*: insulted.
239–40.   *tricks . . . oaths*: tricks to swear oaths that aren't binding (like "by this light" when,
       literally speaking, he insulted Moll by candlelight).
244.   *borne witness on't*: witnessed the assault.
246.   *turn tail*: proverbial: "even the weak will turn upon their attackers."
249–50.   *offered . . . counterbuff*: tried even the lightest blow in return.
253.   *yard*: see note to 2.1.162.
254–55.   *I cannot . . . th'snaffle?*: I can't ride a stallion unless someone leads him by the bridle?
260.   *Tyburn*: site of the gallows, west of London.

LAXTON   Mass, that's out o'town indeed. Thou hang'st so many
jests upon thy friends still. I mean honestly to Brentford,
Staines, or Ware.

MOLL   What to do there?

LAXTON   Nothing but be merry and lie together. I'll hire a coach   265
with four horses.

MOLL   I thought 'twould be a beastly journey. You may leave
out one well; three horses will serve, if I play the jade myself.

LAXTON   Nay, push, thou'rt such another kicking wench! Prithee
be kind and let's meet.   270

MOLL   Tis hard but we shall meet, sir.

LAXTON   Nay, but appoint the place, then. [*He offers money.*]
There's ten angels in fair gold, Moll; you see I do not trifle with
you. Do but say thou wilt meet me, and I'll have a coach ready
for thee.   275

MOLL   Why, here's my hand I'll meet you, sir.

LAXTON [*aside*]   Oh, good gold!—The place, sweet Moll?

MOLL   It shall be your appointment.

LAXTON   Somewhat near Holborn, Moll.

MOLL   In Gray's Inn Fields, then.   280

LAXTON   A match.

MOLL   I'll meet you there.

LAXTON   The hour?

MOLL   Three.

LAXTON   That will be time enough to sup at Brentford.   285
                              Fall from them to the other.

OPENWORK [*to Goshawk*]   I am of such a nature sir, I cannot
endure the house when she scolds. Sh' has a tongue will be
heard further in a still morning than Saint Antholin's bell. She
rails upon me for foreign wenching, that I, being a freeman,
must needs keep a whore i'th'suburbs and seek to   290
impoverish the liberties. When we fall out, I trouble
you still to make all whole with my wife.

262–63. *Brentford . . . Ware*: nearby towns, popular for illicit sexual encounters.
  267. *beastly*: lewd.
  268. *jade*: derogatory term for a horse or for a woman; a hussy.
  269. *such another*: such a.
  271. *Tis . . . meet*: It would be a shame if we didn't meet.
  273. *ten angels*: see note to 2.1.122.
  278. *appointment*: decision.
  279. *Holborn*: a road in central London, near the law schools and offices which consti-
         tuted the Inns of Court; Gray's Inn (l. 280) was one of them.
  281. *match*: deal.
  285. *s.d. Fall . . . other*: Moll and Laxton move to other groups onstage.
  288. *Saint Antholin's*: a central London church with Puritan leanings; its bell rang at 5
         a.m. for an early service.
  291. *impoverish the liberties*: the suburbs, known for their brothels, were areas outside of
         London's municipal jurisdiction, while the "liberties" were areas within it, though
         outside the city proper. Mrs. Openwork scolds her husband, a London citizen ("free-
         man"), for spending his money and sexual energy on a suburban ("foreign") whore
         rather than spending it at home (i.e., on her). Compare 2.1.236–38; *fall out*: quarrel.

GOSHAWK   No trouble at all. Tis a pleasure to me to join things
together.

OPENWORK   Go thy ways. [*Aside*] I do this but to try thy honesty,   295
Goshawk.

The feather shop.

JACK DAPPER [*trying on feathers*]   How lik'st thou this, Moll?

MOLL   Oh, singularly; you're fitted now for a bunch. [*Aside*] He
looks for all the world with those spangled feathers like a
nobleman's bedpost. The purity of your wench would I   300
fain try; she seems like Kent unconquered, and I believe
as many wiles are in her. Oh, the gallants of these times are
shallow lechers! They put not their courtship home enough to a
wench; 'tis impossible to know what woman is throughly honest,
because she's ne'er thoroughly tried. I am of that certain belief   305
there are more queans in this town of their
own making than of any man's provoking. Where lies the
slackness then? Many a poor soul would down, and there's
nobody will push 'em.
Women are courted but ne'er soundly tried;   310
As many walk in spurs that never ride.

The sempster's shop.

MRS. OPENWORK   Oh, abominable!

GOSHAWK   Nay, more: I tell you in private, he keeps a whore
i'th'suburbs.

MRS. OPENWORK   Oh, spittle dealing! I came to him a gentle   315
woman born. I'll show you mine arms when you please, sir.

GOSHAWK [*aside*]   I had rather see your legs, and begin that way.

MRS. OPENWORK   Tis well known he took me from a lady's service
where I was well beloved of the steward. I had my Latin
tongue and a spice of the French before I came to him, and now   320
doth he keep a suburbian whore under my nostrils.

295. *Go thy ways*: carry on what you're doing; *try*: test.
300. *bedpost*: feathers often decorated the tops of bedposts on elaborate four-poster beds;
your wench: Mrs. Tiltyard (compare 2.1.350); Moll does not follow through on this
plan.
301. Kent, a county in southeast England, boasted of being "unconquered," as it resisted
the Norman conquest of 1066 and managed to maintain its own laws and customs.
Whereas Kent was known for its "wilds" (forests), Moll punningly claims that Mrs.
Tiltyard has "wiles;" there may also be a pun on Kent/cunt.
303. *shallow lechers*: lazy or unskilled seducers; *home*: thoroughly.
304. *throughly honest*: chaste through and through.
306. *queans*: whores.
308. *would down*: would like to have an affair.
311. *walk . . . ride*: just like many men wear spurs on their boots for show, but never actually
ride a horse; "as" could also mean "because," in which case the sense is "because many
men act as if they're great sexual 'riders,' but never actually do the deed."
313. *he*: i.e., Openwork.
315. *spittle*: hospital (i.e., where one would go with venereal disease).
316. *mine arms*: coat of arms.
320. *a spice . . . French*: a smattering of French; also suggests syphilis, "the French disease."

GOSHAWK   There's ways enough to cry quit with him. Hark in thine
    ear.   [*He whispers to her.*]
MRS. OPENWORK   There's a friend worth a million.

    [*The feather shop.*]

MOLL [*aside*]   I'll try one spear against your chastity, Mistress   325
    Tiltyard, though it prove too short by the burr.

    Enter Ralph Trapdoor.

TRAPDOOR-[*seeing Moll*]   Mass, here she is. I'm bound already to
    serve her though it be but a sluttish trick. [*To Moll*] Bless
    my hopeful young mistress with long life and great limbs!
    Send her the upper hand of all bailiffs and their hungry adherents!   330
MOLL   How now, what art thou?
TRAPDOOR   A poor ebbing gentleman that would gladly wait for the
    young flood of your service.
MOLL   My service? What should move you to offer your service to
    me, sir?   335
TRAPDOOR   The love I bear to your heroic spirit and masculine
    womanhood.
MOLL   So, sir, put case we should retain you to us. What
    parts are there in you for a gentlewoman's service?
TRAPDOOR   Of two kinds, Right Worshipful: movable and   340
    immovable—movable to run of errands, and immovable to stand
    when you have occasion to use me.
MOLL   What strength have you?
TRAPDOOR   Strength, Mistress Moll? I have gone up into a steeple
    and stayed the great bell as't has been ringing; stopped a   345
    windmill going.
MOLL   And never struck down yourself?
TRAPDOOR   Stood as upright as I do at this present.
                          Moll trips up his heels; he falls.

322. *cry quit*: get even.
326. *though . . . burr*: even though it might prove inadequate; a "burr" is a broad iron ring on
    the handle end of a tilting spear.
328. *sluttish trick*: though my so-called "service" is just a dirty trick. "Sluttish" could simply
    mean "filthy" but could also have its modern sexual meaning; both may be implied
    here.
329. *hopeful*: Trapdoor hopes Moll will employ him.
330. *Send . . . adherents!*: May she have the upper hand over arresting officers and their
    eager employees!
333. *young flood*: flow of the tide up-river; serving Moll would reverse Trapdoor's "ebbing"
    fortunes.
338. *put case*: suppose.
339. *parts*: qualities; but in his response, Trapdoor puns on sexual "parts" with "stand" (to
    have an erection) and "use."
340. *Right Worshipful*: Trapdoor's exceedingly respectful title for Moll, typically used for
    men of rank and importance.
341. *of*: on.
345. *stayed*: stopped.

MOLL   Come, I pardon you for this. It shall be no disgrace to
you; I have struck up the heels of the high German's size ere   350
now.—What, not stand?

TRAPDOOR   I am of that nature where I love, I'll be at my mistress's
foot to do her service.

MOLL   Why, well said. But say your mistress should receive
injury: have you the spirit of fighting in you? Durst you   355
second her?

TRAPDOOR   Life, I have kept a bridge myself, and drove seven
at a time before me.

MOLL   Ay?

TRAPDOOR [aside]   But they were all Lincolnshire bullocks,   360
by my troth.

MOLL   Well, meet me in Gray's Inn Fields between three and
four this afternoon, and upon better consideration we'll
retain you.

TRAPDOOR   I humbly thank Your good Mistress-ship. [Aside] I'll   365
crack your neck for this kindness!   Exit Trapdoor.

    Moll meets Laxton.

LAXTON   Remember: three.

MOLL   Nay, if I fail you, hang me.

LAXTON   Good wench, i'faith.

    Then [Moll meets] Openwork.

MOLL   Who's this?   370

OPENWORK   'Tis I, Moll.

MOLL   Prithee, tend thy shop and prevent bastards.

OPENWORK   We'll have a pint of the same wine, i'faith,
Moll.

        [Exeunt Openwork and Moll.] The bell rings.

GOSHAWK   Hark! The bell rings. Come, gentlemen. Jack Dapper,   375
where shall's all munch?

JACK DAPPER   I am for Parker's ordinary.

LAXTON [aside to the others]   He's a good guest to 'm, he deserves
his board. He draws all the gentlemen in a term-time

350. *high German*: a topical reference: a tall, strong German fencer was well known in
London at the time.
355–56. *Durst you second her*: do you dare to back her up?
357–58. *kept a . . . before me*: guarded a bridge and chased away seven at a time (seven bull
calves, as his aside then clarifies, not seven enemy soldiers).
370. *Who's this*: Openwork is most likely in disguise to elude his wife.
373. *same wine*: "bastard" was a sweet Spanish wine; Openwork plays on Moll's remark
that he should go home to avoid having illegitimate children.
377. *ordinary*: see note to 2.1.112.
379. *board*: i.e., he should get free meals for bringing customers to Parker's. *term-time*:
period of the year when the law courts are in session.

thither.—We'll be your followers, Jack; lead the way.—Look you,   380
by my faith, the fool has feathered his nest well.

Exeunt gallants.

Enter Master Gallipot, Master Tiltyard, and servants with water
spaniels and a duck.

TILTYARD   Come, shut up your shops. Where's Master
Openwork?

MRS. OPENWORK   Nay, ask not me, Master Tiltyard.

GALLIPOT   Where's his water-dog? Pooh—psst!—hur—   385
hur—psst!

TILTYARD Come, wenches, come, we're going all to Hoxton.

MRS. GALLIPOT   To Hoxton, husband?

GALLIPOT   Ay, to Hoxton, pigsney.

MRS. TILTYARD   I'm not ready, husband.   390

TILTYARD   Faith, that's well. [*Spits in the dog's mouth.*]
Hum—psst! psst!

GALLIPOT   Come, Mistress Openwork, you are so long.

MRS. OPENWORK   I have no joy of my life, Master Gallipot.

GALLIPOT   Push, let your boy lead his water spaniel along and we'll   395
show you the bravest sport at Parlous Pond. Hey, Trug, hey, Trug,
hey, Trug! Here's the best duck in England, except my wife. Hey,
hey, hey!
Fetch, fetch, fetch! Come, let's away.
Of all the year, this is the sportful'st day.   [*Exeunt.*]   400

[2.2]

Enter Sebastian solus.

SEBASTIAN   If a man have a free will, where should the use
More perfect shine than in his will to love?
All creatures have their liberty in that;

Enter Sir Alexander and listens to him.

Though else kept under servile yoke and fear,
The very bondslave has his freedom there.   5

---

381. *feathered . . . well*: Jack has evidently bought and is now wearing a spectacular new
feather.
381. s.d. *duck*: decoy.
386. *psst!*: Gallipot is whistling for his dog.
387. *Hoxton*: a village just north of London.
389. *pigsney*: pig's eye, a term of endearment.
391. s.d. a way of rewarding a dog and keeping it subordinate to its trainer, based on the
observation that puppies lick the muzzles of the elder dogs in a pack.
396. *bravest*: best; *Parlous Pond*: a pond on the way to Hoxton, named "parlous" (perilous)
due to drownings; *Trug*: a dog's name.
Scene 2.2 s.d. *solus*: alone.
  4. *else*: otherwise.

Amongst a world of creatures voiced and silent,
Must my desires wear fetters? [*Aside, spying his father*]
　　Yea, are you
So near? Then I must break with my heart's truth,
Meet grief at a back way. [*Aloud*] Well, why suppose   10
The two-leaved tongues of slander or of truth
Pronounce Moll loathsome; if before my love
She appear fair, what injury have I?
I have the thing I like. In all things else
Mine own eye guides me, and I find 'em prosper   15
Life, what should ail it now? I know that man
Ne'er truly loves—if he gainsay't he lies—
That winks and marries with his father's eyes.
I'll keep mine own wide open.

Enter Moll and a Porter with a viol on his back.

SIR ALEXANDER [*aside*]   Here's brave willfulness!
A made match. Here she comes; they met o'purpose.   20
PORTER   Must I carry this great fiddle to your chamber,
Mistress Mary?
MOLL   Fiddle, goodman hog-rubber? [*Aside*] Some of these porters
bear so much for others they have no time to carry
wit for themselves.   25
PORTER   To your own chamber, Mistress Mary?
MOLL [*to the audience*]   Who'll hear an ass speak?—Whither
else, goodman pageant-bearer?—They're people of the worst
memories.   *Exit Porter.*
SEBASTIAN   Why, 'twere too great a burden, love, to have them   30
carry things in their minds and o'their backs together.
MOLL   Pardon me, sir, I thought not you so near.
SIR ALEXANDER [*aside*]   So, so, so.
SEBASTIAN   I would be nearer to thee, and in that fashion that makes
the best part of all creatures honest. No otherwise I wish it.   35

10. *meet . . . back way*: grieve privately, in a hidden place.
11. *two-leaved*: forked; duplicitous.
12. *before my love*: in front of my loving gaze.
15. *Mine own eye . . . prosper*: I find that they (i.e., the things in which my eye guides
　　me) turn out well.
16. *what should ail it now?*: why should there be something wrong with my eyesight
　　now?
17. *gainsay't*: denies it.
18. *winks*: closes his eyes.
19. *s.d. viol*: stringed instrument similar to a modern cello.
19. *brave*: fine (ironic).
20. *made match*: an arranged meeting; possibly, "an agreed-upon betrothal."
23. *hog-rubber*: contemptuous term for a swineherd.
28. *pageant-bearer*: porter who carried the elaborate structures used as backdrops, etc., in
　　pageants celebrating civic occasions.
28–29. *They're . . . worst memories*: porters have bad memories.
34–35. *nearer . . . honest*: I would like to be nearer to you by marriage, which makes the
　　majority of people virtuous and respectable.

MOLL   Sir, I am so poor to requite you, you must look for nothing
but thanks of me. I have no humor to marry. I love to lie o'both
sides o'th'bed myself; and again, o'th'other side, a wife, you
know, ought to be obedient, but I fear me I am too headstrong to
obey; therefore I'll ne'er go about it. I love you so well, sir, for   40
your good will, I'd be loath you should repent your bargain after,
and therefore we'll ne'er come together at first. I have the head
now of myself, and am man enough for a woman. Marriage is
but a chopping and changing, where a maiden loses one head
and has a worse i'th'place.   45

SIR ALEXANDER   [aside] The most comfortable answer from a
roaring girl that ever mine ears drunk in!

SEBASTIAN   This were enough now to affright a fool forever
from thee, when 'tis the music that I love thee for.

SIR ALEXANDER [aside]   There's a boy spoils all again!   50

MOLL   Believe it, sir, I am not of that disdainful temper but I
could love you faithfully.

SIR ALEXANDER [aside]   A pox on you for that word! I like you
not now. You're a cunning roarer; I see that already.

MOLL   But sleep upon this once more, sir. You may chance shift a   55
mind tomorrow. Be not too hasty to wrong yourself. Never,
while you live, sir, take a wife running; many have run out at
heels that have done't. You see, sir, I speak against myself,
and if every woman would deal with their suitor so honestly,
poor younger brothers would not be so often gulled with old   60
cozening widows that turn o'er all their wealth in trust to some
kinsman and make the poor gentleman work hard for a pension.
Fare you well, sir.

                                                [She starts to leave.]

SEBASTIAN   Nay, prithee one word more!

SIR ALEXANDER [aside]   How do I wrong this girl! She puts him   65
off still.

37. *humor*: inclination.
38. *o'th'other side*: on the other hand.
42–43. *head . . . myself*: "the husband is the wife's head" was a commonplace of early mod-
    ern marital ideology; Moll also plays on the expression "to give a horse his head,"
    meaning to loosen hold on the reins and allow the horse to go freely.
44–45. *maiden loses . . . i'th'place*: a virgin loses her hymen (maidenhead) and gets a hus-
    band (head of the household) instead.
51–52. *I am not . . . faithfully*: I am not so disdainful that I wouldn't love you faithfully.
55–56. *shift a mind*: change your mind.
57–58. *run . . . heels*: into poverty (i.e., with the heels worn out of your stockings).
57. *running*: in haste.
60–61. *gulled . . . widows*: cheated by tricky old widows.
61–62. *widows . . . pension*: widows typically inherited at least a third, and often much
    more, of their late husbands' wealth, which made them attractive marriage
    prospects for younger brothers, who inherited little under the system of primogeni-
    ture. As marriage legally transferred all of a woman's wealth to her husband, widows
    sometimes protected their assets by signing everything over to a trusted friend or
    kinsman before remarrying: the kinsman thus "owned" the property in a purely legal
    sense, while the widow continued to have the use of it. Moll imagines the new hus-
    band of such a widow being obliged to please her ("work hard," probably in a sexual
    sense) so she would dole out his stipend ("pension").

MOLL   Think upon this in cold blood, sir; you make as much
haste as if you were a-going upon a sturgeon voyage. Take
deliberation, sir; never choose a wife as if you were going to
Virginia.   [*She moves away from him.*]   70
SEBASTIAN [*declaiming*]   And so we parted. My too cursèd
fate!   [*He stands aside.*]
SIR ALEXANDER [*aside*]   She is but cunning, gives him longer
time in't.

   Enter a Tailor.

TAILOR   Mistress Moll, Mistress Moll! Soho ho, soho!
MOLL   There, boy, there, boy, What, dost thou go a-hawking   75
after me with a red clout on thy finger?
TAILOR   I forgot to take measure on you for your new breeches.
SIR ALEXANDER [*aside*]   Heyday, breeches! What, will he marry
a monster with two trinkets? What age is this! If the wife
go in breeches, the man must wear long coats like a fool.   80
            [*The Tailor takes measurements on Moll.*]
MOLL   What fiddling's here? Would not the old pattern have
served your turn?
TAILOR   You change the fashion. You say you'll have the great
Dutch slop, Mistress Mary.
MOLL   Why, sir, I say so still.   85
TAILOR   Your breeches then will take up a yard more.
MOLL   Well, pray look it be put in, then.
TAILOR   It shall stand round and full, I warrant you.
MOLL   Pray make 'em easy enough.
TAILOR   I know my fault now; t'other was somewhat stiff between 90
the legs. I'll make these open enough, I warrant you.
SIR ALEXANDER [*aside*]   Here's good gear towards! I have
brought up my son to marry a Dutch slop and a French
doublet—a codpiece daughter.
TAILOR   So, I have gone as far as I can go.   95
MOLL   Why, then, farewell.

---

68. *sturgeon voyage*: a long fishing voyage, probably to Russia, to catch sturgeon. Presumably the fisherman could leave the hastily chosen wife behind; by contrast, the settler heading for the American colonies (ll. 69–70) would need a wife—any wife—to help him out.
74. *soho*: a hunting-call, alerting hunters or dogs to the presence of a hare. Moll's "there, boy" continues the call as if pointing out the prey to a dog; both dogs and hawks (l. 75) were used to hunt small game.
76. *clout*: cloth (probably a measuring tape or pincushion).
79. *two trinkets*: both male and female genitals; or, possibly, a set of testicles; *what age is this!*: what are these times coming to?
80. *long coats*: petticoats, worn by small children, women, and jesters.
81. *What fiddling's here?*: what a lot of fussing! (with sexual innuendo).
84. *Dutch slop*: big, baggy breeches.
86. *take . . . yard more*: will need a yard more fabric; the pun on "yard" as "penis" runs through the next five lines with "put in," "stand round and full," and "stiff between the legs."
92. *Here's . . . towards*: Here's a fine state of affairs! (with pun on "gear" as "genitals").
94. *codpiece*, see note to Epistle, l. 16, "daughter" was commonly used for a daughter-in-law.

TAILOR   If you go presently to your chamber, Mistress Mary,
    pray send me the measure of your thigh, by some honest
    body.
MOLL   Well, sir, I'll send it by a porter presently.   *Exit Moll.* 100
TAILOR   So you had need; it is a lusty one. Both of them would
    make any porter's back ache in England.   *Exit Tailor.*
SEBASTIAN [*to himself*]   I have examined the best part of man—
    Reason and judgment—and in love, they tell me,
    They leave me uncontrolled. He that is swayed   105
    By an unfeeling blood, past heat of love,
    His springtime must needs err; his watch ne'er goes right
    That sets his dial by a rusty clock.
SIR ALEXANDER [*coming forward*]   So, and which is that rusty clock,
    sir? You?   110
SEBASTIAN   The clock at Ludgate, sir. It ne'er goes true.
SIR ALEXANDER   But thou goest falser. Not thy father's cares
    Can keep thee right, when that insensible work
    Obeys the workman's art, lets off the hour,
    And stops again when time is satisfied;   115
    But thou run'st on, and judgment, thy main wheel,
    Beats by all stops, as if the work would break
    Begun with long pains, for a minute's ruin,
    Much like a suffering man brought up with care,
    At last bequeathed to shame and a short prayer.   120
SEBASTIAN   I taste you bitterer than I can deserve, sir.
SIR ALEXANDER   Who has bewitched thee, son? What devil
        or drug
    Hath wrought upon the weakness of thy blood
    And betrayed all her hopes to ruinous folly?
    Oh, wake from drowsy and enchanted shame,   125

98–99. *some . . . body*: i.e., by somebody honest.
101. *Both of them*: her thighs; "lusty" means both "strong, robust," and "lustful." A
    man's back was considered the source of his sexual energy, so the backache the
    Tailor imagines the porter suffering after "carrying" Moll's thighs may not be
    solely from heavy lifting.
105. *They . . . uncontrolled*: They (reason and judgment) have no authority over me.
106–07. *blood . . . needs err*: blood, the seat of the passions, was thought to be hotter in
    youth; Sebastian thus claims that the youth who allows an older man ("an unfeel-
    ing blood, past heat of love") to influence him in matters of the heart will end up
    making the wrong decision.
111. *Ludgate*: one of the ancient gates in the city walls.
113. *insensible work*: i.e, the clock at Ludgate.
114. *lets off*: strikes.
116–18. *judgment . . . ruin*: your faulty judgment (driving you as the main wheel drives a
    clock), beats aside all restraints, and after all the trouble ("long pains") I've taken
    to raise you, you're going to destroy yourself in a single minute (i.e., the time it
    takes to marry Moll).
120. *short prayer*: i.e., the prayer said by criminals before the "shame" of execution.
123–24. *thy blood . . . hopes*: Sir Alexander plays on the two meanings of "blood," as both
    "passion" (the source of Sebastian's weakness) and "lineage" (the source of his
    "hopes," or social expectations).

Wherein thy soul sits with a golden dream,
Flattered and poisoned! I am old, my son;
Oh, let me prevail quickly,
For I have weightier business of mine own
Than to chide thee. I must not to my grave   130
As a drunkard to his bed, whereon he lies
Only to sleep, and never cares to rise;
Let me dispatch in time. Come no more near her.
SEBASTIAN   Not honestly, not in the way of marriage?
SIR ALEXANDER   What say'st thou? Marriage? In what place,
      the sessions house?   135
And who shall give the bride, prithee? An indictment?
SEBASTIAN   Sir, now ye take part with the world to wrong her.
SIR ALEXANDER   Why, wouldst thou fain marry to be pointed at?
Alas, the number's great; do not o'erburden't.
Why, as good marry a beacon on a hill,   140
Which all the country fix their eyes upon,
As her thy folly dotes on. If thou long'st
To have the story of thy infamous fortunes
Serve for discourse in ordinaries and taverns,
Thou'rt in the way; or to confound thy name,   145
Keep on, thou canst not miss it; or to strike
Thy wretched father to untimely coldness,
Keep the left hand still, it will bring thee to't.
Yet if no tears wrung from thy father's eyes,
Nor sighs that fly in sparkles from his sorrows,   150
Had power to alter what is willful in thee,
Methinks her very name should fright thee from her,
And never trouble me.
SEBASTIAN   Why, is the name of Moll so fatal, sir?
SIR ALEXANDER   Many one, sir, where suspect is entered,   155
Forseek all London from one end to t'other
More whores of that name than of any ten other.
SEBASTIAN   What's that to her? Let those blush for themselves.

---

129. *weightier business*: i.e., preparing for death, as the next three lines explain.
133. *dispatch*: settle my affairs.
136. *indictment?*: Sir Alexander imagines the wedding taking place in criminal court ("the sessions house") rather than in church.
138. *fain*: desire to.
139. *number's*: i.e., of people who make a spectacle of themselves with notoriously bad choices in marriage.
145. *Thou't in the way*: You're going about it the right way; for "ordinaries," see note to 2.1.112; *confound thy name*: ruin your reputation.
147. *untimely coldness*: early death.
148. *Keep . . . still*: keep going left (i.e., the perverse way that you're going).
150. *sparkles*: sparks.
155. *suspect is entered*: many a woman named Moll has been (rightly) suspected.
156. *Forseek*: seek thoroughly.

Can any guilt in others condemn her?
I've vowed to love her. Let all storms oppose me   160
That ever beat against the breast of man;
Nothing but death's black tempest shall divide us.
SIR ALEXANDER   Oh folly, that can dote on naught but shame!
SEBASTIAN   Put case a wanton itch runs through one name
More than another, is that name the worse   165
Where honesty sits possessed in't? It should rather
Appear more excellent, and deserve more praise,
When through foul mists a brightness it can raise.
Why, there are of the devil's, honest gentlemen,
And well descended, keep an open house,   170
And some o'th'good man's that are arrant knaves.
He hates unworthily that by rote contemns,
For the name neither saves nor yet condemns.
And for her honesty, I have made such proof on't,
In several forms, so nearly watched her ways,   175
I will maintain that strict against an army,
Excepting you, my father. Here's her worst:
Sh' has a bold spirit that mingles with mankind,
But nothing else comes near it, and oftentimes
Through her apparel somewhat shames her birth   180
But she is loose in nothing but in mirth.
Would all Molls were no worse!
SIR ALEXANDER [*turning away*]   This way I toil in vain and
     give but aim
To infamy and ruin. He will fall;
My blessing cannot stay him. All my joys   185
Stand at the brink of a devouring flood
And will be willfully swallowed, willfully!
But why so vain let all these tears be lost?
I'll pursue her to shame, and so all's crossed.
                                        Exit Sir Alexander.

164. *put case*: suppose.
166. *where . . . possessed in't?*: when owned by someone who's virtuous?
169. *there are . . . honest gentlemen*: there are men who share a name with the devil
         (probably "Nick") who are honest gentlemen.
170. *keep an open house*: are hospitable.
171. *good man's*: some men named after Christ (e.g., "Christian").
172. *He hates . . . contemns*: A person hates unfairly when he despises others according
         to mindless rules.
174. *honesty*: chastity; *proof on't*: proof of it.
175. *nearly*: closely.
176. *I will . . . strict*: I will defend [her reputation] rigorously.
178–79. *bold spirit . . . comes near it*: i.e., her spirit is somewhat masculine and/or mixes
         with men, but no other part of her goes near them.
180. *birth*: could refer to either her social status or her "natural" gender.
183. *give . . . aim*: provide a target.
188. *why . . . lost*: why let all these tears be lost in vain?
189. *all's crossed*: everything will be thwarted.

SEBASTIAN   He is gone with some strange purpose, whose effect   190
Will hurt me little if he shoot so wide
To think I love so blindly. I but feed
His heart to this match to draw on th'other,
Wherein my joy sits with a full wish crowned—
Only his mood excepted, which must change   195
By opposite policies, courses indirect;
Plain dealing in this world takes no effect.
This mad girl I'll acquaint with my intent,
Get her assistance, make my fortunes known;
'Twixt lovers' hearts she's a fit instrument,   200
And has the art to help them to their own.
By her advice—for in that craft she's wise—
My love and I may meet, spite of all spies.   *Exit Sebastian.*

[3.1]

Enter Laxton in Gray's Inn Fields with the Coachman.

LAXTON   Coachman!
COACHMAN   Here, sir.
LAXTON   There's a tester more. Prithee drive thy coach to the
hither end of Marybone Park—a fit place for Moll to get in.
COACHMAN   Marybone Park, sir?   5
LAXTON   Ay, it's in our way, thou know'st.
COACHMAN   It shall be done, sir.   [*He starts to leave.*]
LAXTON   Coachman!
COACHMAN   Anon, sir.
LAXTON   Are we fitted with good frampold jades?   10
COACHMAN   The best in Smithfield, I warrant you, sir.

191–92.   *if he shoot . . . blindly:* if he is so far off the mark as to think I'm blind enough to
   love Moll.
192–93.   *I but feed . . . t'other:* I'm feeding him this story about Moll as a ploy to eventually
   marry Mary Fitzallard.
   195.   *mood excepted:* except for his dislike.
   196.   *opposite policies:* stratagems to oppose him.
   199.   *fortunes:* circumstances.
   201.   *their own:* what is rightfully theirs (i.e., marriage to each other).
     3.   *tester:* sixpence.
     4.   *Marybone Park:* now Regent's Park, in north-central London. "Marybone" is a cor-
   ruption of "St. Mary le Bourne," named for a church on the bank of a stream or
   "bourne." Laxton, however, is thinking of "marrowbones" (see note to 2.1.181),
   the delicious aphrodisiac of which Moll (Mary) reminds him.
    10.   *frampold jades:* feisty horses.
    11.   *Smithfield:* London's main livestock market.

LAXTON   May we safely take the upper hand of any coached velvet
cap or tuftaffety jacket? For they keep a vile swaggering in
coaches nowadays; the highways are stopped with them.

COACHMAN   My life for yours, and baffle 'em too, sir. Why, they are   15
the same jades, believe it, sir, that have drawn all your famous
whores to Ware.

LAXTON   Nay, then, they know their business; they need no
more instructions.

COACHMAN   They're so used to such journeys, sir, I never use   20
whip to 'em; for if they catch but the scent of a wench once,
they run like devils.   *Exit Coachman with his whip.*

LAXTON   Fine Cerberus! That rogue will have the start of a
thousand ones, for whilst others trot afoot he'll ride prancing
to hell upon a coach horse.—Stay, 'tis now about the hour of   25
her appointment, but yet I see her not.   [*The clock strikes
three.*] Hark, what's this? One, two, three: three by the clock
at Savoy. This is the hour, and Gray's Inn Fields the place,
she swore she'd meet me. Ha! Yonder's two Inns o'Court
men with one wench, but that's not she: they walk toward   30
Islington out of my way. I see none yet dressed like her. I must
look for a shag ruff, a frieze jerkin, a short sword, and a
safeguard, or I get none. Why, Moll, prithee make haste,
or the coachman will curse us anon.

    Enter Moll like a man.

MOLL [*aside*]   Oh, here's my gentleman. If they would keep their   35
days as well with their mercers as their hours with their harlots,
no bankrupt would give sevenscore pound for a sergeant's
place. For, would you know a catchpole rightly derived, the
corruption of a citizen is the generation of a sergeant.

---

12. *May . . . hand*: i.e., can we safely overtake finely dressed rich people riding in coaches?
13. *tuftaffety*: tufted taffeta, a silk fabric with raised velvet patterns.
15. *baffle'em*: humiliate them.
17. *Ware*: see note to 2.1.285–86.
23. *Cerberus*: In Greek mythology, the three-headed dog who guards the gates of Hades;
the coachman, Laxton may be implying, is a kind of gatekeeper between whores and
their clients; *the start of:* a head start on (i.e., along the road to hell).
28. *Savoy*: a hospital on the north bank of the Thames.
31. *Islington*: a northern suburb of London.
33. *safeguard*: see note to 2.1.165 (stage direction).
37. **s.d.** *dressed like*: she is in full male garb, rather than the combination of masculine
jerkin and feminine safeguard of her previous appearance.
35–39. *if they would keep . . . sergeant*: "If gentlemen would pay the bills for their clothes (a
'mercer' sells fine fabrics) as dependably as they keep appointments with their
whores, bankrupt men wouldn't pay the 140-pound fee it takes to get a job as an
arresting officer (i.e., because such jobs would not be lucrative if there were no
debtors to arrest). If you'd like to know where an arresting officer ('catchpole')
comes from, he's born out of the bankruptcy of a tradesman." Moll describes a kind
of vicious circle, in which tradesmen go bankrupt because gentlemen don't pay
their bills; these tradesmen then find work as sergeants, who arrest gentlemen for
not paying their bills.

How his eye hawks for venery! [*To Laxton*] Come, are you   40
ready, sir?

LAXTON   Ready for what, sir?

MOLL   Do you ask that now, sir? Why was this meeting
'pointed?

LAXTON   I thought you mistook me, sir.   45
You seem to be some young barrister.
I have no suit in law; all my land's sold,
I praise heaven for't; 't has rid me of much trouble.

MOLL   Then I must wake you, sir. Where stands the coach?

LAXTON   Who's this? Moll? Honest Moll?   50

MOLL   So young and purblind? You're an old wanton in your
eyes, I see that.

LAXTON   Thou'rt admirably suited for the Three Pigeons at
Brentford. I'll swear I knew thee not.

MOLL   I'll swear you did not; but you shall know me now.   55
[*She starts to remove her cloak.*]

LAXTON   No, not here. We shall be spied, i'faith. The coach is
better; come.   [*He starts to go.*]

MOLL   Stay!   *She puts off her cloak and draws [her sword].*

LAXTON   What, wilt thou untruss a point, Moll?

MOLL   Yes, here's the point that I untruss. 'T has but one tag; 'twill   60
serve enough to tie up a rogue's tongue.

LAXTON   How?

MOLL [*showing money*]   There's the gold.
With which you hired your hackney; here's her pace.
She racks hard, and perhaps your bones will feel it.   65
Ten angels of mine own I've put to thine;
Win 'em and wear 'em!

LAXTON   Hold, Moll! Mistress Mary—

MOLL   Draw, or I'll serve an execution upon thee
Shall lay thee up till doomsday.   70

LAXTON   Draw upon a woman? Why, what dost mean, Moll?

MOLL   To teach thy base thoughts manners. Thou'rt one of those
That thinks each woman thy fond flexible whore.

---

40. *eye . . . venery*: his eye roves about like a hawk hunting for game; "venery" refers both to the sport of hunting and to sexual activity.
44. *'pointed*: appointed.
51. *purblind*: partially or totally blind.
53–54. *suited*: dressed; the Three Pigeons is a famous Brentford tavern.
55. *know*: Laxton thinks Moll means "know" in the Biblical sense (i.e., sexually).
59. *untruss a point*: undo a tag fastening hose to doublet; Laxton thinks Moll is undressing for sex on the spot. Her response (ll. 60–61) plays on the double meaning of "point": the clothing tag and the pointy end of her unsheathed sword.
64. *hackney*: a horse for hire, figuratively, a prostitute.
65. *racks hard*: she moves briskly; a "rack" is a pace between a trot and a gallop.
67. *Win . . . wear 'em*: Moll matches the money that Laxton gave her at 2.1.297 and challenges him to a winner-takes-all duel.
69–70. *execution*: "to serve an execution" is to seize the goods or person of a debtor in default of payment; Moll uses the term as a metaphor for the physical harm she will inflict on Laxton if he refuses to draw his sword.
73. *fond flexible*: foolish and easily led.

If she but cast a liberal eye upon thee,
Turn back her head, she's thine; or, amongst company, 75
By chance drink first to thee, then she's quite gone,
There's no means to help her; nay, for a need,
Wilt swear unto thy credulous fellow lechers
That thou'rt more in favor with a lady
At first sight than her monkey all her lifetime. 80
How many of our sex by such as thou
Have their good thoughts paid with a blasted name
That never deserved loosely or did trip
In path of whoredom beyond cup and lip?
But for the stain of conscience and of soul, 85
Better had women fall into the hands
Of an act silent than a bragging nothing;
There's no mercy in't. What durst move you, sir,
To think me whorish?—a name which I'd tear out
From the high German's throat, if it lay ledger there 90
To dispatch privy slanders against me!
In thee I defy all men, their worst hates
And their best flatteries, all their golden witchcrafts
With which they entangle the poor spirits of fools.
Distressed needlewomen and trade-fall'n wives. 95
Fish that must needs bite or themselves be bitten,
Such hungry things as these may soon be took
With a worm fast'ned on a golden hook;
Those are the lecher's food, his prey. He watches
For quarreling wedlocks and poor shifting sisters; 100
'Tis the best fish he takes. But why, good fisherman,
Am I thought meat for you, that never yet
Had angling rod cast towards me? 'Cause, you'll say,
I'm given to sport, I'm often merry, jest?

76. *drink . . . thee*: happen to toast you first.
77–78. *for a need . . . wilt swear*: if you need to, you'll swear.
80. *monkey*: a pet salaciously rumored to perform sexual services for its mistress.
82. *paid . . . name*: repaid with a ruined reputation.
83. *deserved loosely*: i.e., deserved to be thought a loose woman.
84. *cup and lip*: alludes to the proverb "there's many a slip betwixt cup and lip" (i.e., things can go wrong at the last minute); Moll's meaning, however, seems to be "women who have never gone further down the path towards being a whore than to put a cup to their lips to toast a man's health" (the innocuous gesture mentioned in l. 76).
85. *But*: except.
86–87. *better had . . . bragging nothing*: women would be better off with a man who successfully seduces them but keeps silent about it than with a man who doesn't seduce them but brags to everyone that he did.
88. *mercy in't*: i.e., in the act of bragging about non-existent sexual exploits.
90. *high German's*: see note to 2.1.377; *ledger*: resident.
91. *privy*: secret.
92. *in thee*: in defying thee.
94. *fools*: innocent or ignorant women.
95. *trade-fall'n wives*: wives impoverished by failing businesses (theirs or their husbands').
100. *quarreling . . . sisters*: unhappy marriages and women struggling to make ends meet; "shifting" means "living by one's efforts, managing to get by."
104. *given to sport*: playful.

Had mirth no kindred in the world but lust?   105
Oh, shame take all her friends, then! But howe'er
Thou and the baser world censure my life,
I'll send 'em word by thee, and write so much
Upon thy breast, 'cause thou shalt bear't in mind:
Tell them 'twere base to yield where I have conquered.   110
I scorn to prostitute myself to a man,
I that can prostitute a man to me,
And so I greet thee.   [*She draws her sword.*]

LAXTON [*drawing in defense*]   Hear me!

MOLL   Would the spirits
Of all my slanderers were clasped in thine,
That I might vex an army at one time!   115

                    They fight. [*Moll wounds Laxton.*]

LAXTON   I do repent me. Hold!

MOLL   You'll die the better Christian, then.

LAXTON   I do confess I have wronged thee, Moll.

MOLL   Confession is but poor amends for wrong,
Unless a rope would follow.

LAXTON   I ask thee pardon.   120

MOLL   I'm your hired whore, sir!

LAXTON   I yield both purse and body.

MOLL   Both are mine and now at my disposing.

LAXTON   Spare my life!

MOLL   I scorn to strike thee basely

LAXTON   Spoke like a noble girl, i'faith. [*Aside*] Heart, I think.
I fight with a familiar, or the ghost of a fencer! She's   125
wounded me gallantly. Call you this a lecherous voyage?
Here's blood would have served me this seven year in broken
heads and cut fingers, and it now runs all out together.
Pox o'the Three Pigeons! I would the coach were here now
to carry me to the chirurgeon's.   *Exit Laxton.*   130

MOLL   If I could meet my enemies one by one thus,
I might make pretty shift with 'em in time,
And make 'em know, she that has wit and spirit
May scorn to live beholding to her body for meat

---

106. *her friends*: Mirth's relatives.
108. *write*: i.e., carve with my sword.
113. *Would*: I wish.
117. *die . . . then*: Moll deliberately misunderstands Laxton to be repenting his sins in preparation for his imminent death, when in fact he's apologizing to her.
120. *a rope*: to hang him.
125. *familiar*: an evil spirit or demon, usually attendant on a witch.
126. *Call you . . . lecherous voyage?*: Is this the sexy out-of-town jaunt I was expecting?
127–28. *broken heads*: i.e., head wounds that break the scalp.
130. *chirurgeon's*: surgeon's.
132. *make pretty shift*: deal effectively.
134. *beholding to*: obligated to; *meat*: food.

Or for apparel, like your common dame   135
That makes shame get her clothes to cover shame.
Base is that mind that kneels unto her body,
As if a husband stood in awe on 's wife!
My spirit shall be mistress of this house
As long as I have time in 't.

Enter Trapdoor [not recognizing Moll].

                              Oh,   140
Here comes my man that would be; 'tis his hour.
Faith, a good well-set fellow, if his spirit
Be answerable to his umbles. He walks stiff,
But whether he will stand to't stiffly, there's the point.
'Has a good calf for't, and ye shall have many a woman   145
Choose him she means to make her head by his calf;
I do not know their tricks in't. Faith, he seems
A man without; I'll try what he is within.

TRAPDOOR   She told me Gray's Inn Fields 'twixt three and four.
I'll fit Her Mistress-ship with a piece of service   150
I'm hired to rid the town of one mad girl.

                                          She jostles him.

[*To Moll*] What a pox ails you, sir?
MOLL [*aside*]   He begins like a gentleman.
TRAPDOOR   Heart, is the field so narrow, or your eyesight?
[*She comes toward him.*] Life, he comes back again!   155
MOLL   Was this spoke to me, sir?
TRAPDOOR   I cannot tell, sir.
MOLL   Go, you're a coxcomb!
TRAPDOOR   Coxcomb?
MOLL   You're a slave!   160
TRAPDOOR   I hope there's law for you, sir!

---

136. *That makes . . . cover shame*: who shamefully prostitutes herself so she can buy
      clothes to cover her private ("shameful") parts.
138. *on's*: of his.
139. *house*: i.e., her body.
141. *my man that would be*: my would-be manservant; *his hour*: the time we agreed on.
142. *well-set*: well-built.
143. *umbles*: literally, his innards; Moll means something like "if his spirit is as robust
      as his physique."
144. *stiffly*: stand up bravely to a challenge; have a stiff erection.
145–47. *ye shall . . . tricks in't*: i.e., many women choose husbands for their nice legs, a
      strategy I've never understood.
148. *without*: in his external appearance.
150. *I'll fit . . . service*: sarcastic: "I'll serve her, all right!"
152. *pox*: an expletive: modern equivalent would be "what the hell's wrong with you?"
      Compare 2.1.233.
158. *coxcomb*: a conceited fool.
160. *slave*: a low-born, worthless fellow. Moll is trying, unsuccessfully, to provoke Trap-
      door into standing up for himself and fighting her.
161. *there's law for you*: Trapdoor is threatening Moll with a lawsuit.

MOLL   Yea, do you see, sir? *Turns his hat.*

TRAPDOOR   Heart, this is no good dealing. Pray let me know
what house you're of.

MOLL   One of the Temple, sir. *Fillips him.*   165

TRAPDOOR   Mass, so methinks.

MOLL   And yet sometimes I lie about Chick Lane.

TRAPDOOR   I like you the worse because you shift your lodging so
often. I'll not meddle with you for that trick, sir.

MOLL   A good shift, but it shall not serve your turn.   170

TRAPDOOR   You'll give me leave to pass about my business, sir?

MOLL   Your business? I'll make you wait on me before I ha' done,
and glad to serve me, too.

TRAPDOOR   How, sir, serve you? Not if there were no more
men in England.   175

MOLL   But if there were no more women in England, I hope you'd
wait upon your mistress then.

                              [*Moll reveals her identity.*]

TRAPDOOR   Mistress!

MOLL   Oh, you're a tried spirit at a push, sir.

TRAPDOOR   What would Your Worship have me do?   180

MOLL   You a fighter?

TRAPDOOR   No, I praise heaven, I had better grace and more manners.

MOLL   As how, I pray, sir?

TRAPDOOR   Life, 't had been a beastly part of me to have drawn my
weapons upon my mistress. All the world would ha' cried shame   185
of me for that.

MOLL   Why, but you knew me not.

TRAPDOOR   Do not say so, mistress. I knew you by your wide
straddle as well as if I had been in your belly.

MOLL   Well, we shall try you further. I'th'meantime we give you   190
entertainment.

TRAPDOOR   Thank Your good Mistress-ship.

MOLL   How many suits have you?

TRAPDOOR   No more suits than backs, mistress.

---

162.   **s.d.** *turns his hat*: an insulting gesture intended to provoke, as is the "fillip" given
in l. 165. To "fillip" is to give a sharp smack with the back of the fingers. Trapdoor's
failure to fight back reveals him as a coward.

165.   *Temple*: the Middle or Inner Temple, two "houses" (l. 165) of the Inns of Court.

167.   *Chick Lane*: a rough street in Smithfield, the market district.

169.   *for*: because of.

170.   *shift*: evasion.

179.   *you're . . . push*: sarcastic: "you're an experienced fighter when push comes to shove."

184.   *part*: action. As "beastly" can mean "lustful" as well as "brutal," Trapdoor probably
intends a sexual innuendo in "drawn my weapons upon my mistress," continued in
ll.188–189 with "I knew you . . . as well as if I had been in your belly" (i.e., as your
sexual partner, though it could also mean "as if you were my own mother").

185–86.   *shame of*: shame on.

191.   *entertainment*: employment.

MOLL   Well, if you deserve, I cast off this next week, and you may   195
    creep into't.
TRAPDOOR   Thank Your good Worship.
MOLL   Come, follow me to Saint Thomas Apostles. I'll put a livery
    cloak upon your back, the first thing I do.
TRAPDOOR   I follow my dear mistress.   *Exeunt omnes.*   200

[3.2]

Enter Mistress Gallipot as from supper, her husband after her.

GALLIPOT   What, Pru! Nay, sweet Prudence!
MRS. GALLIPOT   What a pruing keep you! I think the baby would
    have a teat, it kyes so. Pray be not so fond of me; leave your city
    humors. I'm vexed at you to see how like a calf you come
    bleating after me.   5
GALLIPOT   Nay, honey Pru, how does your rising up before all the
    table show? And flinging from my friends so uncivilly? Fie, Pru,
    fie. Come.
MRS. GALLIPOT   Then up and ride, i'faith.
GALLIPOT   Up and ride? Nay, my pretty Pru, that's far from   10
    my thought, duck. Why, mouse, thy mind is nibbling at
    something. What is't? What lies upon thy stomach?
MRS. GALLIPOT   Such an ass as you! Heyday, you're best turn
    midwife or physician; you're a pothecary already, but I'm none of
    your drugs.   15
GALLIPOT   Thou art a sweet drug, sweetest Pru, and the more thou
    art pounded, the more precious.
MRS. GALLIPOT   Must you be prying into a woman's secrets?
    Say ye?
GALLIPOT   Woman's secrets?   20

---

195. *this*: i.e., the suit I'm wearing; servants often received their employers' used clothes.
198. *Saint Thomas Apostles*: a church in the clothing district.
198–99. *livery cloak*: part of a servant's uniform; distinctive clothing ("livery") would dis-
        tinguish the servants of a particular employer.
    2. *the baby*: i.e., Gallipot.
    3. *kyes*: cries (in baby talk); *fond*; foolishly affectionate.
3–4. *city humors*: whims or affectations befitting a city tradesman or "citizen." Citi-
        zens were stereotyped as excessively fond of, and thus subservient to, their wives.
6–7. *rising . . . show?*: how does it look when you get up before our dinner guests?
    7. *flinging from*: leaving abruptly or angrily.
    9. *up and ride*: an exclamation of impatience; Gallipot, however, takes it in a sexual
        sense (ll. 10–11).
  11. *mouse*: like "duck," an endearment.
  12. *What . . . stomach*: i.e., what's bothering you?
  14. *pothecary*: apothecary, a pharmacist.
  15. *drugs*: declaring herself to be none of his "drugs," Mrs. Gallipot plays on
        "drudge," a menial servant.
  17. *pounded . . . precious*: an apothecary used mortar and pestle to pound medicinal
        ingredients; Gallipot intends a sexual innuendo.
  18. *secrets*: private parts, as well as the modern meaning.

MRS. GALLIPOT   What? I cannot have a qualm come upon me but
your teeth waters till your nose hang over it.

GALLIPOT   It is my love, dear wife.

MRS. GALLIPOT   Your love? Your love is all words; give me
deeds. I cannot abide a man that's too fond over me—so   25
cookish! Thou dost not know how to handle a woman in
her kind.

GALLIPOT   No, Pru? Why, I hope I have handled—

MRS. GALLIPOT   Handle a fool's head of your own. Fie, fie!

GALLIPOT   Ha, ha, 'tis such a wasp! It does me good now to   30
have her sting me, little rogue.

MRS. GALLIPOT   Now, fie, how you vex me! I cannot abide these
apron husbands. Such cotqueans! You overdo your things; they
become you scurvily.

GALLIPOT [aside]   Upon my life, she breeds. Heaven knows   35
how I have strained myself to please her, night and day! I
wonder why we citizens should get children so fretful and
untoward in the breeding, their fathers being for the most
part as gentle as milch kine.—Shall I leave thee, my Pru?

MRS. GALLIPOT   Fie, fie!   40

GALLIPOT   Thou shalt not be vexed no more, pretty kind rogue.
Take no cold, sweet Pru.   *Exit Master Gallipot.*

MRS. GALLIPOT   As your wit has done!—Now, Master Laxton, show
your head. [*She takes out a letter.*] What news from
you? Would any husband suspect that a woman crying "Buy   45
any scurvy grass" should bring love letters amongst her herbs
to his wife? Pretty trick, fine conveyance! Had jealousy a
thousand eyes, a silly woman with scurvy grass blinds
them all.

Laxton, with bays   50
Crown I thy wit for this; it deserves praise.
This makes me affect thee more; this proves thee wise.
'Lack, what poor shift is love forced to devise?—
To th'point.   *She reads the letter.*

21. *qualm:* attack of nausea.
22. *teeth . . . over it:* i.e., your mouth waters with anticipation until you can stick your
nose into my business.
26. *cookish:* like a cook (presumably, fussy and womanish).
26–27. *handle . . . her kind:* as women ought to be handled.
33. *cotqueans:* husbands who meddle in housewifery.
33–34. *You overdo . . . scurvily:* You go too far in your attentions to me; it reflects poorly on you.
35. *she breeds:* she's pregnant (thought to make women bad-tempered and demanding).
37. *get:* beget.
38. *untoward . . . breeding:* difficult in utero.
39. *milch kine:* milk cows.
43. *As . . . done:* i.e., your intelligence has caught a cold.
46. *scurvy grass:* a herb believed to protect against scurvy.
48. *silly:* simple, uneducated.
50. *bays:* laurel leaves, the crown of celebrated warriors and poets.
52. *affect:* like.
53. *shift:* stratagem.

"O sweet creature," (a sweet beginning!) "pardon my long   55
absence, for thou shalt shortly be possessed with my presence.
Though Demophoon was false to Phyllis, I will be to thee as
Pan-da-rus was to Cres-sida; though Aeneas made an ass of
Dido, I will die to thee ere I do so. O sweetest creature, make
much of me, for no man beneath the silver moon shall make   60
more of a woman than I do of thee. Furnish me therefore
with thirty pounds; you must do it of necessity for me. I languish
till I see some comfort come from thee, protesting not to die in
thy debt, but rather to live so, as hitherto I have and will,
                                            Thy true Laxton, ever."   65
Alas, poor gentleman! Troth, I pity him.
How shall I raise this money? Thirty pound?
'Tis thirty, sure, a three before an O;
I know his threes too well. My childbed linen?
Shall I pawn that for him? Then if my mark   70
Be known, I am undone! It may be thought
My husband's bankrupt. Which way shall I turn?
Laxton, what with my own fears and thy wants,
I'm as a needle 'twixt two adamants.

   Enter Master Gallipot hastily.

GALLIPOT   Nay, nay, wife, the women are all up [*Aside*] Ha?   75
How? Reading o' letters? I smell a goose. A couple of capons
and a gammon of bacon from her mother out of the country,
I hold my life. Steal—steal—   [*He sneaks up behind her.*]
MRS. GALLIPOT   Oh, beshrew your heart!
GALLIPOT   What letter's that? I'll see't.   *She tears the letter.*   80
MRS. GALLIPOT   Oh, would thou hadst no eyes to see the downfall
of me and thyself! I'm forever, forever I'm undone!
GALLIPOT   What ails my Pru? What paper's that thou tear'st?
MRS. GALLIPOT   Would I could tear
My very heart in pieces! For my soul   85

57–59. *Though Demophoon . . . do so*: allusions to Greek myth and epic. Ovid's *Heroides*
    relates Demophoon's abandonment of his wife Phyllis (Book 2) and Aeneas's aban-
    donment of Dido, queen of Carthage (Book 7); both women committed suicide.
    Pandarus and Cressida (Mrs. Gallipot hesitates over the unfamiliar names) are
    characters in a medieval adaptation of the Trojan war narrative; the joke is that Pan-
    darus was not Cressida's lover but her uncle, who acted as her go-between with
    Troilus (whom she eventually betrayed). Either Laxton is trying to impress Mrs.
    Gallipot by alluding to stories of which he is ignorant, or (more likely) he is count-
    ing on her own ignorance to have a laugh at her expense.
60–61. *make more of*: cherish; make more money from.
    63. *protesting*: promising; Laxton is insisting that he will repay Mrs. Gallipot as her
         lover. However, there may be a pun on "die," meaning "to have an orgasm," which
         would trickily reverse the sense of his promise.
    69. *childbed linen*: a special and typically expensive set of sheets, nightgowns, baby
         clothes, etc. used by new mothers; the "mark" (l. 70) was an embroidered mono-
         gram or other symbol identifying the owner of these articles.
    74. *two adamants*: magnets.
    78. *hold*: bet; *steal*: sneak.
    79. *beshrew*: a mild curse: "darn you!"

Lies on the rack of shame that tortures me
Beyond a woman's suffering.

GALLIPOT   What means this?

MRS. GALLIPOT   Had you no other vengeance to throw down,
But even in height of all my joys—

GALLIPOT   Dear woman!

MRS. GALLIPOT   When the full sea of pleasure and content   90
Seemed to flow over me?

GALLIPOT   As thou desirest to keep me out of Bedlam, tell what
troubles thee. Is not thy child at nurse fall'n sick, or dead?

MRS. GALLIPOT   Oh, no!

GALLIPOT   Heavens bless me, are my barns and houses   95
Yonder at Hockley Hole consumed with fire?
I can build more, sweet Pru.

MRS. GALLIPOT   'Tis worse,'tis worse.

GALLIPOT   My factor broke, or is the *Jonas* sunk?

MRS. GALLIPOT   Would all we had were swallowed in the waves,
Rather than both should be the scorn of slaves!   100

GALLIPOT   I'm at my wit's end!

MRS. GALLIPOT   Oh, my dear husband,
Where once I thought myself a fixèd star,
Placed only in the heaven of thine arms,
I fear now I shall prove a wanderer.   105
O Laxton, Laxton, is it then my fate
To be by thee o'erthrown?

GALLIPOT   Defend me, wisdom,
From falling into frenzy! On my knees,
Sweet Pru, speak! What's that Laxton who so heavy lies
On thy bosom?

MRS. GALLIPOT   I shall sure run mad.   110

GALLIPOT   I shall run mad for company, then. Speak to me;
I'm Gallipot thy husband.—Pru! Why, Pru!
Art sick in conscience for some villainous deed
Thou wert about to act? Didst mean to rob me?
Tush, I forgive thee. Hast thou on my bed   115
Thrust my soft pillow under another's head?
I'll wink at all faults, Pru; 'las, that's no more

---

88. *you*: i.e., Laxton.
92. *Bedlam*: Bethlehem Hospital, for mental patients.
93. *child at nurse*: i.e., an infant sent out to board with a wet-nurse for breast-feeding; this was a common practice.
96. *Hockley Hole*: a village on the northwest edge of London.
98. *my factor broke*: my agent gone bankrupt; *Jonas*: a ship carrying cargo in which Gallipot is invested.
99. *scorn of slaves*: i.e., a laughingstock to even the lowest members of society.
108. *frenzy*: insanity.
109–10. *so heavy . . . on thy bosom*: who so disturbs or oppresses your heart; with unintended sexual double entendre.
111. *for company*: along with you.
117. *wink at*: overlook.

Than what some neighbors near thee have done before.
Sweet honey Pru, what's that Laxton?
MRS. GALLIPOT   Oh!
GALLIPOT   Out with him!
MRS. GALLIPOT   Oh, he's born to be my undoer!   120
This hand which thou call'st thine to him was given;
To him was I made sure i'th'sight of heaven.
GALLIPOT   I never heard this thunder!
MRS. GALLIPOT   Yes, yes, before
I was to thee contracted, to him I swore.
Since last I saw him twelve months three times told   125
The moon hath drawn through her light silver bow,
For o'er the seas he went, and it was said
(But rumor lies) that he in France was dead.
But he's alive, oh, he's alive! He sent
That letter to me, which in rage I rent,   130
Swearing with oaths most damnably to have me
Or tear me from this bosom. O heavens, save me!
GALLIPOT   My heart will break. Shamed and undone forever!
MRS. GALLIPOT   So black a day, poor wretch, went o'er thee never!
GALLIPOT   If thou shouldst wrestle with him at the law,   135
Thou'rt sure to fall; no odd sleight, no prevention.
I'll tell him thou'rt with child.
MRS. GALLIPOT   Umh!
GALLIPOT   Or give out
One of my men was ta'en abed with thee.
MRS. GALLIPOT   Umh, umh!
GALLIPOT   Before I lose thee, my dear Pru,
I'll drive it to that push.
MRS. GALLIPOT   Worse and worse still!   140
You embrace a mischief to prevent an ill.
GALLIPOT I'll buy thee of him, stop his mouth with gold.
Think'st thou 'twill do?
MRS. GALLIPOT   Oh, me! Heavens grant it would!
Yet, now my senses are set more in tune,
He writ, as I remember in his letter,   145

110. *Out with him!*: i.e., tell me about him!
122. *in'th'sight of heaven*: Mrs. Gallipot claims (falsely) that she was betrothed to Lax-
         ton before she married Gallipot; this "precontract," if proven, would legally invali-
         date the Gallipots' marriage. To be "made sure" to someone is to be formally
         betrothed.
125–26. *twelve . . . silver bow*: a poetic way of saying "three years have passed."
130. *rent*: tore up.
132. *this*: i.e., Gallipot's;
136. *no . . . prevention*: no legal sleight-of-hand could prevent Laxton from winning a
         lawsuit against us.
137–38. *give . . . with thee*: spread a rumor that you were caught in bed with one of my
         servants.
140. *I'll . . . push*: I'll take it that far.

That he in riding up and down had spent,
Ere he could find me, thirty pounds. Send that;
Stand not on thirty with him.
GALLIPOT   Forty, Pru.
Say thou the word, 'tis done. We venture lives
For wealth, but must do more to keep our wives.   150
Thirty or forty, Pru?
MRS. GALLIPOT   Thirty, good sweet;
Of an ill bargain let's save what we can.
I'll pay it him with my tears. He was a man,
When first I knew him, of a meek spirit;
All goodness is not yet dried up, I hope.   155
GALLIPOT   He shall have thirty pound. Let that stop all;
Love's sweets taste best when we have drunk down gall.

Enter Master Tiltyard and his wife, Master Goshawk,
and Mistress Openwork.

Godso, our friends! Come, come, smooth your cheek;
After a storm, the face of heaven looks sleek.
TILTYARD   Did I not tell you these turtles were together?   160
MRS. TILTYARD [*to Mrs. Gallipot*]   How dost thou, sirrah?
Why, sister Gallipot!
MRS. OPENWORK   Lord, how she's changed!
GOSHAWK [*to Gallipot*]   Is your wife ill, sir?
GALLIPOT   Yes, indeed, la, sir, very ill, very ill, never worse.   165
MRS. TILTYARD   How her head burns! Feel how her pulses work!
MRS. OPENWORK [*to Mrs. Gallipot*]   Sister, lie down a little.
That always does me good.
MRS. TILTYARD   In good sadness, I find best ease in that too.
Has she laid some hot thing to her stomach?   170
MRS. GALLIPOT   No, but I will lay something anon.
TILTYARD [*to Mis. Tiltyard*]   Come, come, fools, you trouble
her.—Shall's go, Master Goshawk?
GOSHAWK   Yes, sweet Master Tiltyard.
                    [*He talks privately with Mrs. Openwork.*]
Sirrah Rosamond, I hold my life Gallipot hath vexed his wife.   175
MRS. OPENWORK   She has a horrible high color, indeed.

148. *Stand not on*: Don't quibble about.
149. *lives*: risk our lives.
157. *gall*: bile; figuratively, anything bitter.
158. *Godso*: a mild oath.
160. *turtles*: turtledoves, equivalent to modern "lovebirds."
161. *sirrah?*: see note to 2.1.176.
169. *In . . . sadness*: seriously.
171. *something anon*: the remedies the women suggest can be taken in a sexual sense, as can
    Mrs. Gallipot's response that she will soon ("anon") lay "some hot thing to her stomach."
173. *Shall's*: Shall we.
175. *hold*: bet.
176. *has . . . high color*: is terribly flushed.

GOSHAWK   We shall have your face painted with the same red
soon at night when your husband comes from his rubbers
in a false alley; thou wilt not believe me that his bowls run
with a wrong bias.   180
MRS. OPENWORK   It cannot sink into me that he feeds upon
stale mutton abroad, having better and fresher at home.
GOSHAWK   What if I bring thee where thou shalt see him stand at
rack and manger?
MRS. OPENWORK   I'll saddle him in's kind and spur him till he   185
kick again.
GOSHAWK   Shall thou and I ride our journey, then?
MRS. OPENWORK   Here's my hand.
GOSHAWK   No more. [Aloud] Come, Master Tiltyard, shall we leap
into the stirrups with our women and amble home?   190
TILTYARD   Yes, yes.—Come, wife.
MRS. TILTYARD [to Mrs. Gallipot]   In troth, sister, I hope you will do
well for all this.
MRS. GALLIPOT   I hope I shall. Farewell, good sister, sweet Master
Goshawk.   195
GALLIPOT   Welcome, brother; most kindly welcome, sir.
OMNES   Thanks, sir, for our good cheer.
                              Exeunt all but Gallipot and his wife.
GALLIPOT   It shall be so, because a crafty knave
Shall not outreach me, nor walk by my door
With my wife arm in arm as 'twere his whore.   200
I'll give him a golden coxcomb: thirty pound.
Tush, Pru, what's thirty pound? Sweet duck, look cheerly.
MRS. GALLIPOT   Thou art worthy of my heart; thou buy'st it dearly.

    Enter Laxton, muffled.

LAXTON [aside]   Ud's light, the side's against me. A pox of
Your Pothecaryship! Oh, for some glister to set him going!   205

178–80. *rubbers . . . bias*: Goshawk uses bowling metaphors to claim that Mrs. Openwork's
         husband is cheating on her. "Rubbers" are sets of three games, but the sexual
         innuendo of "a false alley" (i.e., in the wrong vagina) adds the physical sense of
         "rubbing." A bowling ball ("bowl") that "runs with a bias" follows a curved path.
  182. *mutton*: women's flesh; "mutton" alone could mean "prostitutes," but here Mrs.
         Openwork makes a distinction between "stale mutton" (prostitutes) and her own
         "fresher" mutton.
  184. *rack and manger*: implements for holding animal fodder, so "see him feed like a
         farm animal."
  185. *in's kind*: i.e., like the (stud) horse that he is.
  186. *journey*: have an affair; go to spy on Openwork with his prostitutes.
  193. *for*: despite.
  196. *Welcome . . . sir*: i.e., you have been welcome; Gallipot is thanking his guests for coming.
  201. *coxcomb*: fool's cap; Gallipot thinks he is defeating and humiliating Laxton by pay-
         ing him off.
  204. *Ud's*: God's; *side's against me*: they've ganged up on me (Laxton was not expecting
         to see Gallipot).
  205. *glister*: enema (sold by apothecaries).

'Tis one of Hercules' labors to tread one of these city hens,
because their cocks are still crowing over them. There's no
turning tail here; I must on.

MRS. GALLIPOT   Oh, husband, see, he comes!

GALLIPOT   Let me deal with him.   210

LAXTON   Bless you, sir.

GALLIPOT   Be you blessed too, sir, if you come in peace.

LAXTON   Have you any good pudding-tobacco, sir?

MRS. GALLIPOT   Oh, pick no quarrels, gentle sir! My husband
Is not a man of weapon, as you are.   215
He knows all; I have opened all before him
Concerning you.

LAXTON [aside]   Zounds, has she shown my letters?

MRS. GALLIPOT   Suppose my case were yours, what would you do,
At such a pinch, such batteries, such assaults,   220
Of father, mother, kindred, to dissolve
The knot you tied, and to be bound to him?
How could you shift this storm off?

LAXTON [aside]   If I know, hang me.

MRS. GALLIPOT   Besides, a story of your death was read   225
Each minute to me.

LAXTON [aside]   What a pox means this riddling?

GALLIPOT   Be wise, sir. Let not you and I be tossed
On lawyers' pens; they have sharp nibs and draw
Men's very heart-blood from them. What need you, sir,   230
To beat the drum of my wife's infamy,
And call your friends together, sir, to prove
Your precontact, when sh' has confessed it?

LAXTON   Umh, sir—
Has she confessed it?

GALLIPOT   Sh' has, faith, to me, sir,
Upon your letter sending.

MRS. GALLIPOT   I have, I have.   235

LAXTON [aside]   If I let this iron cool, call me slave.—
Do you hear, you dame Prudence? Think'st thou, vile woman,
I'll take these blows and wink?

MRS. GALLIPOT   Upon my knees—

LAXTON   Out, impudence!

---

206.   *tread*: copulate with (said of fowl); in classical mythology, Hercules had to perform
twelve seemingly-impossible tasks or "labors" as penance for having killed his wife and
children in a fit of madness.
207.   *still*: always.
213.   *pudding-tobacco*: tobacco compressed into a sausage shape; a "pudding" is a sausage.
219.   *Suppose . . . yours*: Put yourself in my shoes; Mrs. Gallipot goes on to claim that her
entire family bullied her into breaking her contract to Laxton and marrying Gallipot.
231.   *beat the drum*: publicize.
236.   *iron cool*: alludes to the proverb "strike while the iron is hot," i.e., take an opportunity
when it presents itself.
238.   *wink*: overlook or ignore the blows.

GALLIPOT   Good sir—

LAXTON   You goatish slaves,
  No wild fowl to cut up but mine?

GALLIPOT   Alas, sir,   240
  You make her flesh to tremble. Fright her not;
  She shall do reason, and what's fit.

LAXTON [to Mrs. Gallipot]   I'll have thee,
  Wert thou more common than an hospital
  And more diseased—

GALLIPOT   But one word, good sir.

LAXTON   So, sir.

GALLIPOT   I married her, have lain with her, and got   245
  Two children on her body; think but on that.
  Have you so beggarly an appetite,
  When I upon a dainty dish have fed,
  To dine upon my scraps, my leavings? Ha, sir?
  Do I come near you now, sir?

LAXTON   By' Lady, you touch me.   250

GALLIPOT   Would not you scorn to wear my clothes, sir?

LAXTON   Right, sir.

GALLIPOT   Then pray, sir, wear not her, for she's a garment
  So fitting for my body I'm loath
  Another should put it on; you will undo both.
  Your letter, as she said, complained you had spent   255
  In quest of her some thirty pound; I'll pay it.
  Shall that, sir, stop this gap up 'twixt you two?

LAXTON   Well, if I swallow this wrong, let her thank you.
  The money being paid, sir, I am gone;
  Farewell. Oh women! Happy's he trusts none.   260

MRS. GALLIPOT   Dispatch him hence, sweet husband.

GALLIPOT   Yes, dear wife.—
  Pray, sir, come in. [To his wife] Ere Master Laxton part,
  Thou shalt in wine drink to him.

MRS. GALLIPOT   With all my heart.
                          Exit Master Gallipot.
  How dost thou like my wit?

LAXTON   Rarely! That wile

239–40. *You . . . mine*: You lustful wretches, were there no loose women for you to fornicate
     with other than my fiancée?
  242. *reason . . . fit*: what's reasonable and right.
  243. *common*: public, accessible (i.e., sexually to men).
  250. *come near you*: make an impression on you; *By' Lady*: By Our Lady (a mild oath).
  257. *stop this gap up*: i.e., settle this quarrel.
  258. *I swallow this wrong*: patiently accept the wrong you've done me.
  260. *Happy's he*: happy is he who.
  261. *Dispatch him hence*: settle up and send him away.
  263. *drink to*: toast (as a gesture of goodwill).

By which the serpent did the first woman beguile   265
Did ever since all women's bosoms fill;
You're apple eaters all, deceivers still.   *Exeunt.*

[3.3]

*Enter Sir Alexander Wengrave, Sir Davy Dapper, [and] Sir
Adam Appleton at one door, and Trapdoor at another door.*

SIR ALEXANDER   Out with your tale, Sir Davy, to Sir Adam.
A knave is in mine eye deep in my debt.
SIR DAVY   Nay, if he be a knave, sir, hold him fast.
          [*Sir Alexander takes Trapdoor aside and
                    speaks privately.*]
SIR ALEXANDER   Speak softly: what egg is there hatching now?
TRAPDOOR   A duck's egg, sir, a duck that has eaten a frog. I have   5
cracked the shell and some villainy or other will peep out
presently. The duck that sits is the bouncing ramp, that roaring
girl my mistress; the drake that must tread is your son
Sebastian.
SIR ALEXANDER   Be quick.   10
TRAPDOOR   As the tongue of an oyster-wench.
SIR ALEXANDER   And see thy news be true.
TRAPDOOR   As a barber's every Saturday night. Mad Moll—
SIR ALEXANDER   Ah!
TRAPDOOR   Must be let in without knocking at your back gate.   15
SIR ALEXANDER   So.
TRAPDOOR   Your chamber will be made bawdy.
SIR ALEXANDER   Good.
TRAPDOOR   She comes in a shirt of mail.
SIR ALEXANDER   How, shirt of mail?   20
TRAPDOOR   Yes, sir, or a male shirt, that's to say in man's apparel.
SIR ALEXANDER   To my son.
TRAPDOOR   Close to your son; your son and her moon will be in
conjunction, if all almanacs lie not. Her black safeguard is turned

265. *By which . . . beguile:* by which Satan, in the form of a snake, deceived Eve into eating
      an apple from the Tree of the knowledge of good and evil; an allusion to the story of
      the Fall, Genesis 3:1–7.
  2. *A knave . . . my debt:* I see a scoundrel who owes me money (Sir Alexander's excuse to
      talk privately with Trapdoor).
  5. *A duck's egg . . . a frog:* swallowed the bait; "duck" here may carry the sense of "wild
      fowl" at 3.2.240, i.e., a loose woman.
  7. *bouncing ramp:* big, boisterous tomboy.
  8. *tread:* see note to 3.2.206.
 11. *tongue of an oyster-wench:* a girl who sells oysters; "fishwives" were notoriously talkative.
 13. *As a barber's:* barbers had a reputation for spreading gossip.
 15. *Must be:* will be.
 17. *bawdy:* i.e., will be the site of an illicit sexual encounter.
 19. *mail:* chain-mail, worn as armor; Sir Alexander is understandably surprised.
 23. *her moon:* her genitals; Trapdoor plays on son/sun to describe intercourse between
      Sebastian and Moll in astrological terms (the modern slang sense of "moon" as "but-
      tocks" was not current in this period). For "almanacs," see note to 2.1.40.
 24. *safeguard:* see note to 2.1.164 (stage direction).

into a deep slop, the holes of her upper body to buttonholes,   25
her waistcoat to a doublet, her placket to the ancient seat of a
codpiece, and you shall take 'em both with standing collars.

SIR ALEXANDER   Art sure of this?

TRAPDOOR   As every throng is sure of a pickpocket, as sure as a
whore is of the clients all Michaelmas term and of the pox   30
after the term.

SIR ALEXANDER   The time of their tilting?

TRAPDOOR   Three.

SIR ALEXANDER   The day?

TRAPDOOR   This.   35

SIR ALEXANDER   Away, ply it. Watch her.

TRAPDOOR   As the devil doth for the death of a bawd. I'll watch her;
do you catch her.

SIR ALEXANDER   She's fast. Here, weave thou the nets. Hark!

TRAPDOOR   They are made.   40

SIR ALEXANDER   I told them thou didst owe me money. Hold it up;
maintain't.

TRAPDOOR   Stiffly, as a Puritan does contention: "Fox, I owe thee
not the value of a halfpenny halter!"

SIR ALEXANDER   "Thou shalt be hanged in't ere thou scape so.   45
Varlet, I'll make thee look through a grate!"

TRAPDOOR   "I'll do't presently: through a tavern grate. Drawer!
Pish!"   *Exit Trapdoor.* [*Sir Alexander rejoins the others.*]

SIR ADAM   Has the knave vexed you, sir?

SIR ALEXANDER   Asked him my money;
He swears my son received it. Oh, that boy   50
Will ne'er leave heaping sorrows on my heart
Till he has broke it quite!

SIR ADAM   Is he still wild?

---

25. *slop*: see note to 2.2.84; *holes of her upper body*: eyelets of her bodice.
26. *placket*: slit where a skirt fastens at the waist.
27. *codpiece*: see note to Epistle, l. 14; *standing collars*: high, stiff collars (with a pun on "standing" as "an erection").
30. *Michaelmas term*: the autumn term of the law courts; law-clients visiting London to pursue their suits would give the whore plenty of business, leaving her with syphilis at the term's end.
32. *tilting*: jousting, swordplay (with sexual innuendo).
36. *ply it*: do your job.
37. *bawd*: a brothel madam or pimp.
39. *fast*: trapped.
41. *them*: i.e., Sir Adam and Sir Davy. What follows until Trapdoor's exit is the fake quarrel over the money he supposedly owes Sir Alexander.
42. *maintain't*: back me up, go along with my pretence.
43. *Stiffly . . . contention*: as rigidly as a Puritan defends his controversial religious views.
44. *halfpenny halter*: hangman's noose.
45. *scape*: escape.
46. *grate*: barred window (i.e., in debtors' prison).
47. *I'll do't . . . Drawer!*: "I'll look through a grate right now—one on the window of a tavern. Bartender!" Alehouses were traditionally marked by a latticed window.
49. *Asked him*: asked him for.

SIR ALEXANDER   As is a Russian bear.
SIR ADAM   But he has left
　His old haunt with that baggage?
SIR ALEXANDER   Worse still and worse.
　He lays on me his shame, I on him my curse.   55
SIR DAVY   My son Jack Dapper then shall run with him
　All in one pasture.
SIR ADAM   Proves your son bad too, sir?
SIR DAVY   As villainy can make him. Your Sebastian
　Dotes but on one drab, mine on a thousand.
　A noise of fiddlers, tobacco, wine, and a whore,   60
　A mercer that will let him take up more,
　Dice, and a water spaniel with a duck—oh,
　Bring him abed with these! When his purse jingles,
　Roaring boys follow at 's tail. Fencers and ningles—
　Beasts Adam ne'er gave name to—these horse-leeches suck   65
　My son; he being drawn dry, they all live on smoke.
SIR ALEXANDER   Tobacco?
SIR DAVY   Right, but I have in my brain
　A windmill going that shall grind to dust
　The follies of my son, and make him wise,
　Or a stark fool. Pray lend me your advice.   70
SIR ALEXANDER *and* SIR ADAM   That shall you, good Sir Davy.
SIR DAVY   Here's the springe
　I ha' set to catch this woodcock in: an action
　In a false name—unknown to him—is entered
　I'th'Counter to arrest Jack Dapper.
SIR ALEXANDER *and* SIR ADAM   Ha, ha, he!   75
SIR DAVY   Think you the Counter cannot break him?
SIR ADAM   Break him?
　Yes, and break's heart too, if he lie there long.

---

　54. *His . . . baggage*: hanging around with that hussy.
56–57. *shall run . . . pasture*: will be in the same boat.
　59. *drab*: whore.
　60. *noise*: company.
　61. *take up more*: buy more on credit.
　62. *water spaniel . . . duck*: i.e., for hunting.
　63. *Bring him abed with*: let him be delivered from; the term usually applies to a woman
　　in childbirth being delivered of a baby.
　64. *ningles*: ingles, I.e., young male lovers. Adam gives names to the animals in Genesis
　　2:19–20, but God, Sir Davy implies, created no such beast as an ingle.
　65. *horse-leeches*: a horse-leech is an especially large and insatiable kind of leech.
　66. *drawn*: sucked.
　71. *springe*: snare for trapping birds.
　72. *woodcock*: a proverbially gullible bird.
72–73. *an action . . . is entered*: a lawsuit is registered.
　74. *Counter*: one of London's two debtors' prisons, Wood Street Counter and Poultry
　　Counter.
　78. *lie*: be imprisoned.

SIR DAVY   I'll make him sing a countertenor, sure.

SIR ADAM   No way to tame him like it. There he shall learn   80
  What money is indeed, and how to spend it.

SIR DAVY   He's bridled there.

SIR ALEXANDER   Ay, yet knows not how to mend it.
  Bedlam cures not more madmen in a year
  Than one of the counters does; men pay more dear
  There for their wit than anywhere. A counter,   85
  Why, 'tis an university. Who not sees?
  As scholars there, so here men take degrees
  And follow the same studies—all alike.
  Scholars learn first logic and rhetoric;
  So does a prisoner. With fine honeyed speech,   90
  At 's first coming in, he doth persuade, beseech
  He may be lodged with one that is not itchy,
  To lie in a clean chamber, in sheets not lousy;
  But when he has no money, then does he try,
  By subtle logic and quaint sophistry,   95
  To make the keepers trust him.

SIR ADAM   Say they do?

SIR ALEXANDER   Then he's a graduate.

SIR DAVY   Say they trust him not.

SIR ALEXANDER   Then is he held a freshman and a sot,
  And never shall commence, but being still barred,
  Be expulsed from the Master's Side to th 'Twopenny Ward,   100
  Or else i'th'Hole be placed.

SIR ADAM   When, then, I pray,
  Proceeds a prisoner?

SIR ALEXANDER   When, money being the theme,
  He can dispute with his hard creditors' hearts
  And get out clear, he's then a Master of Arts.
  Sir Davy, send your son to Wood Street College;   105
  A gentleman can nowhere get more knowledge.

SIR DAVY   There gallants study hard.

SIR ALEXANDER   True: to get money.

---

  79. *countertenor*: a high-pitched male singing part, above a tenor; puns on "Counter"
        and may carry an additional suggestion of castration.
  83. *Bedlam*: see note to 3.2.92.
  93. *lousy*: infested with lice.
  95. *quaint*: ingenious.
  96. *trust*: i.e., to pay them later. Prisoners had to pay their jailers for room and board.
  98. *sot*: idiot.
  99. *commence*: graduate with a degree.
100–101. *Be expulsed . . . placed*: the Master's Side, the Twopenny Ward, and the Hole
        were prison lodgings of descending degrees of comfort, from the expensive but
        tolerable "Master's Side" to the dreaded "Hole" for the destitute.
  102. *Proceeds*: Graduates.
  103. *dispute*: "disputes" or formal debates were an important part of a Renaissance
        university education; the imprisoned debtor is thus imagined as having to win a
        debate against his creditors on the "theme" of money.
  105. *Wood Street College*: see note to 3.3.74.

SIR DAVY   'Lies by th' heels, i'faith. Thanks, thanks; I ha' sent
For a couple of bears shall paw him.

Enter Sergeant Curtalax and Yeoman Hanger.

SIR ADAM   Who comes yonder?   110
SIR DAVY   They look like puttocks. These should be they.
SIR ADAM   I know 'em;
They are officers. Sir, we'll leave you.
SIR DAVY   My good knights,
Leave me. You see I'm haunted now with sprites.
SIR ALEXANDER *and* SIR ADAM   Fare you well, sir.
                                 Exeunt Alexander and Adam.
CURTALAX [*to Hanger*]   This old muzzle chops should be he, by the   115
fellow's description.—Save you, sir.
SIR DAVY   Come hither, you mad varlets. Did not my man tell
you I watched here for you?
CURTALAX   One in a blue coat, sir, told us that in this place
an old gentleman would watch for us—a thing contrary to   120
our oath, for we are to watch for every wicked member in
a city.
SIR DAVY   You'll watch then for ten thousand. What's thy name,
honesty?
CURTALAX   Sergeant Curtalax, I, sir.   125
SIR DAVY   An excellent name for a sergeant, Curtalax.
Sergeants indeed are weapons of the law.
When prodigal ruffians far in debt are grown,
Should not you cut them, citizens were o'erthrown.
Thou dwell'st hereby in Holborn, Curtalax?   130
CURTALAX   That's my circuit, sir; I conjure most in that circle.
SIR DAVY   And what young toward whelp is this?
HANGER   Of the same litter; his yeoman, sir. My name's Hanger.

---

108. *'Lies by th' heels*: lies in leg irons.
109. *couple . . . paw him*: sergeants to arrest him (typically, by laying a heavy hand on the
shoulder).
111. *puttocks*: birds of prey, slang for arresting officers.
113. *sprites*: spirits (i.e., the officers).
115. *muzzle chops*: man with protruding jaws ("chops"), like an animal's muzzle.
116. *fellow*: i.e., Sir Davy's manservant (as mentioned in the next line).
118. *watched*: was waiting.
119. *blue coat*: typically worn by serving-men.
121. *watch*: i.e., watch out for, keep an eye on.
124. *honesty*: i.e., you honest fellow.
126. *Curtalax*: Cutlass.
129. *o'erthrown*: bankrupted.
130. *Holborn*: see note to 2.1.280.
131. *circuit*: area of jurisdiction; *circle*: Curtalax compares his job of summoning debtors to
prison to a conjuror calling up spirits within a magic circle.
132. *young . . . whelp*: promising young pup.
133. *yeoman*: assistant; *Hanger*: strap for attaching a sword to a belt (and so an appropriate
name for an assistant to Curtalax); there is perhaps also an allusion to hanging as capital punishment, as suggested in l. 136.

SIR DAVY   Yeoman Hanger!
   One pair of shears, sure, cut out both your coats;   135
   You have two names most dangerous to men's throats.
   You two are villainous loads on gentlemen's backs;
   Dear ware, this Hanger and this Curtalax.
CURTALAX   We are as other men are, sir. I cannot see but he
   who makes a show of honesty and religion, if his claws can   140
   fasten to his liking, he draws blood. All that live in the
   world are but great fish and little fish, and feed upon one
   another. Some eat up whole men; a sergeant cares but for the
   shoulder of a man. They call us knaves and curs, but many
   times he that sets us on worries more lambs one year than   145
   we do in seven.
SIR DAVY   Spoke like a noble Cerberus. Is the action entered?
HANGER   His name is entered in the book of unbelievers.
SIR DAVY   What book's that?
CURTALAX   The book where all prisoners' names stand; and not   150
   one amongst forty when he comes in, believes to come out
   in haste.
SIR DAVY   Be as dogged to him as your office allows you to be.
CURTALAX *and* HANGER   Oh, sir!
SIR DAVY   You know the unthrift Jack Dapper?   155
CURTALAX   I? Ay, sir, that gull? As well as I know my yeoman.
SIR DAVY   And you know his father too, Sir Davy Dapper?
CURTALAX   As damned a usurer as ever was among Jews. If he were
   sure his father's skin would yield him any money, he would when
   he dies, flay it off and sell it to cover drums for children at   160
   Barthol'mew Fair.
SIR DAVY [*aside*]   What toads are these, to spit poison on a man
   to his face! [*To them*] Do you see, my honest rascals? Yonder

135. *One . . . coats*: i.e., you're two of a kind.
138. *Dear ware*: expensive goods.
139–41. *I cannot see . . . he draws blood*: As far as I can see, even a man who appears pious
   will cruelly take advantage of others if he can profit from it.
144. *shoulder of a man*: a sergeant would seize a man by the shoulder to arrest him; the joke
   depends on the difference between eating "whole men" (i.e., ruining them entirely),
   and having only, so to speak, a shoulder roast; *curs*: dogs (a derogatory term).
145. *worries*: mauls.
147. *Cerberus*: see note to 3.1.23; *action entered*: presumably, Sir Davy is asking for
   official confirmation of the lawsuit he mentions registering in 3.3.72–74. "The
   book of unbelievers" suggests the opposite of the Book of Life, in which the names
   of Christian believers are said to be written (Revelations 3:5); the allusion compares debtors' prison to damnation.
153. *dogged*: cruel.
156. *gull*: gullible simpleton.
158. *usurer*: moneylender who charges extortionate interest; as Jews were expelled
   from England in 1290 by Edward I, Curtalax's assumptions about Jewish money-
   lenders are based in prejudice, not known practice.
161. *Barthol'mew Fair*: fair held on St. Bartholomew's day, August 24, where toys and
   other cheap goods were sold.
162–63. *spit . . . face*: Curtalax and Hanger don't realize they are talking to Sir Davy himself; given their opinion of his avarice (ll. 158–61), Sir Davy has good reason not
   to let them know he is having his own son arrested.

Grayhound is the dog he hunts with; out of that tavern Jack Dapper
   will sally. Sa, sa! Give the counter! On, set upon him!   165
CURTALAX *and* HANGER   We'll charge him upo' th'back, sir.
SIR DAVY   Take no bail; put mace enough into his caudle!
   Double your files! Traverse your ground!
CURTALAX *and* HANGER   Brave, sir.
SIR DAVY   Cry arm, arm, arm!   170
CURTALAX *and* HANGER   Thus, sir.
               [*They ineptly execute the manual of arms.*]
SIR DAVY   There, boy, there, boy, away! Look to your prey, my
   true English wolves, and—and so I vanish.   *Exit Sir Davy.*
CURTALAX   Some warden of the sergeants begat this old fellow,
   upon my life. Stand close.   175
HANGER   Shall the ambuscado lie in one place?
CURTALAX   No. Nook thou yonder.   [*They hide separately.*]

   Enter Moll and Trapdoor.

MOLL   Ralph?
TRAPDOOR   What says my brave captain, male and female?
MOLL   This Holborn is such a wrangling street.   180
TRAPDOOR   That's because lawyers walks to and fro in't.
MOLL   Here's such jostling, as if everyone we met were drunk
   and reeled.
TRAPDOOR   Stand, mistress! Do you not smell carrion?
MOLL   Carrion? No, yet I spy ravens.   185
TRAPDOOR   Some poor wind-shaken gallant will anon fall into sore
   labor, and these men-midwives must bring him to bed i'the
   Counter; there all those that are great with child with debts lie in.
MOLL   Stand up.
TRAPDOOR   Like your new maypole.   190

---

164. *Grayhound*: either the name of the tavern Dapper is about to exit, or an actual dog who
    accompanies him; in either case, Sir Davy points offstage.
165. *Sa, sa!*: a cry accompanying a thrust at fencing, or to urge on a fighter; *Give the*
    counter: parry a thrust in fencing, with a pun on "the Counter," debtors' prison.
166. *upo' th' back*: come up on him from behind.
167. *mace . . . caudle*: spice up his drink for him, i.e., give him a hard time. "Mace" is both a
    sergeant's truncheon and a spice derived from nutmeg, used to flavor "caudle," a
    warm, sweet drink of wine or ale mixed with gruel.
168. *Double . . . ground*: military drill commands.
169. *Brave*: well done.
172. *boy*: see note to 2.2.75.
174. *warden*: official who oversees arresting officers.
175. *close*: concealed.
176. *Shall . . . place?*: Shall we lie in ambush together?
177. *Nook*: hide.
184. *Stand*: Stop; *carrion*: rotting carcass.
188. *lie in*: i.e., in childbirth. Trapdoor punningly compares the debt-ridden ("wind-
    shaken") gallant, who will "lie in" prison attended by sergeants until delivered from his
    debts, to a woman in labor who "lies in," attended by midwives.
189. *Stand up*: Get ready to back me.
190. *maypole*: a tall pole decorated with flowers around which people would dance during
    May-day celebrations; as "maypole" was slang for "erection," Trapdoor interprets the
    command to "stand" in a sexual sense. "Your" is probably impersonal, i.e., "a maypole."

HANGER [*signaling to Curtalax*]   Whist! Whew!
CURTALAX [*signaling back*]   Hump, no!
MOLL   Peeping? It shall go hard, huntsmen, but I'll spoil your
game. [*To Trapdoor*] They look for all the world like two infected
maltmen coming muffled up in their cloaks in a frosty morning   195
to London.
TRAPDOOR   A course, Captain! A bear comes to the stake.

Enter Jack Dapper and Gull.

MOLL   It should be so, for the dogs struggle to be let loose.
HANGER [*signaling*]   Whew!
CURTALAX   Hemp!   200
MOLL   Hark, Trapdoor, follow your leader.
JACK DAPPER   Gull?
GULL   Master?
JACK DAPPER   Didst ever see such an ass as I am, boy?
GULL   No, by my troth, sir, to lose all your money, yet have false   205
dice of your own, Why, 'tis as I saw a great fellow used t'other
day: he had a fair sword and buckler, and yet a butcher dry-beat
him with a cudgel.
MOLL *and* TRAPDOOR   Honest sergeant!—Fly, fly, Master
Dapper! You'll be arrested else!   210
                        [*Moll and Trapdoor detain the sergeants.*]
JACK DAPPER   Run, Gull, and draw!
GULL   Run, master! Gull follows you.   *Exit Dapper and Gull.*
CURTALAX [*to Moll*]   I know you well enough. You're but a
whore to hang upon any man.
MOLL   Whores then are like sergeants, so now hang you! [*To*   215
Trapdoor] Draw, rogue, but strike not. For a broken pate, they'll
keep their beds and recover twenty marks damages.

---

192. *Hump*: a code-word between the officers; compare 3.3.200, where "Hemp!"
      means "that's him!"
193. *It shall go hard but*: an expression roughly equivalent to the modern "I'll be
      damned if I don't . . ."; Moll is speaking as if to the officers.
195. *maltmen*: men who transported malt into London; maltmen were at high risk of
      infection with the plague as they also transported rags back to the countryside for
      use as fertilizer, a practice officially forbidden in 1630.
197. *A bear . . . stake*: in the sport of bear-baiting, a bear was tied to a stake to defend
      himself against attacks by dogs; each of these attacks was called a "course." Trap-
      door refers to the officers' imminent "attack" on Dapper, as does Moll in l. 198.
200. *Hemp!*: see note to 3.3.192.
205–06. *To lose . . . false dice*: i.e., Dapper has lost all his money gambling, despite the fact
      that he was cheating with weighted dice.
206. *great*: big.
207. *buckler*: small shield.
207. *dry-beat*: beat thoroughly, without drawing blood.
209–10. *Fly . . . else!*: Moll and Trapdoor distract the officers, then urge Dapper to flee.
215. *Whores . . . sergeants*: i.e., sergeants (physically) hang on to men just like whores do.
216–17. *broken . . . damages*: i.e., for a cut on the head ("a broken pate"), they'll pretend to
      be injured badly enough to be bedridden and then they'll sue us.

CURTALAX   You shall pay for this rescue! [*To Hanger*] Run down
   Shoe Lane and meet him.
TRAPDOOR   Shoo! Is this a rescue, gentlemen, or no?   220
                        [*Exeunt Curtalax and Hanger.*]
MOLL   Rescue? A pox on 'em, Trapdoor. Let's away.
   I'm glad I have done perfect one good work today.
   If any gentleman be in scriveners' bands,
   Send but for Moll; she'll bail him, by these hands.   *Exeunt.*

[4.1]

Enter Sir Alexander Wengrave solus.

SIR ALEXANDER   Unhappy in the follies of a son
   Led against judgment, sense, obedience,
   And all the powers of nobleness and wit!
   Oh, wretched father!

Enter Trapdoor.

                        Now, Trapdoor, will she come?
TRAPDOOR   In man's apparel, sir. I am in her heart now,   5
   And share in all her secrets.
SIR ALEXANDER   Peace, peace, peace!
   Here, take my German watch. Hang't up in sight,
   That I may see her hang in English for't.
                        [*He give a watch*]
TRAPDOOR   I warrant you for that, now; next sessions rids her, sir.
   This watch will bring her in, better than a hundred constables.   10
SIR ALEXANDER   Good Trapdoor, say'st thou so? Thou cheer'st my
      heart
   After a storm of sorrow. My gold chain, too.
   Here, take a hundred marks in yellow links.
                        [*He gives a gold chain.*]
TRAPDOOR   That will do well to bring the watch to light, sir, and
   worth a thousand of your headborough's lanterns.   15

---

218. *rescue*: the forcible taking of a person out of legal custody; now that Dapper is safely gone, Trapdoor "shoos" the officers after him and implies he never took Dapper out of their hands.
223. *scriveners' bands*: i.e., in bondage to a scrivener; the job-title of "scrivener" applied both to a scribe (who would write up bonds between creditors and debtors), and to a broker who lent money out at interest on behalf of a third party.
Scene 4.1 s.d. *solus*: alone.
   5. *in her heart*: in her confidence.
   8. *in English*: under English law.
   9. *next . . . her*: the courts will get rid of her when they're next in session.
   15. *headborough*: a parish constable. Trapdoor puns on "links," meaning both "the links of a chain" and "torches used for outdoor lighting"; he also puns on "watch," meaning both the timepiece and a group of constables on night-duty (called "the watch").

SIR ALEXANDER   Place that o' the court-cupboard. Let it lie
Full in the view of her thief-whorish eye.
                        [*Trapdoor places the objects on a sideboard.*]
TRAPDOOR   She cannot miss it, sir. I see't so plain that I could
steal't myself.
SIR ALEXANDER   Perhaps thou shalt, too—   20
That or something as weighty. What she leaves,
Thou shalt come closely in and filch away,
And all the weight upon her back I'll lay.
TRAPDOOR   You cannot assure that, sir.
SIR ALEXANDER   No? What lets it?   25
TRAPDOOR   Being a stout girl, perhaps she'll desire pressing; then
all the weight must lie upon her belly.
SIR ALEXANDER   Belly or back, I care not so I've one.
TRAPDOOR   You're of my mind for that, sir.
SIR ALEXANDER   Hang up my ruff band with the diamond   30
at it;
It may be she'll like that best.
TRAPDOOR [*aside*]   It's well for her that she must have her
choice; he thinks nothing too good for her! [*To him*] If you
hold on this mind a little longer, it shall be the first work
I do to turn thief myself. Would do a man good to be hanged   35
when he is so well provided for.
                        [*The ruff collar is hung up in plain view.*]
SIR ALEXANDER   So, well said. All hangs well; would she hung
so too!
The sight would please me more than all their glisterings.
Oh, that my mysteries to such straits should run,
That I must rob myself to bless my son!   *Exeunt.* 40

*Enter Sebastian, with Mary Fitzallard like a page, and
Moll [dressed as a man].*

SEBASTIAN [*to Moll*]   Thou hast done me a kind office, without
touch

16. *court-cupboard*: small cabinet used to display plate.
22. *closely*: secretly.
23. *weight*: i.e., of the accusation of theft.
25. *lets*: prevents.
26. *stout*: robust, tough.
26–27. *she'll desire . . . belly*: accused criminals who refused to enter a plea were pressed with
        weights until they either pled or died; such a death allowed the accused's heirs to
        inherit his property, which would be forfeit to the Crown if he were tried and exe-
        cuted. Trapdoor plays on the sexual sense of "pressing"—i.e., beneath a man in inter-
        course.
28. *so I've one*: so long as I get what I want (i.e., to incriminate her); but Trapdoor takes
     him to mean "as long as I get her (sexually)—from the front or from behind."
30. *ruff band*: ruff collar.
37. *well said*: well done.
38. *glisterings*: glitterings.
39. *mysteries*: skills of a trade (here, presumably, the job of fatherhood).
41. *office*: service.

Either of sin or shame; our loves are honest.
MOLL   I'd scorn to make such shift to bring you together
    else.
SEBASTIAN [*to Mary*]   Now have I time and opportunity,
    Without all fear, to bid thee welcome, love.   [*They*] *Kiss.*   45
MARY   Never with more desire and harder venture!
MOLL   How strange this shows, one man to kiss another!
SEBASTIAN   I'd kiss such men to choose, Moll.
    Methinks a woman's lip tastes well in a doublet.
MOLL   Many an old madam has the better fortune then,   50
    Whose breaths grew stale before the fashion came,
    If that will help 'em, as you think 'twill do,
    They'll learn in time to pluck on the hose too.
SEBASTIAN   The older they wax, Moll. Troth, I speak seriously:
    As some have a conceit their drink tastes better   55
    In an outlandish cup than in our own,
    So methinks every kiss she gives me now
    In this strange form is worth a pair of two.
    Here we are safe, and furthest from the eye
    Of all suspicion. This is my father's chamber,   60
    Upon which floor he never steps till night.
    Here he mistrusts me not, nor I his coming.
    At mine own chamber he still pries unto me;
    My freedom is not there at mine own finding,
    Still checked and curbed. Here he shall miss his purpose   65
MOLL   And what's your business, now you have your mind, sir?
    At your great suit I promised you to come;
    I pitied her for name's sake, that a Moll
    Should be so crossed in love, when there's so many

43. *shift*: efforts, with a pun on "shift" meaning "to change clothes."
47. *shows*: looks.
48. *to choose*: by choice.
50–53. *Many an old . . . pluck on the hose too*: i.e., old women who were unkissable before the current fad for masculine fashions are now in luck—if men like kissing women in doublets as much as you say they do, old women will make themselves desirable by putting them on, and will even go the extra step of wearing masculine hose (tight-fitting breeches).
54. *The older they wax*: (i.e., the older they grow) implies a joke to the effect of "the older the better" or "the older they are, the more masculine clothing they'll need to be desirable"; Sebastian then claims that what he says next—about liking Mary's kisses better when she's cross-dressed—is in all seriousness.
55. *conceit*: notion.
56. *outlandish*: foreign, unfamiliar.
62. *mistrusts*: suspects (i.e., he doesn't suspect I'd be here).
63. *still pries unto me*: always spies on me.
64. *freedom . . . finding*: I'm unable to provide for my own freedom there.
65. *checked*: restrained.
66. *have your mind*: have what you wanted.
67. *suit*: earnest request.
68. *Moll*: nickname for Mary.
69. *crossed*: thwarted.

That owes nine lays apiece, and not so little.   70
My tailor fitted her. How like you his work?
SEBASTIAN   So well, no art can mend it for this purpose.
But to thy wit and help we're chief in debt,
And must live still beholding.
MOLL   Any honest pity
I'm willing to bestow upon poor ringdoves.   75
SEBASTIAN   I'll offer no worse play.
MOLL   Nay, an you should, sir,
I should draw first and prove the quicker man.
SEBASTIAN   Hold, there shall need no weapon at this meeting.
But 'cause thou shalt not loose thy fury idle,
Here, take this viol. [*He takes down and hands her a viola da
gamba.*] Run upon the guts   80
And end thy quarrel singing.
MOLL   Like a swan above bridge;
For, look you, here's the bridge and here am I.
SEBASTIAN   Hold on, sweet Moll.
MARY   I've heard her much commended, sir, for one that was
ne'er taught.   85
MOLL   I'm much beholding to 'em. Well, since you'll needs
put us together, sir, I'll play my part as well as I can. It shall ne'er
be said I came into a gentleman's chamber and let his
instrument hang by the walls!
SEBASTIAN   Why, well said, Moll, i'faith. It had been a shame   90
for that gentleman, then, that would have let it hung still
and ne'er offered thee it.
MOLL   There it should have been still, then, for Moll, for, though
the world judge impudently of me, I ne'er came into that
chamber yet where I took down the instrument myself.   95

---

70. *owes nine lays apiece*: meaning uncertain, but most likely "so many women named
    Moll have nine lodgings in which to fornicate (i.e., have nine lovers)."
72. *no art can mend it*: nothing could improve upon it.
74. *beholding*: obligated to you.
75. *ringdoves*: i.e., lovebirds.
76. *no worse play*: i.e., I won't try anything unchaste with Mary; Moll's response is jok-
    ingly ambiguous, implying that if ("an") he did, she would either defend Mary with
    her sword, or she would beat Sebastian to whatever sexual act he had in mind.
79. *But 'cause*: so that; *idle*: in vain.
80–81. *run . . . singing*: play upon catgut strings of the viol, with a pun on running one's
    sword through the guts of an opponent.
81. *Like . . . bridge*: swans were thought to sing before their deaths.
82. *here's the bridge*: Moll puns on two meanings of "bridge": the kind built over rivers,
    and the kind found on musical instruments.
83. *Hold on*: Go ahead [and sing].
86. *beholding*: obliged.
87. *put us*: i.e., me and the viol. The exchange that follows puns bawdily on "instru-
    ment" as "penis."
93. *There it . . . for Moll*: i.e., his instrument would be left hanging, then, as far as I'm
    concerned.
95. *took . . . instrument*: removed the musical instrument from the wall; relieved the
    gentleman of his erection.

SEBASTIAN   Pish, let 'em prate abroad. Thou'rt here where thou art
known and loved. There be a thousand close dames that will call
the viol an unmannerly instrument for a woman, and therefore
talk broadly of thee, when you shall have them sit wider to a
worse quality.   100

MOLL   Push, I ever fall asleep and think not of 'em, sir;
and thus I dream.

SEBASTIAN   Prithee, let's hear thy dream, Moll.

THE SONG

MOLL [*sings*]   I dream there is a mistress,
                                 And she lays out the money.   105
                     She goes unto her sisters;
                     She never comes at any.

Enter Sir Alexander behind them.

                     She says she went to th'Burse for patterns;
                     You shall find her at Saint Kathern's,
                     And comes home with never a penny.   110

SEBASTIAN   That's a free mistress, faith.

SIR ALEXANDER [*aside*]   Ay, ay, ay,
Like her that sings it, one of thine own choosing.

MOLL   But shall I dream again?

[*She sings.*]   Here comes a wench will brave ye,   115
                     Her courage was so great;
                     She lay with one o'the navy;
                     Her husband lying i'the Fleet.
                     Yet oft with him she caviled.
                     I wonder what she ails?   120

96. *let 'em prate abroad*: let the world talk.
97. *close*: secretive.
97–100. *dames that will . . . worse quality*: the viol, like a modern cello, was played
    between the legs; Sebastian observes that women who say lewd things ("talk
    broadly") about Moll because she plays the viol, sit with their own legs even
    more widely apart for far less innocent activities.
101. *Push*: Pish.
The Song. The song, though somewhat ambiguous, seems to be about a married woman
    who lies about going shopping so she can instead spend the household money
    drinking with her female friends—but who, despite what one might expect of
    such a woman, is nonetheless chaste.
107. *she never comes at any*: she never sexually accosts any men.
108. *th'Burse*: the Royal Exchange, a financial center surrounded by fashionable
    shops; *patterns*: models of the clothing, etc. sold in such shops.
109. *Saint Kathern's*: a dockside area in east London, known for its taverns.
111. *free*: generous, free-spending; Sir Alexander takes it to mean "free with her sex-
    ual favors."
115. In contrast to the first song, this one concerns a woman who cheats on her
    imprisoned husband with a sailor and yet has the nerve to call Moll a whore;
    brave ye: challenge or defy you.
118. *Fleet*: Fleet Prison, with a pun on the navy's fleet.
119. *caviled*: found fault with.
120. *what she ails*: what ails her.

> Her husband's ship lay graveled
> When hers could hoise up sails;
> Yet she began, like all my foes,
> To call "whore" first; for so do those.
> A pox of all false tails!   125

SEBASTIAN   Marry, amen, say I.

SIR ALEXANDER [*aside*]   So say I, too.

MOLL [*returning the viola da gamba*]   Hang up the viol now, sir;
all this while I was in a dream. One shall lie rudely then;
but being awake, I keep my legs together.—A watch! what's   130
o'clock here?

SIR ALEXANDER [*aside*] Now, now, she's trapped.

MOLL   Between one and two? Nay, then, I care not. A watch and
a musician are cousin-germans in one thing: they must both
keep time well, or there's no goodness in 'em. The one else   135
deserves to be dashed against a wall, and t'other to have his
brains knocked out with a fiddle case. [*She sees the other
displayed objects.*] What, a loose chain and a dangling
diamond? Here were a brave booty for an evening thief now.
There's many a younger brother would be glad to look twice   140
in at a window for't, and wriggle in and out, like an eel in a
sandbag. Oh, if men's secret youthful faults should judge
'em, 'twould be the general'st execution that e'er was seen
in England! There would be but few left to sing the ballads.
There would be so much work, most of our brokers would be   145
chosen for hangmen! A good day for them: they might renew
their wardrobes of free cost then.

SEBASTIAN [*to Mary*]   This is the roaring wench must do us good.

MARY [*to Sebastian*]   No poison, sir, but serves us for some use,
Which is confirmed in her.

SEBASTIAN   Peace, peace!   150
Foot, I did hear him, sure, where'er he be.

MOLL   Who did you hear?

---

121. *graveled*: beached.
122. *hoise*: hoist (metaphorically, the husband is a beached ship, stuck in prison, while
the wife can hoist her sails—and her skirts—and move freely).
125. *false tails*: Moll puns on "tails/tales" to curse both unchaste women and the false
stories they tell about her.
134. *cousin-germans*: first cousins ("german" = germane).
135. *else*: otherwise.
140–42. *younger brother . . . sandbag*: as eldest sons inherited the family estate under the
system of primogeniture, younger brothers were stereotyped as having to live by
their wits. Compare 2.2.60–63.
144. *sing the ballads*: ballads were written about particularly sensational crimes; Moll
imagines a scenario in which so many are executed for crimes committed in their
youth that few people are left to sing the ballads about them.
146–47. *they . . . cost then*: brokers bought and sold second-hand clothes; hangmen traditionally received the clothes of those they executed. If brokers found work as hangmen, they could replenish their stock free of charge.
149. *No poison . . . use*: i.e., there is no poison that does not have its use (proverbial).
151. *Foot*: by God's foot.

SEBASTIAN   My father;
'Twas like a sigh of his. I must be wary.
SIR ALEXANDER [*aside*]   No? Will't not be? Am I alone so wretched
That nothing takes? I'll put him to his plunge for't.   155
SEBASTIAN [*seeing Sir Alexander*]   Life, here he comes.
[*Aloud to Moll*] Sir, I beseech you take it.
Your way of teaching does so much content me,
I'll make it four pound. Here's forty shillings, sir.
                                    [*He offers money.*]
I think I name it right. [*Aside to Moll*] Help me, good Moll.   160
[*Aloud*] Forty in hand.
MOLL   Sir, you shall pardon me;
I have more of the meanest scholar I can teach.
This pays me more than you have offered yet.
SEBASTIAN   At the next quarter,
When I receive the means my father 'lows me,   165
You shall have t'other forty.
SIR ALEXANDER [*aside*]   This were well now,
Were't to a man whose sorrows had blind eyes,
But mine behold his follies and untruths
With two clear glasses.   [*He comes forward.*]
          [*To Sebastian*] How now?
SEBASTIAN   Sir?
SIR ALEXANDER   What's he there?
SEBASTIAN   You're come in good time, sir. I've a suit to you;   170
I'd crave your present kindness.
SIR ALEXANDER   What is he there?
SEBASTIAN   A gentleman, a musician, sir, one of excellent
fingering.
SIR ALEXANDER   Ay, I think so. [*Aside*] I wonder how they scaped
her.
SEBASTIAN   'Has the most delicate stroke, sir.   175
SIR ALEXANDER [*aside*]   A stroke indeed; I feel it at my heart.
SEBASTIAN   Puts down all your famous musicians.
SIR ALEXANDER [*aside*]   Ay, a whore may put down a hundred of 'em.

---

155. *nothing takes*: nothing works; *put . . . plunge*: put him in a difficult situation.
157. *take it*: i.e., the money he pretends to be offering Moll for teaching viol lessons.
161. *Forty in hand*: forty shillings as a down payment; a pound was worth twenty shillings, so this is half of the "four pound" promised as full payment.
163. *This pays . . . offered yet*: Moll, playing the "music teacher," refuses to take less than full payment; even the poorest ("meanest") students pay more than forty shillings, and as this is the most Sebastian has ever tried to pay, it's unlikely he'd ever pay the remainder.
165. *'lows*: allows.
169. *he*: i.e., the disguised Moll.
173. *fingering*: with its multiple senses of "fingering an instrument," "pilfering," and "sexual touching," a series of sexual double-entendres begins, including "stroke"; "puts down" (puts to shame/lays down on a bed); "mounts"; "stands upon the whole" (insists on the whole amount/has an erection against the "hole"); "be in other tale" (tell another story/be inside another tail); and "stop his mouth" (shut him up/kiss him).
174. *I wonder . . . her*: I wonder how the watch and chain escaped being stolen?

SEBASTIAN   Forty shillings is the agreement, sir, between us.
  Now, sir, my present means mounts but to half on't.   180
SIR ALEXANDER   And he stands upon the whole.
SEBASTIAN   Ay, indeed, does he, sir.
SIR ALEXANDER [*aside*]   And will do still; he'll ne'er be in other tale.
SEBASTIAN   Therefore I'd stop his mouth, sir, and I could.
SIR ALEXANDER   H'm, true. [*Aside*] There is no other way, indeed.   185
  His folly hardens; shame must needs succeed.
  [*To Moll*] Now, sir, I understand you profess music.
MOLL   I am a poor servant to that liberal science, sir.
SIR ALEXANDER   Where is it you teach?
MOLL   Right against Clifford's Inn.   190
SIR ALEXANDER [*aside*]   H'm, that's a fit place for it.   [*To Moll*]
  You have many scholars?
MOLL   And some of worth, whom I may call my masters.
SIR ALEXANDER [*aside*]   Ay, true, a company of whoremasters.
  [*To Moll*] You teach to sing, too?   195
MOLL   Marry, do I, sir.
SIR ALEXANDER   I think you'll find an apt scholar of my son,
  especially for prick-song.
MOLL   I have much hope of him.
SIR ALEXANDER [*aside*]   I am sorry for't; I have the less for that.   200
  [*To Moll*] You can play any lesson?
MOLL   At first sight, sir.
SIR ALEXANDER   There's a thing called "The Witch." Can you
  play that?
MOLL   I would be sorry anyone should mend me in't.   205
SIR ALEXANDER [*aside*]   Ay, I believe thee. Thou hast so bewitched
  my son,
  No care will mend the work that thou hast done.
  I have bethought myself, since my art fails,
  I'll make her policy the art to trap her.
                                        [*He produces four coins.*]
  Here are four angels marked with holes in them,   210
  Fit for his cracked companions. Gold he will give her;

186. *succeed*: follow.
190. *Clifford's Inn*: one of the Inns of Chancery, law schools affiliated with the Inns of
      Court; Clifford's Inn stood near a neighborhood known for prostitution, prompt-
      ing Sir Alexander's aside.
194. *whoremasters*: prostitutes' clients.
198. *prick-song*: music sung from a written ("pricked") score; with bawdy play on "prick."
200. *I have . . . that*: i.e., less hope of him because of that.
203. *"The Witch"*: title of a contemporary song or ballad; Sir Alexander is thinking of
      Moll's "bewitching" of Sebastian (see l. 206).
205. *mend me*: better me.
209. *policy*: craftiness (in posing as a musician).
210–11. *four angels . . . cracked*: an "angel" was a gold coin worth ten shillings; Sir Alexan-
      der gives Sebastian four damaged angels to give Moll, presumably in the hope that
      she will be arrested when she tries to spend them. It was illegal to clip or file metal
      off coins, a tempting practice when coins were still made of gold and silver; a coin
      clipped so far as to damage the ring around the king's head was "cracked," and no
      longer legal tender. "Cracked" was metaphorically applied to women who had lost
      their chastity; an "induction" (l. 212) is a prologue.

These will I make induction to her ruin,
And rid shame from my house, grief from my heart.
[*To Sebastian*] Here, son; in what you take content and pleasure,
Want shall not curb you. Pay the gentleman   215
His latter half in gold.   [*He gives Sebastian the money.*]
SEBASTIAN   I thank you, sir.
SIR ALEXANDER [*aside*]   Oh, may the operation on't end three:
In her, life; shame in him; and grief in me! *Exit Alexander.*
SEBASTIAN [*giving Moll the money*]   Faith, thou shalt have 'em.
'Tis my father's gift.   220
Never was man beguiled with better shift!
MOLL   He that can take me for a male musician,
I cannot choose but make him my instrument
And play upon him.   *Exeunt omnes.*

[4.2]

Enter Mistress Gallipot and Mistress Openwork.

MRS. GALLIPOT   Is then that bird of yours, Master Goshawk, so
wild?
MRS. OPENWORK   A goshawk? A puttock, all for prey! He angles
for fish, but he loves flesh better.
MRS. GALLIPOT   Is't possible his smooth face should have   5
wrinkles in't, and we not see them?
MRS. OPENWORK   Possible? Why, have not many handsome legs
in silk stockings villainous splay feet for all their great roses?
MRS. GALLIPOT   Troth, sirrah, thou say'st true.
MRS. OPENWORK   Didst never see an archer, as thou 'ast walked   10
by Bunhill, look asquint when he drew his bow?
MRS. GALLIPOT   Yes. When his arrows have fline toward
Islington, his eyes have shot clean contrary towards Pimlico.

---

215. *Want*: Lack (of money); the ten angels amount to the forty shillings Sebastian still owes
the "musician."
217. *operation . . . three*: i.e., may the money operate so as to bring three things to an end.
221. *Never . . . shift*: Never was man tricked with a better stratagem.
   3. *puttock*: a bird of prey, especially a kite or a buzzard, compare note to 3.3.111.
5–6. *possible . . . wrinkles in't*. i.e., is it possible his good looks can hide bad intentions?
   8. *villainous splay feet*: ugly, turned-out feet; *for . . . great roses*: despite the large ornamental rosettes on their shoes.
   9. *sirrah*: see note to 2.1.176.
 11. *Bunhill*: a street in northern London, near where the city militia practiced; *asquint*: off
to one side.
 12. *fline*: flown.
 13. *Islington*: a suburb to the northwest; *Pimlico*: a tavern to the northeast. The point is
that the archer looks in one direction while he shoots in another, just as Goshawk pretends to alert Mrs. Openwork to her husband's infidelity when his real intentions are to
get her into bed.

MRS. OPENWORK   For all the world so does Master Goshawk
  double with me.   15
MRS. GALLIPOT   Oh, fie upon him! If he double once, he's not
  for me.
MRS. OPENWORK   Because Goshawk goes in a shag-ruff band,
  with a face sticking up in't which shows like an agate set in a
  cramp-ring, he thinks I'm in love with him.   20
MRS. GALLIPOT   'Las, I think he takes his mark amiss in thee.
MRS. OPENWORK   He has, by often beating into me, made me
  believe that my husband kept a whore.
MRS. GALLIPOT   Very good.
MRS. OPENWORK   Swore to me that my husband this very morning   25
  went in a boat, with a tilt over it, to the Three Pigeons at
  Brentford, and his punk with him under his tilt.
MRS. GALLIPOT   That were wholesome!
MRS. OPENWORK   I believed it; fell a-swearing at him, cursing of
  harlots, made me ready to hoise up sail and be there as soon as he.   30
MRS. GALLIPOT   So, so.
MRS. OPENWORK   And for that voyage Goshawk comes hither
  incontinently. But, sirrah, this water spaniel dives after no
  duck but me; his hope is having me at Brentford to make me
  cry quack.   35
MRS. GALLIPOT   Art sure of it?
MRS. OPENWORK   Sure of it? My poor innocent Openwork came in
  as I was poking my ruff. Presently hit I him i'the teeth with the
  Three Pigeons. He forswore all. I up and opened all, and now
  stands he, in a shop hard by, like a musket on a rest, to hit   40
  Goshawk i'the eye when he comes to fetch me to the boat.
MRS. GALLIPOT   Such another lame gelding offered to carry me
  through thick and thin—Laxton, sirrah—but I am rid of him
  now.

15. *double*: behave deceitfully.
18. *shag-ruff band*: velvet ruff-style collar.
20. *cramp-ring*: a ring believed to have the power to ward off cramp and other maladies.
    The idea seems to be that Goshawk wears a ruff too big for his rather small head,
    under the delusion that it makes him attractive to women.
21. *his mark . . . thee*: i.e., he's mistaken in thinking you to be a good target ("mark").
22. *beating into me*: repeatedly assuring me.
26–27. *Three Pigeons at Brentford*: see note to 3.1.53–54.
27. *punk*: prostitute; *tilt*: awning.
28. *That were wholesome*: How healthy! (sarcastic).
30. *hoise*: hoist; Mrs. Openwork speaks of herself as if she were a ship preparing for
    departure.
33. *incontinently*: immediately.
34–35. *his hope . . . cry quack*: presumably, the cries of sexual pleasure Goshawk hopes Mrs.
    Openwork will make when he "has" her at Brentford; she imagines him pursuing
    her as a hunting dog pursues a duck.
38. *poking*: ironing the pleats of; *Presently hit . . . teeth*: Immediately I accused him.
39. *forswore*: denied; *up and opened all*: told him everything.
40. *hard by*: nearby.
40-41. *to hit . . . eye*: confront Goshawk.
42. *gelding*: castrated horse.

MRS. OPENWORK   Happy is the woman can be rid of 'em all.   45
'Las, what are your whisking gallants to our husbands, weigh 'em
rightly man for man?

MRS. GALLIPOT   Troth, mere shallow things.

MRS. OPENWORK   Idle simple things, running heads. And yet let 'em
run over us never so fast, we shopkeepers, when all's done, are   50
sure to have 'em in our purse-nets at length, and when they are
in, Lord, what simple animals they are! Then they hang the head.

MRS. GALLIPOT   Then they droop.

MRS. OPENWORK   Then they write letters.

MRS. GALLIPOT   Then they cog.   55

MRS. OPENWORK   Then deal they underhand with us, and we
must ingle with our husbands abed, and we must swear they
are our cousins and able to do us a pleasure at court.

MRS. GALLIPOT   And yet when we have done our best, all's but
put into a riven dish; we are but frumped at and libeled upon.   60

MRS. OPENWORK   Oh, if it were the good Lord's will, there were
a law made no citizen should trust any of 'em at all!

Enter Goshawk.

MRS. GALLIPOT [*in a lowered voice*]   Hush, sirrah, Goshawk
flutters.

GOSHAWK [*to Mrs. Openwork*]   How now, are you ready?   65

MRS. OPENWORK   Nay, are you ready? A little thing, you see, makes
us ready.

GOSHAWK   Us? Why, must she make one i'the voyage?

MRS. OPENWORK   Oh, by any means. Do I know how my husband
will handle me?   70

GOSHAWK [*aside*]   Foot, how shall I find water to keep these
two mills going? [*To them*] Well, since you'll needs be clapped

46. *'Las*: alas; *whisking*: lively; *to*: compared to.
49. *running*: giddy, flighty.
51. *in our purse-nets*: indebted financially to us; i.e., caught in our purses. A "purse-net," literally speaking, is a bag-shaped net used for fishing and for snaring rabbits; it also suggests the female sexual anatomy. The women then conflate the gallants' financial inadequacy with male sexual inadequacy in "hang the head" and "droop"; in the discussion that follows, they imply that gallants in debt to shopkeepers make sexual advances to the shopkeepers' wives with the intent that the wives (as their lovers) will persuade their husbands to be lenient.
55. *cog*: flatter, wheedle.
56. *they*: i.e., the gallants.
57. *ingle*: fondle, but also wheedle, coax; here, both meanings seem to be combined: "we must fondle our husbands in bed to wheedle them into doing what the gallants want."
58. *do us a pleasure at court*: win us favors from some royal official.
60. *riven*: cracked; *frumped at*: mocked, insulted.
61–62. *there were a law made*: i.e., there would be a law made decreeing that.
68. *make one*: join us.
69. *any*: all; Mrs. Openwork pretends she wants her friend along for protection when she confronts her cheating husband.
70. *handle me*: treat me.
71–72. *how shall . . . two mills going?*: comparing sexual intercourse to the grinding of a mill, Goshawk wonders how he will have the energy to satisfy two women at once.
72–73. *needs be clapped under hatches*: insist on being stowed below deck.

under hatches, if I sail not with you both till all split, hang me
up at the main yard and duck me. [*Aside*] It's but liquoring
them both soundly, and then you shall see their cork heels fly   75
up high, like two swans when their tails are above water
and their long necks under water diving to catch gudgeons.
[*To them*] Come, come! Oars stand ready; the tide's with
us. On with those false faces. Blow winds, and [*to Mrs.
Openwork*] thou shalt take thy husband casting out his net to   80
catch fresh salmon at Brentford.
MRS. GALLIPOT [*as they put on masks*]   I believe you'll eat of a cod's
head of your own dressing before you reach half way thither.
GOSHAWK   So, so, follow close. Pin as you go.

[*They start to leave.*]

Enter Laxton, muffled.

LAXTON   Do you hear?   [*He takes Mrs. Gallipot aside.*]   85
MRS. GALLIPOT   Yes, I thank my ears.
LAXTON   I must have a bout with Your Pothecaryship.
MRS. GALLIPOT   At what weapon?
LAXTON   I must speak with you.
MRS. GALLIPOT   No.   90
LAXTON   No? You shall.
MRS. GALLIPOT   Shall? Away, soused sturgeon, half fish, half flesh!
LAXTON   Faith, gib, are you spitting? I'll cut your tail, pusscat,
for this.
MRS. GALLIPOT   'Las, poor Laxton! I think thy tail's cut already.   95
Your worst!

---

73. *split*: goes to pieces.
74. *main yard*: boom of the mainsail; *duck me*: dunk me in the water. Using nautical
language, Goshawk proclaims himself ready to undergo punishment if he does not
take on both women to the limits of his physical endurance.
74–75. *liquoring them both soundly*: getting them both thoroughly drunk.
75. *cork heels*: i.e., of their shoes. It is uncertain whether Goshawk hopes that inebria-
tion will make the women more willing, less demanding, or both.
77. *gudgeons*: minnow-like fish.
79. *false faces*: silk or velvet masks commonly worn by women to protect their complex-
ions.
81. *fresh salmon*: i.e., whores.
82–83. *cod's head*: slang for "simpleton."
83. *your own dressing*: i.e., make an idiot of yourself; Mrs. Gallipot plays on preparing
("dressing") a fish head for eating, and unwittingly preparing oneself to be served up
as a fool.
84. *Pin*: i.e., pin on your masks.
84. s.d. *muffled*: wrapped so as to conceal his face.
87. *bout*: round of fighting (with sexual suggestion); *Your Pothecaryship*: Laxton jokingly
turns Gallipot's occupation as apothecary into an aristocratic-sounding title for his
wife.
92. *soused sturgeon*: pickled fish.
93. *gib*: cat (derogatory term for an old woman).
96. *Your worst!*: i.e., do your worst! Mrs. Gallipot taunts Laxton with his supposed emas-
culation; compare 1.2.55–58.

LAXTON   If I do not—   *Exit Laxton.*
GOSHAWK [*to Mrs. Gallipot*] Come, ha' you done?

   Enter Master Openwork.

[*Aside to Mrs. Openwork*] 'Sfoot, Rosamond, your husband!
OPENWORK   How now? Sweet Master Goshawk, none more   100
   welcome!
  I have wanted your embracements. When friends meet,
  The music of the spheres sounds not more sweet
  Than does their conference. Who is this? Rosamond?
  Wife? [*To Mrs. Gallipot*] How now, sister?
GOSHAWK [*aside to Mrs. Openwork*]   Silence, if you love me!   105
OPENWORK   Why masked?
MRS. OPENWORK   Does a mask grieve you, sir?
OPENWORK   It does.
MRS. OPENWORK   Then you're best get you a-mumming.
GOSHAWK [*aside to Mrs. Openwork*]   'Sfoot, you'll spoil all!   110
MRS. GALLIPOT   May not we cover our bare faces with masks
  as well as you cover your bald heads with hats?
OPENWORK   No masks! Why, they're thieves to beauty, that rob eyes
  Of admiration in which true love lies.
  Why are masks worn? Why good? Or why desired?   115
  Unless by their gay covers wits are fired
  To read the vilest looks. Many bad faces,
  Because rich gems are treasured up in cases,
  Pass by their privilege current; but as caves
  Damn misers' gold, so masks are beauties' graves.   120
  Men ne'er meet women with such muffled eyes
  But they curse her that first did masks devise,
  And swear it was some beldam. Come, off with't.
MRS. OPENWORK   I will not.
OPENWORK   Good faces masked are jewels kept by sprites.   125

---

101. *wanted*: missed.
102. *music of the spheres*: in early modern astronomy, the celestial harmony produced by
    motion of the concentric "spheres" that comprised the earth-centered universe.
109. *a-mumming*: mummers' plays, traditional holiday entertainment, were performed
    by amateurs who were both masked and silent. Mrs. Openwork is telling her hus-
    band to shut up.
116–17. *gay covers . . . vilest looks*: i.e., attractive masks fire up men to gaze at otherwise
    vile-looking women.
118–20. *Many bad . . . beauties' graves*: many ugly women are (wrongly) assumed to be
    beautiful when they hide their faces in masks, because so many beautiful women
    wear them, hiding their beauty in masks like jewels are hidden away ("treasured
    up") in jewel-cases. To "pass current" is said of coins acceptable as currency; the
    point is that beautiful women who wear masks unwittingly give ugly women the
    privilege of not being found out as "counterfeits." Beauty hidden in a mask, he
    adds, is as useless as a miser's gold hidden in a cave.
123. *beldam*: ugly old woman.
125. *kept by sprites*: hidden away by spirits.

Hide none but bad ones, for they poison men's sights;
Show them as shopkeepers do their broidered stuff,
By owl-light. Fine wares cannot be open enough.
Prithee, sweet Rose, come, strike this sail.

MRS. OPENWORK   Sail?   130

OPENWORK   Ha?
Yes, wife, strike sail, for storms are in thine eyes.

MRS. OPENWORK   They're here, sir, in my brows, if any rise.

OPENWORK   Ha, brows? [*To Mrs. Gallipot*] What says she, friend?
[*To them both*] Pray tell me why   135
Your two flags were advanced? The comedy?
Come, what's the comedy?

MRS. GALLIPOT   *Westward Ho.*

OPENWORK   How?

MRS. OPENWORK   'Tis *Westward Ho*, she says.   140

GOSHAWK   Are you both mad?

MRS. OPENWORK   Is't market day at Brentford, and your ware not
sent up yet?

OPENWORK   What market day? What ware?

MRS. OPENWORK   A pie with three pigeons in't. 'Tis drawn and 145
stays your cutting up.

GOSHAWK [*aside to Mrs. Openwork*]   As you regard my credit—

OPENWORK [*to Mrs. Openwork*]   Art mad?

MRS. OPENWORK   Yes, lecherous goat! Baboon!

OPENWORK   Baboon? Then toss me in a blanket.   150

MRS. OPENWORK [*aside to Mrs. Gallipot*]   Do I it well?

MRS. GALLIPOT [*aside to Mrs. Openwork*]   Rarely!

GOSHAWK [*to Openwork*]   Belike, sir, she's not well; best leave her.

OPENWORK   No,

---

127. *broidered stuff*: embroidered fabric (implied to be of poor quality). Crooked shopkeep-
     ers would deceive customers by displaying shoddy wares in dim light.
128. *owl-light*: twilight.
129. *strike this sail*: i.e., take off your mask; to "strike" a sail is to lower it.
133. *in my brows, if any rise*: Mrs. Openwork indicates her forehead ("brows"), implying that
     her anger ("storms") stems from her husband's infidelity. A wife's infidelity was said to
     make horns grow on her husband's forehead; here, the idea is extended to the wife of a
     cheating husband.
136. *Your two flags were advanced?*: i.e., your masks were up. Playhouses flew flags when
     open for performances.
138. *Westward Ho*: title of a 1604 comedy by Dekker and Webster; also, the cry of a Thames
     boatman seeking passengers for a westward journey (like the one the women planned
     to Brentford).
145. *drawn*: out of the oven.
146. *stays*: awaits; *cutting up*: Mrs. Openwork alludes to the Three Pigeons tavern at Brent-
     ford and to the prostitutes (*pigeon*, sweetheart) she supposes Openwork will meet
     there. The implication is that he will dig into the prostitutes like a man helping himself
     to a pie.
147. *credit*: reputation.
150. *toss me in a blanket*: a humiliating punishment; Openwork is denying his wife's
     accusation.
152. *Rarely!*: Extremely well!

I'll stand the storm now, how fierce soe'er it blow.   155
MRS. OPENWORK   Did I for this lose all my friends? Refuse
   Rich hopes and golden fortunes, to be made
   A stale to a common whore?
OPENWORK   This does amaze me.
MRS. OPENWORK   Oh, God, oh, God, feed at reversion now?
   A strumpet's leaving?   160
OPENWORK   Rosamond!
GOSHAWK [aside]   I sweat. Would I lay in Cold Harbor!
MRS. OPENWORK   Thou hast struck ten thousand daggers
   through my heart!
OPENWORK   Not I, by heaven, sweet wife.
MRS. OPENWORK   Go, devil, go! That which thou swear'st by damns
   thee.   165
GOSHAWK [aside to Mrs. Openwork]   'Sheart, will you undo me?
MRS. OPENWORK [to Openwork]   Why stay you here? The star by
   which you sail
   Shines yonder above Chelsea; you lose your shore.
   If this moon light you, seek out your light whore.
OPENWORK   Ha?   170
MRS. GALLIPOT   Push! Your western pug!
GOSHAWK [aside]   Zounds, now hell roars!
MRS. OPENWORK   With whom you tilted in a pair of oars this
   very morning.
OPENWORK   Oars?   175
MRS. OPENWORK   At Brentford, sir.
OPENWORK   Rack not my patience.—Master Goshawk, some
   slave has buzzed this into her, has he not?—I run a-tilt in
   Brentford with a woman? 'Tis a lie. What old bawd tells thee
   this? 'Sdeath, 'tis a lie.   180
MRS. OPENWORK   'Tis one to thy face shall justify all that I speak.

---

156. *lose all my friends*: alienate all my relatives; she implies her family opposed her decision
   to marry Openwork instead of a wealthier man.
158. *stale*: a laughingstock, particularly to a sexual rival.
159. *feed at reversion*: eat leftovers.
160. *leaving*: leftovers.
162. *Cold Harbor*: a poor area near London Bridge, known as a haven for debtors avoiding
   arrest; the situation is getting too hot for Goshawk, who wishes he were somewhere
   safe and "cold."
165. *that . . . swear'st by*: i.e., heaven.
169. *light whore*: comparing the whore Openwork follows to a star or moon guiding a ship,
   Mrs. Openwork tells him to go to her before he misses his chance ("lose your shore");
   she puns on the "light" of the moon and "light" meaning "wanton."
171. *push*: pish; *pug*: prostitute.
173. *tilted*: jousted with lances; also a pun on the "tilt" or awning over the boat (see
   4.2.26–27); She is accusing him of having had sex in a rowboat.
177. *Rack*: torture.
178. *slave*: scoundrel; *a-tilt*: see note to 4.2.174.
179. *bawd*: brothel madam, pimp.
180. *'Sdeath*: God's death (an oath).
181. *'Tis one*: There's someone.

OPENWORK   Ud's soul, do but name that rascal.

MRS. OPENWORK   No, sir, I will not.

GOSHAWK [*aside*]   Keep thee there, girl. [*To them*] Then!

OPENWORK [*to Mrs. Gallipot*]   Sister, know you this varlet?   185

MRS. GALLIPOT   Yes.

OPENWORK   Swear true:
Is there a rogue so low damned? A second Judas?
A common hangman? Cutting a man's throat?
Does it to his face? Bite me behind my back?   190
A cur dog? Swear if you know this hellhound.

MRS. GALLIPOT   In truth, I do.

OPENWORK   His name?

MRS. GALLIPOT   Not for the world;
To have you to stab him.

GOSHAWK [*aside*]   Oh, brave girls! Worth gold!

OPENWORK   A word, honest Master Goshawk.

                                        Draw[s] out his sword.

GOSHAWK   What do you mean, sir?

OPENWORK   Keep off, and if the devil can give a name   195
To this new Fury, holla it through my ear,
Or wrap it up in some hid character.
I'll ride to Oxford and watch out mine eyes,
But I'll hear the Brazen Head speak, or else
Show me but one hair of his head or beard,   200
That I may sample it. If the fiend I meet
In mine own house, I'll kill him—the street,
Or at the church door. There, 'cause he seeks to untie
The knot God fastens, he deserves most to die.

MRS. OPENWORK [*to Mrs. Gallipot*]   My husband titles him!

OPENWORK   Master Goshawk, pray, sir,   205
Swear to me that you know him or know him not,
Who makes me at Brentford to take up a petticoat
Besides my wife's.

---

182.   *Ud's soul*: God's soul (an oath).
185.   *varlet*: rascal (i.e., the person who told Mrs. Openwork about the prostitute).
188.   *A second Judas*: Judas Iscariot, the apostle who betrayed Christ.
191.   *cur*: worthless mongrel; *hellhound*: allusion to Cerberus, watch-dog of hell.
192–93.   *Not for . . . stab him*: i.e., I won't give you his name because then you'd stab him.
196.   *Fury*: avenging demon (Openwork assumes the person spreading rumors about him is doing it for revenge); *holla*: shout.
197.   *hid character*: secret code.
198–99.   *watch out . . . speak*: i.e., I'll stay awake until my eyes give out, waiting for the Brazen Head to tell me the rumor-spreader's name. A reference to the legendary speaking brass head of Brasenose College, Oxford.
200.   *his*: i.e., the rumor-spreader.
203–04.   *at the church door . . . most to die*: i.e., he deserves to die at the church door because he's trying to ruin a marriage, "the knot God fastens."
205.   *titles him*: calls him (Goshawk) what he is.
209.   *Who . . . take up a petticoat*: Who claims that I go to Brentford to lift a woman's skirt.

GOSHAWK   By heaven, that man I know not.

MRS. OPENWORK   Come, come, you lie.

GOSHAWK [to Mrs. Openwork]   Will you not have all out?
By heaven I know no man beneath the moon   210
Should do you wrong, but if I had his name,
I'd print it in text letters.

MRS. OPENWORK   Print thine own, then.
Didst not thou swear to me he kept his whore?

MRS. GALLIPOT   And that in sinful Brentford they would commit
That which our lips did water at, sir? Ha?   215

MRS. OPENWORK   Thou spider, that hast woven thy cunning web
In mine own house t'ensnare me, hast not thou
Sucked nourishment even underneath this roof
And turned it all to poison, spitting it
On thy friend's face, my husband—he, as 'twere, sleeping—   220
Only to leave him ugly to mine eyes,
That they might glance on thee?

MRS. GALLIPOT   Speak, are these lies?

GOSHAWK   Mine own shame me confounds.

MRS. OPENWORK   No more, he's stung.
Who'd think that in one body there could dwell
Deformity and beauty, heaven and hell?   225
Goodness, I see, is but outside; we all set,
In rings of gold, stones that be counterfeit.
I thought you none.

GOSHAWK   Pardon me.

OPENWORK   Truth, I do.
This blemish grows in nature, not in you,
For man's creation stick even moles in scorn   230
On fairest cheeks.—Wife, nothing is perfect born.

MRS. OPENWORK   I thought you had been born perfect.

OPENWORK   What's this whole world but a gilt rotten pill?
For at the heart lies the old core still.
I'll tell you, Master Goshawk, ay, in your eye   235
I have seen wanton fire; and then to try
The soundness of my judgment, I told you

---

209. *Will . . . out?*: Don't you want the truth to be known?
211. *Should do*: Who is likely to do.
212. *text letters*: capital letters.
215. *That . . . water*: The deed that made our mouths water (i.e., sex).
220. *sleeping*: i.e., unaware of your slander, as a sleeping man is unaware of a poison-
     ous spider.
223. *me confounds*: defeats me.
228. *I thought you none*: i.e., I thought you were a true gem, not a counterfeit one.
229. *nature*: human nature.
230–31. *man's creation . . . cheeks*: natural human imperfection means that even the fairest
     cheeks have moles on them.
233. *gilt*: gilded, covered in a thin layer of gold.
236. *to try*: to test.

I kept a whore, made you believe 'twas true
Only to feel how your pulse beat, but find
The world can hardly yield a perfect friend.   240
Come, come, a trick of youth, and 'tis forgiven.
This rub put by, our love shall run more even.
MRS. OPENWORK   You'll deal upon men's wives no more?
GOSHAWK   No. You teach me a trick for that.
MRS. OPENWORK   Troth, do not; they'll o'erreach thee.   245
OPENWORK [to Goshawk]   Make my house yours, sir, still.
GOSHAWK   No.
OPENWORK   I say you shall.
Seeing, thus besieged, it holds out, 'twill never fall.

> Enter Master Gallipot, and Greenwit like a summoner [in a
> wig]; Laxton muffled aloof off. [Greenwit seizes Gallipot by
> the shoulder in a gesture of arrest.]

OMNES   How now?
GALLIPOT [to Greenwit]   With me, sir?
GREENWIT   You, sir. I have gone snuffling up and down by your   250
door this hour to watch for you.
MRS. GALLIPOT   What's the matter, husband?
GREENWIT   I have caught a cold in my head, sir, by sitting up late
in the Rose Tavern, but I hope you understand my speech.
GALLIPOT   So, sir.   255
GREENWIT   I cite you by the name of Hippocrates Gallipot,
and you by the name of Prudence Gallipot, to appear upon
Crastino, do you see, Crastino sancti Dunstani, this Easter
term, in Bow Church.
GALLIPOT   Where, sir?—What says he?   260
GREENWIT   Bow: Bow Church, to answer to a libel of
precontract on the part and behalf of the said Prudence and
another. You're best, sir, take a copy of the citation, 'tis but
twelvepence.   [He holds out a citation.]

---

241. *trick of youth*: it's just a youthful indiscretion.
242. *rub*: obstacle.
243. *deal upon*: work on (to seduce).
245. *Troth*: in truth; *o'erreach*: defeat, get the better of.
247. *it*: i.e., the house, a metaphor for his wife and marriage.
247. **s.d.** *summoner*: officer who summoned people to appear in courts operated by the church; *muffled aloof off*: with his face concealed in a scarf, standing aside.
253–54. *cold in my head . . . speech*: to disguise his voice, Greenwit is speaking nasally, claiming to have a bad cold; the others imply at 4.2.267 and 4.2.296–98 that his nose is instead damaged by syphilis.
258. *Crastino sancti Dunstani*: May 20, the day after St. Dunstan's day (Latin).
258–59. *Easter term*: the third of the four legal terms in which law cases could be heard, Easter term lasted through April and May.
259. *Bow Church*: church of St. Mary le Bow, where the Court of Arches was held.
261–62. *libel of precontract*: charge of marrying someone who was already "contracted" or legally betrothed to someone else.
263. *another*: another man, i.e., Laxton; *citation*: written summons, subpoena.

OMNES   A citation?   265
GALLIPOT   You pocky-nosed rascal, what slave fees you to this?
LAXTON [*coming forward*]   Slave? [*Aside to Goshawk*] I ha'
    nothing to do with you, do you hear, sir?
GOSHAWK [*aside*] Laxton, is't not? What vagary is this?
GALLIPOT [*to Laxton*]   Trust me, I thought, sir, this storm long   270
    ago had been full laid, when, if you be remembered, I paid you the
    last fifteen pound, besides the thirty you had first; for then you
    swore —
LAXTON   Tush, tush, sir, oaths—
    Truth, yet I'm loath to vex you. Tell you what;   275
    Make up the money I had an hundred pound,
    And take your bellyful of her.
GALLIPOT   An hundred pound?
MRS. GALLIPOT   What, a hundred pound? He gets none.
    What, a hundred pound?   280
GALLIPOT   Sweet Pru, be calm. The gentleman offers thus:
    If I will make the moneys that are past
    A hundred pound he will discharge all courts
    And give his bond never to vex us more.
MRS. GALLIPOT   A hundred pound? 'Las, take, sir, but threescore.   285
    [*Aside to Laxton*] Do you seek my undoing?
LAXTON   I'll not bate
    One sixpence. [*Aside to Mrs. Gallipot*] I'll maul you, puss, for
    spitting.
MRS. GALLIPOT [*aside to Laxton*]   Do thy worst! [*Aloud*] Will
    fourscore stop thy mouth?
LAXTON   No.
MRS. GALLIPOT   You're a slave!   290
    Thou cheat, I'll now tear money from thy throat.—
    Husband, lay hold on yonder tawny coat.
GREENWIT   Nay, gentlemen, seeing your women are so hot, I must
    lose my hair in their company, I see.
                                        [*He removes his wig.*]

---

266. *pocky-nosed*: with syphilitic pustules on his nose; *what slave . . . this?*: what
      scoundrel is paying you to do this?
269. *vagary*: devious trick.
271. *full laid*: laid to rest.
276. *make up . . . hundred pound*: bring the total sum to a hundred pounds. Laxton has
      evidently bilked Gallipot out of an additional fifteen pounds since receiving the
      thirty-pound payment at the end of 3.2.
283–84. *discharge . . . bond*: give up all lawsuits and sign a legal agreement.
285. *threescore*: sixty (three times twenty); Mrs. Gallipot is willing to give Laxton an
      extra fifteen pounds, but not the fifty-five he demands.
286. *bate*: deduct.
292. *yonder tawny coat*: i.e., the officer in his brown coat, the disguised Greenwit.
293. *so hot*: angry.

MRS. OPENWORK   His hair sheds off, and yet he speaks not so   295
much in the nose as he did before.

GOSHAWK   He has had the better chirurgeon.—Master Greenwit, is
your wit so raw as to play no better a part than a summoner's?

GALLIPOT   I pray, who plays A *Knack to Know an Honest Man*
in this company?   300

MRS. GALLIPOT   Dear husband, pardon me. I did dissemble,
Told thee I was his precontracted wife.
When letters came from him for thirty pound,
I had no shift but that.

GALLIPOT   A very clean shift, but able to make me lousy. On.   305

MRS. GALLIPOT   Husband, I plucked—when he had tempted me to
think well of him—gelt feathers from thy wings, to make him fly
more lofty.

GALLIPOT   O'the top of you, wife. On.

MRS. GALLIPOT   He, having wasted them, comes now for more,   310
Using me as a ruffian doth his whore
Whose sin keeps him in breath. By heaven, I vow,
Thy bed he never wronged more than he does now.

GALLIPOT   My bed? Ha, ha, like enough! A shop board will serve
To have a cuckold's coat cut out upon.   315
Of that we'll talk hereafter. [*To Laxton*] You're a villain!

LAXTON   Hear me but speak, sir. You shall find me none.

OMNES   Pray, sir, be patient and hear him.

GALLIPOT   I am muzzled for biting, sir. Use me how you will.

LAXTON   The first hour that your wife was in my eye,   320
Myself with other gentlemen sitting by
In your shop tasting smoke, and speech being used
That men who have fairest wives are most abused
And hardly scaped the horn, your wife maintained

295–97. *hair sheds off . . . better chirurgeon*: hair loss was a symptom of syphilis; Goshawk
jokes that despite the "loss" of Greenwit's hair, his less nasal (because undisguised)
voice implies he's been cured by a good doctor.
299. *A Knack . . . Man*: title of an anonymous 1594 comedy; Gallipot would like to
know who's telling the truth.
301. *dissemble*: deceive you.
304. *shift*: stratagem; Gallipot then puns on two meanings of "clean shift": "a clever
stratagem" and "a woman's clean undergarment."
305. *On*: Go on.
308. *gelt*: gilded.
309. *O'the top of you*: i.e., he "flew" right on top of you; Gallipot assumes his wife has
had sex with Laxton.
311. *ruffian*: pimp.
312. *in breath*: alive, i.e., through her financial support.
314. *like enough*: very likely; *shop board*: shop counter for displaying goods or measuring
out cloth. Gallipot implies his wife is equivocating, claiming she has not wronged
his bed because she has had sex with her lover on the shop counter instead.
319. *for*: against.
322. *tasting smoke*: smoking.
324. *hardly . . . horn*: could hardly avoid being cuckolded (cuckolds were said to grow
horns).

That only such spots in city dames were stained   325
Justly but by men's slanders. For her own part,
She vowed that you had so much of her heart,
No man, by all his wit, by any wile,
Never so fine spun, should yourself beguile
Of what in her was yours.
GALLIPOT   Yet, Pru, 'tis well.—   330
Play out your game at Irish, sir. Who wins?
MRS. OPENWORK   The trial is when she comes to bearing.
LAXTON   I scorned one woman thus should brave all men,
And, which more vexed me, a she-citizen.
Therefore I laid siege to her. Out she held,   335
Gave many a brave repulse, and me compelled
With shame to sound retreat to my hot lust.
Then seeing all base desires raked up in dust,
And that to tempt her modest ears I swore
Ne'er to presume again, she said her eye   340
Would ever give me welcome honestly;
And, since I was a gentleman, if it run low,
She would my state relieve, not to o'erthrow
Your own and hers; did so. Then, seeing I wrought
Upon her meekness, me she set at naught;   345
And yet to try if I could turn that tide,
You see what stream I strove with. But, sir, I swear,
By heaven and by those hopes men lay up there,
I neither have nor had a base intent
To wrong your bed. What's done is merriment.   350
Your gold I pay back with this interest:
When I had most power to do't, I wronged you least.
GALLIPOT   If this no gullery be, sir—
OMNES   No, no, on my life.
GALLIPOT   Then, sir, I am beholden—not to you, wife,

325–26. *such spots . . . slanders*: city wives' bad reputations ("spots") were fair only if they weren't caused by men's slanders. "But" in this context means "if not."
329–30. *yourself beguile . . . yours*: should cheat you out of what you owned (i.e., her heart).
331. *Irish*: i.e., finish your story; Irish was a board game like backgammon but took longer to play.
332. *bearing*: term for removing a piece from the board at the end of a game of Irish, with pun on "childbearing" and "bearing (sexually) the weight of a man."
333. *brave*: defy.
334. *she-citizen*: city woman.
335. *laid siege*: i.e., attempted to seduce (the military metaphor is carried through the next two lines).
338. *raked . . . dust*: smothered, like a fire covered with ashes to dampen it.
339–40. *to tempt . . . again*: I swore never to be so presumptuous as to tempt her modest ears again.
342–44. *if it run low . . . and hers*: if my finances ran low, she would relieve them, so long as it wouldn't financially ruin herself and you.
345. *meekness*: generosity; *me . . . naught*: she despised me.
353. *gullery*: trickery.
354. *beholden*: indebted.

But, Master Laxton, to your want of doing ill,　　　　　355
Which it seems you have not.—Gentlemen,
Tarry and dine here all.

OPENWORK　Brother, we have a jest
As good as yours to furnish out a feast.

GALLIPOT　We'll crown our table with it. Wife, brag no more　　　360
Of holding out. Who most brags is most whore.

Exeunt omnes.

[5.1]

*Enter Jack Dapper, Moll, Sir Beauteous Ganymede, and
Sir Thomas Long.*

JACK DAPPER　But prithee, Master Captain Jack, be plain and
perspicuous with me: was it your Meg of Westminster's
courage that rescued me from the Poultry puttocks,
indeed?

MOLL　The valour of my wit, I ensure you, sir, fetched you　　　5
off bravely when you were i'the forlorn hope among those
desperates. Sir Beauteous Ganymede here and Sir Thomas Long
heard that cuckoo, my man Trapdoor, sing the note of your
ransom from captivity.

SIR BEAUTEOUS　Uds so, Moll, where's that Trapdoor?　　　10

MOLL　Hanged, I think, by this time. A justice in this town, that
speaks nothing but "Make a mittimus! Away with him to
Newgate!" used that rogue like a firework to run upon a line
betwixt him and me.

OMNES　How, how?　　　15

MOLL　Marry, to lay trains of villainy to blow up my life. I smelt
the powder, spied what linstock gave fire to shoot against the

---

355. *want*: lack.
359. *furnish out*: complete, add to the enjoyment of.
361. *Who*: She who.
　　1. *Jack*: generic term for a man, and apparently a name Moll goes by when in male attire
　　　 (compare 5.1.29 and 5.1.51).
　　2. *perspicuous*: clear; *Meg of Westminster*: heroine of London folklore.
　　3. *puttocks*: arresting officers for a debtors' prison (see note to 3.3.111).
5–6. *fetched . . . bravely*: rescued you handsomely.
　　6. *i'the forlorn hope*: in a desperate situation.
　　7. *desperates*: reckless, violent men (i.e., the officers).
　　8. *cuckoo*: fool.
　10. *Uds so*: God's soul (an oath).
　11. *justice*: justice of the peace, i.e., Sir Alexander.
　12. *mittimus*: document committing a person to prison.
　13. *Newgate*: a famous London prison; *run upon a line*: to run along a fuse before explod-
　　　 ing (i.e., Sir Alexander sent Trapdoor to "blow up" Moll).
　16. *trains*: lines of gunpowder used to convey a spark to an explosive device; Moll speaks
　　　 metaphorically of the traps Sir Alexander laid for her.
　17. *linstock*: forked staff used to hold a gunner's match, i.e., Trapdoor.

poor captain of the galley foist, and away slid I my man like a
shovel-board shilling. He struts up and down the suburbs, I
think, and eats up whores, feeds upon a bawd's garbage.   20
SIR THOMAS   Sirrah Jack Dapper—
JACK DAPPER   What say'st, Tom Long?
SIR THOMAS   Thou hadst a sweet-faced boy, hail-fellow with thee to
your little Gull. How is he spent?
JACK DAPPER   'Troth, I whistled the poor little buzzard off o'my   25
fist, because when he waited upon me at the ordinaries, the
gallants hit me i'the teeth still and said I looked like a painted
alderman's tomb, and the boy at my elbow like a death's-head.
Sirrah Jack, Moll—
MOLL   What says my little Dapper?   30
SIR BEAUTEOUS   Come, come, walk and talk, walk and talk.
JACK DAPPER   Moll and I'll be i'the midst.
MOLL   These knights shall have squires' places, belike, then.
Well, Dapper, what say you?
JACK DAPPER   Sirrah Captain Mad Mary, the gull my own father—   35
Dapper, Sir Davy—laid these London boot-halers, the
catchpoles, in ambush to set upon me.
OMNES   Your father? Away, Jack!
JACK DAPPER   By the tassels of this handkercher, 'tis true; and what
was his warlike stratagem, think you? He thought, because a wicker   40
cage tames a nightingale, a lousy prison could make an ass of me.
OMNES   A nasty plot.
JACK DAPPER   Ay, as though a counter, which is a park in which all
the wild beasts of the city run head by head, could tame me.

18. *galley foist*: a barge used in official celebrations by the Lord Mayor of London; such
occasions often involved fireworks.
18–19. *away slid . . . shovel-board shilling*: I sent Trapdoor away as quickly as a shovel-board
player slides a coin ("shilling") down the board. Shovel-board, precursor of modern
shuffleboard, was played by sliding coins across a polished board to land in num-
bered compartments.
20. *feeds . . . garbage*: lives off the earnings of whores other pimps don't want anymore.
23. *hail-fellow*: on intimate terms.
23. *to*: in (i.e., "you used to have a sweet-faced little servant called Gull"); *How is he
spent?*: How did he end up?
25. *buzzard*: an inferior kind of hawk, a worthless person.
25–26. *whistled . . . off my fist*: dismissed him. Dapper uses terms from falconry.
26. *ordinaries*: eating-houses.
27. *hit me i'the teeth still*: insulted me continually.
27–28. *painted alderman's tomb*: i.e., the carved and painted effigy of the deceased which
commonly adorned the tomb of a wealthy person, in this case, a high-ranking city
official.
28. *death's-head*: a skull, a common motif in funerary art.
33. *knights . . . places*: the knights, Sir Beauteous and Sir Thomas, will walk on the outside of the foursome, where lower-ranking squires would traditionally walk; *belike*:
in all likelihood.
35. *gull*: simpleton.
36. *boot-halers*: marauders, highwaymen.
37. *catchpoles*: arresting officers.
38. *Away*: Get out! (expression of disbelief).
43. *counter*: debtor's prison.

Enter the Lord Noland.

MOLL   Yonder comes my Lord Noland.   45
OMNES   Save you, my lord.
LORD NOLAND   Well met, gentlemen all, good Sir Beauteous
   Ganymede, Sir Thomas Long. And how does Master Dapper?
JACK DAPPER   Thanks, my lord.
MOLL   No tobacco, my lord?   50
LORD NOLAND   No, faith, Jack.
JACK DAPPER   My Lord Noland, will you go to Pimlico with us? We
   are making a boon voyage to that nappy land of spice-cakes.
LORD NOLAND   Here's such a merry ging, I could find in my
   heart to sail to the World's End with such company. Come,   55
   gentlemen, let's on.
JACK DAPPER   Here's most amorous weather, my lord.
OMNES   Amorous weather?   *They walk.*
JACK DAPPER Is not "amorous" a good word?

   Enter Trapdoor, like a poor soldier, with a patch o'er one eye,
   and Tearcat with him, all tatters.

TRAPDOOR [*to Tearcat*]   Shall we set upon the infantry, these troops   60
   of foot? Zounds, yonder comes Moll, my whorish master and
   mistress. Would I had her kidneys between my teeth!
TEARCAT   I had rather have a cow-heel.
TRAPDOOR   Zounds, I am so patched up, she cannot discover me;
   We'll on.   65
TEARCAT   *Alla corago*, then.
TRAPDOOR [*to the group*]   Good Your Honours and Worships,
   enlarge the ears of commiseration, and let the sound of a
   hoarse military organ-pipe penetrate your pitiful bowels to
   extract out of them so many small drops of silver as may give   70
   a hard straw-bed lodging to a couple of maimed soldiers.
JACK DAPPER   Where are you maimed?
TEARCAT   In both our nether limbs.
MOLL   Come, come, Dapper, let's give 'em something. 'Las, poor
   men! What money have you? By my troth, I love a soldier with   75
   my soul.

   52. *Pimlico*: an inn at Hoxton.
   53. *boon voyage*: fortunate journey (from French "bon voyage"); *nappy*: frothy, heady (in
      reference to the strong ale for which Pimlico was famous).
   54. *ging*: gang.
   55. *World's End*: tavern on the outskirts of London, but Noland puns on its name to
      imply "to the ends of the earth."
   57. *amorous*: lovely. The response indicates that "amorous weather" sounded as bizarre
      then as it does now.
   59. s.d. *all tatters*: dressed in rags.
   60–61. *troops of foot*: i.e., Jack Dapper and his friends; Trapdoor speaks of his fraudulent
      begging as if it were an attack on enemy soldiers.
   63. *cow-heel*: cow's foot, stewed to a nutritious jelly.
   64. *discover*: recognize.
   66. *Alla corago*: take courage (slang, based on Italian "coraggio").
   69. *bowels*: thought to be the seat of compassion.
   70. *drops of silver*: coins.

SIR BEAUTEOUS   Stay, stay.—Where have you served?

SIR THOMAS   In any part of the Low Countries?

TRAPDOOR   Not in the Low Countries, if it please your manhood,
but in Hungary against the Turk at the siege of Belgrade.   80

LORD NOLAND   Who served there with you, sirrah?

TRAPDOOR   Many Hungarians, Moldavians, Valachians, and
Transylvanians, with some Sclavonians, and retiring home, sir,
the Venetian galleys took us prisoners, yet freed us, and suffered
us to beg up and down the country.   85

JACK DAPPER   You have ambled all over Italy, then?

TRAPDOOR   Oh, sir, from Venice to Roma, Vecchio, Bononia,
Romania, Bologna, Modena, Piacenza, and Tuscana with all her
cities, as Pistoia, Valteria, Mountepulchena, Arrezzo, with the
Siennois, and divers others.   90

MOLL   Mere rogues. Put spurs to 'em once more.

JACK DAPPER [to Tearcat]   Thou look'st like a strange creature, a fat
butter-box, yet speak'st English. What are thou?

TEARCAT   *Ick, mine here? Ick bin den ruffling Tearcat, den brave
soldado. Ick bin dorick all Dutchlant gewesen. Der shellum das*   95
meere ine beasa, ine woert gaeh. Ick slaag um stroakes ou tom cop,
dastick, den hundred touzun divell halle; frollick, mine here.

SIR BEAUTEOUS   Here, here, let's be rid of their jabbering.

                    [He starts to offer money to the beggars.]

MOLL   Not a cross, Sir Beauteous.—You base rogues, I have taken
measure of you, better than a tailor can, and I'll fit you, as you—   100
monster with one eye—have fitted me.

TRAPDOOR   Your Worship will not abuse a soldier!

MOLL   Soldier? Thou deserv'st to be hanged up by that tongue
which dishonors so noble a profession. Soldier, you

---

78. *Low Countries*: region corresponding to present-day Holland, Belgium, and Luxem-
    bourg.
80. *siege of Belgrade*: an impossible claim, as it has been almost a hundred years since the
    Turkish emperor seized Belgrade, capital of Serbia, from the Hungarians in 1522.
82–83. *Hungarians . . . Sclavonians*: soldiers from other Hungarian-ruled regions.
84. *suffered*: permitted.
87–90. *Venice to Roma . . . Siennois*: Italian cities and regions; Trapdoor's inclusion of both
    "Bononia" and "Bologna"—one and the same place—betrays that he's just reeling
    off as many Italian place-names as he can think of.
91. *Put spurs to 'em*: i.e., chase them away.
93. *butter-box*: derogatory term for a Dutchman.
94–97. *Ick, mine here? . . . frollick, mine here*: Tearcat speaks a garbled mixture of Dutch
    and English, more to convince Dapper he is a Dutchman than to be literally under-
    stood. It translates roughly as "I, my lord? I am the ruffling Tearcat, the brave sol-
    dier. I have been through all of Dutch-land (or Deutschland, i.e., Germany). [He is]
    the greater scoundrel that gives an angry word. I beat him directly on the head, that
    you take out a hundred thousand devils. A pleasure, my lord."
99. *cross*: low-value coin, stamped with a cross.
101. *have fitted me*: I'll treat you the way you treated me (with pun on the idea of a tailor
    "fitting" him with clothes).

skeldering varlet? Hold, stand; there should be a trapdoor   105
hereabouts.   *Pull off his patch.*
TRAPDOOR   The balls of these glaziers of mine—mine eyes—shall
be shot up and down in any hot piece of service for my invincible
mistress.
JACK DAPPER   I did not think there had been such knavery in black   110
patches as now I see.
MOLL   Oh, sir, he hath been brought up in the Isle of Dogs, and can
both fawn like a spaniel and bite like a mastiff as he finds occasion.
LORD NOLAND [*to Tearcat*]   What are you, sirrah? A bird of this
feather too?   115
TEARCAT   A man beaten from the wars, sir.
SIR THOMAS   I think so, for you never stood to fight.
JACK DAPPER   What's thy name, fellow soldier?
TEARCAT   I am called, by those that have seen my valor, Tearcat.
OMNES   Tearcat?   120
MOLL   A mere whip-jack, and that is, in the commonwealth of
rogues, a slave that can talk of sea-fight, name all your chief
pirates, discover more countries to you than either the Dutch,
Spanish, French, or English ever found out; yet indeed all his
service is by land, and that is to rob a fair, or some such   125
venturous exploit. Tearcat! Foot, sirrah, I have your name, now I
remember me, in my book of horners—horns for the thumb, you
know how.
TEARCAT   No indeed, Captain Moll—for I know you by sight—I am
no such nipping Christian, but a maunderer upon on the pad, I   130
confess; and meeting with honest Trapdoor here, whom you had
cashiered from bearing arms, out at elbows under your colors, I
instructed him in the rudiments of roguery, and by my map made
him sail over any country you can name, so that now he can
maunder better then myself.   135
JACK DAPPER   So then, Trapdoor, thou art turned soldier now.
TRAPDOOR   Alas, sir, now there's no wars, 'tis the safest course of
life I could take.

---

105. *skeldering:* begging by pretending to be a wounded soldier; *varlet:* rascal.
107. *glaziers:* eyes (thieves' slang). Once Moll removes his disguise, Trapdoor claims to be
her loyal servant who will always stand watch for her.
112. *Isle of Dogs:* peninsula on the Thames, east of London, known as a rough area where
people hid out from their creditors.
113. *fawn:* flatter, behave with servile fondness.
121. *whip-jack:* beggar pretending to be a destitute sailor.
123. *discover:* reveal, describe.
125. *service . . . rob a fair:* i.e., all the service he's ever done has been on land—stealing
goods at fairs.
127. *horns for the thumb:* thimbles made of horn, worn by thieves to protect the thumb from
the purse-cutting knife; "horner" could also mean "cuckold-maker."
130. *nipping:* purse-cutting; *maunderer . . . pad:* beggar on the road.
132. *cashiered . . . arms:* dismissed from your service; *out at elbows under your colors:* in
ragged livery.

MOLL   I hope then you can cant, for by your cudgels, you, sirrah,
are an upright man.   140

TRAPDOOR   As any walks the highway, I assure you.

MOLL   And Tearcat, what are you? A wild rogue, an angler, or a
ruffler?

TEARCAT   Brother to this upright man, flesh and blood, ruffling
Tearcat is my name, and a ruffler is my style, my title, my   145
profession.

MOLL   Sirrah, where's your doxy? Halt not with me.

OMNES   Doxy, Moll? What's that?

MOLL   His wench.

TRAPDOOR   My doxy? I have, by the solomon, a doxy that carries a   150
kinchin-mort in her slate at her back, besides my dell and my
dainty wild dell, with all whom I'll tumble this next darkmans in
the strommel, and drink ben booze, and eat a fat gruntling cheat,
a cackling cheat, and a quacking cheat.

JACK   Here's old cheating!   155

TRAPDOOR   My doxy stays for me in a boozing ken, brave Captain.

MOLL   He says his wench stays for him in an alehouse. [*To
Trapdoor and Tearcat*] You are no pure rogues.

TEARCAT   Pure rogues? No, we scorn to be pure rogues, but if you
come to our libken, or our stalling ken, you shall find neither   160
him nor me a queer cuffin.

MOLL   So, sir, no churl of you.

TEARCAT   No, but a ben cove, a brave cove, a gentry cuffin.

LORD NOLAND   Call you this canting?

JACK DAPPER   Zounds, I'll give a schoolmaster half a crown a week   165
and teach me this peddler's French.

---

139. *cant*: speak underworld slang; "upright man," is a cant term for a sturdy rogue at
the top of the supposed underworld hierarchy, usually depicted carrying a staff or
cudgel. Much of the dialogue that follows is in cant.

142. *wild rogue*: one born and raised in the underworld; *angler*: thief who steals with a
hooked pole.

143. *ruffler*: rogue ranked just below (or in some sources, above) the upright man.

145. *style*: official title.

147. *doxy*: female vagabond. The difference between a "doxy" and a "dell" (see 5.1.151)
is that a "doxy" is sexually experienced, while a "dell" is a virgin; *Halt not with me*:
Don't lie to me.

150–55. In this passage Tearcat is demonstrating his ability at canting; *by the solomon*: by
the mass (an oath); *kinchin-mort*: little girl; *slate*: sheet; *dell*: virgin girl; *wild dell*:
virgin girl born and raised in the underworld; *tumble*: have sex; *darkmans*: night;
strommel: straw; *ben booze*: good liquor; *gruntling cheat*: pig; *cackling cheat*: roos-
ter; *quacking cheat*: duck.

155. *old*: plenty of.

158. *pure rogues*: genuine members of the underworld. Moll seems to be criticizing
their canting, perhaps to incite them to further demonstrations. Tearcat, however,
takes "pure" to mean "morally uncorrupted."

160. *libken*: sleeping quarters; *stalling ken*: house for receiving stolen goods.

161. *queer cuffin*: worthless fellow.

162. *no churl of you*: you're not a bad guy.

163. *ben cove*: good fellow; *gentry cuffin*: gentleman. "Cove" and "cuffin" both mean "man."

166. *und*: to; *peddler's French*: thieves' slang.

TRAPDOOR   Do but stroll, sir, half a harvest with us, sir, and you
    shall gabble your bellyful.
MOLL   Come, you rogue, cant with me.
SIR THOMAS   Well said, Moll.—Cant with her, sirrah, and you shall   170
    have money; else not a penny.
TRAPDOOR   I'll have a bout, if she please.
MOLL   Come on, sirrah.
TRAPDOOR   Ben mort, shall you and I heave a booth, mill a ken, or
    nip a bung? And then we'll couch a hogshead under the ruffmans,   175
    and there you shall wap with me, and I'll niggle with you.
MOLL   Out, you damned impudent rascal!   [*She flails at him.*]
TRAPDOOR   Cut benar whids, and hold your fambles and your stamps!
LORD NOLAND   Nay, nay, Moll, why art thou angry? What was his
    gibberish?   180
MOLL   Marry, this, my lord. Says he: "Ben mort"—good wench—
    "shall you and I heave a booth, mill a ken, or nip a bung?"—
    shall you and I rob a house, or cut a purse?
OMNES   Very good!
MOLL   "And then we'll couch a hogshead under the ruffmans"—   185
    and then we'll lie under a hedge.
TRAPDOOR   That was my desire, Captain, as 'tis fit a soldier should
    lie.
MOLL   "And there you shall wap with me, and I'll niggle with
    you"—and that's all.   190
SIR BEAUTEOUS   Nay, nay, Moll, what's that "wap"?
JACK DAPPER   Nay, teach me what "niggling" is. I'd fain be niggling.
MOLL   Wapping and niggling is all one. The rogue my man can tell
    you.
TRAPDOOR   'Tis fadoodling, if it please you.   195
SIR BEAUTEOUS   This is excellent! One fit more, good Moll.
MOLL   Come, you rogue, sing with me.

                          THE SONG

MOLL   A gage of ben Rom-booze
                     In a boozing ken of Rom-ville
TEARCAT   Is benar than a caster,   200

    167. *half a harvest*: half a thieving season.
    168. *your bellyful*: as much as you want.
    172. *bout*: session, round (with sexual double-entendre).
174–76. Moll translates this speech at 5.1.181–83.
    178. *Cut benar . . . your stamps*: Speak better words and hold back your hands and feet!
187–88. *fit a . . . lie*: i.e., as it's an appropriate place for a soldier to sleep.
    193. *all one*: the same thing.
    195. *fadoodling*: nonsense word, but implies sexual fooling around.
    196. *fit*: round of canting (literally, a section of a song, a piece of music).
The song. Moll provides a paraphrase of the song at 5.1.240–250, but the literal meaning is: "A
    quart pot of good wine / In a tavern in London / Is better than a cloak / Meat, bread,
    buttermilk, or porridge / Which we steal in the country. / Oh, I would lie all the day. /
    Oh, I would lie all the night, / By the mass, under the bushes, / By the mass, in the
    stocks, / And wear fetters / And lie there till a scabby beggar screwed my girl / As long
    as my drunken head could drink wine well. / Ahoy, to the road, let us go."

	Peck, pannam, lap, or poplar
	Which we mill in Deuse-a-ville.
MOLL *and* TEARCAT	Oh, I would lib all the lightmans.
	Oh, I would lib all the darkmans,
	By the solomon, under the ruffmans, 205
	By the solomon, in the harmans,
TEARCAT	And scour the queer cramp-ring,
	And couch till a palliard docked my dell,
	So my boozy nab might skew Rome-booze
	well. 210
MOLL *and* TEARCAT	Avast, to the pad let us bing,
	Avast, to the pad let us bing.

OMNES   Fine knaves, i'faith.

JACK DAPPER   The grating of ten new cart-wheels and the gruntling of five hundred hogs coming from Romford market cannot make 215 a worse noise than this canting language does in my ears. Pray, my Lord Noland, let's give these soldiers their pay.

SIR BEAUTEOUS   Agreed, and let them march.

LORD NOLAND [*giving money*]   Here, Moll.

MOLL [*to Trapdoor and Tearcat*]   Now I see that you are stalled 220 to the rogue and are not ashamed of your professions. Look you, my Lord Noland here and these gentlemen bestows upon you two two bords and a half: that's two shillings sixpence.   [*She gives them each money.*]

TRAPDOOR   Thanks to Your Lordship. 225

TEARCAT   Thanks, heroical Captain.

MOLL   Away!

TRAPDOOR   We shall cut ben whids of your masters and mistress-ship wheresoever we come.

MOLL [*to Trapdoor*]   You'll maintain, sirrah, the old justice's plot to 230 his face?

TRAPDOOR   Else trine me on the cheats: hang me.

MOLL   Be sure you meet me there.

TRAPDOOR   Without any more maundering I'll do't.—Follow, brave Tearcat. 235

---

215. *Romford*: town northeast of London, with a famous hog market.
220–21. *stalled to the rogue*: fully initiated as rogues; the initiation or "stalling" ceremony was said to involve pouring a pot of beer over the initiate's head.
223. *two bords*: shillings, worth twelve pence.
228. *cut ben whids*: speak good words.
230–31. *maintain . . . his face?*: i.e., you'll tell the truth about Sir Alexander's plot to his face?
232. *trine*: hang; *cheats*: gallows.
234. *maundering*: grumbling.

TEARCAT   *I prae, sequor.* Let us go, mouse.
                                    Exeunt they two; manet the rest.
LORD NOLAND   Moll, what was in that canting song?
MOLL   Troth, my lord, only a praise of good drink, the only milk
    which these wild beasts love to suck; and thus it was:

>   A rich cup of wine,   240
>   Oh, it is juice divine,
>   More wholesome for the head
>   Than meat, drink, or bread.
>   To fill my drunken pate
>   With that, I'd sit up late;   245
>   By the heels would I lie,
>   Under a lousy hedge die,
>   Let a slave have a pull
>   At my whore, so I be full
>   Of that precious liquor—   250

and a parcel of such stuff, my lord, not worth the opening.

> *Enter a Cutpurse very gallant, with four or five men*
> *after him, one with a wand.*

LORD NOLAND   What gallant comes yonder?
SIR THOMAS   Mass, I think I know him; 'tis one of Cumberland.
FIRST CUTPURSE [*aside to his companions*]   Shall we venture to
    shuffle in amongst yon heap of gallants, and strike?   255
SECOND CUTPURSE   'Tis a question whether there be any silver
    shells amongst them, for all their satin outsides.
ALL THE CUTPURSES   Let's try.
MOLL [*to the gentlemen*]   Pox on him! A gallant? Shadow me?
    I know him: 'tis one that cumbers the land indeed. If he swim 260
    near to the shore of any of your pockets, look to your purses.
ALL THE GENTLEMEN   Is't possible?
MOLL   This brave fellow is no better than a foist.
ALL THE GENTLEMEN   Foist? What's that?
MOLL   A diver with two fingers: a pickpocket. All his train study 265
    the figging law, that's to say, cutting of purses and foisting. One
    of them is a nip; I took him once i'the twopenny gallery at the
    Fortune. Then there's a cloyer, or snap, that dogs any new

---

228. *I prae, sequor*: go first, I'll follow; *mouse*: term of endearment, typically addressed
    to women.
236. **s.d.** *manet the rest*: the rest remain.
251. *opening*: explaining.
251. **s. d.** *gallant*: finely dressed; *wand*: light walking-stick or riding switch.
253. *Cumberland*: a northern county.
256–57. *silver shells*: coins.
260. *cumbers*: encumbers, burdens (with pun on "Cumberland").
265. *train*: companions.
266. *figging law*: code of the cutpurse.
267. *nip*: cutpurse.
267–68. *took him . . . the Fortune*: caught him [stealing] in the medium-priced seats at the
    Fortune (Bankside theatre where *The Roaring Girl* was first performed).
268. *snap*: thief to whom the "nip" hands the goods.

brother in that trade, and snaps will have half in any booty. He
with the wand is both a stale, whose office is to face a man i'the   270
streets whilst shells are drawn by another; and then, with his
black conjuring rod in his hand, he, by the nimbleness of his eye
and juggling stick, will, in cheaping a piece of plate at a goldsmith's
stall, make four or five rings mount from the top of his caduceus,
and, as if it were at leapfrog, they skip into his hand presently.   275

SECOND CUTPURSE   Zounds, we are smoked!

ALL THE CUTPURSES   Ha?

SECOND CUTPURSE   We are boiled. Pox on her! See Moll, the
roaring drab.

FIRST CUTPURSE   All the diseases of sixteen hospitals boil her!   280
Away!   [They start to leave, but Moll intercepts them.]

MOLL [to the First Cutpurse]   Bless you, sir.

FIRST CUTPURSE   And you, good sir.

MOLL   Dost not ken me, man?

FIRST CUTPURSE   No, trust me, sir.   285

MOLL   Heart, there's a knight to whom I'm bound for many favors,
lost his purse at the last new play i'the Swan—seven angels in't.
Make it good, you're best; do you see? No more.

FIRST CUTPURSE   A synagogue shall be called, Mistress Mary.
Disgrace me not. Pacus palabros. I will conjure for you;   290
farewell.   [Exeunt Cutpurses.]

MOLL   Did not I tell you, my lord?

LORD NOLAND   I wonder how thou cam'st to the knowledge of
these nasty villains.

SIR THOMAS   And why do the foul mouths of the world call thee   295
Moll Cutpurse? A name, methinks, damned and odious.

MOLL   Dare any step forth to my face and say,
"I have ta'en thee doing so, Moll"? I must confess,
In younger days, when I was apt to stray,
I have sat amongst such adders, seen their stings—   300

---

270. *stale*: decoy; *face*: confront.
271. *shells are drawn*: coins are taken [out of his pocket].
273. *cheaping*: bargaining for.
274. *caduceus*: wand (specifically, the wand of the Roman god Mercury, patron of thieves).
    Moll describes a trick in which the thief slips several gold rings over the end of his
    walking stick while distracting the goldsmith by bargaining for another item.
276. *smoked*: smoked out, detected.
278. *boiled*: done for.
279. *drab*: whore.
280. *boil*: inflame, with suggestion of the hot-bath treatments used for syphilis.
284. *ken*: know.
285. *trust*: believe.
286. *bound*: obligated.
287. *the Swan*: a Bankside theatre; *seven angels*: gold coins worth ten shillings.
288. *make . . . best*: you'd better get it back for him.
289. *synagogue*: assembly (i.e., of thieves, to discover who took the purse).
290. *Pacus palabros*: few words (corruption of Spanish *pocas palabras*); *conjure*: perform
    magic to retrieve lost objects.
293. *to the knowledge of*: to know.
298. *"I have . . . Moll"*: i.e., I have caught you cutting a purse.

As any here might—and in full playhouses
Watched their quick-diving hands, to bring to shame
Such rogues, and in that stream met an ill name.
When next, my lord, you spy any one of those,
So he be in his art a scholar, question him,   305
Tempt him with gold to open the large book
Of his close villainies; and you yourself shall cant
Better than poor Moll can, and know more laws
Of cheaters, lifters, nips, foists, puggards, curbers,
Withal the devil's black guard, than it is fit   310
Should be discovered to a noble wit.
I know they have their orders, offices,
Circuits, and circles, unto which they are bound,
To raise their own damnation in.

JACK DAPPER   How dost thou know it?   315

MOLL   As you do. I show it you; they to me show it.
Suppose, my lord, you were in Venice.

LORD NOLAND   Well.

MOLL   If some Italian pander there would tell
All the close tricks of courtesans, would not you
Hearken to such a fellow?

LORD NOLAND   Yes.

MOLL   And here,   320
Being come from Venice, to a friend most dear
That were to travel thither, you would proclaim
Your knowledge in those villainies to save
Your friend from their quick danger: must you have
A black ill name because ill things you know?   325
Good troth, my lord, I am made Moll Cutpurse so.
How many are whores in small ruffs and still looks?

302–03. to shame . . . ill name: i.e., by going among rogues with the intention of exposing them, I myself got a bad reputation.
305. in his art a scholar: i.e., an expert thief.
307. close: secret.
309. cheaters: crooks who gamble with false dice; lifters and puggards: thieves; curbers: thieves who steal goods out of windows, using a hooked pole (compare "angler" at 5.1.142); for nips and foists, see 5.1.265 and 267.
310. Withal the devil's black guard: and all the rest of Satan's servants.
311. discovered: revealed.
312. offices: official positions.
313. bound: officially indentured, like an apprentice, but with a suggestion of "in bondage."
314. To raise their own damnation in: Moll puns on a "circle" or group of thieves and the magic circle which conjurors use to summon or "raise" spirits; the thieves are summoning up only their own damnation.
318. pander: pimp.
319. close: secret; courtesans: high-class prostitutes.
320. hearken: listen.
324. quick: lively, real.
325. name: reputation.
327. small ruffs and still looks: narrow collars (worn by Puritans) and sober faces.

How many chaste, whose names fill Slander's books?
Were all men cuckolds whom gallants in their scorns
Call so, we should not walk for goring horns.   330
Perhaps for my mad going some reprove me;
I please myself, and care not else who loves me.

ALL THE GENTLEMEN   A brave mind, Moll, i'faith!

SIR THOMAS   Come, my lord, shall's to the ordinary?

LORD NOLAND   Ay, 'tis noon, sure.   335

MOLL   Good my lord, let not my name condemn me to you or to
the world. A fencer, I hope, may be called a coward; is he so for
that? If all that have ill names in London were to be whipped
and to pay but twelvepence apiece to the beadle, I would rather
have his office than a constable's.   340

JACK DAPPER   So would I, Captain Moll. 'Twere a sweet tickling
office, i'faith!   *Exeunt.*

[5.2]

Enter Sir Alexander Wengrave, Goshawk,
and Greenwit, and others.

SIR ALEXANDER   My son marry a thief? That impudent girl
Whom all the world stick their worst eyes upon?

GREENWIT   How will your care prevent it?

GOSHAWK   'Tis impossible.
They marry close; they're gone, but none knows whither.

SIR ALEXANDER   Oh, gentlemen, when has a father's heartstrings   5
Held out so long from breaking?

Enter a Servant.

                                    Now, what news, sir?

SERVANT   They were met upo' th'water an hour since, sir,
Putting in towards the Sluice.

---

330. *not walk for goring horns*: i.e., we wouldn't be able to walk around without getting
    gored by all the horned cuckolds. Compare 4.2.134.
331. *mad going*: eccentric behavior.
334. *shall's to the ordinary?*: shall we go to the eating-house?
336. *my name*: reputation, but also the nickname "Moll Cutpurse."
337. *hope*: trust; *for*: because of.
338–40. *If all that have . . . than a constable's*: a "beadle" was a parish official whose job
    included whipping petty offenders; he was ranked below and paid less than a con-
    stable. Moll's point is that if the beadle were to whip and collect a fine of twelve
    pence from all persons merely *reputed* to have done wrong, his job would be more
    lucrative than his superior's.
341. *'Twere*: It would be.
341–42. *sweet tickling office*: gratifying job, with a pun on being "tickled" (i.e., lashed) by
    the whip.
    4. *close*: secretly.

SIR ALEXANDER   The Sluice? Come, gentlemen,
'Tis Lambeth works against us.   [*Exit Servant.*]

GREENWIT   And that Lambeth joins more mad matches than your   10
six wet towns 'twixt that and Windsor Bridge, where fares lie
soaking.

SIR ALEXANDER   Delay no time, sweet gentlemen! To Blackfriars!
We'll take a pair of oars and make after 'em.

    Enter Trapdoor.

TRAPDOOR   Your son, and that bold masculine ramp, my mistress,   15
are landed now at Tower.

SIR ALEXANDER   Heyday, at Tower?

TRAPDOOR   I heard it now reported.   [*He retires.*]

SIR ALEXANDER   Which way, gentlemen, shall I bestow my care?
I'm drawn in pieces betwixt deceit and shame.   20

    Enter Sir [Guy] Fitzallard.

SIR GUY   Sir Alexander,
You're well met, and most rightly served:
My daughter was a scorn to you.

SIR ALEXANDER   Say not so, sir.

SIR GUY   A very abject she, poor gentlewoman!
Your house had been dishonored. Give you joy, sir,   25
Of your son's gaskin-bride. You'll be a grandfather shortly
To a fine crew of roaring sons and daughters;
'Twill help to stock the suburbs passing well, sir.

SIR ALEXANDER   Oh, play not with the miseries of my heart!
Wounds should be dressed and healed, not vexed or left   30
Wide open, to the anguish of the patient,
And scornful air let in; rather let pity
And advice charitably help to refresh 'em.

---

8. *the Sluice*: the embankment on the Thames at Lambeth, south of London, where pas-
sengers ("fares," l. 11) would disembark from water-taxis.

9. *Lambeth*: an area outside the city's jurisdiction, known as a destination for clandestine
marriages ("mad matches") and sexual assignations.

12. *soaking*: a joke on "wet" towns beside the river but also refers to the hot baths used to
treat syphilis, which the "fares" might have caught on one of their excursions.

13. *Blackfriars*: location of a landing stage for water-taxis.

14. *a pair of oars*: i.e., a boat.

15. *ramp*: tomboy.

16. *Tower*: landing stage at the Tower of London; from Blackfriars, Tower and Lambeth are
in opposite directions.

17. *Heyday*: exclamation of surprise.

23. *scorn*: object of scorn.

24. *abject*: worthless.

25. *dishonored*: i.e., your family would have been dishonored had Sebastian married her
(sarcastic).

26. *gaskin-bride*: bride in knee-breeches.

28. *stock the suburbs*: replenish the areas outside city limits, known for their low-life inhabitants; *passing*: surpassingly, exceedingly.

32. *scornful air*: air was thought to be bad for (thus "scornful" to) wounds.

33. *refresh 'em*: heal them (i.e., the wounds).

SIR GUY   Who'd place his charity so unworthily,
　　Like one that gives alms to a cursing beggar?   35
　　Had I but found one spark of goodness in you
　　Toward my deserving child, which then grew fond
　　Of your son's virtues, I had eased you now.
　　But I perceive both fire of youth and goodness
　　Are raked up in the ashes of your age,   40
　　Else no such shame should have come near your house,
　　Nor such ignoble sorrow touch your heart.
SIR ALEXANDER   If not for worth, for pity's sake, assist me!
GREENWIT   You urge a thing past sense. How can he help you?
　　All his assistance is as frail as ours,   45
　　Full as uncertain. Where's the place that holds 'em?
　　One brings us water news; then comes another
　　With a full-charged mouth, like a culverin's voice,
　　And he reports the Tower. Whose sounds are truest?
GOSHAWK [to Sir Guy]   In vain you flatter him.—Sir Alexander—   50
SIR GUY   I flatter him? Gentlemen, you wrong me grossly.
GREENWIT [aside to Goshawk]   He does it well, i'faith.
SIR GUY   Both news are false,
　　Of Tower or water. They took no such way yet.
SIR ALEXANDER   Oh, strange! Hear you this, gentlemen? Yet more
　　plunges?
SIR GUY   They're nearer than you think for, yet more close   55
　　Than if they were further off.
SIR ALEXANDER   How am I lost in these distractions!
SIR GUY   For your speeches, gentlemen,
　　In taxing me for rashness: 'fore you all,
　　I will engage my state to half his wealth,   60

37. *which*: who.
38. *eased*: helped.
40. *raked up*: smothered.
41. *such shame*: i.e., Sebastian's marriage to Moll.
43. *if not for worth*: i.e., even if I don't deserve it.
44. *You . . . past sense*: i.e., your demand is pointless.
46. *Where's . . . holds 'em*: i.e., where are Sebastian and Moll?
48. *culverin*: cannon.
50. *flatter him*: give him (Sir Alexander) false hopes; Goshawk implies that Sir Guy should
　　stop pretending that he *could* tell Sir Alexander the couple's whereabouts if he wanted to.
52. *He does it well*: i.e., plays his part in the trick; Sir Guy, Greenwit, Goshawk, and Trap-
　　door are all in on a plot to make Sir Alexander believe that Sebastian is marrying Moll.
54. *plunges*: lurches, twists.
57. *distractions*: confusions pulling me in different directions.
59. *taxing*: reproving; *rashness*; i.e., in claiming I could help Sir Alexander if I wanted to. Sir
　　Guy says: "With all of you as witnesses, I will wager ("engage") everything I own against
　　half of Sir Alexander's wealth—no, against his son's income, which is even less, and in
　　fact is non-existent until Sir Alexander gives it to him—that I could prevent this mar-
　　riage if my desire ("will") to do so matched my ability." Being in on the plot, Sir Guy can
　　be absolutely certain that he will win this wager: he is thus unafraid to bet everything he
　　owns, and he stakes it against what he is sure to "win"—namely, Sebastian's income,
　　which his daughter Mary will share as Sebastian's wife.

Nay, to his son's revenues, which are less,
And yet nothing at all till they come from him,
That I could, if my will stuck to my power,
Prevent this marriage yet, nay, banish her
Forever from his thoughts, much more his arms.   65
SIR ALEXANDER   Slack not this goodness, though you heap
      upon me
Mountains of malice and revenge hereafter!
I'd willingly resign up half my state to him,
So he would marry the meanest drudge I hire.
GREENWIT [to Sir Alexander]   He talks impossibilities, and you
      believe 'em!   70
SIR GUY   I talk no more than I know how to finish;
My fortunes else are his that dares stake with me.
The poor young gentleman I love and pity;
And to keep shame from him—because the spring
Of his affection was my daughter's first,   75
Till his frown blasted all—do but estate him
In those possessions which your love and care
Once pointed out for him, that he may have room
To entertain fortunes of noble birth,
Where now his desperate wants casts him upon her;   80
And if I do not, for his own sake chiefly,
Rid him of this disease that now grows on him,
I'll forfeit my whole state, before these gentlemen.
GREENWIT   Troth, but you shall not undertake such matches.
We'll persuade so much with you.
SIR ALEXANDER [giving a ring to Sir Guy]   Here's my ring;   85
He will believe this token. 'Fore these gentlemen,
I will confirm it fully: all those lands
My first love 'lotted him he shall straight possess
In that refusal.

---

64. *her*: i.e., Moll.
66. *Slack not*: Don't hold back.
68. *state*: estate; *to him*: to Sebastian (or, possibly, to Sir Guy as proposed in the wager).
69. *so he*: if he, Sebastian; *meanest drudge*: lowliest maidservant (i.e., anyone but Moll).
72. *My fortunes . . . stake with me*: i.e., I'll bet everything I own against anyone who claims I can't keep my promise (to prevent the marriage).
74–76. *the spring . . . blasted all*: i.e., Sebastian's young ("spring") love was the first offered to my daughter, until Sir Alexander's disapproval ruined everything.
76–77. *estate him in*: let him inherit.
78. *pointed out*: designated.
78–79. *room . . . noble birth*: opportunities to marry gentlewomen.
80. *his desperate . . . upon her*: his desperate financial need (since he's been disinherited) throws him together with Moll. The point may be that he can live off of her, or that she's the best a penniless man can get.
82. *Rid . . . disease*: i.e, cure him of his desire for Moll.
84. *before these gentlemen*: with these gentlemen as witnesses.
84. *matches*: wagers.
85–86. *Here's my ring . . . token*: i.e., to be shown to Sebastian as proof that Sir Guy is relaying a genuine message from Sir Alexander.
88. *My first love 'lotted him*: that I allotted to him when he still had my fatherly love.
89. *In that refusal*: when he refuses to marry Moll.

SIR GUY   If I change it not,
Change me into a beggar.
GREENWIT   Are you mad, sir?   90
SIR GUY   'Tis done.
GOSHAWK   Will you undo yourself by doing,
And show a prodigal trick in your old days?
SIR ALEXANDER   'Tis a match, gentlemen.
SIR GUY   Ay, ay, sir, ay.
I ask no favor, trust to you for none.
My hope rests in the goodness of your son.   *Exit Fitzallard.*   95
GREENWIT [*aside to Goshawk*]   He holds it up well yet.
GOSHAWK [*aside to Greenwit*]   Of an old knight, i'faith.
SIR ALEXANDER   Curst be the time I laid his first love barren,
Wilfully barren, that before this hour
Had sprung forth fruits of comfort and of honor!
He loved a virtuous gentlewoman.   100

    Enter Moll [dressed as a man].

GOSHAWK   Life, here's Moll.
GREENWIT   Jack!
GOSHAWK   How dost thou, Jack?
MOLL   How dost thou, gallant?
SIR ALEXANDER [*to Moll*]   Impudence, where's my son?
MOLL   Weakness, go look him.
SIR ALEXANDER   Is this your wedding gown?
MOLL   The man talks monthly.
Hot broth and a dark chamber for the knight;   105
I see he'll be stark mad at our next meeting.   *Exit Moll.*
GOSHAWK   Why, sir, take comfort now, there's no such
    matter:
No priest will marry her, sir, for a woman
Whiles that shape's on; and it was never known
Two men were married and conjoined in one.   110
Your son hath made some shift to love another.
SIR ALEXANDER   Whate'er she be, she has my blessing
    with her.

---

89. *If I change it not*: i.e., Sebastian's decision to marry Moll.
91. *undo*: bankrupt, ruin.
92. *prodigal*: recklessly extravagant.
96. *Of*: for.
97. *laid . . . barren*: thwarted his first love.
99. *had sprung forth*: would have brought forth.
102. *Jack*: Moll's name when dressed as a man; compare 5.1.1.
103. *look*: look for.
104. *wedding gown*: Sir Alexander gestures at her male clothing; *monthly*: like a lunatic (influenced by the monthly changes of the moon).
105. *Hot broth and a dark chamber*: treatments prescribed for madmen.
108. *for*: as.
111. *shift*: stratagem, device.

May they be rich and fruitful, and receive
Like comfort to their issue as I take in them!
He's pleased me now, marrying not this;   115
Through a whole world he could not choose amiss.
GREENWIT   Glad you're so penitent for your former sin, sir.
GOSHAWK   Say he should take a wench with her smock-dowry,
No portion with her but her lips and arms?
SIR ALEXANDER   Why, who thrive better, sir? They have most
blessing,   120
Though other have more wealth, and least repent.
Many that want most know the most content.
GREENWIT   Say he should marry a kind youthful sinner?
SIR ALEXANDER   Age will quench that. Any offence but theft
And drunkenness—nothing but death can wipe away;   125
Their sins are green even when their heads are gray.
Nay, I despair not now; my heart's cheered, gentlemen.
No face can come unfortunately to me.

Enter a Servant.

Now, sir, your news?
SERVANT   Your son with his fair bride
Is near at hand.
SIR ALEXANDER   Fair may their fortunes be!   130
GREENWIT   Now you're resolved, sir, it was never she?
SIR ALEXANDER   I find it in the music of my heart.

*Enter Moll [dressed as a woman], masked, in Sebastian's
hand, and [Sir Guy] Fitzallard.*

See where they come.
GOSHAWK   A proper lusty presence, sir.
SIR ALEXANDER   Now has he pleased me right. I always
counseled him
To choose a goodly personable creature.   135

114. *comfort to their issue*: similar happiness from their children.
116. *whole world . . . choose amiss*: i.e., he could marry anyone in the world (except
     Moll) and not make the wrong choice.
118. *smock-dowry*: owning nothing but her undergarments.
119. *portion*: dowry, the money a bride brought with her to the marriage.
120–21. *have . . . least repent*: i.e., poor couples who marry for love have the most bless-
     ings and regret their marriages the least.
122. *want*: lack.
123. *kind youthful sinner*: a sexually promiscuous girl.
124–26. *age . . . heads are gray*: i.e., maturity will put an end to sexual sin, and in fact to
     any sin other than theft and drunkenness—these end only when you die, and are
     lively and flourishing ("green") even in gray-haired old people.
128. *no face . . . unfortunately*: i.e., no woman he chooses will be unwelcome.
131. *it was never she?*: now you're certain it was never Moll (that Sebastian meant to
     marry)?
132. *s.d. masked*: see 4.2.85 and 4.2.114–137; *in . . . hand*: holding his hand.
133. *proper lusty presence*: good-looking, healthy young woman.

Just of her pitch was my first wife, his mother.
SEBASTIAN [*kneeling*]   Before I dare discover my offence,
    I kneel for pardon.
SIR ALEXANDER   My heart gave it thee
    Before thy tongue could ask it.
    Rise. Thou hast raised my joy to greater height   140
    Than to that seat where grief dejected it.   [*Sebastian rises*]
    Both welcome to my love and care forever!
    Hide not my happiness too long; all's pardoned.
    Here are our friends.—Salute her, gentlemen.
                                    They unmask her.
OMNES   Heart, Who's this, Moll?   145
SIR ALEXANDER   Oh, my reviving shame! Is't I must live,
    To be struck blind? Be it the work of sorrow,
    Before age take't in hand!
SIR GUY [*to Sir Alexander*]   Darkness and death!
    Have you deceived me thus? Did I engage
    My whole estate for this?
SIR ALEXANDER   You asked no favor,   150
    And you shall find as little. Since my comforts
    Play false with me, I'll be as cruel to thee
    As grief to fathers' hearts.
MOLL   Why, what's the matter with you,
    'Less too much joy should make your age forgetful?   155
    Are you too well, too happy?
SIR ALEXANDER   With a vengeance!
MOLL   Methinks you should be proud of such a daughter—
    As good a man as your son.
SIR ALEXANDER   Oh, monstrous impudence!
MOLL   You had no note before, an unmarked knight;
    Now all the town will take regard on you,   160
    And all your enemies fear you for my sake.
    You may pass where you list, through crowds most thick,
    And come off bravely with your purse unpicked.
    You do not know the benefits I bring with me:
    No cheat dares work upon you, with thumb or knife,   165
    While you've a roaring girl to your son's wife.

---

136. *pitch*: stature.
137. *discover*: reveal.
140–41. *joy to greater . . . dejected it*: i.e., you've given me more joy now than you gave me
        grief before.
144. *salute*: greet, i.e. with a kiss, which requires the "bride" to remove her mask.
147–48. *Be it . . . in hand*: May sorrow blind me before age does!
152. *as cruel to thee*: i.e., I'll take everything you own. Sir Alexander assumes Sir Guy
        has lost his bet that he could prevent Sebastian from marrying Moll.
155. *'Less*: unless.
159. *note*: notice (taken of you); *unmarked*: unremarked, unnoticed.
162. *pass where you list*: go wherever you like.
166. *to*: as.

SIR ALEXANDER   A devil rampant!
SIR GUY [*to Sir Alexander*]   Have you so much charity
   Yet to release me of my last rash bargain,
   An I'll give in your pledge?
SIR ALEXANDER   No sir, I stand to't.
   I'll work upon advantage, as all mischiefs   170
   Do upon me.
SIR GUY   Content.—Bear witness all, then:
   His are the lands, and so contention ends.
   Here comes your son's bride, 'twixt two noble friends.

> *Enter the Lord Noland and Sir Beauteous Ganymede with Mary*
> *Fitzallard between them, the citizens [Tiltyard, Openwork,*
> *Gallipot] and their wives with them.*

MOLL [*to Sir Alexander*]   Now are you gulled as you would be.
   Thank me for't;
   I'd a forefinger in't.
SEBASTIAN [*kneeling*]   Forgive me, father.   175
   Though there before your eyes my sorrow feigned,
   This still was she for whom true love complained.
SIR ALEXANDER   Blessings eternal, and the joys of angels,
   Begin your peace here to be signed in heaven!
                      [*Sebastian rises.*]
   How short my sleep of sorrow seems now to me   180
   To this eternity of boundless comforts,
   That finds no want but utterance and expression!
   [*To Lord Noland*] My lord, your office here appears so
     honorably,
   So full of ancient goodness, grace, and worthiness,
   I never took more joy in sight of man   185
   Than in your comfortable presence now.
LORD NOLAND   Nor I more delight in doing grace to virtue
   Than in this worthy gentlewoman, your son's bride,
   Noble Fitzallard's daughter, to whose honor

---

167. *rampant*: unrestrained; "rampant" is a heraldic term denoting a creature standing
     on its hind legs.
169. *give in your pledge*: release you from your side of the wager.
170–71. *I'll work . . . upon me*: I'll take whatever advantage I can, since evils are taking
     advantage of me.
172. *His*: i.e., Sebastian's; *contention*: quarrelling.
174. *gulled as you would be*: tricked the way you would like to be.
177. *This still . . . love complained*: Mary was always the woman for whom my true love
     pined.
181. *to*: compared to.
182. *no want . . . expression*: that lacks nothing but the words to express it.
183. *office*: role, position.
184. *ancient*: venerable.
186. *comfortable*: comforting.

And modest fame I am a servant vowed;   190
So is this knight.
SIR ALEXANDER   Your loves make my joys proud.
[*To Servant*] Bring forth those deeds of land my care laid
        ready,   [*The Servant fetches the deeds.*]
[*To Sir Guy*] And which, old knight, thy nobleness may
        challenge,
Joined with thy daughter's virtues, whom I prize now
As dearly as that flesh I call mine own.   195
[*To Mary*] Forgive me, worthy gentlewoman; 'twas my blindness.
When I rejected thee, I saw thee not;
Sorrow and willful rashness grew like films
Over the eyes of judgment, now so clear
I see the brightness of thy worth appear.   200
MARY   Duty and love may I deserve in those,
And all my wishes have a perfect close.
SIR ALEXANDER   That tongue can never err, the sound's so sweet.
                        [*He gives Sebastian the deeds.*]
Here, honest son, receive into thy hands
The keys of wealth, possession of those lands   205
Which my first care provided; they're thine own.
Heaven give thee a blessing with 'em! The best joys
That can in worldly shapes to man betide
Are fertile lands and a fair fruitful bride,
Of which I hope thou'rt sped.
SEBASTIAN   I hope so too, sir.   210
MOLL   Father and son, I ha' done you simple service here.
SEBASTIAN   For which thou shalt not part, Moll, unrequited.
SIR ALEXANDER   Thou art a mad girl, and yet I cannot now
Condemn thee.
MOLL   Condemn me? Troth, and you should, sir,
I'd make you seek out one to hang in my room: 215
I'd give you the slip at gallows, and cozen the people.
[*To Lord Noland*] Heard you this jest, my lord?
LORD NOLAND   What is it, Jack?
MOLL   He was in fear his son would marry me,
But never dreamt that I would ne'er agree.
LORD NOLAND   Why? Thou hadst a suitor once. Jack, when   220
wilt marry?

190. *modest fame*: chaste reputation.
192. *my care laid ready*: I carefully made ready.
193. *may challenge*: deserves.
201. *Duty . . . in those*: May I always be worthy, in your eyes, of duty and love.
207–08. *best joys . . . betide*: the best earthly joys that can come to a man.
210. *sped*: provided.
211. *simple service*: a straightforward good deed.
216. *cozen*: defraud (of the spectacle of seeing her hanged).

MOLL   Who, I, my lord? I'll tell you when, i'faith.
         When you shall hear
         Gallants void from sergeants' fear,
         Honesty and truth unslandered,   225
         Woman manned but never pandered,
         Cheaters booted but not coached,
         Vessels older ere they're broached.
         If my mind be then not varied,
         Next day following, I'll be married.   230
LORD NOLAND   This sounds like doomsday.
MOLL   Then were marriage best,
         For if I should repent, I were soon at rest.
SIR ALEXANDER   In troth, thou'rt a good wench. I'm sorry now
         The opinion was so hard I conceived of thee.
         Some wrongs I've done thee.

         Enter Trapdoor.

TRAPDOOR [*aside*]   Is the wind there now?   235
         'Tis time for me to kneel and confess first,
         For fear it come too late, and my brains feel it.—
         Upon my paws I ask you pardon, mistress.   [*He kneels.*]
MOLL   Pardon? For what, sir? What has Your Rogueship done
         now?   240
TRAPDOOR   I have been from time to time hired to confound you,
         by this old gentleman.
MOLL   How?
TRAPDOOR [*rising*]   Pray forgive him;
         But, may I counsel you, you should never do't.   245
         Many a snare to entrap Your Worship's life
         Have I laid privily—chains, watches, jewels—
         And when he saw nothing could mount you up,
         Four hollow-hearted angels he then gave you,
         By which he meant to trap you, I to save you.   250

224. *void . . . fear*: unafraid of sergeants who would arrest them for debt.
226. *manned*: several possible meanings, including "provided with or escorted by a man,"
      "supplied with servants," "mastered (by a husband)," and "made manly"; *pandered*:
      pimped out.
227. *Cheaters . . . coached*: con-men walking around in boots, not riding in luxurious
      coaches. The distinction may be between the petty crimes of the poor and the more
      serious, more lucrative dishonesty of the rich.
228. *vessels*: casks of liquor, women; *broached*: tapped, penetrated sexually.
231. *doomsday*: Judgement Day, the end of the world.
232. *repent*: regret (getting married); *were*: would be.
235. *Is the wind there now?*: Is that the way things are going now?
237. *my brains feel it*: i.e., I get beaten about the head.
241. *confound*: ruin.
242. *old gentleman*: i.e., Sir Alexander.
245. *But, may . . . do't*: But—if I may advise you—you never will forgive him.
247. *privily*: secretly.
248. *mount you up*: i.e., on the gallows.
249. *hollow-hearted angels*: gold coins with holes in them.

SIR ALEXANDER   To all which shame and grief in me cry guilty.
   Forgive me now! I cast the world's eyes from me,
   And look upon thee freely with mine own.
   I see the most of many wrongs before thee
   Cast from the jaws of Envy and her people,   255
   And nothing foul but that. I'll nevermore
   Condemn by common voice, for that's the whore
   That deceives man's opinion, mocks his trust,
   Cozens his love, and makes his heart unjust.
MOLL [*showing money*]   Here be the angels, gentlemen; they were
   given me   260
   As a musician. I pursue no pity;
   Follow the law. An you can cuck me, spare not!
   Hang up my viol by me, and I care not.
SIR ALEXANDER   So far I'm sorry, I'll thrice double 'em
   To make thy wrongs amends.—   265
   Come, worthy friends, my honorable lord,
   Sir Beauteous Ganymede, and noble Fitzallard,
   And you, kind gentlewomen, whose sparkling presence
   Are glories set in marriage—beams of society,
   For all your loves give lustre to my joys.   270
   The happiness of this day shall be remembered
   At the return of every smiling spring;
   In my time now 'tis born, and may no sadness
   Sit on the brows of men upon that day,
   But as I am, so all go pleased away! [*Exeunt, except Moll.*]   275

Epilogus

MOLL   A painter, having drawn with curious art
   The picture of a woman—every part
   Limned to the life—hung out the piece to sell.
   People who passed along, viewing it well,
   Gave several verdicts on it. Some dispraised   5

---

252. *I cast . . . from me*: i.e., I reject the way society looks at you.
254. *wrongs before thee*: wrongs of which you are accused.
255. *her people*: Envy's followers.
262. *An you . . . spare not*: if you can legally punish me with the cucking-stool, go right
   ahead; "cucking," typically used to punish women who disturbed the peace, involved
   strapping the offender into a chair and repeatedly plunging her into a pond or river;
264. *'em*: the coins.
268. *kind gentlewomen*: i.e., the citizens' wives.
273. *'tis born*: i.e., this happiness is born.
275. *But as I . . . away!*: May everyone leave as pleased as I am!
  1. *curious*: skillful.
  3. *limned*: depicted.
  5. *several*: various.

The hair; some said the brows too high were raised;
Some hit her o'er the lips, misliked their color;
Some wished her nose were shorter; some, the eyes fuller;
Others said roses on her cheeks should grow,
Swearing they looked too pale; others cried no.   10
The workman still, as fault was found, did mend it,
In hope to please all; but this work being ended
And hung open at stall, it was so vile,
So monstrous, and so ugly, all men did smile
At the poor painter's folly. Such we doubt   15
Is this our comedy. Some perhaps do flout
The plot, saying, 'tis too thin, too weak, too mean;
Some for the person will revile the scene,
And wonder that a creature of her being
Should be the subject of a poet, seeing   20
In the world's eye, none weighs so light; others look
For all those base tricks published in a book—
Foul as his brains they flowed from—of cutpurses,
Of nips and foists, nasty, obscene discourses,
As full of lies, as empty of worth or wit,   25
For any honest ear or eye unfit.
And thus,
If we to every brain that's humorous
Should fashion scenes, we, with the painter, shall,
In striving to please all, please none at all.   30
Yet for such faults as either the writers' wit
Or negligence of the actors do commit,
Both crave your pardons. If what both have done
Cannot full pay your expectation,
The Roaring Girl herself, some few days hence,   35
Shall on this stage give larger recompense;
Which mirth that you may share in, herself does woo you,
And craves this sign: your hands to beckon her to you.
                                        [*Exit.*]

FINIS.

11. *still*: continually.
15–16. *Such we . . . comedy*: We're afraid our comedy is like this.
16. *flout*: insult;
17. *mean*: low, poor.
18. *person*: character (i.e., of Moll).
21. *in the world's . . . light*: i.e., nobody is held by society to be more worthless.
28. *humorous*: whimsical, capricious.
33. *Both crave your pardons*: i.e., both writer and actors beg your pardons.
36. *give larger recompense*: see introduction, p.ix.
37. *which mirth . . . woo you*: i.e., Moll the character invites you to come back and enjoy the real Moll's performance.
38. *hands*: applause.

CONTEXTS

THOMAS DEKKER

Along with writing plays, Thomas Dekker turned his hand to a variety of prose publications. The first of these, *The Bellman of London* (1608), belongs to the genre of rogue pamphlets, purporting to expose the habits and language (the slang known as "cant") of thieves, beggars, and other underworld figures. The "bellman" of the title is the London nightwatchman, who would encounter such characters during his rounds. Dekker's *Bellman* relies heavily on an earlier pamphlet of the same genre, Thomas Harman's *A Caveat for Common Cursitors* (1567). Whether the underworld was actually organized according to the intricate hierarchies ascribed to it by the pamphleteers is highly debatable. In the excerpt below, the first paragraph is spoken by the rogues' leader to a new recruit; the remainder is spoken by the hostess of the tavern where the rogues have met, explaining their hierarchy to the narrator.

Underworld Cant in *The Bellman of London*[†]

We have amongst us some eighteen or nineteen several offices[1] for men, and about seven or eight for women. The chiefest of us are called Upright-men[2] (O, my dear sunburnt brother, if all those that are the chiefest men in other companies were Upright-men too, what good dealing would there be in all occupations?); the next are Rufflers; then have we Anglers, but they seldom catch fish till they go up westward for flounders;[3] then are there Rogues, then Priggers, then Palliards, then Fraters, then Tom of Bedlam's band of madcaps, otherwise called Poor Tom's stock of wild geese (whom here thou seest by his black and blue naked arms to be a man beaten to the world), and those wild geese or hare-brains are called Abraham-men; in the next squadron march our brave Whipjacks, at the tail of them come crawling our counterfeit Cranks; in another troop are gabbling

---

† *The Bellman of London*, STC # 6482, is held at the British Library and is accessible through Early English Books Online. Spelling and punctuation have been modernized.
1. Different ranks.
2. Upright-men, Anglers, Rogues, Whipjacks, and Curtals are explained in detail in the rest of the excerpt. Priggers are thieves; Palliards are men who beg, accompanied by women who pose as their wives; Fraters pretend to collect money for charitable foundations such as hospitals; Abraham-men (also known as Tom of Bedlam's madcaps or Poor Tom's wild geese) feign insanity; Cranks feign epilepsy (called "the falling sickness"); Dummerers feign muteness; Irish-toils and Swigmen pose as pedlars; Jarkmen are literate beggars who fabricate licenses and passes; Patricoes are beggar-priests who marry beggars to each other; Kinchin-coes are little boys, useful for breaking into houses through small windows.
3. To catch fools.

Dummerers, then Curtals follow at their heels, and they bring along with them strange Engineers, called Irish-toils. After whom follow the Swigmen, the Jarkmen, the Patricoes, and last the Kinchin-coes. These are the tottered[4] regiments that make up our main army. The victuallers to the camp are women, and of those some are Glimmerers, some Bawdy-baskets, some Autem-morts, others Walking-morts; some Doxies, others are Dells, the last and least are called Kinchinmorts,[5] with all which, Comrades, thou shalt in thy beggarly peregrination[6] meet, converse, and be drunk, and in a short time know their natures and roguish conditions without the help of a tutor.

* * *

An Upright-man

You shall understand, then, (quoth she), that the chiefest of those that were my table-men today are called Upright-men, whose picture I will draw to the life before you. An Upright-man is a sturdy, big-boned knave, that never walks but (like a commander) with a short truncheon in his hand, which he calls his Filchman. At markets, fairs, and other meetings, his voice among beggars is of the same sound that a constable's is of: it is not to be controlled.[7] He is free of all the shires in England, but never stays in any place long: the reason is, his profession is to be idle, which being looked into, he knows is punishable, and therefore to avoid the whip,[8] he wanders. If he come to a farmer's door, the alms he begs is neither meat nor drink, but only money: if anything else be offered to him, he takes it with disdain and lays it under a hedge for any that comes next, but in revenge of this, if he spy any geese, hens, ducks, or such like walking spirits haunting the house, with them he conjures about midnight,[9] using them the next morning like traitors, either beheading them or quartering them in pieces, for which purpose, this band of Uprightmen seldom march without five or six in a company, so that country people rather give them money for fear than out of any devotion. After this bloody massacre of the poor innocent pullen, the actors

---

4. Tattered.
5. Doxies, Dells, and Kinchin-morts are explained in detail in the rest of the excerpt; *victuallers to the camp*: literally, those who provide food to an army; the women described here satisfy other appetites as well. Glimmerers are people who claim to have lost their houses and belongings in a fire; Bawdy-baskets are female pedlars who engage in opportunistic thievery and prostitution; Autem-morts are married women (an "autem" is a church); Walking-morts claim to be widows.
6. Travel.
7. Challenged or restrained.
8. Vagrants were punished by whipping; *free of*: a citizen of.
9. I.e., he makes the poultry disappear at midnight like a conjurer makes ghosts ("walking spirits") disappear from a haunted house.

in their bloody tragedy repair to their stalling-kens, and those are tippling houses,[1] which will lend money upon any stolen goods, and unto which none but such guests as they resort. There, the spits go round and the cans[2] walk up and down; there have they their Morts and Doxies, with whom (after they have boozed profoundly) they lie (instead of featherbeds upon litters of clean straw) to increase the generation of rogues and beggars. For these Upright-men stand so much upon their reputation, that they scorn any Mort or Doxy should be seen to walk with them, and indeed what need they care for them, when he may command any Doxy to leave another man and to lie with him, the other not daring to murmur against it? An Upright-man will seldom complain of want, for whatsoever any one of his profession doth steal, he may challenge a share in it, yea and may command any inferior Rogue to fetch in booty[3] to serve his turn. These carry the shapes of soldiers and can talk of the Low-Countries, though they never were beyond Dover.[4]

A Ruffler

The next in degree to him is called a Ruffler. The Ruffler and the Upright-man are so like in conditions that you would swear they are brothers: they walk with cudgels alike, they profess arms alike, though they be both out at elbows,[5] and will swear they lost their limbs in their country's quarrel, when either they are lame by diseases, or have been mangled in some drunken quarrel. These commonly are fellows that have stood aloof in the wars, and whilst others fought, they took their heels and ran away from their captain, or else they have been servingmen, whom for their behaviour, no man would trust with a livery.[6] If they cannot spend their days to their minds[7] by their own begging or robbing of country people that come late from markets (for upon those they most usually exercise their trade) then do they compel the inferior subjects of their commonwealth (as Rogues, Palliards, Morts, Doxies, etc.) to pay tribute unto them. A Ruffler after a year or two takes state upon him,[8] and becomes an Upright-man (but no honest man).

---

1. Taverns; *pullen*: poultry.
2. Drinking vessels.
3. Stolen goods.
4. A port in southeast England; *carry the shapes of soldiers*: are disguised as soldiers; *Low-Countries*: modern-day Holland, Belgium, and Luxembourg, sites of religious wars throughout the period.
5. With holes in the elbows of their clothing; *profess arms*: claim to be soldiers.
6. Servant's uniform.
7. As they like.
8. Assumes a superior rank.

An Angler

An Angler is a limb of an Upright-man, as being derived from him. The apparel in which they walk is commonly frieze jerkins and galley slops.[9] In the day time they beg from house to house, not so much for relief, as to spy what lies fit for their nets, which in the night following they fish for. The rod they angle with is a staff of five or six foot in length, in which, within one inch of the top, is a little hole bored quite through, into which hole they put an iron hook, and with the same do they angle at windows about midnight, the draught[1] they pluck up being apparel, sheets, coverlets, or whatsoever their iron hooks can lay hold of, which prize when they have gotten, they do not presently[2] make sale of it, but after four or five days or according as they suspect inquiry will be made after it, do they bring such goods to a Broker (traded up[3] for the purpose) who lends upon them half so much money as they be worth, which notwithstanding serves the Angler awhile for spending money, and enriches him[4] that buys it for a long time after.

A Rogue

A Rogue is known to all men by his name, but not to all men by his conditions.[5] No Puritan[6] can dissemble[7] more than he, for he will speak in a lamentable tune, and crawl along the streets (supporting his body by a staff) as if there were not life enough in him to put strength into his legs. His head shall be bound about with linen, loathsome to behold and as filthy in colour as the complexion of his face. His apparel is all tattered, his bosom naked, and most commonly no shirt on: not that they are given to this misery by mere want, but that if they had better clothes given them, they would rather sell them to some of their own fraternity than wear them, and wander up and down in that piteous manner, only to move people to compassion, and to be relieved with money, which being gotten, at night is spent as merrily and as lewdly as in the day it was won by counterfeit villainy. Another sect there be of these, and they are called Sturdy Rogues: these walk from country to country under colour of travelling to their friends,[8] or to find out some kinsman, or else to deliver some letter to one gentleman or other, whose name he

---

9. Sleeveless jackets of coarse woollen cloth and baggy breeches like those worn in the galleys (ships rowed by slaves or condemned criminals).
1. Haul of fish caught in a net.
2. Immediately.
3. Trained.
4. I.e., the broker.
5. I.e, all men know the word "rogue," but they don't know exactly what a rogue is or does.
6. Puritans were commonly denigrated as hypocrites.
7. Deceive.
8. Relatives; *colour*: pretext.

will have fairly endorsed on paper, folded up for that purpose, and handsomely sealed. Others use this shift, to carry a certificate or passport[9] about them, with the hand and seal of some Justice to it, giving notice how he hath been whipped for a vagabond, according to the laws of the realm, and that he is now to return to such a place where he was born, or dwelt last, by a certain day limited, which is sure to be set down long enough,[1] for all these writings are but counterfeit, they having among them (of their own rank) that can write and read, who are their Secretaries in this business. These fellows have fingers as nimble as the Upright-man, and have their wenches and meeting-places, where whatsoever they get, they spend, and whatsoever they spend is to satisfy their lust. Some of this brood are called Curtals,[2] because they wear short cloaks. Their company is dangerous, their lives detestable, and their ends miserable.

A Wild Rogue

The Tame Rogue begets a Wild Rogue, and this is a spirit that cares not in what circle he rises,[3] nor into the company of what devils he falls. In his swaddling clouts is he marked to be a villain, and in his breeding is instructed to be so.[4] The mother of him (who was delivered of her burden under a hedge) either travelling with him at her back, or else leading him in her hand, and will rather endure to see his brains beaten out, than to have him taken from her to be put to an honest course of life, so envious[5] they are and so much do they scorn any profession but their own. They have been Rogues themselves, and disdain that their children should be otherwise. These Wild Rogues (like wild geese) keep in flocks, and all the day loiter in the fields (if the weather be warm), and at brick-kilns, or else disperse themselves in cold weather to rich men's doors, and at night have their meetings in barns or other out-places, where (twenty or more in a company) they engender,[6] male and female, every one catching her whom he doth best fancy, the stronger and more sturdy keeping the weaker in subjection. Their language is bawdy talk, damned oaths, and plots where to filch the next morning, which they perform betimes, rising as early as the sun, and enjoining their punks to look out for cheats,[7] to make their meeting at night the merrier.

* * *

9. A document permitting him to pass through the country without being arrested for vagrancy.
1. I.e., the deadline by which he has to have arrived is set a long time off.
2. Literally, a horse with a docked tail.
3. Conjurers would draw magic circles in which to summon (evil) spirits.
4. I.e., as an infant, he is selected to be a villain, and he is brought up to be one; *swaddling clouts*: bands of fabric used to wrap a baby.
5. Spiteful.
6. Copulate.
7. Instructing their whores to look out for goods to be stolen; *betimes*: early.

A Whipjack

Then there is another sort of nimble-fingered knaves, and they are called Whipjacks, who talk of nothing but fights at sea, piracies, drownings, and shipwrecks, travelling both in the shapes and names of mariners, with a counterfeit licence[5] to beg from town to town, which licence they call a gybe, and the seals to it, jarks. Their colour of wandering from shire to shire, especially along the sea coasts) is to hearken after their ship that was overthrown, or for the merchandise stolen out of her, but the end[6] of their land voyages is to rob booths at fairs, which they call "heaving of the booth." These Whipjacks will talk of the Indies, and of all countries that lie under heaven, but are indeed no more but freshwater soldiers.[7]

* * *

[Morts, Dells, and Doxies]

Thus have I opened unto you half the nest of this generation of vipers, now will I discover the other half, wherein sits a brood of serpents, as dangerous and as loathsome as these, of which the young ones and the least[8] are called Kinchin-morts, and those are girls of a year or two old, which the Morts (their mothers) carry at their backs in their slates (which in the canting tongue are sheets); if they have no children of their own they will steal them from others, and by some means disfigure them, that by their parents they shall never be known. The second bird of this feather is a Dell, and that is a young wench, ripe for the act of generation,[9] but as yet not spoiled of her maidenhead; these Dells are reserved as dishes for the Upright-men, for none but they must have the first taste of them, and after the Upright-men have deflowered them (which commonly is when they are very young), then are they free for any of the brotherhood, and are called Dells no more but Doxies. Of these Dells some are termed Wild-dells, and those are such as are born and begotten under a hedge: the other are young wenches that either by death of parents, the villainy of executors,[1] or the cruelty of masters or mistresses, fall into this infamous and damnable course of life. When they have gotten the title of Doxies, then are they common for any, and walk for

---

5. The Crown issued temporary licences to injured or impoverished seamen entitling them to beg for alms; *shapes and names of mariners*: disguised as, and calling themselves sailors.
6. Goal; *colour of*: pretext for; *hearken after . . . over thrown*: to hear news of their ship which was seized by pirates.
7. Literally, inexperienced soldiers; the term plays on the Whipjacks' lack of "saltwater" experience.
8. Smallest, lowest in rank.
9. Sexual intercourse.
1. I.e., executors of their parents' wills, who have deprived the girls of their inheritances.

the most part with their betters (who are a degree above them) called Morts, but whensoever an Upright-man is in presence, the Doxy is only at his command. These Doxies will for good victuals[2] or a small piece of money, prostitute their bodies to servingmen if they can get into any convenient corner about their master's houses, and to ploughmen in barns, haylofts, or stables. They are common pickpockets, familiars with the baser sorts of cutpurses, and oftentimes secret murderers of those infants which are begotten of their bodies. These Doxies have one special badge to be known by, for most of them go working of laces and shirt strings, or such like stuff, only to give colour to[3] their idle wandering.

2. Food.
3. As a pretext for; *go working of*: walk around while knitting.

Women in Men's Clothing: Fads and Controversies

PHILIP STUBBES

The Anatomy of Abuses by Philip Stubbes (c. 1555–c. 1610) first appeared in 1583 and was popular enough to be republished twice (1584 and 1595) with revisions and additions. Stubbes's book "anatomizes" (i.e., dissects) an enormous array of contemporary "abuses," or vices, ranging from adultery and drunkenness to playing football on Sundays. The *Anatomy* is in the form of a dialogue between Philoponus ("lover of hard work"), who has returned to his unnamed country from travels in England, and Spudeus ("zealous student"), who is curious to hear about the immorality he encountered there. The excerpt below, from the 1595 edition, is part of a longer diatribe against costly and elaborate apparel, both male and female.

Doublets for Women in England[†]

PHILOPONUS: The women also there have doublets and jerkins, as men have here, buttoned up to the breast, and made with wings, welts, and pinions[1] on the shoulder points, as man's apparel is in all respects, and although this be a kind of attire proper only to man, yet they blush not to wear it: and if they could as well change their sex, and put on the kind[2] of man, as they can wear apparel assigned only to man, I think they would as verily become men indeed, as now they degenerate from godly sober women in wearing this wanton lewd kind of attire, proper only to man. It is writted in the 22 of Deuteronomy[3], that what man soever weareth woman's apparel is

---

† *The Anatomy of Abuses*, STC# 23379, is held at the Huntington Library and is accessible through Early English Books Online. Spelling and punctuation have been modernized.
1. Decorative flaps of fabric; *doublets*: men's close-fitting jackets, fastening up the front; *jerkins*: sleeveless outer jackets, usually leather, worn over doublets.
2. Nature.
3. Deuteronomy 22:8: "The woman shall not wear that which pertaineth unto a man, neither shall a man put on a woman's garment: for all that do so are abomination unto the Lord thy God."

accursed, and what woman weareth man's apparel is accursed also. Now whether they be within the compass of that curse, let they themselves judge. Our apparel was given as a sign distinctive, to discern betwixt sex and sex, and therefore one to wear the apparel of another sex, is to participate with the same, and to adulterate the verity[4] of his own kind. Wherefore these women may not improperly be called Hermaphroditi, that is monsters of both kinds, half women, half men. Who if they were natural women, and honest matrons, would blush to go in such wanton and lewd attire, that is incident only to men.

SPUDEUS: I never read nor heard of any people, except drunken with Circe's cups,[5] or poisoned with the exorcisms of Medea, that famous and renowned sorceress, that ever would wear such kind of attire, as is not only stinking before the face of God, and offensive to man, but also such as painteth out to the whole world the dissoluteness of their corrupt conversation.[6]

---

4. Truth; *participate*: share qualities in common.
5. *Circe's cups*: In Greek mythology, Circe was an enchantress who used potions to turn men into animals.
6. Behavior; *exorcisms of Medea . . . sorceress*: In Greek mythology, Medea, Circe's niece, killed a rival by means of a poisoned dress. "Exorcisms" here seems to mean "spells," not "casting out of demons."

JOHN CHAMBERLAIN

From 1597 to 1628, John Chamberlain (1553–1628), a wealthy Londoner and prolific correspondent, relayed political news, court gossip, and the current events of the city in a series of over 450 letters to his friend Sir Dudley Carleton, a diplomat stationed abroad. The first excerpt below describes Mary Frith's 1612 penance for her performance at the Fortune playhouse; the second two are contemporaneous with the *Hic Mulier* and *Haec Vir* pamphlets (1620, see pages 123–46) and refer to the same then-current fad for women to wear masculine clothing.

From The Letters[†]

London, February 12, 1612

The other week a young minion of Sir Pexall Brockas did penance at Paul's Cross,[1] whom he had entertained and abused[2] since she was twelve years old, and this last Sunday, Moll Cutpurse, a notorious baggage (that used to go in men's apparel and challenged the field of diverse gallants[3]) was brought to the same place, where she wept bitterly and seemed very penitent, but it is since doubted she was maudlin drunk, being discovered to have tippled of three quarts of sack[4] before she came to her penance. She had the daintiest preacher or ghostly father that I ever saw in pulpit, once Ratcliffe of Brazen Nose[5] in Oxford, a likelier man to have led the revels in some Inn of Court[6] then to be where he was, but the best is he did extreme badly, and so wearied the audience that the best part went away, and the rest tarried[7] rather to hear Moll Cutpurse than him.

London, January 25, 1620

Yesterday the bishop of London called together all his clergy about this town, and told them he had express commandment from the King to will them to inveigh vehemently and bitterly in their sermons

† From *The Letters of John Chamberlain,* ed. Norman Egbert McClure, 2 vols. (Greenwood Press: Westport, Conn, 1979) (rpt. of the 1939 publication of the American Philosophical Society, Philadelphia). Spelling and punctuation have been modernized and new footnotes have been added.
1. An open-air pulpit in the grounds of St. Paul's Cathedral. Penance, imposed by the church courts for minor (mainly sexual) offences, consisted of the guilty party appearing publicly in church dressed in a white sheet, while a clergyman preached a sermon against the offence he or she had committed; *minion*: lover.
2. Employed in his household and sexually exploited.
3. Challenged various gallants to duels; *baggage*: hussy.
4. Sherry; *doubted*: suspected.
5. Brasenose College; *ghostly*: spiritual.
6. Holiday celebrations with dancing, feasting, etc., held at the Inns of Court, London institutions for legal training and practice.
7. Stayed; *best part*: majority.

against the insolency of our women, and their wearing of broad-brimmed hats, pointed doublets, their hair cut short or shorn, and some of them stilettoes or poniards, and other such trinkets of like moment,[8] adding withal that if pulpit admonitions will not reform them he would proceed by another course. The truth is, the world is very far out of order, but whether this will mend it, God knows.

London, February 12, 1620

Our pulpits ring continually of the insolence and impudence of women: and to help the matter forward, the players have likewise taken them to task, and so too the ballads and ballad-singers, so that they can come nowhere but their ears tingle: and if this will not serve, the King threatens to fall upon their husbands, parents, or friends[9] that have or should have power over them, and make them pay for it.

JOHN WILLIAMS

John Williams's *A Sermon of Apparel* was first preached on February 22, 1619, about a year before James I commanded the London clergy to "inveigh vehemently and bitterly in their sermons" against the "insolency" of women in male attire (see Chamberlain letters, above); it was published the following year, as its title page notes, "by his Majesty's especial, Commandment." While most of the sermon castigates sartorial excess in both sexes, the following excerpt begins with men who show off their finery in church, and moves to a specific condemnation of women who flaunt the latest in masculine fashions.

A Sermon of Apparel[†]

When thou comest thus rigged to the house of God, (for that's nowadays the Theater of all this vanity), *velut gladium te & venenum videntibus prebes*[1] (saith St. Cyprian) thou art no better than poison in the veins and a sword in the heart of all thy brethren. Thy colours glitter in their rolling eyes, when they should be reading. Thy silks do rattle in their itching ears, when they should be hearing. Thy fashions swim in their idle brains, when they should be thinking. And thou

---

8. Significance; *stilettoes or poniards*: types of daggers, with thick and slim blades respectively.
9. Relatives.
† Published in 1620, *A Sermon of Apparel*, STC# 25728, is held at Cambridge University Library and is accessible through Early English Books Online. Spelling and punctuation have been modernized.
1. The Latin is translated in the rest of the sentence.

takest up all the powers of their souls, when they should be praying.
And thus (instead of worshipping God), they worship (with Jeroboam)
a golden calf, as though their coming hither was only to see thy self
clothed in soft raiments.[2] Lastly, suppose the people were so attentive
as not to regard this vanity of men; what flesh and blood hath his
thoughts so staunch but must be distracted[3] in his Church-devotions
at the prodigious apparition of our women? *Monstrum a monstrando*
(say the Grammarians), monsters are therefore so termed, because
men cannot for their hearts[4] but run out to see them. For a woman
therefore to come unto a Church, Chimaera-like, half male and half
female, or as the priests of the Indian Venus, half black, half white,[5]
as it were, and there (it is St. Chrysostom's observation) first to profess repentance and remorse for sin. But how? By holding up to God
a pair of painted hands, and by lifting towards his throne two plas-
tered eyes and a polled head?[6] Secondly, to humble herself. But how?
In satin (I warrant you) instead of sackcloth, and covered with pearls
instead of ashes.[7] Thirdly, to move[8] God to be gracious. But how?
With a face and countenance he never saw before, composed for smiling more than for sorrowing, and purled with unions[9] instead of tears.
Lastly, to protest[1] amendment and newness of life. But how? As standing most manly upon her points,[2] by wagging a feather to defy the
world, and carrying a dagger to kill (no doubt) the flesh and the
devil.[3] To come thus a-begging (saith Theophilact) as if she came a-
marrying, and to enter God's house, as if it were a Play-house: *Quis
tam ferreus ut teneat se*, what devotion in the world but must start
aside and step out to see a suitor[4] clothed in such raiments?

2. A reference to the sermon's key text, Matthew 11:8: "But what went you out to see? A
   man clothed in soft raiment? Behold, they that wear soft clothing are in kings' houses.";
   golden calf: King Jeroboam caused the Israelites to turn away from God and instead worship two golden images of calves (1 Kings 12:26–33).
3. I.e., what person has a mind so steady as not to be distracted?
4. Can't help themselves. *Grammarians*: scholars of grammar, philologists; *Monstrum a
   monstrando*: literally, "monstrum, from something to be shown."
5. In *The Life of Apollonius of Tyana*, the Greek philosopher Philostratus claimed that Apollonius had travelled to India, where he met a woman black from the waist up and white
   from the waist down who was sacred to a goddess he described as the "Indian Venus."
   Chimaera: mythical beast, part lion, part goat, and part serpent.
6. Eyes smeared with makeup, and a head with a short haircut.
7. Sackcloth and ashes were the traditional garb of the penitent.
8. Beg, persuade.
9. Adorned with pearls.
1. Solemnly promise.
2. *points*: tags for attaching hose to doublet (both articles of male clothing); pun on standing
   (i.e., insisting) upon a point in a debate.
3. The world, the flesh, and the devil were the three traditional enemies of the human soul;
   Williams is being sarcastic.
4. I.e., one who begs for God's grace; *Quis . . . ut teneat se*: the Latin is translated in the rest
   of the sentence.

ANONYMOUS

The 1620 fad for masculine fashions on women, which provoked the ire of James I (see the Chamberlain letters, pp. 120–21), became the subject of a pair of anonymous pamphlets: *Hic Mulier; or The Man-Woman* and, in response, *Haec Vir; or The Womanish Man.* While the radical ideals of gender equality espoused (at least initially) by the female speaker of the latter make it tempting to speculate about the sex of its author, nothing is known about the author of either pamphlet. It was not unheard of for the same writer to capitalize on a controversial subject by publishing arguments both "for" and "against."

Hic Mulier; or, The Man-Woman:[†]

Being a Medicine
to cure the Coltish Disease of the Staggers
in the Masculine-Feminines of our Times,
Expressed in a brief Declamation:
Non omnes possumus omnes.[1]

Hic Mulier:[2] How now? Break Priscian's[3] head at the first encounter? But two words, and they false Latin? Pardon me, good Signor Construction, for I will not answer thee as the pope did, that I will do it in despite of the Grammar. But I will maintain, if it be not the truest Latin in our Kingdom, yet it is the commonest. For since the days of Adam women were never so Masculine: Masculine in their genders and whole generations, from the Mother to the youngest daughter; Masculine in Number, from one to multitudes; Masculine in Case, even from the head to the foot; Masculine in Mood, from bold speech to impudent action; and Masculine in Tense[4] for without redress they were, are, and will be still most Masculine, most mankind, and most monstrous. Are all women then turned Masculine? No, God forbid, there are a world full of holy thoughts, modest carriage, and severe chastity. To these let me fall on my knees and say,

---

† From Katherine Usher Henderson and Barbara F. McManus, *Half Humankind: Contexts and Texts of the Controversy about Women in England, 1540–1640* (University of Illinois Press, 1985). Notes are by Henderson and McManus.
1. "We cannot all be everybody." This is a clever variation on Vergil, *Eclogue* 8.63 ("non omnia possumus omnes," "we cannot all do everything"), underlining the author's contention that women who dress like men are really trying to *become* men. "The Staggers" is a disease of horses and other animals which causes reeling and falling.
2. Deliberately incorrect Latin for "this woman," coupling the masculine form of the adjective with the feminine noun ("this mannish woman").
3. Priscian was a sixth-century A.D. Roman grammarian; "to break his head" was to violate his rules of grammar.
4. A series of puns on the root meaning of the grammatical terms *gender, number, case, mood,* and *tense* (at this time the word *case* could refer to clothing).

Title page, *Hic Mulier: Or, The Man-Woman* (1620). Reproduced by permission of the Huntington Library, San Marino, California.

"You, oh you women, you good women, you that are in the fullness of perfection, you that are the crowns of nature's work, the complements of men's excellences, and the Seminaries[5] of propagation; you that maintain the world, support mankind, and give life to society; you that, armed with the infinite power of Virtue, are Castles impregnable, Rivers unsailable, Seas immovable, infinite treasures, and invincible armies; that are helpers most trusty, Sentinels most careful, signs deceitless, plain ways fail-less, true guides dangerless, Balms that instantly cure, and honors that never perish. Oh do not look to find your names in this Declamation, but with all honor and reverence do I speak to you. You are Seneca's Graces,[6] women, good women, modest women, true women—ever young because ever virtuous, ever chaste, ever glorious. When I write of you, I will write with a golden pen on leaves of golden paper; now I write with a rough quill and black Ink on iron sheets the iron deeds of an iron generation."

Come, then, you Masculine women, for you are my Subject, you that have made Admiration an Ass and fooled him with a deformity never before dreamed of; that have made yourselves stranger things than ever Noah's Ark unloaded or Nile engendered;[7] whom to name, he that named all things might study an Age to give you a right attribute; whose like are not found in any Antiquary's study, in any Seaman's travel, nor in any Painter's cunning. You that are stranger than strangeness itself; whom Wise men wonder at, Boys shout at, and Goblins themselves start at; you that are the gilt dirt which embroiders Play-houses, the painted Statues which adorn Caroches,[8] and the perfumed Carrion that bad men feed on in Brothels: 'tis of you I entreat[9] and of your monstrous deformity. You that have made your bodies like antic Boscadge or Crotesco work,[1] not half man/half woman, half fish/half flesh, half beast/half Monster, but all Odious, all Devil; that have cast off the ornaments of your sexes to put on the garments of Shame; that have laid by the bashfulness of your natures to gather the impudence of Harlots; that have buried silence to revive slander; that are all things but that which you should be, and nothing less than[2] friends to virtue and

---

5. Seed plots, nurseries.
6. In his treatise On Benefits (de Beneficiis), Seneca, an ancient Roman moral philosopher and playwright, presented the mythological Graces (three beautiful virgins depicted dancing hand in hand) as symbols of kindness and gratitude.
7. According to Ovid's Metamorphoses, some strange and monstrous creatures emerged from the slime left by the receding waters after the great flood, creatures similar to those thought to be produced in the mud of the Nile's annual floods.
8. Stately coaches.
9. Treat.
1. Boscadge is a decorative design imitating branches and foliage; crotesco is painting or sculpture that fantastically combines human and animal forms interwoven with foliage and flowers.
2. Anything rather than.

goodness; that have made the foundation of your highest detested work from the lowest despised creatures that Record can give testimony of: the one cut from the Commonwealth at the Gallows; the other is well known.[3] From the first you got the false armory of yellow Starch (for to wear yellow on white or white upon yellow is by the rules of Heraldry baseness, bastardy, and indignity), the folly of imitation, the deceitfulness of flattery, and the grossest baseness of all baseness, to do whatever a greater power will command you. From the other you have taken the monstrousness of your deformity in apparel, exchanging the modest attire of the comely Hood, Cowl, Coif, handsome Dress or Kerchief, to the cloudy Ruffianly broad-brimmed Hat and wanton Feather; the modest upper parts of a concealing straight gown, to the loose, lascivious civil embracement of a French doublet, being all unbuttoned to entice, all of one shape to hide deformity, and extreme short waisted to give a most easy way to every luxurious action; the glory of a fair large hair, to the shame of most ruffianly short locks; the side, thick gathered, and close guarding Safeguards[4] to the short, weak, thin, loose, and every hand-entertaining short bases;[5] for Needles, Swords; for Prayerbooks, bawdy legs; for modest gestures, giantlike behaviors; and for women's modesty, all Mimic and apish incivility. These are your founders, from these you took your copies, and, without amendment, with these you shall come to perdition.

Sophocles, being asked why he presented no women in his Tragedies but good ones and Euripides none but bad ones, answered

---

3. Some background is necessary to understand this reference to a scandal that rocked English society in the early seventeenth century. The scandal revolved around Lady Frances Howard who, although married to the earl of Essex while both were still children, had by January 1613 embarked on an affair with Robert Carr, earl of Somerset and the king's favorite. Somerset's political and personal mentor, the writer Sir Thomas Overbury, convinced of the fundamental wickedness of Lady Frances, determined to end the relationship, but Somerset was deeply infatuated with his mistress and broke with Overbury over the issue. Both King James and his queen detested Overbury for his intrusive arrogance, and in April 1613 James found an excuse to have him imprisoned in the Tower. In September 1613 Lady Frances succeeded in obtaining an annulment of her marriage to Essex on grounds of his supposed impotence, and three months later, with the king's blessing, she married Robert Carr at Whitehall in a lavish ceremony. In September of the same year Sir Thomas Overbury had died in the Tower, but not until the summer of 1615 did the fact emerge that he had been murdered by Lady Frances with the help of her close friend Mrs. Anne Turner. History leaves no doubt as to the guilt of the two women, for eventually all who had assisted them confessed freely. Mrs. Turner, a dressmaker who had introduced the fashion of the yellow ruff and cuffs into the court (a fashion that James despised), was sentenced to be hung. Lady Frances was also sentenced to death, but her sentence was commuted by James and after a term of imprisonment she was pardoned. The author of *Hic Mulier* links the crime of these two women with their mode of dress. James insisted that Mrs. Turner, "the one cut from the Commonwealth at the Gallows," go to her death wearing a dress, cuffs, and a ruff that had been starched with yellow; although Lady Frances may not have worn all the masculine fashions attributed to her by the author, we know from a famous portrait in the National Gallery that she wore ruffs with extremely low-cut, revealing gowns.
4. Long outer petticoats.
5. Plaited, knee-length, open skirts.

he presented women as they should be, but Euripides, women as they were.[6]

[These "Mermaids or rather Mer-Monsters" who dress bizarrely in men's fashions probably never practiced "comeliness or modesty." Although they may associate with or be related to persons of gentle birth, they themselves are "but rags of Gentry,[7] torn from better pieces for their foul stains." Some are not even descended from gentry but are rather "the stinking vapors drawn from dunghills"; these people may exist on the fringes of good society for a time, but eventually they will fall back "to the place from whence they came, and there rot and consume unpitied and unremembered."]

And questionless it is true that such were the first beginners of these last deformities, for from any purer blood would have issued a purer birth; there would have been some spark of virtue, some excuse for imitation. But this deformity hath no agreement with goodness, nor no difference against the weakest reason. It is all base, all barbarous: base, in respect it offends man in the example and God in the most unnatural use; barbarous, in that it is exorbitant from Nature and an Antithesis to kind,[8] going astray with ill-favored affectation both in attire, in speech, in manners, and, it is to be feared, in the whole courses and stories of their actions. What can be more barbarous than with the gloss of mumming Art[9] to disguise the beauty of their creations? To mould their bodies to every deformed fashion, their tongues to vile and horrible profanations, and their hands to ruffianly and uncivil actions? To have their gestures as piebald and as motley-various as their disguises, their souls fuller of infirmities than a horse or a prostitute, and their minds languishing in those infirmities? If this be not barbarous, make the rude Scythian, the untamed Moor, the naked Indian, or the wild Irish, Lords and Rulers of well-governed Cities.[1]

But rests this deformity then only in the baser, in none but such as are the beggary of desert, that have in them nothing but skittishness and peevishness, that are living graves, unwholesome Sinks, quartan Fevers for intolerable cumber,[2] and the extreme injury and wrong of

6. The author twists this reference to his own purpose, for the Greek philosopher Aristotle in his *Poetics* actually quotes Sophocles as saying that he presented men as they ought to be and Euripides, men as they were.
7. The society of Renaissance England consisted of the titled, leisured classes (the nobility and the gentry) and the commons (yeomen, husbandmen, craftsmen, etc.), who worked for their living and were not considered "wellborn." The distinction was a real and important one, though somewhat fuzzy at the dividing line between gentry and commons, and merchants and yeomen in the upper echelons of the commonalty were sometimes quite wealthy.
8. Natural disposition, nature.
9. Like actors in costume and mask.
1. Many Elizabethans considered these nationalities to be fundamentally uncivilized.
2. Destruction.

nature? Are these and none else guilty of this high Treason to God and nature?

Oh yes, a world of other—many known great, thought good, wished happy, much loved and most admired—are so foully branded with this infamy of disguise. And the marks stick so deep on their naked faces and more naked bodies that not all the painting in Rome or Fauna[3] can conceal them, but every eye discovers them almost as low as their middles.

It is an infection that emulates the plague and throws itself amongst women of all degrees, all deserts, and all ages; from the Capitol to the Cottage are some spots or swellings of this disease. Yet evermore the greater the person is, the greater is the rage of this sickness; and the more they have to support the eminence of their Fortunes, the more they bestow in the augmentation of their deformities. Not only such as will not work to get bread will find time to weave herself points[4] to truss her loose Breeches; and she that hath pawned her credit to get a Hat will sell her Smock to buy a Feather; she that hath given kisses to have her hair shorn will give her honesty to have her upper parts put into a French doublet. To conclude, she that will give her body to have her body deformed will not stick to give her soul to have her mind satisfied.

But such as are able to buy all at their own charges, they swim in the excess of these vanities and will be manlike not only from the head to the waist, but to the very foot and in every condition: man in body by attire, man in behavior by rude complement,[5] man in nature by aptness to anger, man in action by pursuing revenge, man in wearing weapons, man in using weapons, and, in brief, so much man in all things that they are neither men nor women, but just good for nothing.

[Neither great birth nor great beauty nor great wealth can save these foolish women from "one particle of disgrace." To support this point, the author includes two stanzas by the poet S. T. O.;[6] the speaker in the poem attests that he would love a virtuous woman above one of high birth, beauty, or wealth.]

Remember how your Maker made for our first Parents coats—not one coat, but a coat for the man and a coat for the woman, coats of several fashions, several forms, and for several uses—the man's coat

---

3. Probably signifies "nature" here.
4. Ties ending in metal tags.
5. Personal quality or accomplishment.
6. The stanzas are from "A Wife" by Sir Thomas Overbury, probably written in an effort to dissuade his friend Robert Carr from marrying the divorced Frances Howard (see p. 126, note 3).

fit for his labor, the woman's fit for her modesty.[7] And will you lose the model left by this great Workmaster of Heaven?

The long hair of a woman is the ornament of her sex, and bashful shamefastness her chief honor; the long hair of a man, the vizard[8] for a thievish or murderous disposition. And will you cut off that beauty to wear the other's villainy? The Vestals[9] in Rome wore comely garments of one piece from the neck to the heel; and the Swordplayers,[1] motley doublets with gaudy points. The first begot reverence; the latter, laughter. And will you lose that honor for the other's scorn? The weapon of a virtuous woman was her tears, which every good man pitied and every valiant man honored; the weapon of a cruel man is his sword, which neither Law allows nor reason defends. And will you leave the excellent shield of innocence for this deformed instrument of disgrace? Even for goodness' sake, that can ever pay her own with her own merits, look to your reputations, which are undermined with your own Follies, and do not become the idle Sisters of foolish Don Quixote,[2] to believe every vain Fable which you read or to think you may be attired like Bradamant, who was often taken for Ricardetto, her brother; that you may fight like Marfiza and win husbands with conquest; or ride astride like Claridiana and make Giants fall at your stirrups.[3] The Morals[4] will give you better meanings, which if you shun and take the gross imitations, the first will deprive you of all good society; the second, of noble affections; and the third, of all beloved modesty. You shall lose all the charms of women's natural perfections, have no presence to win respect, no beauty to enchant men's hearts, nor no bashfulness to excuse the vilest imputations.

The fairest face covered with a foul vizard begets nothing but affright or scorn, and the noblest person in an ignoble disguise attains to nothing but reproach and scandal. Away then with these disguises and foul vizards, these unnatural paintings and immodest discoveries! Keep those parts concealed from the eyes that may not be touched with the hands; let not a wandering and lascivious

---

7. In fact the passage in Genesis 3.21 does not differentiate clothing by sex: "Unto Adam also and to his wife did the Lord God make coats of skins and clothed them."
8. Mask.
9. Virgin priestesses who tended the sacred fire of the goddess Vesta in ancient Rome.
1. Probably Roman gladiators.
2. The hero of Miguel de Cervantes' satiric romance who tries to act out all the fantasies of chivalry.
3. These are heroines of romances who play masculine roles. In the romantic epic *Orlando Furioso* by the Italian poet Ariosto, Bradamant is a brave and virtuous woman who engages in feats of knighthood, and Marfiza is a pagan warrior.
4. Allegories (the author advises women to view these female figures as symbols rather than as literal role models).

thought read in an enticing Index the contents of an unchaste volume. Imitate nature, and, as she hath placed on the surface and superficies of the earth all things needful for man's sustenance and necessary use (as Herbs, Plants, Fruits, Corn and suchlike) but locked up close in the hidden caverns of the earth all things which appertain to his delight and pleasure (as gold, silver, rich Minerals, and precious Stones), so do you discover[5] unto men all things that are fit for them to understand from you (as bashfulness in your cheeks, chastity in your eyes, wisdom in your words, sweetness in your conversation, and severe modesty in the whole structure or frame of your universal composition). But for those things which belong to this wanton and lascivious delight and pleasure (as eyes wandering, lips billing, tongue enticing, bared breasts seducing, and naked arms embracing), oh, hide them, for shame hide them in the closest prisons of your strictest government! Shield them with modest and comely garments, such as are warm and wholesome, having every window closed with a strong Casement and every Loophole furnished with such strong Ordinance that no unchaste eye may come near to assail them, no lascivious tongue woo a forbidden passage, nor no profane hand touch relics so pure and religious. Guard them about with Counterscarps[6] of Innocence, Trenches of humane Reason, and impregnable walls of sacred Divinity, not with Antic disguise and Mimic fantasticalness, where every window stands open like the *Subura*,[7] and every window a Courtesan with an instrument, like so many Sirens, to enchant the weak passenger to shipwreck and destruction. Thus shall you be yourselves again and live the most excellent creatures upon earth, things past example, past all imitation.

Remember that God in your first creation did not form you of slime and earth like man, but of a more pure and refined metal, a substance much more worthy: you in whom are all the harmonies of life, the perfection of Symmetry, the true and curious consent of the most fairest colors and the wealthy Gardens which fill the world with living Plants. Do but you receive virtuous Inmates (as what Palaces are more rich to receive heavenly messengers?) and you shall draw men's souls unto you with that severe, devout, and holy adoration, that you shall never want praise, never love, never reverence.

But now methinks I hear the witty offending great Ones reply in excuse of their deformities: "What, is there no difference among women? No distinction of places, no respect of Honors, nor no regard of blood or alliance? Must but a bare pair of shears pass

---

5. Reveal.
6. The exterior slopes of a ditch. In this somewhat confused metaphor, female sexuality is compared to precious metals to be buried, shameful evils to be imprisoned, and the contents of a besieged city to be defended—all by the proper clothing.
7. A poor district abounding in prostitutes in ancient Rome.

between Noble and ignoble, between the generous spirit and the base Mechanic?[8] Shall we be all coheirs of one honor, one estate, and one habit? Oh Men, you are then too tyrannous and not only injure Nature but also break the Laws and customs of the wisest Princes. Are not Bishops known by their Miters, Princes by their Crowns, Judges by their Robes, and Knights by their spurs? But poor Women have nothing, how great soever they be, to divide themselves from the enticing shows or moving Images which do furnish most shops in the City. What is it that either the Laws have allowed to the greatest Ladies, custom found convenient, or their bloods or places challenged, which hath not been engrossed into the City with as great greediness and pretense of true title as if the surcease from the Imitation were the utter breach of their Charter everlastingly?[9]

"For this cause these Apes of the City have enticed foreign Nations to their cells and, there committing gross adultery with their Gewgaws, have brought out such unnatural conceptions[1] that the whole world is not able to make a Democritus[2] big enough to laugh at their foolish ambitions. Nay, the very Art of Painting,[3] which to the last Age shall ever be held in detestation, they have so cunningly stolen and hidden amongst their husbands' hoards of treasure that the decayed stock of Prostitution, having little other revenues, are hourly in bringing their action of Detinue[4] against them. Hence, being thus troubled with these Popinjays and loath still to march in one rank with fools and Zanies, have proceeded these disguised deformities, not to offend the eyes of goodness but to tire with ridiculous contempt the never-to-be-satisfied appetites of these gross and unmannerly intruders. Nay, look if this very last edition of disguise, this which is so full of faults, corruptions, and false quotations, this bait which the Devil hath laid to catch the souls of wanton Women, be not as frequent in the demi-Palaces of Burgers and Citizens as it is either at Masque, Triumph, Tilt-yard[5] or Playhouse. Call but to account the Tailors that are contained within the Circumference of the Walls of the City and let but their Hells[6] and their hard reckonings be justly summed together, and it will be found they have

---

8. A member of the lower classes; a manual worker.
9. Noblewomen (the "offending great Ones") defend their masculine style of dress as a response to the fact that there is no distinction of attire to separate high- and low-born women; women of the mercantile classes in the City of London constantly ape their betters' fashions and carry them to ridiculous extremes. Hence the nobility invented this style of dress to bring contempt on their lower-class imitators.
1. A sexual metaphor—their outlandish costumes are the offspring ("conceptions") of adultery with foreign styles of dress and gross imitations of court styles.
2. A fifth-century B.C. philosopher who laughed at the pretensions of his time.
3. The coloring of the face with cosmetics.
4. An action at law to recover something wrongfully detained by the defendant; in other words, prostitutes are suing these women for wrongful use of their stock in trade, cosmetics.
5. Public celebrations and tournaments especially frequented by the upper classes.
6. Containers for a tailor's discarded material.

raised more new foundations of this new disguise and metamorpho-
sized more modest old garments to this new manner of short base and
French doublet only for the use of Freeman's[7] wives and their children
in one month than hath been worn in Court, Suburbs, or Country
since the unfortunate beginning of the first devilish invention.

"Let therefore the powerful Statute of apparel[8] but lift up his
Battle-Ax and crush the offenders in pieces, so as everyone may be
known by the true badge of their blood or Fortune. And then these
Chimeras[9] of deformity will be sent back to hell and there burn to
Cinders in the flames of their own malice."

Thus, methinks, I hear the best of offenders argue, nor can I
blame a high blood to swell when it is coupled and counterchecked
with baseness and corruption. Yet this shows an anger passing near
akin to envy and alludes much to the saying of an excellent Poet:

> Women never
> Love beauty in their Sex, but envy ever.

They have Caesar's ambition and desire to be one and alone, but
yet to offend themselves to grieve others is a revenge dissonant to
Reason. And, as Euripides saith, a woman of that malicious nature is
a fierce Beast and most pernicious to the Commonwealth, for she
hath power by example to do it a world of injury.

[A woman's disposition should be gentle; her thoughts, according
to a poet cited by the author, should be "attended with remorse." In
contrast to the ideal woman, those who indulge in the new fashion
have given "a shameless liberty to every loose passion." In their
attempt to control the men who should rule them, they endanger
their personal fortunes and reputations as well as those of their families and their sex. The author includes a stanza by Edmund Spenser
from the Book of Justice of *The Faerie Queene*:

> Such is the cruelty of womenkind,
> When they have shaken off the shamefast band
> With which wise Nature did them strongly bind
> T'obey the hests[1] of man's well ruling hand,
> That then all rule and reason they withstand
> To purchase a licentious liberty.

---

7. Here the term *freeman* apparently designates a freeborn individual who is not a member
   of the gentry.
8. Laws governing what each class may or may not wear; the noblewomen claim that the
   fashion of masculine attire would disappear if dress distinctions between classes of
   women were maintained and enforced by law.
9. In Greek mythology, the chimera was a fire-breathing female monster with the head of a
   lion, the body of a goat, and a serpent for a tail.
1. Behests, commands.

But virtuous women wisely understand
That they were born to base humility,
Unless the heavens them lift to lawful sovereignty.[2]]

To you therefore that are Fathers, Husbands, or Sustainers of these new Hermaphrodites belongs the cure of this Imposture.[3] It is you that give fuel to the flames of their wild indiscretion; you add the oil which makes their stinking Lamps defile the whole house with filthy smoke, and your purses purchase these deformities at rates both dear and unreasonable. Do you but hold close your liberal hands or take strict account of the employment of the treasure you give to their necessary maintenance, and these excesses will either cease or else die smothered in the Tailor's Trunk for want of Redemption.

Seneca, speaking of liberality, will by no means allow that any man should bestow either on friend, wife, or children any treasure to be spent upon ignoble uses, for it not only robs the party of the honor of bounty and takes from the deed the name of a Benefit, but also makes him conscious and guilty of the crimes which are purchased by such a gratuity. Be, therefore, the Scholars of Seneca, and your Wives, Sisters, and Daughters will be the Coheirs of modesty.

Lycurgus[4] the law-giver made it death in one of his Statutes to bring in any new custom into his Commonwealth. Do you make it the utter loss of your favor and bounty to have brought into your Family any new fashion or disguise that might either deform Nature or be an injury to modesty. So shall shamefastness and comeliness ever live under your roof, and your Wives and Daughters, like Vines and fair Olives, ever spread with beauty round about your Tables.

The Lacedaemonians,[5] seeing that their children were better taught by examples than precepts, had hanging in their houses in fair painted tablets all the Virtues and Vices that were in those days reigning with their rewards and punishments. Oh, have you but in your houses the fashions of all attires constantly and without change held and still followed through all the parts of Christendom! Let them but see the modest Dutch, the stately Italian, the rich Spaniard, and the courtly French with the rest according to their climates, and

---

2. Book 5, canto 5, stanza 25. The stanza describes the tyranny of the Amazon queen Radigund over Artegall, the hero of the Book of Justice. As a symbol of Artegall's enslavement, Radigund forces him to wear women's clothing and to spend his time spinning and carding. The relationship causes both of them misery, for Radigund is secretly in love with Artegall but cannot bring herself "to serve the lowly vassal of her might." The last line of the stanza cited refers, of course, to Queen Elizabeth, regarded by most Elizabethan thinkers as a legitimate exception to the ideal of female submission.
3. Pride or insolence.
4. Traditional founder of the constitution of ancient Sparta.
5. Citizens of ancient Sparta.

they will blush that in a full fourth part of the world there cannot be found one piece of a Character to compare or liken with the absurdity of their Masculine Invention. Nay, they shall see that their naked Countryman, which had liberty with his Shears to cut from every Nation of the World one piece or patch to make up his garment, yet amongst them all could not find this Miscellany or mixture of deformities which, only by those which whilst they retained any spark of womanhood were both loved and admired, is loosely, indiscreetly, wantonly, and most unchastely invented.

And therefore, to knit up this imperfect Declamation, let every Female-Masculine that by her ill examples is guilty of Lust or Imitation cast off her deformities and clothe herself in the rich garments which the Poet bestows upon her in these Verses following:

> Those Virtues that in women merit praise
> Are sober shows without, chaste thoughts within,
> True Faith and due obedience to their mate,
> And of their children honest care to take.[6]

---

6. From John Harington's 1591 translation of Ariosto's *Orlando Furioso* (*Editor's note*).

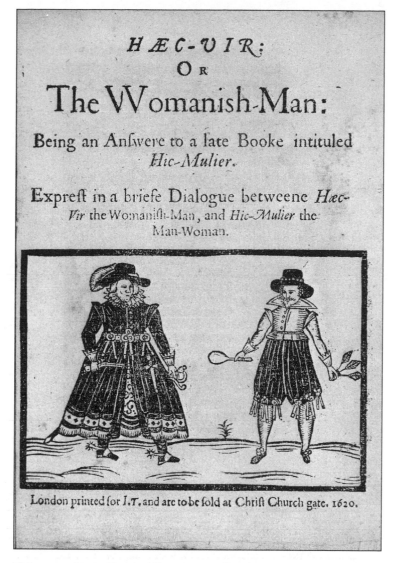

HÆC-VIR:
OR
The Womanish-Man:

Being an Anſwere to a late Booke intituled
Hic-Mulier.

Expreſt in a briefe Dialogue betweene *Hæc-Vir* the Womaniſh-Man, and *Hic-Mulier* the Man-Woman.

London printed for I.T. and are to be ſold at Chriſt Church gate. 1620.

Title page, *Haec-Vir: Or, The Womanish Man* (1620). Reproduced by permission of the Huntington Library, San Marino, California.

ANONYMOUS

Haec Vir; or, The Womanish Man:†

Being an Answer to a late Book entitled
Hic Mulier, Expressed in a briefe Dialogue between
Haec Vir, the Womanish Man, and
Hic Mulier, the Man-Woman.

HAEC VIR:[1]   Most redoubted and worthy Sir (for less than a Knight I cannot take you), you are most happily given unto mine embrace.

HIC MULIER:[2]   Is she mad or doth she mock me? Most rare and excellent Lady, I am the servant of your virtues and desire to be employed in your service.

HAEC VIR: Pity of patience, what doth he behold in me, to take me for a woman? Valiant and magnanimous Sir, I shall desire to build the Tower of my Fortune upon no stronger foundation than the benefit of your grace and favor.

HIC MULIER: Oh, proud ever to be your Servant.

HAEC VIR: No, the Servant of your Servant.

HIC MULIER: The Tithe of your friendship, good Lady, is above my merit.

HAEC VIR: You make me rich beyond expression. But fair Knight, the truth is I am a Man and desire but the obligation of your friendship.

HIC MULIER: It is ready to be sealed and delivered to your use. Yet I would have you understand I am a Woman.

HAEC VIR: Are you a Woman?

HIC MULIER: Are you a Man? O Juno Lucina,[3] help me!

HAEC VIR: Yes, I am.

HIC MULIER: Your name, most tender piece of Masculine.

HAEC VIR: Haec Vir, no stranger either in Court, City, or Country. But what is yours, most courageous counterfeit of Hercules and his Distaff?[4]

---

† From Katherine Usher Henderson and Barbara F. McManus, *Half Humankind: Contexts and Texts of the Controversy about Women in England, 1540–1640* (University of Illinois Press, 1985). Notes are by Henderson and McManus.
1. Deliberately incorrect Latin for "this man," coupling the feminine form of the adjective with the masculine noun ("this womanish man").
2. Deliberately incorrect Latin for "this woman," coupling the masculine form of the adjective with the feminine noun ("this mannish woman").
3. The Roman goddess of childbirth.
4. For one of his misdeeds, the strongman hero Hercules was condemned to serve for one year as the slave of Omphale, queen of Lydia. To humiliate him, he was dressed in women's clothes and made to sit spinning and weaving with the female slaves (a distaff is an implement used in spinning).

HIC MULIER: Near akin to your goodness, and compounded of fully as false Latin. The world calls me Hic Mulier.

HAEC VIR: What, Hic Mulier, the Man-Woman? She that like an Alarm Bell at midnight hath raised the whole Kingdom in Arms against her? Good, stand and let me take a full survey, both of thee and all thy dependents.

HIC MULIER: Do freely and, when thou hast daubed me over with the worst colors thy malice can grind, then give me leave to answer for myself, and I will say thou art an accuser just and indifferent.[5] Which done, I must entreat you to sit as many minutes that I may likewise take your picture, and then refer to censure whether[6] of our deformities is most injurious to Nature or most effeminate to good men in the notoriousness of the example.

HAEC VIR: With like condition of freedom to answer, the Articles are agreed on. Therefore, stand forth, half Birchenlane, half Saint Thomas Apostle's (the first lent thee a doublet, the latter a nether-skirt);[7] half Bridewell, half Blackfriars (the one for a scurvy Block, the other for a most profane Feather);[8] half Mulled Sack the Chimney Sweeper, half Garrat the Fool at a Tilting (the one for a Yellow Ruff, the other for a Scarf able to put a Soldier out of countenance);[9] half Bedlam, half Brimendgham (the one for a base sale Boot, the other for a beastly Leaden gilt Spur);[1] and, to conclude, all Hell, all Damnation for a shorn, powdered, borrowed Hair; a naked, lascivious, bawdy Bosom; a Leadenhall Dagger; a Highway Pistol; and a mind and behavior suitable or exceeding every repeated deformity. To be brief, I can but in those few lines delineate your proportion for the paraphrase or compartment to set out your ugliness to

5. Impartial.
6. Which.
7. Your doublet (or the fabric from which it was made) was purchased in Birchenlane (a lane in London which boasted many drapers' shops); your nether-skirt (underskirt) was purchased in the parish of St. Thomas the Apostle (an area associated with hosiers).
8. You obtained your hat in Bridewell (an area in London near the famous prison of that name) and the feather for your hat in the Blackfriars area ("block" is a pun referring both to the wood on which criminals were beheaded and the wood on which hats were formed). The insult is heightened by the fact that prostitutes were imprisoned in Bridewell.
9. The yellow ruff, an object of scorn and ridicule at the court of King James, was made popular in England by Anne Turner, who was executed in 1615 for her part in the murder of Sir Thomas Overbury. James insisted that Mrs. Turner wear her yellow ruff to the gallows. Mulled sack, a kind of hot, spiced wine, is also the title of another pamphlet purporting to answer Hic Mulier (Mulled Sack; or, The Apology of Hic Mulier to the late Declamation against her, 1620); moreover, "the sack" was a method of execution involving drowning in a sack. Garrat, while probably a real person, is also a pun on garrote, the Spanish method of capital punishment by strangulation. Thus the "Scarf able to put a Soldier out of countenance" is the garrotte—a reference both to the stick twisted to effect the execution and to the weapon carried by Hic Mulier.
1. Bedlam was an institution for the insane in London; Hic Mulier apparently bought her boots "on sale" near this asylum. This may also contain a reference to "the boot," an instrument of torture used to extract confessions. Brimendgham may possibly be Birmingham.

the greatest extent of wonder.[2] I can but refer you to your Godchild that carries your own name—I mean the Book of *Hic Mulier*. There you shall see your character and feel your shame with that palpable plainness, that no Egyptian darkness[3] can be more gross and terrible.

HIC MULIER: My most tender piece of man's flesh, leave this lightning and thunder and come roundly to the matter; draw mine accusation into heads, and then let me answer.

HAEC VIR: Then thus. In that Book you are arraigned and found guilty, first, of Baseness, in making yourself a slave to novelty and the poor invention of every weak Brain that hath but an embroidered outside; next, of unnaturalness, to forsake the Creation of God and Customs of the Kingdom to be pieced and patched up by a French Tailor, an Italian Babymaker, and a Dutch Soldier beat from the Army for the ill example of Ruffianly behavior;[4] then of Shamefulness, in casting off all modest softness and civility to run through every desert and wilderness of men's opinions like careless untamed Heifers or wild Savages; lastly, of foolishness, in having no moderation or temper[5] either in passions or affections, but turning all into perturbations and sicknesses of the soul, laugh away the preciousness of your Time and at last die with the flattering sweet malice of an incurable consumption. Thus Baseness, Unnaturalness, Shamefulness, Foolishness are the main Hatchments[6] or Coat-Armors which you have taken as rich spoils to adorn you in the deformity of your apparel; which, if you can execute, I can pity and thank Proserpina[7] for thy wit, though no good man can allow of the Reasons.

HIC MULIER: Well then, to the purpose. First, you say I am Base, in being a Slave to Novelty. What slavery can there be in freedom of election, or what baseness to crown my delights with those pleasures which are most suitable to mine affections? Bondage or Slavery is a restraint from those actions which the mind of its own accord doth most willingly desire, to perform the intents and purposes of another's disposition, and that not[8] by mansuetude or sweetness of entreaty, but by the force of authority and strength of compulsion. Now for me to follow change according to the limitation of mine

2. I will sketch the outline of your ugliness; it must remain for others to fill in the details (a "paraphrase" is an amplification of a passage or a commentary on a text).
3. In Renaissance England, comparing someone's dark complexion to that of an Egyptian was a way of calling him shamefully ugly.
4. Hic Mulier's style of attire is not only irreligious, it is also foreign; a "Babymaker" is probably a maker of dolls.
5. Restraint within due limits.
6. Panels bearing the coat of arms of a man who has recently died, displayed before his house.
7. Daughter of the goddess Demeter/Ceres, she was carried off by Hades and became queen of the underworld for part of each year.
8. Original text reads "not *but* by mansuetude."

own will and pleasure, there cannot be a greater freedom. Nor do I
in my delight of change otherwise than as the whole world doth, or
as becometh a daughter of the world to do. For what is the world but
a very shop or warehouse of change? Sometimes Winter, sometimes
Summer; day and night; they hold sometimes Riches, sometimes
Poverty; sometimes Health, sometimes Sickness; now Pleasure,
presently Anguish; now Honor, then contempt; and, to conclude,
there is nothing but change, which doth surround and mix with all
our Fortunes. And will you have poor woman such a fixed Star that
she shall not so much as move or twinkle in her own Sphere? That
were true slavery indeed and a Baseness beyound the chains of the
worst servitude! Nature to everything she hath created hath given a
singular delight in change: as to Herbs, Plants, and Trees a time to
wither and shed their leaves, a time to bud and bring forth their
leaves, and a time for their Fruits and Flowers; to worms and creep-
ing things a time to hide themselves in the pores and hollows of the
earth, and a time to come abroad and suck the dew; to Beasts liberty
to choose their food, liberty to delight in their food, and liberty to
feed and grow fat with their food; the Birds have the air to fly in, the
waters to bathe in, and the earth to feed on; but to man both these
and all things else to alter, frame, and fashion, according as his will
and delight shall rule him. Again, who will rob the eye of the variety
of objects, the ear of the delight of sounds, the nose of smells, the
tongue of tastes, and the hand of feeling? And shall only woman,
excellent woman, so much better in that she is something purer, be
only deprived of this benefit? Shall she be the Bondslave of Time,
the Handmaid of opinion, or the strict observer of every frosty or
cold benumbed imagination? It were a cruelty beyond the Rack or
Strappado.[9]

But you will say it is not Change, but Novelty, from which you
deter us, a thing that doth avert the good and erect the evil, prefer
the faithless and confound desert, that with the change of Opinions
breeds the change of States, and with continual alterations thrusts
headlong forward both Ruin and Subversion. Alas, soft Sir, what can
you christen by that new imagined Title, when the words of a wise
man are, "That what was done, is but done again; all things do
change, and under the cope of Heaven there is no new thing." So
that whatsoever we do or imitate, it is neither slavish, Base, nor a
breeder of Novelty.

Next, you condemn me of Unnaturalness in forsaking my creation
and contemning[1] custom. How do I forsake my creation, that do all
the rights and offices due to my Creation? I was created free, born

9. Instruments of torture.
1. Scorning.

free, and live free; what lets[2] me then so to spin out my time that I may die free?

To alter creation were to walk on my hands with my heels upward, to feed myself with my feet, or to forsake the sweet sound of sweet words for the hissing noise of the Serpent. But I walk with a face erect, with a body clothed, with a mind busied, and with a heart full of reasonable and devout cogitations, only offensive in attire, inasmuch as it is a Stranger to the curiosity of the present times and an enemy to Custom. Are we then bound to be the Flatterers of Time or the dependents on Custom? Oh miserable servitude, chained only to Baseness and Folly, for than custom, nothing is more absurd, nothing more foolish.

It was a custom amongst the Romans that, as we wash our hands before meals, so they with curious and sweet ointments anointed all their arms and legs quite over, and by succession of time grew from these unguents to baths of rich perfumed and compound waters in which they bathed their whole bodies, holding it the greatest disgrace that might be to use or touch any natural water, as appears by these Verses:

> She shines with ointments to make hair to fall,
> Or with sour Chalk she overcovers all.
>   (Martial[3])

It was a custom amongst the Ancients to lie upon stately and soft beds when either they delivered Embassies or entered into any serious discourse or argument, as appears by these Verses:

> Father Aeneas thus gan say,[4]
> From stately Couch whereon he lay.
>   (Virgil, *Aeneid*)

Cato Junior[5] held it for a custom never to eat meat but sitting on the ground; the Venetians kiss one another ever at the first meeting; and even at this day it is a general received custom amongst our English that when we meet or overtake any man in our travel or journeying, to examine him whither he rides, how far, to what purpose,

---

2. Hinders.
3. Martial was an ancient Roman poet known for his biting and often scurrilous epigrams. Although the Romans copiously rubbed oils on their bodies, they did frequently bathe in plain water; in fact, this line (6.93.9) appears in a poem highly critical of the hygiene of the lady in question.
4. Spoke. Virgil's *Aeneid* was the great national epic of ancient Rome; this is a translation of *Aeneid* 2.2.
5. Marcus Porcius Cato the Younger, the conservative Roman statesman of the first century B.C.

and where he lodgeth. Nay, and with that unmannerly boldness of inquisition that it is a certain ground of a most insufficient quarrel not to receive a full satisfaction of those demands which go far astray from good manners or comely civility. And will you have us to marry ourselves to these Mimic and most fantastic customs? It is a fashion or custom with us to mourn in Black; yet the Aegean and Roman Ladies ever mourned in White[6] and, if we will tie the action upon the signification of colors, I see not but we may mourn in Green, Blue, Red, or any simple color used in Heraldry. For us to salute strangers with a kiss is counted but civility, but with foreign Nations immodesty; for you to cut the hair of your upper lips, familiar here in England, everywhere else almost thought unmanly. To ride on Sidesaddles at first was counted here abominable pride, etc. I might instance in a thousand things that only Custom and not Reason hath approved. To conclude, Custom is an Idiot, and whosoever dependeth wholly upon him without the discourse of Reason will take from him his pied coat and become a slave indeed to contempt and censure.

But you say we are barbarous and shameless and cast off all softness to run wild through a wilderness of opinions. In this you express more cruelty than in all the rest. Because I stand not with my hands on my belly like a baby at Bartholomew Fair that move not my whole body when I should, but only stir my head like Jack of the Clockhouse which hath no joints;[7] that am not dumb when wantons court me, as if, Asslike, I were ready for all burdens; or because I weep not when injury grips me, like a worried Deer in the fangs of many Curs, am I therefore barbarous or shameless? He is much injurious that so baptized us. We are as freeborn as Men, have as free election and as free spirits; we are compounded of like parts and may with like liberty make benefit of our Creations. My countenance shall smile on the worthy and frown on the ignoble; I will hear the Wise and be deaf to Idiots; give counsel to my friend, but be dumb to flatterers. I have hands that shall be liberal to reward desert, feet that shall move swiftly to do good offices, and thoughts that shall ever accompany freedom and severity. If this be barbarous, let me leave the City and live with creatures of like simplicity.

To conclude, you say we are all guilty of most infinite folly and indiscretion. I confess that Discretion is the true salt which seasoneth every excellence, either in Man or Woman, and without it

---

6. Actually, black was associated with mourning in Greece and Rome, although there was no mandate or fixed period for its wearing.
7. The baby dolls sold at the stalls of Bartholomew Fair, a huge annual fair held in August in the suburbs west of London, were apparently designed with the doll's hands resting on its abdomen; they resembled Jack of the Clockhouse, a male figure which struck the bell of a clock, in that only their heads moved.

nothing is well, nothing is worthy; that want[8] disgraceth our actions, staineth our Virtues, and indeed makes us most profane and irreligious. Yet it is ever found in excess, as in too much or too little. And of which of these are we guilty? Do we wear too many clothes or too few? If too many, we should oppress Nature; if too few, we should bring sickness to Nature; but neither of these we do, for what we do wear is warm, thrifty, and wholesome. Then no excess, and so no indiscretion—where is then the error? Only in the Fashion, only in the Custom. Oh, for mercy sake, bind us not to so hateful a companion, but remember what one of our famous English poets says:

> Round-headed Custom th' apoplexy is
> Of bedrid Nature, and lives led amiss,
> And takes away all feelings of offense.
>   (G.C.[9])

Again, another as excellent in the same Art saith:

> Custom the World's Judgment doth blind so far,
> That Virtue is oft arraigned at Vice's Bar.
>   (D'Bart.[1])

And will you be so tyrannous then to compel poor Woman to be a mistress to so unfaithful a Servant? Believe it, then we must call up our Champions against you, which are Beauty and Frailty, and what the one cannot compel you to forgive, the other shall enforce you to pity or excuse. And thus myself imagining myself free of these four Imputations, I rest to be confuted by some better and graver Judgement.

[Haec Vir responds by claiming that the freedom that Hic Mulier has assumed is merely "a willful liberty to do evil." According to Divines of the Church, a woman may dress like a man only to avoid persecution, and Hic Mulier does not have this excuse. It would be better had "the first inventor of your disguise perished with all her complements about her," for her invention has caused infinite scandal and sin. To delight in sin is to yield to baseness, and to yield to baseness is foolish and barbarous. Thus, until Hic Mulier returns to traditional dress, she is base, unnatural, shameful, and foolish.]

HIC MULIER: Sir, I confess you have raised mine eyelids up, but you have not clean taken away the film that covers the sight. I feel, I confess, cause of belief and would willingly bend my heart to entertain

---

8. Lack (of discretion).
9. Probably George Chapman, a poet and playwright best known for his translations of Homer's *Iliad* and *Odyssey* into rhymed couplets.
1. Probably Guillaume DuBartas, a French religious poet admired and translated by the English in the sixteenth century.

belief, but when the accuser is guilty of as much or more than that he accuseth, or that I see you refuse the potion and are as grievously infected, blame me not then a little to stagger.[2] And till you will be pleased to be cleansed of that leprosy which I see apparent in you, give me leave to doubt whether mine infection be so contagious as your blind severity would make it.

Therefore, to take your proportion[3] in a few lines, my dear Feminine-Masculine, tell me what Charter, prescription, or right of claim you have to those things you make our absolute inheritance? Why do you curl, frizzle, and powder your hairs, bestowing more hours and time in dividing lock from lock, and hair from hair, in giving every thread his posture, and every curl his true sense and circumference, than ever Caesar did in marshalling his Army, either at Pharsalia, in Spain, or Britain? Why do you rob us of our Ruffs, of our Earrings, Carcanets,[4] and Mamillions,[5] of our Fans and Feathers, our Busks, and French bodies,[6] nay, of our Masks, Hoods, Shadows, and Shapinas?[7] Not so much as the very Art of Painting,[8] but you have so greedily engrossed it that were it not for that little fantastical sharp-pointed dagger that hangs at your chins, and the cross hilt which guards your upper lip, hardly would there be any difference between the fair Mistress and the foolish Servant. But is this theft the uttermost of our Spoil? Fie, you have gone a world further and even ravished from us our speech, our actions, sports, and recreations. Goodness leave me, if I have not heard a Man court his Mistress with the same words that Venus did Adonis, or as near as the Book could instruct him.[9] Where are the Tilts and Tourneys and lofty Galliards[1] that were danced in the days of old, when men capered in the air like wanton kids on the tops of Mountains and turned above ground as if they had been compact of Fire or a purer element? Tut, all's forsaken, all's vanished.

[Hic Mulier claims that men have stolen women's pastimes, especially shuttlecock,[2] which had been "a very Emblem of us and our

---

2. Begin to doubt or waver (probably also a reference to the pamphlet *Hic Mulier*, which accuses the masculine women of being afflicted with the disease of the staggers).
3. Form, shape.
4. Ornamental collars or necklaces usually set with gold and jewels.
5. Items of clothing that covered the breasts.
6. Corsets and whalebone bodices.
7. Various headdresses; "Shadows" projected forward to shade the face.
8. The coloring of the face with cosmetics.
9. The book is doubtless Shakespeare's *Venus and Adonis*, a popular narrative poem which had been reprinted in nine successive quartos by 1616. In this erotic Ovidian poem Venus woos the bashful Adonis with conventional feminine wiles, including sighs, tears, and considerable self-pity. The goddess of love stresses her physical charms, pointing out to Adonis that her "flesh is soft and plump" and offering to "like a fairy, trip upon the green" if he will but respond to her entreaties.
1. Lively dances in triple time for two dancers.
2. A game similar to badminton.

lighter despised fortunes." Having relinquished the arms that "would shake all Christendom with the brandish," men now languish in "softness, dullness, and effeminate niceness."] To see one of your gender either show himself in the midst of his pride or riches at a Playhouse or public assembly: how, before he dare enter, with the Jacob's Staff[3] of his own eyes and his Page's, he takes a full survey of himself from the highest sprig in his feather to the lowest spangle that shines in his Shoestring; how he prunes and picks himself like a Hawk set aweathering, calls every several garment to Auricular confession,[4] making them utter both their mortal great stains and their venial and lesser blemishes, though the mote be much less than an Atom. Then to see him pluck and tug everything into the form of the newest received fashion, and by Dürer's[5] rules make his leg answerable to his neck, his thigh proportionable with his middle, his foot with his hand, and a world of such idle, disdained foppery. To see him thus patched up with Symmetry, make himself complete and even as a circle and, lastly, cast himself amongst the eyes of the people as an object of wonder with more niceness than a Virgin goes to the sheets of her first Lover, would make patience herself mad with anger and cry with the Poet:

> O Hominum mores, O gens, O Tempora dura,
> Quantus in urbe Dolor; Quantus in Orbe Dolus![6]

Now since according to your own Inference, even by the Laws of Nature, by the rules of Religion, and the Customs of all civil Nations, it is necessary there be a distinct and special difference between Man and Woman, both in their habit and behaviors, what could we poor weak women do less (being far too weak by force to fetch back those spoils you have unjustly taken from us), than to gather up those garments you have proudly cast away and therewith to clothe both our bodies and our minds?

[Hic Mulier asserts that women adopted masculine clothing and behavior reluctantly, only to preserve "those manly things which you have forsaken." To prove that men were dressing in an effeminate manner long before women assumed masculine dress, she recites two stanzas by the Italian poet Ariosto[7] describing a bejeweled man

---

3. An instrument for measuring height and distance.
4. Confession told privately in the ear (a pun on religious confession, since "stains," "blemishes," and "mote" can refer to moral flaws as well as spots on clothing).
5. Albrecht Dürer was a painter and engraver of Renaissance Germany.
6. "O morals of men, O race, O harsh times! How much anguish in the city; how much treachery in the world!"
7. Lodovico Ariosto was an Italtan Renaissance poet best known for his long narrative poem *Orlando Furioso*.

who "was himself in nothing but in name." Because the "deformity" of the effeminate man has a longer history than that of the masculine woman, it will be more difficult to eradicate; men must return to traditional dress and behavior, however, before women can be expected to do so.]

Cast then from you our ornaments and put on your own armor; be men in shape, men in show, men in words, men in actions, men in counsel, men in example. Then will we love and serve you; then will we hear and obey you; then will we like rich Jewels hang at your ears to take our Instructions, like true friends follow you through all dangers, and like careful leeches[8] pour oil into your wounds. Then shall you find delight in our words, pleasure in our faces, faith in our hearts, chastity in our thoughts, and sweetness both in our inward and outward inclinations. Comeliness shall be then our study, fear our Armor, and modesty our practice. Then shall we be all your most excellent thoughts can desire and having nothing in us less than[9] impudence and deformity.

HAEC VIR: Enough. You have both raised mine eyelids, cleared my sight, and made my heart entertain both shame and delight in an instant—shame in my Follies past, delight in our Noble and worthy Conversion. Away then from me these light vanities, the only Ensigns of a weak and soft nature, and come you grave and solid pieces which arm a man with Fortitude and Resolution: you are too rough and stubborn for a woman's wearing. We will here change our attires, as we have changed our minds, and with our attires, our names. I will no more be Haec Vir, but Hic Vir; nor you Hic Mulier, but Haec Mulier. From henceforth deformity shall pack to Hell, and if at any time he hide himself upon the earth, yet it shall be with contempt and disgrace. He shall have no friend but Poverty, no favorer but Folly, nor no reward but shame. Henceforth we will live nobly like ourselves, ever sober, ever discreet, ever worthy: true men and true women. We will be henceforth like well-coupled Doves, full of industry, full of love. I mean not of sensual and carnal love, but heavenly and divine love, which proceeds from God, whose inexpressable nature none is able to deliver in words, since it is like his dwelling, high and beyond the reach of human apprehension, according to the saying of the Poet[1] in these Verses following:

> Of love's perfection perfectly to speak,
> Or of his nature rightly to define,
> Indeed doth far surpass our reason's reach

8. Physicians.
9. Anything in us rather than.
1. Edmund Spenser (1552–1599); the verses are adapted from *Colin Clout's Come Home Again* (*Editor's note*).

And needs his Priest t'express his power divine.
For long before the world he was yborn[2]
And bred above its highest celestial Sphere,
For by his power the world was made of yore,
And all that therein wondrous doth appear.

2. Born.

The Life of Mary Frith:
Records and Documents

Mary Frith's Appearance at the Consistory Court
January 27, 1612[†]

On the twenty-seventh day of the month of January in the year of
our Lord, according to the reckoning of the English Church, 1611,[1]
before the most reverend bishop, John Lord Bishop of London, in
his episcopal London palace, sitting judicially together with Master
Thomas Edwards, Doctor of Laws, his vicar general in spiritual matters and principal officer etc., in the presence of Master Robert
Christian, notary public.[2]

This day and place the said Mary appeared personally and then and
there voluntarily confessed that she had long frequented all or most of
the disorderly and licentious places in this city, as namely she hath
usually in the habit of a man resorted to alehouses, taverns, tobacco
shops, and also to playhouses, there to see plays and prizes,[3] and
namely being at a play about three quarters of a year since, at the Fortune, in man's apparel, and in her boots and with a sword by her side,
she told the company there present that she thought many of them
were of opinion that she was a man, but if any of them would come to
her lodging, they should find that she is a woman, and some other
immodest and lascivious speeches she also used at that time. And also
sat there upon the stage in the public view of all the people there present, in man's apparel, and played upon her lute and sang a song. And
she further confessed that she hath for this long time past usually blas-
phemed and dishonoured the name of God by swearing and cursing

---

† Mary Frith's appearance before the Bishop of London on January 27, 1612, is recorded in
   The Consistory of London Correction Book for November 1611 to October 1613 (London
   Metropolitan Archives, DL/C/310, folios 19-20). The record is transcribed by Paul A.
   Mulholland, in *"The Date of The Roaring Girl."* From *Review of English Studies* 28. 109
   (1977): 18–31, pp. 30–31. Reprinted by permission of Oxford University Press. Spelling
   and punctuation have been modernized and abbreviations have been silently expanded.
1. This is according to Old Style dating, under which the new year was taken to commence
   on March 25th.
2. In the original document, this paragraph is in Latin. The translation is Mulholland's.
3. Fencing or wrestling matches.

and by tearing God out of His kingdom if it were possible, and hath also usually associated herself with ruffianly swaggering and lewd company, as namely with cutpurses, blasphemous drunkards, and others of bad note and of most dissolute behaviour with whom she hath to the great shame of her sex often times [fallen into the detestable and hateful sin of drunkeness][4] (as she said) drunk hard and distempered her head with drink. And further confesseth that since she was punished for the misdemeanours aforementioned in Bridewell she was since upon Christmas day at night taken in Paul's church with her petticoat tucked up about her in the fashion of a man, with a man's cloak on her, to the great scandal of diverse[5] persons who understood the same, and to the disgrace of all womanhood. [And she confesseth that she is commonly termed Moll Cutpurse for her cutting of purses.] And she sayeth and protesteth that she is heartily sorry for her foresaid licentious and dissolute life and giveth her earnest promise to carry and behave herself ever from hence forward honestly, soberly, and womanly, and resteth ready to undergo any censure or punishment for her misdemeanours aforesaid in such manner and form as shall be assigned to her by the Lord Bishop of London, her Ordinary.[6] And then she being pressed to declare whether she had not been dishonest of her body and hath not also drawn other women to lewdness by her persuasions and by carrying herself like a bawd,[7] she absolutely denied that she was chargeable with either of these imputations. And thereupon his Lordship thought fit to remand her to Bridewell from whence she now came until he might further examine the truth of the misdemeanours enforced against her[8] without laying as yet any further censure upon her.

Mary Frith's Appearance at the Court of Star Chamber, June 4, 1621[†]

On June 4, 1621, Mary Frith appeared in the Court of Star Chamber as a defendant in a lawsuit brought against her by a couple named Richard and Margaret Dell. One Henry Killigrew had had his pocket picked by a woman during an anonymous nocturnal sexual encounter in the streets of London; like the knight mentioned in act

4. Bracketed lines in original document are crossed out but legible.
5. Several. *Paul's church*: St. Paul's cathedral, a popular meeting place.
6. Judge; *honestly*: chastely.
7. Pimp; *dishonest*: unchaste.
8. Of which she was accused.
† From Margaret Dowling, "A Note on Moll Cutpurse—'The Roaring Girl'" *Review of English Studies* 10 (1934): 67–71, 69–70. Reprinted by permission of Oxford University Press. Spelling and punctuation have been modernized and abbreviations have been silently expanded.

5, scene 1, lines 286–88 of *The Roaring Girl*, he turned to Frith for help. Once Killigrew had shown Frith where the pickpocket lived, Margaret Dell was arrested and brought to Frith' house, where she was held for Killigrew to identify her. These proceedings infuriated Richard Dell, who demanded that his wife be removed from the house of such a "notorious infamous person, and such a one as was well known and acquainted with all thieves and cutpurses." Frith, according to Dell, retorted that she had a royal commission to examine such offenders. Nonetheless, Dell prosecuted her, Killigrew, and others involved in Margaret's arrest, for wrongful imprisonment. The suit appears to have been dropped before a verdict was reached. The records of this case can be found in the National Archives, STAC 8/124/4.

The said defendant for plea unto the said bill of complaint[1] saith that true it is that Henry Killigrew, in the bill of complaint mentioned, came unto this defendant and told her how a woman had met with him the night before in the street, and asked him if he would give her a quart or a pint of wine, and he consenting, they went down Blackhorse alley and there as they went, he proffering her some kindness, she showed him a window and said she durst[2] not stay there where they were because that was her husband's lodging, but she would go with him some other where further off, which they did, and at last staying in another place and growing more private, whilst he was in private familiarity with her she privily took forth of his pocket certain pieces of gold and some seals and other things, and suddenly, as he was trussing his points,[3] she was gone, and he, putting his hand in his pocket and finding his gold and other things gone, the next day became[4] to this defendant and desired her to do her endeavour to try if she could by any means find out the pickpocket or help him to his money, he being before of this defendant's acquaintance and having heard how by this defendant's means many that had had their purses cut or goods stolen had been helped to their goods again, and divers[5] of the offenders taken or discovered. And the said Henry Killigrew then described the woman and showed unto this defendant and others the window where she said her husband lodged, which was in truth the window of the complainant[6] then lodging (as this defendant hath been more certainly informed),

---

1. In answer to the charges against her (the "bill of complaint" would be filed by the plaintiff), *defendant*: i.e., Mary Frith.
2. Dared; *proffering . . . kindness*: making sexual advances to her.
3. Refastening the tags attaching his hose to his doublet; *private*: intimate; *privily*: secretly; *seals*: small embossed metal stamps used to imprint sealing wax.
4. Came.
5. Several.
6. Plaintiff, i.e., Richard Dell.

and he told also of some other private mark whereby she might be, as he thought, discovered, and thereupon the warrant[7] in the bill of complaint mentioned was, as this defendant thinketh, procured, and by the descriptions, the complainant's wife being a well-known woman, and her conversation not to be so absolute good as her[8] pretendeth in his bill, she was strongly suspected to be the woman who had so picked the said Henry Killigrew's pocket, and not long after the constable, as this defendant was informed, did by virtue of the said warrant apprehend her and then brought her to this defendant and left her in this defendant's lodging for some time until the said Henry Killigrew, being sent for to see her whether she were the woman that picked his pocket as aforesaid, came and he seeing her confidently affirmed that he thought her to be the woman, and thereupon the said constable then carried her before Sir Thomas Bennett in the bill mentioned, as this defendant thinketh, but this defendant meddled no further with her. But it may be that this defendant might and did give them some reply in some tart or angry manner again, which being all that this defendant hath done without any unlawful plot, practice, confederacy, or conspiracy, this defendant doth humbly demand and pray the judgment of this noble court whether she shall be to make any other or further answer to the said bill, and humbly prayeth to be hence dismissed with her costs and charges in this behalf wrongfully sustained.

Last Will and Testament of Mary Frith, June 6, 1659[†]

In the name of God, Amen.

I, Mary Markham, alias Frith, of the parish of St. Bride, alias Bridget, in Fleet street, London, Widow,[1] being aged and sick and weak in body, but of good mind and memory and understanding, for all which I do most humbly thank my most gracious and merciful Creator, for the quieting of my mind and the settling of the small part and remainder of that mean[2] estate which it hath pleased God of his great mercy and goodness to lend to me in this world of sorrows, do make this my last will and testament in manner and form following. (That is to say,) First, I do give and bequeath my soul into the hands of my most

---

7. I.e., for Margaret Dell's arrest.
8. She; *conversation*: behavior.
† A transcript of Mary Frith's last will and testament, which she signed on June 6, 1659, is held in the National Archives in London (PROB 11/299, pp. 106–107). Spelling and punctuation have been modernized, and abbrevations have been expanded.
1. On Frith's marriage, see Introduction, pp. x–xi; *alias*: also called; "alias" does not have its modern connotations of a false name.
2. Small, poor.

gracious Creator, who by his only power breathes the breath of life into me, hoping and confidently believing that all my manifold and grievous sins are and shall be freely pardoned and washed away in, by, and through the shedding and pouring out of the most precious blood and the bitter sufferings and passion of my most blessed redeemer and saviour, Jesus Christ, and that after this transitory and mortal life is ended, my soul and body shall be reunited and enjoy everlasting bliss and felicity with him in his heavenly kingdom for ever and ever, Amen. My body I leave unto the earth, whence it came, to be decently buried in Christian burial within the parish church or churchyard of St. Bride's aforesaid in such sort and manner as my executrix hereafter named in her discretion shall think most fitting.

Item, I give unto my kinsman Abraham Robinson twenty pounds of lawful money of England. And I give unto James Robinson, father of the said Abraham, twelve pence. All the rest and remainder of my personal estate whatsoever, my just debts by me owing and my legacies in this my will given and bequeathed, being first paid and discharged, I fully and wholly give and bequeath the same unto my niece and kinswoman Frances Edmonds, wife of George Edmonds, with my will and desires that they shall be and remain unto her own sole use, benefit, and behoof so long as she liveth. And I do make the said Frances Edmonds sole executrix of this my last will and testament.

In witness whereof I, the said Mary Markham, alias Frith, have hereunto set my hand and seal the sixth day of June in the year of our Lord God one thousand six hundred fifty nine. The mark[2] of Mary Markham, alias Frith, subscribed, sealed, and published by her the said Mary Markham, alias Frith, as and for her last will and testament in the presence of us, Richard Hulet, Ralph Warfeild, Abraham Robinson.

This will was proved at London before the Right Worshipful William Metcalf, Doctor of Laws, Master Keeper or Commissary of the Prerogative Court of Canterbury[4] lawfully constituted the four and twentieth day of July in the year of our Lord God according to the computation of the Church of England one thousand six hundred and sixty. By the oath of Frances Edmonds, the sole executrix named in the said will, to whom admin. of all and singular the goods, chattels, and debts of the said deceased was granted and committed, she being first sworn truly to administer the same according to the tenor and effect of the said will.

---

2. A person who was illiterate or semi-literate (able to read but not write) would have signed documents with an X or perhaps with her initials. The original will being lost, we do not know what Mary Frith's "mark" looked like.
3. Until 1858, the court which dealt with the probate of wills for southern England and Wales.

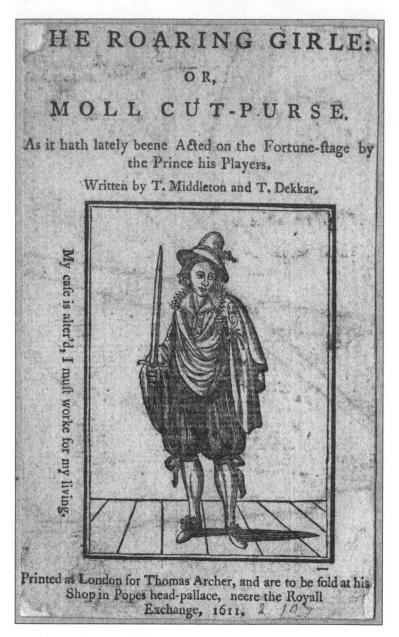

HE ROARING GIRLE:

OR,

MOLL CUT-PURSE.

As it hath lately beene Acted on the Fortune-stage by
the Prince his Players.

Written by T. Middleton and T. Dekkar.

My cafe is alter'd, I muft worke for my living.

Printed at London for Thomas Archer, and are to be fold at his
Shop in Popes head-pallace, neere the Royall
Exchange, 1611.

Variant title page. © National Portrait Gallery, London.

Moll Cutpurse in the Popular Imagination

NATHAN FIELD

Nathan Field's *Amends for Ladies* (c. 1611) staged a virtuous maid, wife, and widow—plus a cameo appearance by Moll Cutpurse—to make "amends" for his earlier satirical depictions of women in *A Woman is a Weather-cock* (c. 1609). *Amends* was first published in 1618 under the title *Amends for Ladies, With the Humour of Roaring*, the subtitle alluding to a subplot in which a cowardly gentleman gets drunk and learns to brawl like a "roaring boy." When reprinted in 1639, the play was titled *Amends for Ladies, With the Merry Prankes of Moll Cut-Purse, Or, the Humour of Roaring: A Comedy full of Honest Mirth and Wit.* The new title, which may confuse Moll's brief appearance with the roaring scenes, suggests that Moll in 1639 was a popular enough figure for a publisher to hope that advertising her "merry pranks" might help bring new readers to an old play. The shopkeeper Seldome and his wife Grace are minor characters who function primarily as examples of a trusting husband and virtuous wife, foils for the jealous husband and virtuous wife featured in one of the three main plots.

From Amends for Ladies†

ACT TWO, SCENE ONE

Enter SELDOME *[and] his wife* [GRACE] *working as*[1] *in their shop.*

GRACE: Husband, these gloves are not fit[2] for my wearing. I'll put 'em into the shop and sell 'em; you shall give me a plain pair for[3] them.

---

† *Amends for Ladies*, STC # 10851, is held at the British Library and is accessible through Early English Books Online. Spelling and punctuation have been modernized.
1. As if.
2. Suitable.
3. In exchange for.

SELDOME: This is wonderful, wonderful! This is thy sweet care and judgment in all things; this goodness is not usual in our wives. Well, Grace Seldome, that thou art fair is nothing, that thou art well-spoken is nothing, that thou art witty is nothing, that thou art a citizen's wife is nothing; but Grace, that thou art fair, that thou art well-spoken, that thou art witty, that thou art a citizen's wife, and that thou art honest,[4] I say, and let any man deny it that can, it is something, it is something, I say, it is Seldome's something, and for all the sunshine of my joy, mine eyes must rain upon thee.

Enter MOLL *with a letter.*

MOLL: By your leave, Master Seldome, have you done the hangers I bespake[5] for the Knight?

SELDOME: Yes, marry, have I, Mistress hic and haec,[6] I'll fetch 'em to you.

Exit [SELDOME].

MOLL: 'Zounds,[7] does not your husband know my name? If it had been somebody else, I would have called him cuckoldly[8] slave.

GRACE: If it had been somebody else, perhaps you might.

MOLL: Well, I may be even with him. All's clear[9]. Pretty rogue[1], I have longed to know thee this twelve months, and had no other means but this to speak with thee. There's a letter to thee from the party.

GRACE: What party?

MOLL: The knight, Sir John Lovall.

GRACE: Hence, lewd impudent
I know not what to term thee, man or woman,
For nature, shaming[2] to acknowledge thee
For either, hath produced thee to the world
Without a sex. Some say thou art a woman,
Others, a man; and many thou art both
Woman and man, but I think rather neither,
Or man and horse, as the old centaurs were feigned.[3]

MOLL: Why how now, Mistress What-Lack-Ye?[4] Are you so fine, with a pox?[5] I have seen a woman look as modestly as you, and speak

4. Chaste; *citizen's*: a London craftsman's or tradesman's.
5. Custom ordered; *By your leave*: a polite expression, "If I may"; *hangers*: straps to attach a sword to a belt.
6. "Hic" is the masculine form of "this" in Latin; "haec" is the feminine: "Mistress He and She"; *Marry*: by the Virgin Mary (a mild oath).
7. God's wounds (an oath).
8. A cuckold is a husband whose wife has cheated on him.
9. The coast is clear (for Moll to speak to Grace alone).
1. A term of endearment.
2. Ashamed.
3. As centaurs (creatures with the head and torso of a man and the body of a horse) were depicted in mythology.
4. "What lack ye?" ("what do you need?") was the typical cry of a shopkeeper; Moll is insulting Grace's social status.
5. An insult; "the pox" was syphilis.

as sincerely, and follow the Friars as zealously, and she has been
as sound a jumbler as e're paid for't.[6] 'Tis true, Mistress Fipenie;[7]
I have sworn to leave this letter.

GRACE: D'ye hear, you sword and target[8] (to speak in
your own key), Marie Umbree, Long-Meg,[9]
Thou that in thy self (me think'st) alone
Look'st like a rogue and a whore under a hedge:
Bawd[1], take your letter with you and begone,
When next you come (my husband's constable)
And Bridewell is hard by;[2] y'have a good wit,
And can conceive.[3]

Enter SELDOME *with hangers.*

SELDOME: Look you, here are the hangers.
MOLL: Let's see them.
Fie, fie, you have mistook[4] me quite,
They are not for my turn[5] (bye, Mistress Seldome).

Exit [MOLL].

THOMAS DEKKER

Written shortly after *The Roaring Girl*, Thomas Dekker's *If This Be Not
A Good Play, The Devil Is In It* (1612) alludes to Moll's stint as a prisoner
in Bridewell, which she served as punishment for her performance at
the Fortune. *If This Be Not A Good Play* is a didactic comedy about three
devils—Rufman, Shacklesoul, and Lurchall—who are sent to earth to
recruit more souls for Hell, as Charon, Hell's ferryman, is threatening to
quit for lack of wealthy customers. The excerpt below is from the final
scene, where the devils and Pluto (standing in for Satan) celebrate their
success and the arrival in Hell of the newly damned souls.

6. As complete a strumpet as ever got what she deserved; *the Friars*: Puritans living in the
   Blackfriars neighborhood of London.
7. Fivepence, or perhaps a misprint for "fripcric" (a second-hand clothes shop); either one is
   another gibe at Grace's status as a shopkeeper.
8. Shield.
9. Mary Ambree and Long Meg of Westminster, women of English history and folklore
   famed for their masculine exploits.
1. Pimp.
2. Bridewell (a prison for prostitutes, vagrants, and other petty criminals) is nearby; *my husband's constable*: my husband is a constable.
3. Understand what I mean.
4. Misunderstood.
5. They are not what I wanted.

From If This Be Not A Good Play, The Devil Is In It[†]

PLUTO   Fetch whips of poisoned steel, strung with glowing wires,
And lash these saucy hell-hounds: duck their souls
Nine times to the bottom of our brimstone lakes,
From whence up pull them by their singéd hair,
Then hang 'em in ropes of ice nine times frozen o'er.
Are they scarce hot in hell, and must they roar?
What holiday's this, that here's such grinning, ha?
Is hell a dancing school? Y'are in extremes:
Snoring, or else horn-mad?[1] Who are set on shore,
On this vast land of horror, that it resounds
With laughter 'stead of shrieks? Who are come to our bounds, ha?

RUFMAN   Dread Lord of this lower tartary, to thy jail
Have we thy busy catch-poles (prisoners) brought
Souls,[2] for whose coming all hell long hath sought.

PLUTO   Their names? Is Ward and Dantziker[3] then come?

OMNES   Yes, Dantziker is come.

PLUTO   Where's the Dutch Schellum?[4] Where's hell's factor,[5] ha?

RUFMAN   Charon has bound him for a thousand years
To tug at's oar;[6] he scoured the seas so well,
Charon will make him ferryman of hell.

PLUTO   Where's Ward?

RUFMAN   The merchants are not pilled nor pulled[7] enough;
They are yet but shaven. When they are flayed, he'll come
And bring to hell fat booties[8] of rich thieves,
A crew of swearers and drinkers, the best that lives.

OMNES   Ward is not ripe for damning yet.

PLUTO   Who is it then?
Cutlar the Sergeant,[9] ha? He come?

RUFMAN   Yes, Pluto.
Cutlar has been here long, sent in by a carman,
But his stern looks the fiends did so displease,
Bound hand and foot, he howls in little ease,

---

† *If This Be Not a Good Play, The Devil Is In It*, STC # 6507, is held at the British Library
and is accessible through Early English Books Online.
1. I.e., you go from one extreme to another: if you're not asleep, you're acting like lunatics.
2. I.e., have brought souls as prisoners; *tartary*: Tartarus, the underworld of Greek and
Roman mythology; *catch-poles*: slang for officers who arrest debtors or other criminals.
3. John Ward and Simon Danziker, famous pirates. The death of Danziker, a Dutchman, was
reported in January 1611; Ward, an Englishman, lived on until at least 1615.
4. Scoundrel (Dutch).
5. An agent who supplies goods to a merchant; while alive, Dantziker supplied Hell with the
souls of his victims.
6. I.e., Charon (the ferryman in Greek and Roman mythology who rows souls across the
river Styx to the underworld) has made Dantziker enter into a thousand-year contract to
be his apprentice; "bound" also suggests "bound in chains," like a prisoner sentenced to
row in the galleys.
7. Stripped clean (literally, of skin and hair; figuratively, of money).
8. I.e., Ward will bring "rich thieves" (his crew of pirates) to hell with him as "booty," or
plunder.
9. An arresting officer; a "catch-pole."

Having only mace[1] to comfort him: he does yell
And rave because he cannot rest in hell.
SHACKLESOUL   'Tis not for him that we this holiday hold.
PLUTO   The bawd of Shoreditch,[2] is that hellcat come?
RUFMAN   No, but she's been a long time launching forth
In a Rosa-Solis bark.[3]
PLUTO   Devils! Who is it then?
Moll Cutpurse: is she come?
OMNES   Our cousin come? No.
SHACKLESOUL   Tis not yet fit Moll Cutpurse here should howl.
She has been too late a sore-tormented soul.
PLUTO   Where is our daughter, ha? Is she idle?
OMNES   No.
She was beating hemp in Bridewell to choke thieves,
Therefore to spare this she-ramp she beseeches,
Till, like herself, all women wear the breeches.[4]
LURCHALL   Moll Cutpurse plies her task and cannot come.
PLUTO   For whom then is this wild Shrove-Tuesday[5] kept?
RUFMAN   See, King of gloomy shades, what souls resort
To this thy most just and least-fying[6] court.
PLUTO   Stay: since our jail is with brave fellows stored,
Bid Charon that no more yet come aboard.

THOMAS FREEMAN

Thomas Freeman's *Rub, and a Great Cast* (1614) is a collection of 200 epigrams, some in tribute to contemporary writers such as Edmund Spenser, Shakespeare, and John Donne, but most satirizing figures who have now faded into obscurity, or simply skewering contemporary vices. The peculiar title comes from the game of bowls (lawn bowling): a "rub" is an impediment in the course of the ball, and a "cast" is one's throw. "Rub and a good cast" was thus a proverb equivalent to "slow and steady wins the race" or "haste makes waste." As the *Oxford English Dictionary*'s earliest recorded use of "cast" in its theatrical sense dates from 1631, it is possible that the title puns on the "Great Cast" of characters assembled in the epigrams.

1. a) the fragrant rind of a nutmeg; b) the club carried by a sergeant; *carman*: cart-driver; *little ease*: a cramped prison cell.
2. A London neighborhood known for its taverns and brothels; *bawd*: pimp, usually female.
3. A boat made out of "Rosa Solis," a liqueur. The bawd is slowly drinking herself to death.
4. I.e. Moll beseeches that she be spared from hell until all women wear breeches like she does; *beating hemp . . . choke thieves*: manual labor performed by prisoners in Bridewell, a house of correction for prostitutes, vagrants, and other petty offenders; hemp was used to make rope, which would hang ("choke") thieves; *she-ramp*: a tomboy.
5. The day before Ash Wednesday, the start of Lent; an occasion for feasting and disorderly behavior.
6. Perhaps, the court in which one is least likely to cry "fie!" at miscarriages of justice; *gloomy shades*: ghosts; also darkness.

From Rub, and a Great Cast[†]

Epigram 90

Of Moll Cut-purse *disguised going.*

They say Moll's honest, and it may be so,
But yet it is a shrewd[1] presumption, no?
To touch but pitch,[2] 'tis known it will defile;
Moll wears the breech, what may she be the while?
Sure she that doth the shadow so much grace,
What will she when the substance comes in place?[3]

JOHN TAYLOR

A waterman by trade, John Taylor (known as "the water-poet") was also a prolific author in a wide variety of genres, from nonsense verse to travel narratives. *The water-cormorant his complaint against a brood of land-cormorants: divided into fourteen satires* (1622) includes verse sketches of a drunkard, an extortioner, a lawyer, a Jesuit, and other traditional targets of Jacobean satire as well as the "prodigal country gallant" of the excerpt below. As Taylor explains in a preface, the cormorant (a voracious sea-bird) is a fit metaphor for both the satirist himself ("His colour is black, I discover deeds of darkness") and for the insatiable appetites of his satiric targets.

From The Water-Cormorant[†]

From *A Prodigal Country Gallant and his new made Madam*

His father (a good house-keeper) being dead
He scorns his honest block[1] should fit his head,
And though he be not skilled in magic art,

---

†   *Rub, and a Great Cast*, STC # 11370, is held at the Huntington Library and is accessible through Early English Books Online.
1. Difficult, troublesome; *honest*: chaste.
2. Tar.
3. I.e., If Moll is so fond of breeches (the "shadow" or image of a man), what will she do when an actual man ("the substance") appears?
†   *The Water-Cormorant*, STC # 23813, is held at the Bodleian Library and is accessible through Early English Books Online. Spelling and punctuation have been modernized.
1. Literally, the style of a hat; the son scorns to follow in his father's footsteps; *good house-keeper*: generous host and charitable landlord.

Yet to a coach he turned his father's cart,
Four teams of horses, to four Flanders mares,
With which to London he in pomp repairs,
Woos a she-gallant,[2] and to wife he takes her,
Then buys a knighthood, and a madam makes her,
And yearly they upon their backs o'er wear
That which oft fed five hundred with good cheer,
Whilst in the country all good bounty's spilt.[3]
His house, as if a juggler it had built,
For all the chimneys, where great fires were made,
The smoke at one hole only is conveyed.
No times observed, nor charitable laws,
The poor receive their answer from the daws,[4]
Who in their cawing language call it plain
Mockbeggar Manor, for they came in vain.
They that devour what charity should give
Are both at London, there the Cormorants live,
But so transformed of late, do what you can,
You'll hardly know the woman from the man.
There Sir Tim Twirlepipe and his Lady Gay,[5]
Do prodigally spend the time away,
Being both exceeding proud and scornful too,
And anything but what is good they'll do.
For incubus and succubus[6] have got
A crew of fiends, which the old world knew not:
That if our grandfathers and grand-dams should
Rise from the dead, and these mad times behold,
Amazéd they (half madly) would admire
At our fantastic[7] gestures and attire;
And they would think that England in conclusion
Were a mere babble Babel[8] of confusion,
That a Muld-sack[9] for his unfashioned fashions

2. fashionable young woman.
3. Spoiled.
4. Jackdaws; times: festival times, when the poor customarily would receive handouts from
   their landlord.
5. I.e., the newly knighted gallant and his wife.
6. I.e., the gallant and his wife. An incubus is a demon believed to prey sexually on women;
   a succubus is his female counterpart, who preys on men.
7. Bizarre; grand-dams: grandmothers; admire: wonder.
8. According to Genesis 11:1–9, the place where God split the common language of
   humankind into numerous mutually incomprehensible languages.
9. Nickname of a flamboyantly dressed chimney-sweeper, thief, and would-be gallant named
   John Cottington, hanged in 1659. Muld Sack, or The Apologie of Hic Mulier is also
   the title of a 1620 pamphlet responding to Hic Mulier and Haec Vir (excerpted on
   pp. 123–46). Purporting, like Haec Vir, to be the Hic Mulier figure's own defence of her
   cross-dressing, Muld Sack cashes in on public interest in the earlier pamphlets to satirize
   an array of conventional vices, most of which have nothing to do with cross-dressing. In a
   dedication to "My professed Friend, Muld Sacke," Hic Mulier praises Muld Sack's "yellow
   bands, feathers, scarves . . . garters, roses, and other . . . feminine masculine fashions."

Is the fit pattern of their transformations,
And Mary Frith doth teach them modesty,
For she doth keep one fashion constantly,
And therefore she deserves a matron's praise,
In these inconstant moon-like changing days.

JEAN RIOLAN

Encheiridium Anatomicum et Pathologicum (1648), an anatomical treatise by the French doctor Jean Riolan, was translated from Latin into
English and published in 1657 as *A sure guide, or, The best and nearest
way to physick and chyrurgery*. Its translator, the English physician and
astrologer Nicholas Culpeper, was evidently reminded of Moll Cutpurse
when he translated the section describing the thigh muscles, for he
added her name to what was, in the Latin original, a nameless "muliere
robustissima Viragine" ("very stout virago"). In *The Roaring Girl*, Moll's
muscular thighs are made much of in the scene where she is measured
for breeches (2.2.75–102).

From A sure guide, or, The best and nearest way to physick, and chyrurgery[†]

Translated by Nicholas Culpeper

I have in men oftimes found a little muscle spread over this [the
main thigh muscle, or *psoas*], which in its original, being of the
length and thickness of a man's little finger, and fleshy, with a small
and flat tendon, is carried above the *psoas*, and when it comes to the
iliac, it looses itself into a broad and very strong *aponeurosis*,[1] which
firmly combines the *iliac* and *psoas* muscles. And therefore I conceive it is added, in strong men, that it might straitly embrace the
psoas and hold it firmly in its seat.

It is called the *parvus psoas*, and is more rarely found in women
than in men: howbeit in the year 1631, in a very stout virago[2] or kind
of Moll Cut-Purse, it was my hap to see one of these muscles, she
having been hanged for robberies and murders by her committed.

---

† *A sure guide*, Wing R1525, is held at Cambridge Univerity Library and is accessible
through Early English Books Online.
1. A membrane sheathing a muscle or connecting a muscle to a tendon.
2. Robust, masculine woman.

ANONYMOUS

Published in 1662, about three years after Frith's death, *The Life and Death of Mrs. Mary Frith* consists of three parts: first, a brief preface titled "To the Reader"; second, a longer introduction describing Moll's early years and her general characteristics; and third, the bulk of the document, written in the first person and labelled "Moll Cutpurse's Diary." Scholars have debated how much, if any of it, was in fact written or dictated by Frith herself; fact mixes with folklore and pure invention, and the text's status as any kind of authoritative biography, let alone autobiography, is highly dubious (for further discussion, see the Introduction, p. xi). Oddly enough, there is no reference in *The Life and Death* to *The Roaring Girl*, although Moll's immortalization on the stage would seem to be at least as noteworthy as some of the other events recounted. The first excerpt below is from the introduction; the remainder is from "Moll Cutpurse's Diary."

From The Life and Death of Mrs. Mary Frith[†]

The Life and Death of Mistress Mary Frith, *alias Moll Cutpurse*

To write this woman's history (a task for the clerk of Newgate, if he had no worser thing to do) many strong and sufficient reasons and impulses there are, and those partly from the strangeness and newness of the subject, and her unparalleled practices and courses, and manner of life and livelihood (which in their time were the talk and discourse of the town, and therefore may not be unworthy of a reducing them to memory), and partly out of a pleasant officiousness to the public good, which has been advantaged (according to information) by such kind of essays.

Equally distant it is from the purport and intent of this piece to favor her ashes, or to rake her in her grave, but as she lived in a kind of mean betwixt open, professed dishonesty and fair and civil deportment, being an hermaphrodite in manners as well as in habit, with the same indifferency shall she be used here, by avoiding all partiality.

She was indeed a perfect *ambidexter*,[1] being mistress of that thriving art: no doubt Mercury was lord of the ascendant at her birth, and with his influences did so endow her that from her very cradle she gave signs of a very towardly and pregnant wench, manifested by

---

† From *The Life and Death of Mrs. Mary Frith*, ed. Randall S. Nakayama (New York: Garland, 1993). Reprinted by permission. Footnotes are Nakayama's and have been renumbered and edited.
1. One able to use both hands; hence, a double dealer.

Frontispiece, *The Life and Death of Mrs. Mary Frith, Commonly Called Moll Cut-purse* (1662). © National Portrait Galley, London.

several petty strategems and designs as oft as occasion and opportunity presented, at her neighbors' as well as at home.

She was born *Anno Domini* 1589,[2] in Barbican, at the upper end of Aldersgate street (a very ancient street, and probably of as ancient a house, and from thence she may challenge gentility). This place was formerly a defense or bulwark of the city, such rampires[3] and fortifications in our ancestors' days being called barbicans. It is since a magazine,[4] but of pawns[5] altogether, being a brokery,[6] which made her extraction so well suit with her condition of life afterward. Plants and trees do relish in their fruit of the ground and earth they grow in, as we see in wines and tobacco, and our Moll had a very great smack and tincture (which lasted throughout the whole course of her life) of that most laudable quality and profession exercised in the place of her nativity; though to give her her due she was not altogether so unconscionable and cruel as those vultures, harpies and wolves which follow that trade; and it is wonder they are allowed to have any other signs, and that in order thereunto it is not publicly decreed. But some few honest men, and rare they are, keep off that brand from the other. But this has another place herein, where it will be properly resumed.

I do not find that any remarkable thing happened at her nativity, such as the flattering soothsayers pretend in eclipses and other the like motions above, or tides, and whales, and great fires, adjusted and timed to the genitures of great statesmen: though for a she-politic, she be not much inferior to Pope Joan;[7] for she was in her time the great cabal and oracle of the mystery of diving into pockets, and was very well read and skilled in the affairs of the placket[8] too among the great ones. There being no such notable accidents falling out then as aforesaid, I cannot ascertain the week nor month of her nativity.

She was born of honest parentage, her father being by his trade a shoemaker living in good esteem and repute in the world and in love and friendly familiarity with his neighbors, a fair and square conditioned man, that loved a good fellow next to himself, which made his issue be so sociable: we do not here dispute the company, for she kept all sorts.

Both of her parents were very tender of this daughter, but especially the mother, according to the tenderness of that sex, which is

---

2. The correct date must be 1584 or 1585, since she died in 1659 and gives her age as 74, threescore and fourteen (p. 181).
3. Ramparts.
4. Business district.
5. The term means both shops and pawnshops.
6. District of second-hand dealers.
7. Legendary female transvestite pope.
8. Petticoat, slang for a prostitute.

naturally more indulgent than the male; most affectionate she was to her in her infancy, most careful of her in her youth, manifested especially in her education, which was the stricter and diligentlier attended by reason of her boisterous and masculine spirit, which then showed itself, and soon after became predominant above all breeding and instruction.

A very tomrig or rumpscuttle[9] she was, and delighted and sported only in boys' play and pastime, not minding or companying with the girls: many a bang and blow this hoiting[1] procured her, but she was not so to be tamed or taken off from her rude inclinations; she could not endure that sedentary life of sewing or stitching; a sampler was as grievous as a winding-sheet; her needle, bodkin and thimble she could not think on quietly, wishing them changed into sword and dagger for a bout at cudgels. For any such exercise, who but she! Where she would not fail, tide what would, if she heard of any such thing, to be a busy spectator; so that she was very well known by most of the rougher sort of people thereabouts when she was yet very young and little.

Her headgear and handkerchief (or what the fashion of those times were for girls to be dressed in) was alike tedious to her, wearing them as handsomely as a dog would a doublet, and so cleanly that the driven pothooks would have blushed at the comparison,[2] and always standing the Bear Garden way, or some other rabble-rout assemblies.

This perplexed her friends, who had only this proverb favorable to their hope, that *an unhappy girl may make a good woman*; but they lived not to the length of that expectation, dying in her minority, and leaving her to the swing and sway of her own unruly temper and disposition.

She would fight with boys, and courageously beat them, run, jump, leap or hop with any of them or any other play whatsoever: in this she delighted, this was all she cared for, and had she not very young, being of a pregnant docible wit, been taught to read perfectly, she might well through her over addicition to this loose and licentious sporting have forgot and blotted out any easy impression. But this learning stood her much in stead afterwards.

She had an uncle, brother to her father, who was a minister, and of him she stood in some awe, but not so powerful as to restrain her in these courses; so that seeing he could not effectually remedy that inveterating evil in her manners, he resigned her to time, which

9. Both terms for tomboy.
1. 'To act the hoyden, to romp inelegantly' (*OED* 1).
2. Playing on 'pure as the driven snow': the pothooks, black and unclean, become white in comparison with Moll and blush at being likened to her.

bringing with it discretion and judgment would certainly at last reclaim her and bring her to right sense and reason.

This uncle, the parson, had a whimsy too (for I am not informed that it was out of any settled serious persuasion, or nonconformity to the church or its customs) which few of the priests have ever been troubled with; that is, he refused to take tithe of his parishioners, but received his maintenance from them under the notion of contribution; and yet a jolly fat fellow he was, and would take of his cup merrily: but it seems it ran in a blood, each of the family had his particular freak, and so had our Mary. But in her trade afterward, she would not be contented with the tithe, but commonly a full half, or such large composition; for *to give the devil his due* was one of her chief maxims, improved beyond the bare letter of a proverb.

I have thus traced her from her originals[3] to show in what proportions she differed from and approached to them, and that neither the derivations of the same blood, the assimilation and resemblance of parts, can conform the mind and the faculties thereof or endue it with the like qualities, but that there is a prevalent power of our stars which overrules all, and resists and subdues the additional and auxiliary strength and reserves of education: and this I have said to be Mercury in conjunction with, or rather in the house of, Venus at her nativity.

This planet Mercury you must know (if you have not well studied Lilly)[4] is of a thievish, cheating, deceitful influence, which is not so powerful in citizens' shops, warehouses, bargains and sales, merchandizing and bartering; nevertheless some little finger it has as with a ray to point at them, so that seldom but some cozenage or lying at the least intervenes in those affairs. In great fairs and markets this planet operates exceedingly, but it violently rages in great throngs and concourses of people at any great show, pomp or solemnity, as coronations, my Lord Mayor's Day, and the like, where it doth so whet and set such an edge on the knives and cutting instruments, so quicken and expedite their fingers, and lastly, so vigorously incite and stir up the minds of those whose genitures have relation thereunto, and with such conveyance too, that it were impossible to be done without the connivance of this star, under the position whereof Turnmill Street[5] is directly fixed.

For the other of Venus, most men and women know without teaching what are her properties. She has dominion over all whores, bawds, pimps &c., and joined with Mercury, over all trapanners[6] and

---

3. Forebears.
4. William Lilly (1602–81), astrologer.
5. Off Clerkenwell Road (E.C. 1), a notoriously dangerous neighborhood.
6. The practice of trapanning is described in the Diary. It is a form of blackmail that involves a husband 'catching' his wife having intercourse with another man; the mortified third party pays the husband to keep the affair quiet.

hectors.[7] She has indeed a more general influence than all the other
six put together, for no place nor person is exempted from it, invad-
ing alike both sacred and profane, nunneries and monasteries as
well as the common places of prostitution, Cheapside and Cornhill
as well as Bloomsbury or Covent Garden.

Under these benevolent and kind stars she grew up to some maturity of years, seasoned all along with such rudiments as these, to be
put in use as soon as occasion should present; she was now a lusty
and sturdy wench, and fit to put out to service, having not a competency of her own left her by friends to maintain her of herself; but
this went against the grain and the hair, as we use to say: she was too
great a libertine and lived too much in common to be enclosed in the
limits of a private domestic life.

A quarterstaff was fitter to her hand than a distaff, stave and tail
instead of spinning and reeling; she would go to the alehouse when
she had made shift for some little stock, and spend her penny, and
come into anyone's company, and club another till she had any left,
and then she was fit for any enterprise.

She could not endure the bakehouse, nor that magpie chat of the
wenches; she was not for mincing obscenity, but would talk freely
whatever came uppermost; a spice she had even then of profane dissolute language, which in her old days amounted to downright
swearing, which was in her not so malicious as customary.

Washing, wringing and starching were as welcome as fasting days
unto her; or in short, any household work; but above all she had a
natural abhorrence to the tending of children, to whom she ever had
an averseness in her mind equal to the sterility and barrenness in
her womb, never being made a mother to our best information.

At this age we spoke of before, she was not much taxed with any
looseness or debauchery in that kind; whether the virility and manliness of her face and aspect took off any man's desires that way
(which may be very rational and probable), or that besides her
uncompliable and rougher temper of body and mind also, which in
the female sex is usually persuasive and winning, not daring or
peremptory (though her disposition can hardly find a suitable term
for an indifferent expression of the manage of her life), she herself
also from the more importunate and prevailing sway of her inclinations, which were masculine and robust, could not intend those
venereal impurities and pleasures: as stronger meats are more palatable and nutritive to strong bodies than *quelque choses*[8] and things

---

7. Swaggerers, bullies, but specifically 'in the second half of the 17th c., . . . a set of disorderly young men who infested the streets of London' (*OED s.* hector 2).
8. Delicacies.

of variety, which may perchance move an appetite, provoke a longing, but are easily refrained from by any considerate good fellow that
knows what is the lastingest friend to *good drink and good company*:
her motto.

She could not but know, moreover (for I suppose her of a very
competent discretion and sagacity of mind as well as maturity and
suitable growth at those years), that such prostitutions were the
most unsatisfactory, that like an accidental scuffle or broil might end
in danger, but never in love, to which she was no way so happily
formed, nor was so much a woman as vainly to expect it.

Several romances there are of many knights who carried their
ladies away in disguise from their parents and native countries, most
commonly in the habits of a page or some such manservant: certainly
it must be a stupified and far advanced affection which can admire,
or fancy, or but admit the view of so unnatural a shape, the reverse of
sexes in the most famed beauties, and to whose excellencies and luster the world were devoted. How unsightly and dreadful is the hinder
region of the air in the sable breeches of a dropping cloud? What an
uncomely mantle is that heap of waters which covers the ground, and
deluges and invades the dry land? That which so much offends us in
the boisterousness of the elements cannot but be disgustful to
mankind in the immodesty of either sex's attire and dress.

Hercules, Nero and Sardanapalus,[9] how are they laughed at and
exploded for their effeminacy and degenerated dissoluteness in this
extravagant debauchery? The first is portrayed with a distaff in his
hand, the other recorded to be married as a wife and all the conjugal
and matrimonial rites performed at the solemnity of the marriage,
the other lacks the luxury of a pen as loose as his female riots to
describe them. These were all monsters or monster killers, and have
no parallels either in old or modern histories till such time as our
Moll Cutpurse approached this example; but her heroic impudence
has quite undone every romance—for never was any woman so like
her in her clothes.

Generally we are so much acquainted with ourselves, and so often
do dislike the effect of too much familiarity, that though we cannot
alter the inside, yet we diversify the outside with all the borrowed
pomp of art in our habits; no doubt Moll's converse with herself
(whose disinviting eyes and look sank inwards to her breast when
they could have no regard abroad) informed her of her defects, and
that she was not made for the pleasure or delight of man; and therefore since she could not be honored with him she would be honored

9. Hercules wore the clothes of Omphale and did her work; Nero and the Assyrian king Sardanapalus were noted for their effeminacy.

by him in that garb and manner of raiment he wore—some wenches have been got with child with the only shaking of the breeches; whereof having no great hopes, she resolved to usurp and invade the doublet, and vie and brave manhood, which she could not tempt nor allure.

I have the rather insisted on this because it was the chief remark of her life, as beginning and ending it; for from the first entrance into a competency of age she would wear it, and to her dying day she would not leave it off till the infirmity and weakness of nature had brought her abed to her last travail, changed it for a waistcoat and her petticoats for a winding sheet.

These were no amiable or obliging vests, they wanted of a mutual correspondence and agreement with themselves, so unlikely were they to beget it abroad and from others: they served properly as a fit covering, not any disguise of her (according to the primitive invention of apparel), wherein every man might see the true dimensions and proportions of body, only hers showed the mind too.

So that by this odd dress it came that no man can say or affirm that ever she had a sweetheart, or any such fond thing to dally with her. A good mastiff was the only thing she then affected and joyed in, in whose fawnings and familiarity she took as much delight as the proudest she ever gloried in the courtship, admiration, attraction and flatteries of her adored beauty. She was not wooed nor solicited by any man, and therefore she was honest,[1] though still in a reserved obedience and future service, either personally or by proxy to Venus.

Her nuptials and wedding grew to be such a proverb as the kisses of Jack Adams,[2] any one he could light upon, that is to say, as much design of love in one as in the other: all the matches she ever intended was at bearbaiting, whose pastimes afforded not leisure or admittance to the weak recreations and impertinencies of lust.

She never had the green sickness,[3] that epidemical disease of maidens after they have once passed their puberty; she never ate lime, oatmeal, coals or suchlike trash, nor never changed complexion; a great felicity for her vocation afterwards that was not to be afraid nor ashamed of anything, neither to wax pale or to blush.

No sighs or dejected looks or melancholy clouded her vigorous spirit or suppressed her joviality in the retired thoughts and despair of a husband; she was troubled with none of those longings which poor maidens are subject to: she had a power and strength (if not the

---

1. Chaste.
2. The proverb is untraced, but Adams was obviously a lover who was indiscriminate in his affections.
3. An anemic condition thought to affect only virgins, and indicating a readiness for marriage; the 'trash' subsequently cited are attempted cures.

will) to command her own pleasure of any person of reasonable ability of body, and therefore she needed not whine for it as long as she
was able to beat a fellow to a compliance without the unnecessary
trouble of entreaties. Nor in all her lifetime was it ever known that
by mere request, and precariously, she ever designed or obtained any
favor whatsoever, but by a strong hand carried and performed all her
enterprises.

She made much of for awhile, and was very often in company with
a shoemaker (a profession for her father's sake she always favored),
to whose expenses she contributed all she could wrap and run
(which is a term of art belonging to that trade whose factor afterwards she was), until she found the fellow made an absolute prey of
her friendship and squandered away the money she with difficulty
enough provided.

This and some such other like chouses[4] and tricks, to which a
freeness of nature subjected her, not only took her off from the consideration or thought of wedlock, but reduced her to some advise-
ment which way she might maintain herself single.

She cast about therefore what course of life she should betake
herself to, and long she was not in the determination, choosing that
which was the most easy, and by a good management would prove
also the most profitable, called living by the quick. As you may perceive by what is already said, she had a numerous acquaintance, and
among others, her company was known to some of the fortune
tellers of the town (from whom she then learned some snatch and
relish of that cheat), and by their schemes and figure-flinging[5] was
further encouraged in that her hopeful occupation.

For a while, therefore, she gave law to her former open licentious-
ness, and seemingly betook herself to a civiller life, that is, to a
closer and cunninger way of living, not being so much in the eye of
all people, by whom she was already defamed beyond remedy. But
there is nothing so bad which thinks not by shows and pretenses to
impose upon and deceive the vulgar.

This her sudden reclaimedness was more admired than credited
by her neighbors, who mused what it would turn to or what strange
effect it would have. She had learned to curtsey and some other
such beginning of manners, but yet very abrupt, which showed they
were troublesome to her and her new designs, however she framed
and formed herself to them for their better accomplishment.

She continued in this sort for some space of time, having entered
and initiated herself into a private crew of some loose women, who

4. Cheats.
5. Casting of horoscopes.

had undertaken to manage the promptness and dexterity of her wit to some notable advantage. Their trade being to receive goods which were lifted, that is to say, stolen by thieves, and so in a fair way sell them again; Moll Cutpurse's insight was very little at first in this kind of dealing, and before she came to practice for herself, or do the like business for those pilfering customers, most of that gang were either hanged or run away; so that it was high time for Mary to leave that dangerous and uncertain course.

But being thus seasoned, she was fit for any employment, and indeed she did but for a while forbear from entering into some such like occupation. Doing still she was, though never so little, otherwise it were impossible she should have ever attained and arrived to that eminence and extraordinary faculty, having an absolute incontrollable power, more than ever the law or justice had over that Mercurial tribe, they being entirely at her beck and command, submitting themselves and their stolen purchases to her only order, will and pleasure.

It will be high time now to recount to you the many notable passages of her life which from this foundation rose to these ensuing stories.

The remaining varieties and shapes of her life, which were no way so constant as her habit (the beloved disguise of her strange humors) are here presented according to that tract of her own genius with which she pleasured herself and her discourses in all company, fitted and suited to the gust and palate of her different converses, and shall therefore re-assume her person for the better grace of this discourse in the ensuing account of her manner of livelihood, from the time of her womanhood.

Which estate having seriously considered of, and duly weighed her propensity and inclinations to the inordinacies and unruliness of her mind, not to be guided either by the reservedness and modesty of her own sex or the more imperious command of the other, she resolved to set up in a neutral or hermaphrodite way of profession, and stand upon her own legs, fixed on the basis of both concerns and relations, like the Colossus of female sublety in the wily arts and ruses of that sex, and of manly resolution in the bold and regardless rudeness of the other, so blended and mixed together that it was hard to say whether she were more cunning or more impudent.

As you may see in this diary of her own here following.

Moll Cutpurse's Diary

All people do justly owe to the world an account of their lives passed; and therefore mine being a greater debt than any other, as I have drawn more observation by unknown practices upon me, I shall dispense with reputation and credit, and following the laudable example of others who have in part preceded me, as Señor Guzman[1] and the Spanish tribe of cheaters, I will freely declare myself to all my loving neighbors, and whomsoever this relation of mine shall happen to meet with, entreating them with all fairness and candor, and the pity of a Sessions House jury, to hear me in this my defense and apology, which my faults do not exceed.

I beheld myself more obnoxious to my fate, and to have a greater quarrel with that than the world can have against me; the universe consists and is made up of cheaters and cheatees, says the learned Albumazar,[2] and there is no great difference below between them; to be excellent and happy in villainy has been always reputed equal with a good fame, whose wings being short, and reaching not beyond the memory of a person, can little prejudice the fortunate achievements of new undertakers. My devices were all of my own spinning, nor was I beholding to any stale artifice whatsoever of any woman preceding me which I have not bettered, and so far forth as became the principles of such mysteries, facilitated and accommodated to the more ingenious moderns.

I will not therefore reckon my childish ignorances and those extravagant sallies[3] of an undisciplined wench for anything, for it is no matter to know how I grew up to this, since I have laid it as a maxim that it was my fate not me; I do more wonder at myself than others can do, and dare assure them that nature does sometimes disport herself not only in the careless nativities of dwarves, changelings, and such naturals, but also in her more considerate productions; for I am confident I can boast of as much human policy in acquisitions, revenges, dissemblings, &c., as any of the grandees of the world, if proportionably considered.

[Moll's relatives try to send her to Virginia.]

I was hardly twenty, from whence I date myself, when viewing the manners and customs of the age, I see myself so wholly distempered and so estranged from them as if I had been born and bred in the Antipodes; but yet such was the kindness of my stars that for all the noise of the New World and the plantations and incredibly rich mines of gold and silver said to be found there, which seemed to have been allotted for me, the discovery so patly then happening, and my friends very willing to humor it so they might have been rid of me, yet nevertheless I escaped the voyage, alike hating Virginia (the first land

---

1. *Guzman de Alfaranche*, a Spanish picaresque romance translated into English in 1622.
2. Arabian astronomer; in Thomas Tomkis' comedy *Albumazar*, performed at Cambridge before James I in 1615, a knavish magician.
3. Outbursts.

possessed by the English in America) and my virginity, the manner this.

My friends perceiving my untoward dispositions designed me[4] thither, where there was no doubt of such manly work and sport I affected, and where the necessity of women, be they what they would, could not but commend me to some Jack as good as myself, whose dominion over me might subdue that violence of my spirit, or else I should be so broke by hard labor that I would of my own accord return to a womanly and civil behavior. There was then no noise or talk of spirits, and I was so generally known that I thought there could be no such tricks shown me; but poor silly wench as I was, being under the pretense of a fair, and some matches at Gravesend trained down and invited thither by water, I was carried aboard a New England man[5] to drink strong waters, which were nothing else but the distillation of mine eyes boiling with fury and impatience, for in my grief there was nothing womanly.

[Moll cajoles and bribes her way off the ship, and finds herself alone in London.]

*   *   *

[Moll makes her living among thieves.]

I had but very little choice, so I listed myself of another colony or plantation (but who neither sow nor reap) of the divers or file-clyers.[6] A cunning nation being a kind of land pirates, trading altogether in other men's bottoms[7] for no other merchandises than bullion and ready coin, and keep most of the great fairs and marts of the world. They are very expert mathematicians, but also excellently good at dialling,[8] as also they are rare figure flingers, and most dexterous at the tactics;[9] they had been long incorporated, and had their governors and assistants as other worshipful companies, and had a good stock for the maintenance of their trade. At my admission among them, I was examined to several questions relating to my fitness and capacity of being a member, to which I gave such satisfactory answers as rendered me very acceptable to be one of their community. I remember they viewed my hands, not only to see whether I had not been manumitted[1] at Sessions, but if they were not naturally fitted

---

4. A marginal note reads, 'Moll Cutpurse spirited for New England.'
5. Ship.
6. Divers, file-clyers, both terms for pickpockets.
7. Ships, with a pun on breeches.
8. ?Picking locks.
9. The science of touch; hence, whatever can be done with the fingers.
1. Literally, freed, but also Moll's hand is being examined to be see if she has been branded, i.e., convicted of theft.

and made convenient for the exercise of the trade, being indeed the
neatest manufacture of the world.

* * *

I had no great promising symptoms of a lucky Mercurial in my fingers, for they had not been used to any sleight and fine work; but I
was judged by these palmisters from the hardness and largeness of
the table of my hand to be very well qualified for a receiver and
entertainer of their fortunate achievements, and was thereupon,
with the usual customs and ceremonies, admitted. Now I bethought
myself how I should govern myself in this condition of life; I could
not but foresee the danger, but was loath to relinquish the profit;
every snip or share I got as accessory to the theft was like green fruit
to me, sour and sweet, nor did I ever digest it but with a conceited
sore throat; yet I could not forsake my company, though I was very
wary how far I engaged, till a year's impunity or more had so stocked
me that I resolved to run no longer the desperate hazard of these
courses (which I see so many of my comrades monthly expiate with
their lives, &c., at least by whipping and the satisfaction of Bridewell
workhouse), but to address myself to a very fair expedient whereby I
might live, if not honestly, yet safely, a mean betwixt the strokes of
justice and the torments of poverty.

I was well known to all the gang, and by my good dealing with them
not a little in their favor; I never wrangled for a share, or when I had
the dividend to make[2] did I ever withhold any of their dues; so that I
was commonly an umpire in their quarrels, and thereby did save
them from the malicious discovery of[3] one another, which they were
sensible of, and did therefore look upon me with more than an ordinary respect. I would now and then too, out of my own pocket, lend
some of the most desperate of them a crown or two, to keep them
from apparent hazards of doing such robberies which fatal necessity
prompted them to, whereby I saved them often out of the hangman's
clutches; so that among all the thieveries they did, my name was
never heard of; for they made it the chiefest of their religion to conceal me and to conceal nothing of their designs from me; nor did I
ever openly accompany with them, save at our own retreats and
places of meeting, where we had all possible privacy and security.

I held very good correspondence now also with those grandees of
this function of thievery, the blades and hacks of the highway,[4] who
having heard from their inferior tribe this repute of my equitable

2. When I divided the spoils.
3. Informing upon.
4. *Blades . . . highway*, highwaymen.

dealing, did deposit in my hands some of their coin against a rainy day. Money was a portable and as partable a commodity, but the luggage and lumber of goods purchased by burglary I was shy to deal withal, for they serve commonly as the traces and scents to the owners to recover them; and I thank my fates, I had still the luck to avoid that inconvenience, though I have been enticed with movables of good value, which I abandoned to other receptories.

* * *

[The first woman to use tobacco]

Among the rest tobacco was grown to be the great mode, and much in use, and a sect of swaggerers there were which from thence were denominated the puffers and high huffers; I was mightily taken with this vanity because of its affected singularity, and no woman before me ever smoked any, though I had a great many to follow my example, how commendably I know not. I had nothing or would have nothing to do but what might better be left undone; all easy and proffering deceit was my business, and my recreations or pastime was suitable and like it; for I grew to be more reserved in my boisterous exercises of baiting, &c., and could content to be a spectator and a bettor only, where a pipe of tobacco did much accommodate me.

One time, an unlucky knave, at a grocer's shop where I used to sit and talk in the intervals of my trade, which I could not patiently await at home, at my demand of a pipe of smoke, presented me with a pipe full of gunpowder covered at top with tobacco, which little suspecting I took, and suddenly it fired in my mouth with such a blast and stench, belching and throwing out the ashes, that it was a little resemblance of Mount Etna. I was all aghast at present, but perceiving it was a boy's roguery, I restrained my passion further than flinging the pipe at his head, but forsook the shop, resolving of no less satisfaction than blowing up both of master and man by engines and devices in convenient time.

[Moll's brokery for the recovery of stolen goods.]

In my house, I should have told you, I set up a kind of brokery or a distinct factory for jewels, rings and watches which had been pinched or stolen any manner of way, at never so great distances from any person; I might properly enough call it the 'insurance office' for such merchandise, for the losers were sure upon composition[5] to

5. Payment.

recover their goods again, and the pirates were as sure to have good ransom, and I so much in the gross[6] for brokerage without any more danger, the hue and cry being always directed to me for the discovery of the goods, not the takers.

A lawless vocation yet bordering between illicit and convenient, more advantageous by far to the injured than the courts of justice and benefits of the law, and more equal to the wrongdoers, who by such an hazardous seizure have, as themselves think, an equal propriety[7] in their spoil, by yielding and restoring it upon such indifferent[8] terms as my markets and prizes usually were.

Sometimes I met with obstinate thieves who would by no means part with their purchases, but would stand to their possession as stiffly as if it had by right accrued to them, yet such a hank[9] I had upon them by working with their partakers and using my authority that I always prevailed, and made them stand to my agreement and arbitrament. Nor could ever your thief catchers do any good upon these sort of people. My house was the Algiers[1] where they trafficked in safety without the bribes to those fellows, and publicly exposed what they had got without the danger of inquisition or examination or fees of silence. I could have told in what quarter of the town a robbery was done the evening before by very early day next morning, and had a perfect inventory of what they had taken as soon as it came to the dividend; nor were ever the custom house bills showing what goods and from whence they are imported more duly published for the advantage of the trade than was the account of those robberies entered with me for the satisfaction of the owners.

So that I may be said to have made a perfect regulation of this thievish mystery,[2] and reduced it to certain rules and orders, which during my administration of the mistresship and government thereof was far better managed than afterwards it was.

* * *

[Penance for cross-dressing.]

While I thus reigned, free from the danger of the common law, some promoting apparitor[3] set on by an adversary of mine, whom I could

---

6. *I . . . gross,* I got my share of the payment.
7. Ownership.
8. Impartial, fair.
9. 'A restraining or curbing hold' (*OED* 4.a.).
1. Center of operations of the Barbary pirates.
2. Craft.
3. Summons server.

never punctually know, cited me to appear in the Court of the Arches, where was an accusation against me for wearing undecent and manly apparel.[4] I was advised by my proctor[5] to demur to the jurisdiction of the court, as for a crime, if such, not cognizable there or elsewhere; but he did it to spin out my cause and get my money, for in the conclusion I was sentenced there to stand and do penance in a white sheet at Paul's Cross during morning sermon on a Sunday.

They might as soon have shamed a black dog as me with any kind of such punishment; for saving the reverence due to those who enjoined it, for a half penny I would have travelled to all the market towns in England with it, and been as proud of it as that citizen who rode down to his friends in his livery gown and hood,[6] or that parson who being enjoined to wear the surplice contrary to his will, when he had once put it on wore it constantly in his own and other towns, while he was complained of for abusing that decent ministerial garment. I am sure there were some few who had no cause to be merry or sport themselves at the sight, for my emissaries were very busy without any regard to the sacredness of the place, but in revenge of this disgrace intended me, spoiled a good many clothes by cutting of part of their cloaks and gowns and sending them home as naked behind as an ape's tail.

* * *

I did not say as much, whatever I thought, when my penance was over; but this dealing with me was therefore so far from reclaiming me to the sobriety of decent apparel, that I was [one] offended with it, or others [of my s]ex:[7] I could by no means endure at any time before the finical and modish excesses of attire into which women were then, as in all ages, very curious, to the wasting and impoverishing their husbands, beyond what they are able to afford towards such lavish and prodigal gallantry.

* * *

4. Sumptuary legislation had no provisions concerning cross-dressing, though James I attempted to institute codes governing this issue and pamphlets and sermons from the period attest to the controversy surrounding the matter. However, one could be prosecuted for wearing indecent apparel by an ecclesiastical court, as appears to be the case here. Mary Frith is known to have done penance at St. Paul's in 1612 upon a conviction of indecent behavior.
5. 'One whose profession is to manage the cases of others in a court administering civil or canon law' (*OED* 4); the term also, given the results of the proctor's advice, may have the cant sense of a 'knave that doth feign tales' (Awdeley).
6. *I.e.*, having been admitted to a guild, he inappropriately wore the ceremonial robes for social occasions.
7. *That . . . sex,* The text is damaged here, but following the sentiments of the context, this conjectural reading suggests that Frith was offended by the garment she was forced to wear and all other garments assigned to women.

[An hermaphrodite and a shamelesss jade.]

There was also a fellow, a contemporary of mine as remarkable as myself, called Aniseed-water Robin, who was clothed very near my antic mode, being an hermaphrodite, a person of both sexes; him I could by no means endure, being the very derision[8] of nature's impotency, whose redundancy in making him man and woman had in effect made him neither, having not the strength nor reason of the male, nor the finesse nor subtlety of the female, being but one step removed from a natural changeling,[9] a kind of mockery (as I was upbraided) of me, who was then counted for an artificial one. And indeed I think nature owed me a spite in sending that thing into the world to mate and match me, that nothing might be without a peer, and the vaccum of society be replenished, which is done by the likeness and similitude of manners; but contrariwise it begot in me a natural abhorrence of him with so strange an antipathy that what by threats and my private instigating of the boys to fall upon and throw dirt at him, I made him quit my walk and habitation that I might have no further scandal among my neighbors, who used to say, 'Here comes Moll's husband.'

* * *

There was a shameless jade, as noted in this town as myself at this time, but for far more enormous actions; she was called Abigail, her way of living (she being a kind of natural)[1] was by ringing the bells with her coats[2] for a farthing, and coming behind any gentleman for the same hire, and clapping him on the back as he turned his head, to kiss him, to the enraging of some gentlemen so far as to cause them to draw their swords and threaten to kill her. This stinking slut, who was never known to have done so to any woman, by somebody's setting her on to affront me, served me in the same manner. I got hold of her and being near at home, dragged her to the Conduit, where I washed her polluted lips for her, and wrenched her lewd petticoats to some purpose, tumbling her under a cock and letting the water run till she had not a dry thread about her, and had her soundly kicked to boot.

* * *

8. The ultimate contemptible instance.
9. Idiot.
1. Half-wit.
2. *Ringing . . . coats* having sex while fully clothed: compare 'her lewd petticoats' below. 'Ringing the bells' is a slang term for sexual intercourse.

[*Moll runs a male prostitution ring.*]

You must know, therefore, that among other my large acquaintance I had some familiarity with the mad girls and the venerable matrons of the kind motion;[3] among the rest, I was very intimate with the abbess of the Holland Leaguer[4] on the Bankside, and with Damaris Page, newly then from a whore-rampant[5] separated to the office of a procurer or provider, and other notable and the ancientest traders in that profession. Now seeing how little hopes there were of my interloping in stolen goods, I thought it the best course to keep me in my old age, which grew apace upon me, to deal altogether in prohibited wares, not doubting but that pleasure would invite as many consumers as profit, there being always, which I considered both in war and peace, good vent of such commodities. The voluptuous bed is never the less frequented for those hard and painful lodgings in the camp.

I saw also that the former traffickers this way were very straight-laced and too narrow in their practice, as confining their industry in this negotiation to one sex, like women tailors[6] that if they were to be hanged cannot make a doublet for themselves. In this I was a little prosperous, though to make good the simile, I could never fit myself. One time (you may spare me this digression, for since there was nothing serious in the whole course of my life save the very anticness thereof, which always kept the same tenor, it is no great matter how I place my words and manner) as I was going down Fleetbridge I espied one of my neighbors, Mr. Drake, a tailor, God bless him, and to my purpose he was altogether for the women; quoth I in droll, 'Mr. Drake, when shall you and I make ducklings?' He quacked again, and told me, that I looked as if some toad had ridden me and poisoned me into that shape, that he was altogether for a dainty duck, that I was not like that feather, and that my eggs were addle.[7] I contented myself with the repulse and walked quietly homeward.

To return, I had new and strange faces now frequenting and haunting my house quite contrary from those before; I began to think myself a *generalissima* or some great military officer, such a troop of gallants and soldier-like men using to me for employment and preferment; among the rest I was cruelly troubled with Frenchmen, who were very solicitous with me for orders, with such confidence that I could not any way be rid of them; one of them whom I ventured upon

---

3. *Girls . . . motion* prostitutes; *the kind motion* is sexual intercourse, the 'natural' activity, or the activity that produces (man)kind.
4. 'Dutch Camp,' apparently the name of a brothel.
5. Practicing prostitute, as opposed to a bawd who is a supplier of prostitutes.
6. Tailors who specialize in women's clothing.
7. Rotten.

a finical madam I saw afterwards in a splendid condition, and generally all whom I set at work were ever afterwards very seldom idle or
needed my assistance. I never well knew the knack of it (for they were
very sordid and ingrateful and courted not, when they were served,
my acquaintance that advanced them), but if I did I should modestly
forbear it; for I love it not myself, and therefore will restrain others so
through their forced ignorance thereof. But without great wrong to
civility, it is imputable chiefly to the *mignardises*[8] and more effeminate wantonness of the *monsieur*, whose soft dalliances and
courtships and impudent bold flatteries are in that preferable before
the rude and downright attempts of the English.

* * *

Generally, I therefore chose the sprucest fellows the town afforded,
for they did me reputation at home and service abroad, my neighbors admiring what this retinue and attendance meant, nor would I
now discover it but to unburden my conscience and shame the private practices of some great women, who to this very purpose keep
emissaries and agents to procure stallions to satiate their desires as
confidently as they entertain grooms and launderers. I will stir this
puddle no longer, nor dive into the depth of it any further, lest I pol-
lute and inquinate[9] the reader with the filth hereof.

* * *

[*Moll's final illness and death.*]

He runs long, we use to say, that never turns: it was therefore high
time for me of thinking of the way by which I should turn, and that
presently offered itself to me; for being grown crazy in my body and
discontented in my mind, I yielded to the next distemper that
approached me, which by my bustling and active spirit I had kept off
a good while from seizing me; it was a dropsy, a disease whose cause
you will easily guess from my past life, but it had such strange and
terrible symptoms that I thought I was possessed and that the devil
was got within my doublet.

For what all the ecclesiastical quirks with their canons and
injunctions could not do, this boisterous malady soon effected. I was
forced to leave off that upper part of my garment and do penance
again in a blanket, a habit distant from the Irish rug and the Scotch
plaid, their national vests for women of quality, whom my scoffing

8. Affected behavior.
9. Defile.

neighbors said I did very much resemble. As for my belly, from a withered, dried and wrinkled piece of skin, it was grown the tightest, roundest globe of flesh that ever any beauteous young lady strutted with, to the ostentation of her fertility and the generosity of her nature. I must tell you I could not but proud myself in it, and thought nature had reserved that kindness for me at the last, insomuch that I could have almost been impregnated (as Spanish jennets are said to be begotten by the wind) with my own fancy and imagination, my conceit proving the same with conception, and to please and maintain me in this delusion a woman of my age then living in London was brought to bed of a son, which was very certainly true; and an old parson in the north, one Mr. Vivan, of near a hundred years old, was juvenilized again, and his age renewed as to all his senses he enjoyed before at fifty.

* * *

I cannot further anatomize my body, for I dared not look on my legs with the swan[1] (though I had nothing in my whole any way amiable), they did so represent a bull or bear's stake, and my head so wrapped up with cloths that I looked like Mother Shipton,[2] so that among all the looking glasses my house was furnished with for ornaments, I had never a one big enough to see it altogether and at once. But myself was indeed the best mirror to my self; for every afflicted part and member of me did represent and point out the wickedness every one of them had been instrumental in, so that I could not but acknowledge the justice of my punishment. My hands indeed escaped this vengeance, and I think they were the most innocent; for I never actually or instrumentally cut any man's purse, though I have often restored it; but oh my plotting, matchmaking head in those sorceries of lust I practiced! The lewdness and bastardies that ensued, and those frequent trottings and runnings up and down to facilitate and bring about those debaucheries! These I cannot but acknowledge were indicated to me so plainly that I was forced to take notice of them, and I hope with a real penance and true grief to deplore my condition and former course of life I had so profanely and wickedly led.

As an advantage thereto, this disease lingered with me a long time, which I had solitude enough to improve, all people but some of my old and nearest acquaintance forsaking me. I will not boast of my

---

1. *I.e.*, the swan's legs too are ugly.
2. A legendary witch and seer of the time of Henry VIII. Along with her skill at prophesying, she was known for her extraordinary physical characteristics: fiery eyes and a crooked nose with multi-colored, phosphorescent warts, and an unusually long head.

conversion lest I encourage other vile people to persist in their sins to the last, but I dare assure the world I never lived a happy moment in it till I was leaving of it, and so I bid it adieu this threescore and fourteenth year of my age.

* * *

Later Representations of
Moll Cutpurse

Following the 1662 publication of *The Life and Death of Mrs. Mary Frith*, Moll's reputation as a colorful underworld character continued through the eighteenth and nineteenth centuries. The accounts from this period typically offer a condensed, paraphrased version of *The Life and Death's* narrative, revised and embellished as each author saw fit. The three excerpts below are from such accounts. The first, from *A general history of the lives and adventures of the most famous highwaymen, murderers, street-robbers, etc.* (1734) by "Captain Charles Johnson" (probably a pseudonym), grants Moll an epitaph supposedly authored by the famous poet John Milton. The second, from James Caulfield's *Portraits, memoirs, and characters of remarkable persons, from the reign of Edward the Third, to the Revolution* (1794) adds "hermaphrodite," "prostitute," and "fortune-teller" to her charge, along with an oft-repeated but highly unlikely bit of folklore about her robbery of Sir Thomas Fairfax, a general in the parliamentarian army (Moll would have been about sixty at the time). The third, from an 1895 edition of *Macmillan's Magazine*, includes a digression on cross-dressing from a distinctly nineteenth-century perspective.

CHARLES JOHNSON

From A general history of the lives and adventures of the most famous highwaymen, murderers, street-robbers, etc.[†]

From *The Life of Mol Cutpurse, a Pickpocket and Highway-woman*

And now, the time of her dissolution drawing near, she desired to be buried with her breech upwards,[1] that she might be as preposterous in her death as she had been all along in her infamous life. When she was dead, she was interred in St. Bridget's church-yard, having a fair marble-stone put over her grave; on which was cut the following epitaph, composed by the ingenious Mr. Milton, but destroyed in the great conflagration[2] of London.

> Here lies, under this same marble
> Dust, for time's last sieve to garble;
> Dust, to perplex a Sadducee,
> Whether it rise a he or she,
> Or two in one, a single pair,
> Nature's sport, and now her care.[3]
> For how she'll clothe it at last day
> Unless she sighs it all away;
> Or where she'll place it, none can tell:
> Some middle place 'twixt Heav'n and Hell—
> And well 'tis Purgatory's[4] found,
> Else she must hide her underground.
> These relics do deserve the doom
> Of that cheat Mahomet's fine tomb;[5]
> For no communion she had
> Nor sorted with the good or bad;

[†] *A general history*, ESTC # T112552, is held at the British Library and is accessible through Eighteenth Century Collections Online. Spelling and punctuation have been modernized.

1. I.e., face down; *dissolution*: death.
2. The great fire of London occurred in 1666; *Mr. Milton*: John Milton (1608–1674), author of *Paradise Lost*; it is highly unlikely that he wrote this epitaph.
3. Nature's amusement, but now her dilemma; *Sadducee*: member of an ancient Jewish sect, represented in the New Testament (Matthew 22:29–32; Acts 23:8) as disbelieving in the resurrection of the body.
4. In Roman Catholic doctrine, a place of temporary punishment and purification for the souls of the dead; *last day*: Judgment Day; in Christian doctrine, the day on which the dead will be resurrected and sent to their eternal reward or punishment.
5. A legend of uncertain origin claimed that the prophet Mohammed's coffin was suspended between heaven and earth by means of magnets; from the eighteenth-century Christian author's perspective, Mohammed is a false prophet or "cheat"; *doom*: fate.

That when the world shall be calcined,[6]
And the mixed mass of humankind
Shall sep'rate by that melting fire,
She'll stand alone, and none come nigh her.
Reader, here she lies till then,
When, truly, you'll see her again.

JAMES CAULFIELD

From Portraits, memoirs, and characters
of remarkable persons, from the reign of Edward
the Third, to the Revolution[†]

Moll Cut-purse

Mary Frith, or Moll Cut-purse, a woman of a masculine spirit and make, who was commonly supposed to have been a hermaphrodite, practised, or was instrumental to, almost every crime and wild frolic, which is notorious in the most abandoned[1] and eccentric of both sexes. She was infamous as a prostitute and procuress, a fortune-teller, a pick-pocket, a thief, and a receiver of stolen goods; she was also concerned with a dexterous scribe in forging hands[2]. Her most signal exploit was robbing General Fairfax, upon Hounslow Health, for which she was sent to Newgate[3]; but was, by the proper application of a large sum of money, soon set at liberty. She well knew, like other robbers in high life, how to make the produce of her accumulated crimes the means of her protection, and to live luxuriously upon the spoils of the public. She died of the dropsy[4] in the 75th year of her age, but probably would have died sooner if she had not smoked tobacco, in the frequent use of which she long indulged herself. It was, at this time, almost as rare a sight to see a woman

---

6. Reduced to ash (at Judgment Day); *communion*: commonality [with other people]; *nor sorted with*: nor can she be categorized with.
† *Portraits, memoirs, and characters* (vol.1), ESTC # T139234, is held at the British Library and is accessible through Eighteenth Century Collections Online. Spelling and punctuation have been modernized.
1. Immoral; *make*: physique.
2. She worked together with a skillful scribe to forge handwriting; *procuress*: female pimp.
3. London's main prison; *signal*: remarkable; *General Fairfax*: Sir Thomas Fairfax (1612–1671), a general in the parliamentarian army; *Hounslow Heath*: a stretch of open land to the southwest of London, notorious for highway robberies.
4. A disease which causes swelling due to fluid retention.

with a pipe as to see one of the sex in man's apparel. Nat. Field[5], in
his comedy called *Amends for The Ladies*, has displayed some of the
Merry Pranks of Moll Cut-Purse. She is also mentioned by Butler
and Swift[6], in the following lines:

> He Trulla lov'd, Trulla more bright
> Than burnished armour of her Knight;
> A bold Virago, stout and tall
> As Joan of France[7], or English Moll. (*Hudibras*)

> The ballads pasted on the wall
> Of Joan of France, and English Moll. (*Baucis and Philemon*)

* * *

ANONYMOUS

From Macmillan's Magazine, Moll Cutpurse[†]

"Enter Moll in a frieze jerkin and a black safeguard." Thus in the old
comedy she comes upon the stage; and truly it was by her clothes
that she was first notorious. By accident a woman, by habit a man,
she must needs invent a costume proper to her pursuits. But she was
no shrieking reformer, no fanatic spying regeneration in a pair of
breeches.[1] Only in her attire she showed her wit; and she went to a
bull-baiting in such a dress as well became her favourite sport. She
was not of those who "walk in spurs but never ride." The jerkin, the
doublet, the galligaskins[2] were put on to serve the practical purposes
of life, not to attract the policeman or the spinster. And when a petticoat spread its ample folds beneath the doublet, not only was her
array handsome, but it symbolised the career of one who was neither

---

5. Nathan Field's *Amends for Ladies* (1618) was reprinted in 1639 under the title *Amends for
   Ladies, With the merry prankes of Moll Cut-Purse: Or, the humour of rouring: A Comedy
   full of honest mirth and wit.* The excerpt featuring Moll is on pp. 153–55 of this Norton
   Critical Edition.
6. Samuel Butler's *Hudibras*, published in three installments between 1662 and 1678, sati-
   rizes the parliamentary factions of the civil war; Jonathan Swift's *Baucis and Philemon*
   (1708) adapts a tale from Ovid's *Metamorphoses*.
7. Joan of Arc; *Virago*: female warrior.
† From *Macmillan's Magazine* 72 (May–Oct. 1895): 411–12.
1 A reference to the Victorian dress reform movement.
2. Wide breeches.

man nor woman, and yet both. After a while, however, the petticoat seemed too tame for her stalwart temper, and she exchanged it for the great Dutch slop, habited in which unseemly garment she is pictured in the ancient prints. Up and down the town she romped and scolded, earning the name which Middleton gave her in her green girlhood. "She has the spirit of four great parishes," says the wit in the comedy, "and a voice that will drown all the city." But she was no mere braggart, and knew well how to carry her threats into action. If a gallant stood in the way she drew upon him in an instant, and he must be a clever swordsman to hold his ground against the tomboy who had laid low the German fencer himself. A good fellow always, she had ever a merry word for the passer-by, and so sharp was her tongue that none ever put a trick upon her. Not to know Moll was to be inglorious, and she "slipped from one company to another like a fat eel between a Dutchman's fingers." Now at Parker's Ordinary, now at the Bear-Garden, she frequented only the haunts of men, and not until old age came upon her did she endure patiently the presence of women. Her voice and speech were suited to the galligaskin. She was a true disciple of Maître François[3], hating nothing so much as mincing obscenity, and if she flavoured her discourse with many a blasphemous quip, the blasphemy was "not so malicious as customary." Like the blood[4] she was, she loved good ale and wine; and she regarded it among her proudest titles to renown that she was the first of women to smoke tobacco. Many was the pound of best Virginian that she bought of Mistress Gallipot, and the pipe, with monkey, dog, and eagle, is her constant emblem. Her antic attire, the fearless courage of her pranks, now and again involved her in disgrace or even jeopardised her freedom; but her unchanging gaiety made light of disaster, and still she laughed and rollicked in defiance of prude and pedant.

3. François Rabelais (1494–1553), forthright in his depictions of human sensuality.
4. Rake, swaggering young man.

CRITICISM

A. H. BULLEN

From the introduction to
The Works of Thomas Middleton, 1885[†]

The Roaring Girl, written in conjunction with Dekker, was published in 1611. Of Mary Frith, the Roaring Girl, whose adventures are so graphically described by the dramatists, I have given some account in a prefatory note to the play. In the Address to the Reader Middleton says:—"Worse things, I must needs confess, the world has taxed her for than has been written of her;" and he concludes with the very proper observation—"We rather wish in such discoveries, where reputation lies bleeding, a slackness of truth than fulness of slander." Under this judicious treatment the Amazon of the Bankside becomes an attractive figure. She moves among rowdies and profligates without suffering any contamination; she has the thews of a giant and the gentleness of a child. Secure in her "armed and iron maidenhood," and defying the breath of scandal, she daffs the world aside and chooses a life of frolic freedom. She can converse with rogues and cheats in their cant language, and knows all their tricks and subterfuges. Her hand is heavy on swaggerers, but she has a woman's ear for a tale of lovers' distress, and is quick to render efficient aid. The conception is strikingly fresh and original.

* * *

HAVELOCK ELLIS

From the preface to *Thomas Middleton*, 1887[‡]

Middleton wrote the comedy of *The Roaring Girl* in conjuction with Dekker. The play is chiefly the work of Middleton, but we detect Dekker's hand in occasional fantastic or imaginative passages, as well as by the copious knowledge of thieves and their slang which somewhat deforms the concluding scenes. To that tender-hearted poet we probably owe much of the charity shed over the central figure in this delightful play. Mary Frith, commonly called Moll Cutpurse, was a noted character of the period, and her reputation was

---

† From *The Works of Thomas Middleton*, vol. 1. London: John C. Nimmo, 1885. Rpt. New York: Ams, 1964.
‡ From *Thomas Middleton*, vol. 2. London: Vizetelly, 1887–90. Rpt. London: Unwin, 1904.

none of the best. She was about twenty-five years old at the time that she gave her name to this play, and only a few months later she had to do penance at Paul's Cross. But this is not the Moll that our dramatists saw. She is strong and courageous, indeed, a "goodly personable creature," and her sword is the match of any man's, but it is never drawn save in a good cause. She is frank and free-spoken when among friends the mood takes her, she can even sing a wanton song and accompany it on the viol; but she is modest for all that, and woe to the man who attempts to take liberties! She is acquainted with the shapes of iniquity, but she moves among them uncontaminated, and uses her knowledge not to practise but to defeat vice. She is a knight-errant who goes about succouring distressed lovers in the way of honesty, and she would like in her own person to avenge all the wrongs of women. She declares at the end that she will not marry until many wrongs are righted;

> "Honesty and truth unslandered,
> Women manned but never pandered."

"This sounds like doomsday," Lord Noland remarks. But Moll is content.

* * *

ALGERNON CHARLES SWINBURNE

From The Age of Shakespeare[†]

* * * The style of 'The Roaring Girl' is full of Dekker's peculiar mannerisms; slipshod and straggling metre, incongruous touches or flashes of fanciful or lyrical expression, reckless and awkward inversions, irrational and irrepressible outbreaks of irregular and fitful rhyme. And with all these faults it is more unmistakably the style of a born poet than is the usual style of Middleton. Dekker would have taken a high place among the finest if not among the greatest of English poets if he had but had the sense of form—the instinct of composition. Whether it was modesty, indolence, indifference, or incompetence, some drawback or shortcoming there was which so far impaired the quality of his strong and delicate genius that it is impossible for his most ardent and cordial admirer to say or think of his very best work that it really does him justice—that it adequately

[†] From *The Age of Shakespeare*. 1908. New York: AMS Press, 1965.

represents the fullness of his unquestionable powers. And yet it is certain that Lamb[1] was not less right than usual when he said that Dekker 'had poetry enough for anything.' But he had not constructive power enough for the trade of a playwright—the trade in which he spent so many weary years of ill-requited labour. This comedy in which we first find him associated with Middleton is well written and well contrived, and fairly diverting—especially to an idle or an uncritical reader: though even such an one may suspect that the heroine here represented as a virginal virago must have been in fact rather like Dr. Johnson's fair friend Bet Flint; of whom the Great Lexicographer[2] 'used to say that she was generally slut and drunkard; occasionally whore and thief' (Boswell, May 8, 1781). The parallel would have been more nearly complete if Moll Cutpurse 'had written her own Life in verse,' and brought it to Selden or Bishop Hall[3] with a request that he would furnish her with a preface to it.

T. S. ELIOT

[Middleton's Realism in *The Roaring Girl*][†]

* * *

But if Middleton understood woman in tragedy better than any of the Elizabethans—better than the creator of the Duchess of Malfy, better than Marlowe, better than Tourneur, or Shirley, or Fletcher,[1] better than any of them except Shakespeare alone—he was also able, in his comedy, to present a finer woman than any of them. *The Roaring Girl* has no apparent relation to Middleton's tragedies, yet it is agreed to be primarily the work of Middleton. It is typical of the comedies of Middleton, and it is the best. In his tragedies Middleton employs all the Italianate horrors of his time, and obviously for the purpose of pleasing the taste of his time; yet underneath we feel always a quiet and undisturbed vision of things as they are and not 'another thing'. So in his comedies. The comedies are long-winded; the fathers are heavy fathers, and rant as heavy fathers should; the

1. Charles Lamb (1775–1834).
2. Samuel Johnson (1709–1784).
3. John Selden (1584–1654); Joseph Hall (1574–1656).
† From *Elizabethan Essays* (1934; Haskell House/Faber and Faber, 1964), pp. 95–97, 99. Reprinted by permission.
1. Playwrights John Webster (c.1578–c.1638), author of *The Duchess of Malfi*; Christopher Marlowe (1564–1593), Cyril Tourneur (d. 1626); James Shirley (1596–1666); John Fletcher (1579–1625).

sons are wild and wanton sons, and perform all the pranks to be expected of them; the machinery is the usual Elizabethan machinery; Middleton is solicitous to please his audience with what they expect; but there is underneath the same steady impersonal passionless observation of human nature. *The Roaring Girl* is as artificial as any comedy of the time; its plot creaks loudly; yet the Girl herself is always real. She may rant, she may behave preposterously, but she remains a type of the sort of woman who has renounced all happiness for herself and who lives only for a principle. Nowhere more clearly than in *The Roaring Girl* can the hand of Middleton be distinguished from the hand of Dekker. Dekker is all sentiment; and, indeed, in the so admired passages of *A Fair Quarrel*, applauded by Lamb, the mood if not the hand of Dekker seems to the unexpert critic to be more present than Middleton's. *A Fair Quarrel* seems as much, if not more, Dekker's than Middleton's. Similarly with *The Spanish Gypsy*, which can with difficulty be attributed to Middleton. But the feeling about Moll Cut-Purse of *The Roaring Girl* is Middleton's rather than anybody's. In Middleton's tragedy there is a strain of realism underneath, which is one with the poetry; and in his comedy we find the same thing.

* * *

As a social document the comedy of Middleton illustrates the transition from government by a landed aristocracy to government by a city aristocracy gradually engrossing the land. As such it is of the greatest interest. But as literature, as a dispassionate picture of human nature, Middleton's comedy deserves to be remembered chiefly by its real—perpetually real—and human figure of Moll the Roaring Girl. That Middleton's comedy was 'photographic', that it introduces us to the low life of the time far better than anything in the comedy of Shakespeare or the comedy of Jonson, better than anything except the pamphlets of Dekker and Greene and Nashe,[2] there is little doubt. But it produced one great play—*The Roaring Girl*—a great play in spite of the tedious long speeches of some of the principal characters, in spite of the clumsy machinery of the plot: for the reason that Middleton was a great observer of human nature, without fear, without sentiment, without prejudice.

* * *

2. Ben Jonson (1572–1637); Thomas Dekker (c. 1572–1632); Robert Greene (1558–1592); Thomas Nashe (1567–1601).

M. C. BRADBROOK

From The Anatomy of Knavery[†]

In *The Roaring Girl*, Middleton and Dekker brought upon the stage an actual personage, Moll Firth, commonly called Moll Cutpurse, who in 1612 did penance at Paul's Cross for an unknown offence, with apparent contrition; it was discovered, however, that 'she had tippled off three quarts of sack before she came to her penance'. In this play she is allowed to characterize herself at the opening in a noble passage that does *not* suggest a portrait from life.

> 'Sir, I am so poor to requite you, you must look for nothing but thanks of me: I have no humour to marry: I love to lie a both sides a' the bed myself: and again, a' the other side, a wife, you know, ought to be obedient, but I fear me I am too headstrong to obey: therefore I'll ne'er go about it. I love you so well, sir, for your good will, I'd be loth you should repent your bargain after: and therefore we'll ne'er come together at first. I have the head now of myself, and am man enough, for a woman: marriage is but a chopping and a changing.' 2.2.

The dignified self-knowledge which her rejection of a rich suitor implies is counter-balanced in the last sentence by a quibbling play upon her masculine appearance, which may have provided the spectators with that kind of entertainment which is now furnished in reports by the popular press of sexual freaks and abnormalities. In her masculine attire—which the real Moll wore—she is addressed as Jack: she fights a duel, rescues a spendthrift from the catchpoles who would arrest him, and talks mysterious canting language with thieves, from whom she has the power to extract stolen goods for her friends. The final justification which she gives—that a knowledge of evil is necessary at times—

> 'You'd proclaim
> Your knowledge in those villainies, to save
> Your friend from their quick danger' 5.1.

is spoken to a Lord, implying that a knowledge of Venetian courtesans would be useful to him in his travels; and it is identical with the argument of Old Hoard's courtesan to excuse her previous way of living. When therefore Moll ends the play with an old-fashioned riddling prophecy that she will marry when various impossibilities

---

† From *The Growth and Structure of Elizabethan Comedy*. (London: Chatto & Windus), 1973. Originally published in 1955. Reprinted by permission of The Random House Group Ltd.

take place, the accent is no longer quite so noble, or her character quite so unequivocal as it was. She has appeared as a kind of feminine Robin Hood, aiding the weak against the strong, and in her final disguise as 'bride' to Wengrave she is deputizing for Mary Fitzallard, whose pathetic self-characterization has been instanced already as amongst Middleton's most poignant lines. The two, Moll and Mary, appear together in male dress in the most significant scene of the play: Mary is disguised as a page, in a suit made by Moll's tailor, but as she takes up this Shakespearean role, that of a Jessica or a Rosalind, her lover abruptly destroys the old decorum with an innocently ironic remark that reduces her to Epicoene

> 'I'd kiss such men to choose, Moll:
> Methinks a woman's lip tastes well in a doublet. . . .
> Every kiss she gives me now
> In this strange form is worth a pair of two.'   4.1.

The identities and roles of Moll and Mary are so intertwined that the rest of the story is of very minor significance: it consists indeed largely of merriments or jests which serve to show off Moll's virtuosity, from her skill in singing bawdy songs to the viol de gambois to her ability in talking canting jargon. She provides entertainment for her betters, seemingly a harmless jester: but the edge of Middleton's writing was seldom keener than here.

* * *

ALEXANDER LEGGATT

From Chaste Maids and Whores[†]

* * *

None of [city comedy's previous] attempts to complicate the conventional opposition of chaste maid and vicious whore really amounts to much: they are all minor effects, frequently uncertain and apologetic. The stereotype, in other words, seems difficult to break. But it *does* break, with a satisfying crash, in Middleton and Dekker's *The Roaring Girl* (Prince Henry's, c. 1610), where female chastity is embodied, not in a virtuous shopgirl, but in Moll Cutpurse, whose racy speech and intimate knowledge of the underworld might seem more appropriate to a conventional whore. The theatrical surface of

† From *Citizen Comedy in the Age of Shakespeare*. (Toronto: University of Toronto Press), 1973, pp. 109–10. Reprinted with permission of the publisher.

one figure is superimposed on the moral values of the other, and the result establishes that virtue is not merely a matter of conventional images. This idea is asserted in various ways throughout the play, by other characters defending Moll—'He hates unworthily, that by rote contemns, / For the name neither saves, nor yet condemns' (II.ii.163–4)—and by Moll herself:

> 'cause you'll say
> I'm given to sport, I'm often merry, jest,
> Had mirth no kindred in the world but lust? (III.i.99–101)

> How many are whores, in small ruffs, and still looks?
> How many chaste, whose names fill slander's books?
>   (V.i.314–5)

Moll's language provides a deliberate reversal of the expected image of the chaste woman. She takes part in ribald conversations, as when she jokes with a tailor about putting a yard in her breeches (II.ii.80–9), and even her assertions of chastity can be racy: 'all this while I was in a dream; one shall lie rudely then, but being awake, I keep my legs together' (IV.i.122–4). She is chaste, despite appearances; but her chastity is not obedience to a social or religious code: it is the assertion of an individual will. The independence that makes her scorn the usual images of respectability is also the key to her sexual behaviour. As she says when rejecting a proposal of marriage, 'I love to lie o' both sides o' th' bed myself' (II.ii.35–6).

We see this most clearly in the scene in which Laxton, a typical would-be seducer, finds that Moll is not so easy a target as he had assumed. She rebukes the gallant for his ill-founded vanity, and goes on to a broader denunciation of men of his type who assume that any woman will yield to them, and who destroy their reputations whether they do or not (III.i.68–80).[1] Moll declares herself above the snares of men, which trap more feeble-minded women, proudly rejects the name of whore and the censure of the world, and scorns the idea of submitting herself to any man. She then translates these assertions into action by fighting with Laxton and defeating him. In the soliloquy that follows, she takes the idea of independence a stage further. She refuses submission not only to men, but to her own physical nature:

> she that has wit, and spirit,
> May scorn to live beholding to her body for meat,
> Or for apparel like your common dame,
> That makes shame get her clothes, to cover shame.
> Base is that mind, that kneels unto her body,

---

1. This is a standard charge against gallants, whose vanity is such that rather than appear as unsuccessful seducers they will slander women they have never lain with. See also *The Fair Maid of the Exchange*, II.691–8, and Dekker and Webster's *Northward Ho*, I.i.

As if a husband stood in awe on's wife,
My spirit shall be mistress of this house,
As long as I have time in't. (iii.i.133–40)

The idea of chastity is embodied in a colourful, individual personality, and even restraint and self-discipline become positive, not negative qualities. Like Simon Eyre, but in a more surprising way, she provides a thoroughly theatrical embodiment for a set of moral values. The play as a whole is a tired, conventional piece of work by two writers who had done the same thing before, and done it better; but Moll herself springs to life, and lingers in the memory.[2]

* * *

THEODORE B. LEINWAND

From Wives, Whores, Widows, and Maids[†]

The women's issues in [Thomas Dekker and John Webster's *Westward Ho* and *Northward Ho*. (c. 1604–1605)] are also explored in *The Roaring Girl*, at the Fortune. Once again, we have to do with a trio of citizen wives and a woman who is able to look out for herself. Mistresses Openwork, Gallipot, and Tiltyard are less resourceful than the wives in *Westward Ho*, and there is less mutual support among Middleton and Dekker's women. Self-assertiveness is intermixed with lechery as once again the women, understandably dissatisfied with their husbands, are deemed incontinent when they act on their dissatisfaction. Thus the sexual economy of the City is not especially happy: because citizen husbands are "cotqueans," citizen wives turn to "whisking gallants" who are but "lame gelding[s]" or "mere shallow things." The wives admit that it is best to return to their citizens (4.2); but their final rejection of the gallants is motivated by bourgeois solidarity, not the hope of contented sexual relations with their husbands.[1] It is significant that despite the conventional, unflattering portraits of citizen husbands and idle gal-

2. T. S. Eliot, *Elizabethan Dramatists* (London, 1963), pays just tribute to Moll as 'a real and unique human being' (p.85), though his claim that she has 'renounced all happiness for herself' (p.90) seems curious in view of the gusto with which she follows her chosen, eccentric way of life.
† From *The City Staged: Jacobean Comedy*, 1603–1613. © 1986 by the Board of Regents of the University of Wisconsin System. Reprinted by permission of The University of Wisconsin Press. Notes have been edited.
1. I stress the social and economic aspects because the wives do: Mistress Openwork insults the gallants, refers to the women as "we shop-keepers," and concludes on a note of citizen pride ("Oh if it were the good Lords wil, there were a law made, no Cittizen should trust any of 'em all"—4.2.57–58).

lants, the women still seem forward and independent. They speak in a language of double entendres that rivals the bawdy of the gallants. Mistress Gallipot, who has the least appealing husband, comes off the worst in her dealing with (the least appealing) gallant Laxton. And if the gallants are finally tricked, it is because Masters Gallipot and Openwork are enlisted into the fray. Middleton and Dekker protect us from the effects of fully independent, sympathetic city wives by giving us as much of them to laugh at as to laugh with.

The citizen wives in *The Roaring Girl* offer us a convenient yardstick to measure the presentation of such women in the public theater against those in the private theaters. However, it is obvious that the consequential woman in the play is Moll, the roaring girl. Middleton and Dekker create a "considerably romanticized version" of the woman who dressed as a man, fought, smoked, and generally scandalized her contemporaries by refusing marriage, motherhood, and conventional femininity.[2] Moll in *The Roaring Girl* is a defender of virtue and a debunker of prejudice against women. She is perfectly confident in herself ("I please my selfe, and care not else who loue mee"—5.1.319), and she is uncompromisingly independent ("I scorne to prostitute my selfe to a man, / I that can prostitute a man to me"—3.1.107–8). When she reproaches the lecherous gallant Laxton, she strikes out for all contemporary women at all such men:

> In thee I defye all men, their worst hates,
> And their best flatteries, all their golden witchcrafts,
> With which they intangle the poore spirits of fooles,
> Distressed needlewomen and trade-fallne wiues.
>   (3.1.88–91)

When Moll converts old Alexander Wengrave to her side, she proves that "common voice," or the very prejudices the city playwrights were staging, is "the whore / That deceiues mans opinion; mockes his trust, / Cozens his loue, and makes his heart vniust" (5.2.248–50). She is tough, spirited, good-humored, and morally upright. She champions the weak (Mary Fitz-allard), and she defeats evil (Laxton, Trapdoor).

All this makes Moll sound like Superwoman, and not a portrayal of a flesh-and-blood woman; and this impression must not be passed over lightly. There is another Moll in *The Roaring Girl*—Moll (or Mary) Fitz-allard is the victimized romantic heroine—and as the editor of the Mermaid edition of the play points out, this "doubling is a deliberate, if elementary, device to establish the identity of purpose in the two."[3] Mary would like to be free of male domination (in the form

---

2. Caroline Cherry, *The Most Unvaluedst Purchase: Women in the Plays of Thomas Middleton*, Salzburg Studies in English Literature (Salzburg: Universität Salzburg, 1973), p.102.
3. Andor Gomme, Introduction, *The Roaring Girl* (New York: Norton, 1976), p. xxiii.

of Sir Alexander's refusal to permit his son to marry her), and while
she is off stage through most of the play, her namesake acts as her
surrogate. But Moll is more than just a stand-in. She is a fantasy, an
embodiment of what an oppressed woman would imagine herself to
be in a time or land in which she has real power. As in the fantasies of
actual oppressed peoples, the champion takes on the traits of the
oppressor. Moll wears breeches and can handle a cudgel. She smokes
and consorts with (and in the language of) shady underworld types.
Moll is even that ultimate and perverse fantasy of the avenging
woman, a castrator (3.1.65–66).

When we finally come upon a "forceful embodiment of female
virtue," we find that she must act like a man.[4] Real women are like
Mary Fitz-allard; independent women are freaks, or outcasts, or
monsters (1.2.138; "Some will not sticke to say shees a man and
some both man and woman"—2.1.186–87). Moll knows that she
cannot marry because no man would tolerate her independence:
"I haue the head now of my selfe, and am man enough for a woman,
marriage is but a chopping and changing, where a maiden looses
one head, and has a worse ith place" (2.2.40–43). But she is wrong
when she asserts that a woman "that has wit, and spirit, / May scorne
to liue beholding to her body for meate" (3.3.133–34). Wit and spirit
are not enough, since even in the best of situations, the witty wife
must return obediently to her husband (and his whims). Total independence comes, as Moll illustrates, at the expense of a real self.
The poles are Mary and Moll, recognizable, dependent woman and
fantastic superwoman, victim and monster. A woman may call attention to herself only in the extreme: as infinitely patient, as sexually
incontinent, or as Amazonian.[5] If she is outrageous, she can help herself, if she is mindful of her place, she must wait for her lover (Sebastian Wengrave) or her fantasy surrogate to protect her. This is the
no-win dilemma staged at the Fortune. It is at once an elaboration of
Swetnam's attack on women and the unspoken implication of Sow-
ernam's defense. Middleton and Dekker can speak out (in the person of Moll) against the injustices done to women, and their attitude
seems to be, as Caroline Cherry has written, "basically affirmative
and liberal."[6] However, they have solved very little for contemporary
women, and what looks liberal is in fact rather conservative. A clear
affirmation of the rights and dignity of women would have meant an
unequivocal portrayal of the citizen wives. As it stands, the audience
may remain something of a Caesar to Middleton and Dekker's
Cleopatra/Moll. The truly spirited woman was best encountered as a

4. Cherry, *Most Unvaluedst Purchase*, p. 105.
5. Celeste T. Wright presents a survey of Elizabethan Amazons in "The Amazons in
Elizabethan Literature," *Studies in Philology*, 37 (1940), 433–56.
6. Cherry, *Most Unvaluedst Purchase*, p. 105.

male actor, playing a roaring girl in male attire, safely set off within the imaginary space of the theater.

Moll Cutpurse is an extravagant representation of an independent woman: her example is of value only to the extent that women can bring Moll's energy and self-confidence back into the mainstream of society. If Moll remains a freak, then she is good only for entertainment.

* * *

SIMON SHEPHERD

From Roaring Girls: Long Meg of Westminster and Moll Cutpurse[†]

Before Spenser's creation of Britomart appeared in print, there existed in folk literature another type of fighting woman. What is interesting about this type is that she inhabits a less chivalric, less aristocratic milieu, but that she still shares similar features in common with the Spenserian warrior woman.[1]

It is apparent that the existence of 'masculine' women was a social reality, in that female fashion tended to imitate that of males. 'I have met with some of these trulles in London so disguised, that it passed my skill to discerne whether they were men or women' (Harrison, *Description of England*, 1877, ii.171). There was a variety of attributes of the costume, many of which trespassed on role division:

> The Women also there have dublets & Ierkins, as men have heer, buttoned up the brest, and made with wings, welts, and pinions on the shoulder points, as mans apparel is for all the world: & though this be a kinde of attire appropriate onely to man, yet they blush not to wear it; and if they could as wel chaunge their sex, & put on the kinde of man, as they can weare apparel assigned onely to man, I think they would as verely become men indeed,
>
> (Stubbes, *Anatomy of Abuses*, 1877, p. 73)

The scandal of women wearing 'male' clothing was that, as we would expect, it upset the ordered scheme that depended on each sex

---

[†] From *Amazons and Warrior Women: Varieties of Feminism in Seventeenth-Century Drama.* (London: Palgrave McMillan, 1981), pp. 67–74, 77–83. Reprinted by permission.
1. The phrase 'roaring girl' is constructed from the Jacobean name for aggressive gallants about town, roaring boys; a female teddy boy, if you like.

maintaining its proper place: 'Our Apparell was given us as a signe
distinctive to discern betwixt sex and sex, & therfore one to weare
the Apparel of another sex is to participate with the same, and to
adulterate the veritie of his owne kinde' (ibid., p. 73). The blurring
of fashion raises important questions about what it is to be a woman.
The resultant confusion issues in something that can't be accommodated, a monster, women who

> from the top to the toe, are so disguised, that though they be in
> sexe Women, yet in attire they appeare to be men, and are like
> Androgini, who counterfayting the shape of either kind, are in
> deede neither, so while they are in condition women, and would
> seeme in apparell men, they are neither men nor women, but
> plaine Monsters.
>
> (Averell, Mervailous Combat, 1588, sig. Biv)

What we discover are Amazons of the streets. Gosson says of
women's 'privie coates':

> Were they for use against the foe
> Our dames for Amazones might goe.
>
> (Pleasant Quippes, 1596, p. 8)

Twenty years later Thomas Adams was again to remark on the Amazon
beneath the man-woman. The clothing scandal is irresistibly like a
seventeenth century version of those famous complaints in the
nineteen-sixties about boys with long hair. We knew then that clothing
and hair could be, and were to be, interpreted as social gesture.
Appearance and dress operate as political shorthand. I suspect much
of the Jacobean discussion went on at this level of gut-reaction.

My quotations so far date form the fifteen-eighties, but worry continued. In 1606, Dekker noted women were 'Mens Shee Apes'
(Dekker, 1963, p. 59). Much later, in 1620, James himself intervened; on 25 January that year Chamberlain records:

> Yesterday the bishop of London called together all his Clergie
> about this towne, and told them he had expresse commaundment
> from the king to will them to inveigh vehemently and bitterly in
> theyre sermons against the insolencie of our women, and theyre
> wearing of brode brimd hats, pointed dublets, theyre haire cut
> short or shorne, and some of them stillettaes or poinards, and such
> other trinckets of like moment, adding withall that yf pulpit admo-
> nitions will not reforme them he wold proceed by another course;
>
> (Chamberlain, 1939, ii.286–7)

The previous year John Williams had preached before the king at
Theobalds Palace on the subject of clothes; it was printed as A Sermon
of Apparell. He spoke of the woman with 'plaister'd eyes and a polled

head' and 'standing most manly upon her points, by wagging a Feather to defie the World, and carrying a dagger' (Williams, 1620, pp. 21–2) ('polled': cropped). The alliteration, the tactful innuendo on 'stand-ing', 'points', even 'Feather', seem calculated to entertain the royal audience. It may be likely that Williams already knew of James's obsessions, for he was to be one of the most canny clerical climbers of the decade. The same year as James's public outburst, and cashing in on it perhaps, there appeared a trio of pamphlets about manly women: Hic Mulier, Haec Vir, Muld Sacke: or the Apologie of Hic Mulier.

The 'masculine' woman of 1620 is described thus:

> till you weare hats to defend the Sunne, not to cover shorne locks, Caules to adorne the head, not Gregorians to warme idle braines, till you weare innocent white Ruffes, not iealous yellow iaundis'd bands, well shapt, comely and close Gownes, not light skirts and French doublets, for Poniards, Samplers, for Pistols Prayer-bookes, and for ruffled Bootes and Spurres, neate Shooes and cleane-garterd Stockings
> (Hic Mulier, 1620, sig. B4v) (Caule: cap or net; Gregorian:
>   a type of wig)

One of the most important elements is those 'shorne locks'. For women of the seventeenth century to cut their hair short was to make a gesture against the role that had been designed for them. The homily on Matrimony talks of the symbolism of long hair: the woman is reminded of her submissive role 'by the apparel of her head, whereby is signified that she is under covert and obedience of her husband. And, as that apparel is of nature so appointed to declare her subjection, so biddeth St. Paul that all other of her rai-ment should express both shamefastness and sobriety' (p. 541). Mas-culine women have exchanged 'the glory of a faire large hayre, to the shame of most ruffianly short lockes' (Hic Mulier, 1620, sig. A4v). That aggressive Presbyterian, Prynne, saw hair fashions as a symp-tom of social decadence. He wrote The Unlovelinesse of Love-Lockes mainly against poncey male fashions, but also asked: 'Whence is it, that our Immodest, Impudent, and mannish Viragoes, or audacious Men-women, doe unnaturally clip, and cut their Haire;' (p. 35). He cites the 'Councell of Gangra' which enacted that the woman who cut her hair, her 'naturall vaile', should be 'accursed, as an infringer of the precept of subiection:' (p. 36).

The crime of clothes involves more than a trespass on maleness. In 1631, Brathwait is still asking: 'That distinction which decency found out for habits virile and feminine, what commixture hath it found in latter times? What near resemblance and relation hath womans to mans: suting their light feminine skirts with manlike doublets?' (Brathwait, 1631, p. 10). Similarly Hic Mulier had spoken of 'nether skirts' that are 'light'. That lightness implies sensuality. The man-woman not only impinges on the role of the male but she is said to display the typical female failing of sexual looseness. We are back with the combination of qualities found in the Amazon Radigund; and 'virago', like 'Amazon', has become a dirty word. The result of the combination is a peculiarly aggressive female threat. The short-haired woman is like the whore in that both refuse subjection to a permanent male partner. Men-women 'have laid by the bashfulnesse of your natures, to gather the impudence of Harlots;' (*Hic Mulier*, sig. A4R). It's a traditional female sexuality that has become 'manly', or aggressive; and one deals with it as one deals with a whore, by sweeping it under the moral carpet.

The scandal about hair-length, clothing and whorishness finds specific focus in the folk figure of Long Meg of Westminster. The earliest printed pamphlet life of her appeared in 1582. The story seems to have been a popular one in that it enjoyed several reprint-ings between 1590 and 1635. There was a ballad entered in the Sta-tioners' Register on 27 August 1590; and a play, now lost, performed by the Admiral's Men on 14 February 1594/5.

The story of Long Meg's life runs like this: in the reign of Henry VIII she arrived in London from Lancashire and was given a job serving in the Eagle tavern at Westminster. After several victorious clashes with debtors, thieves and braggarts, she went with soldiers to Boulogne. Here she defeated the champion of the French and was honoured by the king. Then she returned to England, married a soldier and set up a tavern of her own in Islington.

When we meet references to her outside the pamphlet life she is closely associated with whores: 'O doost remember, howe that Bastard *Iunior* complaines of brothels, and talkes of long *Megg* of *Westminster*' (Lyly, *Works*, ii.403). Or again: 'It is said, that long Meg of Westmin-ster kept alwaies 20 Courtizans in her house, whom by their pictures she sold to all commers' (Deloney, 1912, p.532). *Hollands Leaguer* calls her not only a brothel-keeper but an Amazon. Frequently, how-ever, the name is simply used as an imprecise term of comic abuse.

Against the charges of whorishness and the comedy the popular pamphlet life gives us a different Meg. (I have pieced together the details of her life from the several printed versions.) We learn how her job at the Eagle tavern involves her in various scuffles with the clien-tele. As soon as she is employed she is put to the test by the bragging Sir James de Castile, and she knocks him to the ground. Sir James, it turns out, is the suitor of Meg's mistress, the Hostess of the Eagle. The Hostess dislikes Sir James's attentions and Meg is set up to fight him. She dresses in man's clothes, meets him and defeats him. The forfeit he must pay is 'that this night, at this woman's house, thou wait on my trencher at supper' (*Life of Long Meg*, p. 9). At the supper, James discovers Meg is a woman. She enters the room dressed as a

man, then, to the amusement of all, lets down her hair. The beating by
a woman effectively subdues Sir James's sexual ambitions.

The episode is full of telling details. We have met before the
woman who tames a braggart male's sexual aspirations by physical
punishment. We have met before the sudden, theatrical, release of
long female hair. These are the archetypal attributes of the warrior
woman. Given that the first appearance of Meg's pamphlet was in
1582, the story could not have been influenced by Spenser's Britomart, who appeared in print in 1590. The Meg author *may* have
known the Italian epics: certainly there is a (later) comic habit of
comparing aggressive women to romance warriors. Jonson's Dol
Common is jokingly compared to Claridiana and Bradamante; Doll
Tearsheet is a 'she knight-errant'. *Hic Mulier* tells men-women not
to 'thinke you may be attired like *Bradamant*, who was taken for
Ricardetto her brother; that you may fight like *Marfiza*, and winne
husbands with conquest or ride astride like *Claridiana*, and make
Gyants fall at your stirrops' (sig. B3r).

Although an imitation of the Italian cannot be demonstrated, it is
easy to see how close Long Meg of Westminster is to the image of
the warrior woman. When Meg is asked, at the Eagle, what work she
can do, she replies that she is 'little used to the needle, but to handy
labour; as to wash, to wring, to brew, to bake, to make clean a house
or any such Drudgery' (*Life and Pranks*, sig. A3r). Tasso's Clorinda's

> lofty hand would of itself refuse
> To touch the dainty Needle, or nice Thread;
> She hated Chambers, Closets, secret Mews,
> And in broad Fields preserv'd her Maidenhead:
>
> (*GL* II.39)

Needle-rejection is a symbolic gesture. Meg insists on woman's
work, and duels in open fields, rather than decorative sewing.

One of the versions of the life has her encounter 'huffing Dick' (the
name implies a braggart). He makes trouble in her tavern, and beats
her maid, and Meg punishes him. The penalty involves an elaborate
piece of role-swapping: 'thou shalt put my maid's petticoats on, and
follow me to day to dinner with a sword and a buckler; and I will be
drest in mans apparel.' (*The Life*, ed. Hindley, p. 42). By contrast, Meg
encounters a destitute soldier and decides to try him in physical combat. He proves too strong, 'being a marvellous tall fellow, and one that
feared not his flesh, laid on such a load, that *Meg* was feign to bid him
stay his hand, and discover who she was' (*Life*, pp. 17–8). Proper
manly power forces Meg to be a submissive woman. Thus Meg, like
the warrior woman, sorts out for us the proper man from the braggart.

Again like the warrior, she reinforces the institution of marriage.
When she returns from her fighting in France, she marries a soldier.

He immediately offers to 'trie her manhood' (*Life and Pranks*, sig. B2v). She refuses to fight and 'in all submission fell down upon her knees, desiring him to hold his hands and to pardon her' (*Life*, p. 36). He promptly beats her, and she, without protest, promises her obedience: 'never shall it be said, though I can cudgell a knave that wrongs me, that Long Meg shall be her Husbands master, and therfore use me as you please;' (*Life and Pranks*, sig. B3r).

This sudden marital submission is the most disconcerting part of Meg's life: it follows so suddenly from what has preceded it. The goal of the marital union, and in Meg's case the severe stress on submission, are the most difficult aspects of the warrior woman to take. What we have to remember is the religious, and sexual political, importance of a stress on true partnership in a world of arranged marriages and potentially institutionalised adultery. The warrior women do believe in marriage, they believe also in its corollary, proper government, but they believe in these ideals in a world improperly governed and where the alternative to marriage is much more humiliating. The situation to our eyes is painfully compromised and ambivalent. It is a world of he for God only, she for God in him. But for warrior women it is also a world of he for God only, she for God in him, as long as he can prove God is in him.

Meg, like Britomart, tests men on their own ground, sorts them out for us. She becomes literally a warrior in the French campaign. Here she shows herself able to outsoldier the soldiers and amazes a press-gang with her skill at pike drill. The highspot of her military career is a single-handed fight with the French champion. She defeats him and 'pulling out her Scymeter cut off his head, then taking off her Burganet, her hair did fall about her ears' (*Life and Pranks*, sig. B2v). Again the hair falls at the crucial moment.

Meg's fight against the French reveals the patriotic dimension. Very early she is matched against a 'Spanish knight' whose name, Castile, recalls the country. Just as Britomart in effect challenges the British to be properly aggressive, so Meg is upset to find a soldier who is destitute: 'A proper man and live in distresse'. To which he replies: 'Oh *Meg* quoth he you may say what you please because you are a woman, but divers in this city have seen the day when I lived like a man, but falling into sicknesse lost my service' (*Life and Pranks*, sig. A5r–v). The world is one that no longer values soldiers, that mistreats its proper men.

While Britomart's targets and ambitions were confined to the chivalric world, Meg is supplied with an everyday English context. This context, as with much of this Tudor 'low-life' literature, is double-edged. Firstly, Meg's activities are carefully removed from the present and set back in the reign of Henry VIII—a golden time when England *was* England, when they always sent in the Tudor equivalent of a gun-boat. There is much period colour. The Eagle tavern counts among its topers Dr Skelton and Will Summers; Sir Thomas More is one of the (somewhat unlikely) guests at the humiliation of James de Castile. The effortless class-mingling is a favourite motif of one sort of portrayal of Elizabethan society. Having defeated Sir James, and revealed herself a woman, Meg 'sat in state like her Majesty' (*Whole Life*, p. 10). Presumably, despite the nominal date of the history, this is Elizabeth. She is once again brought close to a warrior type. In the Eagle tavern the queen sits by proxy among those who are lower in the hierarchy than herself. It recalls those scenes where monarch and workers hobnob at banquets. Meg's life is part of the Elizabethan myth-making.

Against this happy muddle, the other side of Meg's world reveals a through-going attack on exploiters and officials. Meg is actually given a type of political awareness: when she tests the destitute soldier she chooses to wear a 'blew Coat, and a white Satten doublet' (*Life and Pranks*, sig. A5v). This clothing is loaded with class values: the blue coat was very often worn by serving men; the white satin doublet is frequently worn by the ornamental rich (see Middleton's young landlord in *Father Hubburd's Tales*, or his Scottish social climber, Andrew Lethe). When she fights a man Meg wears the coat of the servant over the doublet of the rich; when she leaves her proper sex status her clothes deliberately evoke a social hierarchic muddle.

Meg is employed in the Eagle tavern to make people pay their bills and to enforce common justice. Her protection of the tavern leads to conflict with the state's law officers. When a bailiff comes to arrest a man in the tavern, and warns 'the company to keep peace' (*Whole Life*, p. 11), Meg punishes him. She puts him in a pond and then cudgels him. The slapstick celebrates her attack. Later in her own pub in Islington, she confronts a constable: 'coming one night, he would needs search Meg's house, whereupon she came down in her shift, with a cudgel' (*Whole Life*, p. 23). The woman roused from bed holding a weapon recalls Britomart in Malecasta's house: this detail is not in the 1582 version of Meg's life, but was added later.

The fun with bailiffs, constables and officers of the watch extends into mockery of those other moral guardians, clerics: 'One of the lubbers of the Abbey had a mind to try her strength' (*Whole Life*, p. 6). He refuses to pay his bill and she beats the 'Vicar's' head against a wooden post. When she later forces thieves to swear to her conditions, since she has no bible, they swear by the skirt of her smock.

Meg stands for a form of lower-class resistance against the dominant order of society. Her 'programme' is outlined in the conditions she imposes on the thieves whom she punishes for their attempted robbery of her friends:

1. that you never hurt woman, nor any company that a woman is in.
2. that you never hurt poore or impotent man.
3. That you rob no children nor Innocents.
4. That you rob no Pack-men nor Carryers: for their goods and money is none of their own.
5. That you rob no manner of distressed persons: but of this I give you this exception, that as for every rich Farmer and Currish chuff that hoords up money, such spare not; for they let the poore want, therefore let them feele your fingers.

(*Life and Pranks*, sig. A8v)

The last of these conditions becomes less political in a later printing: 'That you rob no manner of poor or distressed' (*Whole Life*, p. 17).

I have spent some time on Meg because she is an interesting figure. She *is* a type of warrior, and this image of her exists alongside the charges elsewhere of whorishness and the man-woman clothing scandal. The warrior morality offers a different perspective on the sensationalised anti-feminism, and in part resists it.

* * *

Moll is carefully associated with the tradition of Long Meg. Moll, like Meg, helps a man escape from debt. He asks her whether it was 'your Meg of Westminster's courage' (V.i.2) that helped him escape. When Sir Alexander's agent, Trapdoor, greets Moll he says: 'Bless my hopeful young mistress with long life and great limbs, send her the upper hand of all bailiffs' (II.i.314–6). Meg was 'long', she was famous for her height; the mention of bailiffs seems again to recall Meg. Just as Meg deliberately tests the manliness of the impoverished soldier, so Moll tries out Trapdoor's 'virility'. When she tells him 'I'll make you wait on me before I ha'done, and glad to serve me too' (III.i.172–3), we are reminded of what Meg did to Sir James and huffing Dick. When she is to fight, Moll appoints to meet in Gray's Inn Fields, the place where Meg meets. Moll's general hostility to officers of the law, and her support for sons against aristocratic fathers seems to recall Meg's championing of poor against rich. Middleton's play arranges deliberately a clash of classes: the aristocrats of the main plot, the citizens of the sub-plot, the roaring girl: the type has her class role.

Part of the tradition of Meg is the sexual monstrosity: the play elaborates on this:

It is a thing
One knows not how to name: her birth began

Ere she was all made: 'tis woman more than man,
Man more than woman, and (which to none can hap)
The sun gives her two shadows to one shape:
Nay more, let this strange thing walk, stand or sit,
No blazing star draws more eyes after it.

(I.ii.128–34)

To increase the scandal Moll is early on contrasted with the other women in the play. Sebastian explains to his lover Mary Fitzallard that he is pretending to love Moll:

a creature
So strange in quality, a whole city takes
Note of her name and person:

(I.i.95–7)

Mary is the romantic heroine, belonging not to the city but to the private world of young love. Moll by contrast first appears in a scene where Laxton the gallant is flirting with shop-keepers' wives, who are expected to delight in the virility of gallants. They say of Moll:

Some will not stick to say she is a man
And some both man and woman.

(II.i.190–1)

Moll, by implication, doesn't have the means to sexual fulfilment available to the citizen wife. Yet Moll upstages both sets of women. Mary Fitzallard is ineffectual in furthering her own private romance. The citizen wives for all their adulterous intrigue end up exploited by both husbands and lovers. Moll has both effectiveness and freedom.

But your freedom is limited if the world thinks of you as peculiar. Sir Alexander Wengrave warns his son that he will be the subject of gossip. The play seems to invite us to see Moll as a comic, knock-about figure. She has a hilarious scene when her tailor measures her for newly fashioned breeches:

TAILOR: Your breeches then will take up a yard more.
MOLL: Well, pray look it be put in then.
TAILOR: It shall stand round and full, I warrant you.

(II.ii.82–4)

The puns on 'yard' (penis) and 'stand' (erection) allow us to laugh at Moll's aspirations, a laughter she encourages: 'I have no humour to marry, I love to lie o' both sides o'th'bed myself, and again o'th'other side; a wife you know ought to be obedient, but I fear me I am too headstrong to obey, therefore I'll ne'er go about it' (II.ii.36–9). Moll articulates the tension that hovers around most women in these plays: she knows what marriage should be but she survives by being

headstrong, thus she finds unsatisfactory the available moral structure. The independence also incorporates a criticism of marriage: 'I
have the head now of myself, and am man enough for a woman; marriage is but a chopping and changing, where a maiden loses one head
and has a worse i'th'place' (42–4). The pun on 'head' (maindenhead/
penis/head of household) connects the chastity and the freedom.

Moll likes, and needs, to be outside male society. And this 'outsi-
deness' is convenient to that society: Sir Alexander is pleased that
she doesn't want to marry Sebastian. Yet she does intervene because
she is used in Sebastian's trick. The comic narrative thus brings us
into tension with the moral labelling: Moll is useful but monstrous.
Here we can recognise at work the Middleton technique. He has us
shift our attitude to Moll, as to Mistress Purge, through our comic
expectations. This narrative trick is a means of inverting our moral
responses. We desire, at the moment of Sir Alexander's triumph, that
Moll intervenes, not just to help Sebastian but to attack Sir Alexander. His influence is much more oppressive and nasty than Moll's,
although of course he is 'normal' and she is 'monstrous'.

Middleton characterises Sir Alexander's 'normality' in two ways.
First, in order to convince his friends how afflicted he is by his son he
tells them a 'story'. This story of supposed filial disobedience is told in
conventional 'tragic' language, but the convention is used to justify
selfish aggression. Sir Alexander's opposition to his son's marriage is
based only on financial considerations. Second, and by way of corollary to the 'tragic' self-image, he intends to use the process of law to
remove Moll from his son's life, and kill her. Law, the institution
which legislates about what is 'normal' can be employed by such 'normal' people as Sir Alexander to further their own aggressive ends.

Sir Davy Dapper, like Sir Alexander, plans to tame his son by law,
by imprisoning him for debt. In this society lack of money is a form
of madness: law is sanity, imprisonment an education:

> Bedlam cures not more madmen in a year
> Than one of the counters does: men pay more dear
> There for their wit than anywhere; a counter,
> Why 'tis an university, who not sees?
> As scholars there, so here men take degrees,
>   (III.iii.79–83) (counter: debtors' prison)

The cynical manipulation of the law combines with the verbal polish
of the sustained imagery and couplets. This is aesthetically 'pleasing'
and socially 'normative'. Against it we must set Moll's monstrosity,
and then allow our sympathies to decide. What these two knights
do, however, is by no means confined to them alone. The play is
careful to enlarge its social criticism. The sergeant employed by Sir
Davy tells us: 'all that live in the world are but great fish and little
fish, and feed upon one another . . . they call us knaves and curs,

but many times he that sets us on worries more lambs one year than
we do in seven' (135–9).

The play notes corruption at all levels of 'normal' society. And it
particularly concerns itself with sexual crime. Moll indicts the entire
libertine outlook on the world:

> Distressed needlewomen and trade-fallen wives,
> Fish that must needs bite or themselves be bitten,
> Such hungry things as these may soon be took
> With a worm fastened on a golden hook:
> Those are the lecher's food, his prey, he watches
> For quarrelling wedlocks, and poor shifting sisters,
> 'Tis the best fish he takes: but why, good fisherman,
> Am I thought meat for you, that never yet
> Had angling rod cast towards me? 'cause, you'll say,
> I'm given to sport, I'm often merry, jest:
> Had mirth no kindred in the world but lust?
>
> (III.i.93–103)

She sees the male exploitation of women, coupled with the insecurities
of women's work and the fact that women have no way of expressing or
defending themselves. And then she moves on to indict that stand-by
of libertine culture, the idea that all is sport, all sexual relations,
never mind how painful, are merry. The sub-plot, about shop-keeping
wives, ends with their husbands being merry with their attempted lovers,
to the exclusion of the women, who remain used and dissatisfied.

The world around Moll manipulates ideas of normality, and makes
assumptions about the exploitation of women and sex. Moll, the supposed deviant, is much more sympathetic than what surrounds her.
But the point is more political than moral. Moll cannot be contained
by male society as it is presently constructed; Middleton makes her
difficult. This is a toughening of the Meg-Moll legend. Meg was, in
many ways, a device for sorting out men, like the warrior woman. She
was a way of 'normalising', in male terms, sexual relationships. Middleton refuses Moll this role, and in doing so activates the tension
between Britomart and Radigund. Moll is, like Radigund, self-willed,
but she is, like Britomart, more just than those around her.

Moll apparently is suspicious of the lecherous shop-keepers'
wives. She lectures Mistress Openwork.

> you that prick out a poor living
> And sews many a bawdy skin-coat together,
> Thou private pandress between shirt and smock,
> I wish thee for a minute but a man:
>
> (II.i.215–8)

What happens immediately after this is that a fellow enters 'with a
long rapier by his side' so Moll picks a fight with him. Moll is not

interested in pursuing the punishment of a woman; she instead
vents her anger on a man, an apparently inoffensive stranger. This
seems somewhat to question Moll's role as just arbiter—it seems
that any man is worse than a lecherous woman. But the man is carrying both the literal and symbolic image of male power: rapier,
penis. Here we need to look again at what Moll said. Mistress Openwork has a 'poor living' which needs to be 'pricked' out: sex is necessary to the economics. This analysis is like her later sympathetic
complaint about what men do to 'Distressed needlewomen and
trade-fallen wives'. Women do have special difficulties. Moll recog-
nises that it is morally inaccurate to treat Mistress Openwork as if
she were a man. Women are trying to survive in a male world run by
male laws that rest on double standards. As such, an aggressive
armed male can be worse than a lecherous woman.

There is a constant awareness of the relationship between female
lechery and the male world which conditions women:

> oh, the gallants of these times are shallow lechers, they put not
> their courtship home enough to a wench, 'tis impossible to
> know what woman is thoroughly honest, because she's ne'er
> thoroughly tried: I am of that certain belief there are more
> queans in this town of their own making than of any man's pro-
> voking; where lies the slackness then? many a poor soul would
> down, and there's nobody will push 'em:
> Women are courted but ne'er soundly tried,
> As many walk in spurs that never ride.
>
> (II.i.290–9)

It is an Ovidian idea that women are not demonstrably chaste ('honest') until 'tried'. It is an argument often used to seduce women; but
Moll tells us here that men don't want sex. They only court, they don't
copulate (the second meaning of 'tried'). This is true of the gallant Laxton. Lines that seem to question the genuineness of female chastity
become an attack on men. The virility of the Ovidian position is undercut, by being spoken by a woman and by the women's open sexual
activity. Women become whores because they want to, not because
men persuade them; men cannot manage sex anyway. The double-
edged quality of the whole piece comes together in the word 'slackness'. Queans as whores are morally slack: but they make themselves
whores because their men are physically slack, they don't have erec-
tions. Consequently, the women are disappointed because the men
won't push them down (onto a bed). There is a suggestion that in the
face of female moral slackness, or sexual challenge, the men become
physically slack. The speech becomes a celebration of female sexuality
against male pretensions. The phrase 'their own making' can also
imply the use of dildoes: the women can literally do without the men.

Moll's honesty about physical sexuality connects with her insistence on getting the spiritual side correct. She scorns a relationship that elevates the physical into a false religion:

> Base is that mind that kneels unto her body,
> As if a husband stood in awe on's wife;
>
> (III.i.137–8)

Male libertine attitudes refuse to admit the challenge of female sexuality; they confuse the physical and spiritual, and make an object of the female body. Moll would like to meet her enemies one by one

> And make 'em know, she that has wit and spirit
> May scorn
> To live beholding to her body for meat,
>
> (III.i.132–4)

She is a woman who, like the warrior, can insist on the sexual duel; she can insist on equal conditions of battle, whether physical or intellectual. To do this revalues the woman. But such equal battles are too often denied by the male world. Males assume a dominance that is physical, intellectual and sexual; they assume that they are the norm, that their value judgements are correct. (This is why so many contemporary feminists attacked slanderers: slander is a way of judging without trial.) It is rare that the male assumptions are put to the trial of strength. Moll wants to test male supremacy empirically. Typically, in doing so she is regarded as a 'monster'.

When Moll confronts males, she plays up to the archetypal male images for women: she exposes the sexually oppressive nature of the customary language. This is most marked in her dealings with Laxton. It is the archetype of the tough woman meeting the libertine male. Laxton wants to meet with Moll, so he offers her gold, which she accepts: 'Why, here's my hand I'll meet you sir' (II.i.265). For him the meeting is sexual, for her a duel. When they meet she challenges:

> Draw, or I'll serve an execution on thee
> Shall lay thee up till doomsday.
>
> (III.i.67–8)

She puns on 'draw' (expose the penis) and 'execution' (sexual intercourse). Moll reverses the Ovidian use of battle images for sex, and thus exposes the power relationship of this 'casual' sexual flirtation. Eventually it is not sex but proprietary male assumptions that Moll attacks:

> th'art one of those
> That thinks each woman thy fond flexible whore:

> If she but cast a liberal eye upon thee,
> Turn back her head, she's thine:

(70–3)

Moll acts the whore and yet insists on her right to choose. Thus she shows males that female sexual activity is not a declaration of subservience.

Moll reveals the contradiction of male attitudes. When she disguises as Sebastian's bride, Sir Alexander likens her to 'my first wife his mother'. There is horror when she unmasks, but she feigns surprise: 'Methinks you should be proud of such a daughter, / As good a man as your son' (V.ii.152–3). The sexual contradictions relate back to economic contradictions: Moll mocks a system of inheritance that privileges children because of their gender rather than their worth. She is manly in honour, but not a biological man. Meg's marriage accepts male power, Moll's fake marriage reveals and laughs at male power. She ends the play single, rejecting Sir Alexander's 'pity', careless of male morality and law.

WORKS CITED

Averell, W. *A Mervailous Combat of Contrarieties*, London, 1588.
Brathwait, R. *The English Gentlewoman*, London, 1631.
Chamberlain, J. *The Letters*, ed. N. E. McClure, 2 vols, American Philosophical Society, 1939.
Dekker, T. *Non-Dramatic Works*, ed. A. B. Grosart. 2nd edn, 5 vols, Russell, 1963.
Deloney, T. *Works*, ed. F. O. Mann, Oxford, 1912.
Goodman, N. *Hollands Leaguer*, London, 1632.
Gosson, S. *Pleasant Quippes for Upstart Newfangled Gentlewomen*, London, 1596.
Harrison, W. *Harrison's Description of England in Shakespere's Youth*, ed. F. J. Furnivall, vol, 2, N. Trubner, 1877.
Hindley, C. *The Life of Long Meg of Westminster*, Reeves and Turner, 1871.
Hic Mulier, or The Man-Woman, London, 1620.
"Homily on the State of Matrimony," *Certain Sermons or Homilies* (1547), London, 1890.
The Life and Death of Long Meg of Westminster, n.d.
The Life and Pranks of Long Meg of Westminster, 1582.
The Life and Merry Pranks of Long Meg of Westminster, Newcastle, 1775.
The Life of Long Meg, of Westminster, n.d.
Lyly, J. *Complete Works of John Lyly*, ed. R. W. Bond, 3 vols, Clarendon, 1902.
Prynne, W. *The Unlovelinesse of Love-Locks*, London, 1628.
Spenser, E. *Poetical Works*, ed. J. C. Smith and E. de Selincourt, 2nd edn, Oxford University Press, 1970.
———.*The Faerie Queene*, ed. E. Greenlaw, et al, 2nd edn, 6 vols, Johns Hopkins University Press, 1958.
Stubbes, P. *Anatomy of the Abuses in England* (1583), ed. F. J. Furnivall, N. Trubner, 1877.
The Whole Life and Death of Long Meg, of Westminster, n.d.
The Whole Life and Death of Long Meg of Westminster, London, 1750.
Williams, J. *A Sermon of Apparell*, London, 1620.

PATRICK CHENEY

Moll Cutpurse as Hermaphrodite in Dekker and Middleton's *The Roaring Girl*†

In his 1927 essay on Middleton, T. S. Eliot praised *The Roaring Girl* as Middleton's "best" comedy. What Eliot valued was the Roaring Girl herself, Moll Cutpurse, whom he finds

> always real. She may rant, she may behave preposterously, but she remains a type of the sort of woman who has renounced all happiness for herself and who lives only for a principle. . . . Middleton's comedy deserves to be remembered chiefly by its real—perpetually real—and human figure of Moll. . . . [*The Roaring Girl* is the] one comedy which more than any Elizabethan comedy realizes a free and noble womanhood[1]

Eliot is thus able to forgive the play's weaknesses for its powerful portrayal of a central figure who is, paradoxically, both "perpetually real" and the embodiment of an ideal (a "type of . . . free and noble womanhood").

Despite Eliot's enthusiasm for *The Roaring Girl*, subsequent criticism has not been so forgiving; it certainly has not been so enthusiastic. Between 1927 and 1970, the criticism confined itself largely to very limited or technical problems, such as the relationship between Moll and the historical Mary Frith, the manuscript of the quarto edition, or the "double" names of two of the characters, Moll and Mary Fitzallard. In the 1970's, however, Middleton (and Dekker) scholarship flourished, resulting in several book-length studies. At one extreme is Anthony Covatta, who mentions merely in passing that *The Roaring Girl* is "much overrated" and that it is "sentimental and topical." At the other extreme is David M. Holmes, who devotes a chapter to the play, focusing on identifying Middleton's contribution and on a plot summary. In between are critics like Norman Brittin, who offers a brief commentary: the play is "largely a vindication of Moll" (who, as the historical Mary Frith, needed a good deal of vindication), and its patterns are "mainly romantic and satirical," the romantic parts being written by Dekker and the satirical by Middleton. Perhaps, however, the most significant work done during the decade is the 1976 New Mermaids edition of the play,

† From *Renaissance and Reformation/Renaissance et Réforme* 7.2 (Centre for Reformation and Renaissance Studies, 1983), pp. 120–34. Reprinted by permission.
1. *Elizabethan Dramatists* (London: Faber and Faber, 1963). pp. 89–93. Eliot still considered the 1927 essay of value in 1963 when he included it in his edition of selected essays.

edited by Andor Gomme, who in an introduction focuses on Moll as the unifying moral force in the play[2]

Aside from Eliot's enthusiasm, missing in recent criticism is a detailed analysis of Moll Cutpurse, the figure Eliot claimed was a "finer woman" than any we find in Webster, Marlowe, Tourneur, Shirley, Fletcher, or even Shakespeare,[3] in the play Eliot claimed was the "best" of Middleton's comedies. I should presently like to build on Eliot's implied remark that Moll's power as a character depends on her being, paradoxically, both realistic and idealistic. She is realistic in that she is endowed with a complex personality, both benign and irascible. She is idealistic (in the sense of being romantic and mythical) in that she is endowed with a hermaphroditic nature, both male and female. I shall argue that Moll's hermaphroditic nature helps explain her dual personality, for her benign manner is traditionally a feminine trait (as in the goddess of beauty, Venus), and her irascible manner is traditionally a masculine trait (as in the god of war, Mars). Moreover, the two sides of Moll's nature and her personality help explain her role in the plot: she is both a moderator-reuniter and an inciter-exposer. Moll's hermaphroditism also helps explain much of the imagery in the play, for in it she is a creature of both the land and the sea, a subject and an object of desire.

Moll's hermaphroditism, I shall also suggest, derives from a Platonic and Neoplatonic tradition, popularized by Spenser, in which the hermaphrodite is a figure of love representing the union of contraries, or the pagan mystery of *concordia discors*. Moll is most akin to that hermaphroditic figure of love, Venus, particularly in the form of *Venus armata* (Venus wearing the armor of Mars), who signifies the warfare of love. In her role as such an *eros* figure, Moll comes to represent, as the play's preface implies, the spirit of comedy—in particular, a new form of comedy then coming into vogue. Although *The Roaring Girl* is at times a very funny play, containing many lewd sexual innuendoes, it has a most serious central theme: love as the power that unites contraries.

2. For notes and articles on the technical problems of the play, see M. Dowling, "A Note on Moll Cutpurse: The Roaring Girl," *RES*, 10 (January 1934), 67–71; James G. McManaway, "Fortune's Wheel," *TLS*, (April 16, 1938), p. 264, George R. Price, "The Manuscript and Quarto of *The Roaring Girl*," *Library*, 11(1956), 182–3; William Power, "Double, Double," *N&Q*, 6(1959), 4–8; and two recent articles by P.A. Mulholland: "The Date of *The Roaring Girl*," *RES*, 28(1977), 18–31 (which fixes the date at 1611, rather than the conventional 1605), and "Some Textual Notes on *The Roaring Girl*," *Library*, 32(1977), 333–43. For comments in books, see Anthony Covatta, *Thomas Middleton's City Comedies* (Lewisburg: Bucknell Univ. Press, 1973), pp. 10 and 137; David M. Holmes, *The Art of Thomas Middleton* (Oxford: Clarendon Press, 1970), pp. 100-110; Norman A. Brittin, *Thomas Middleton* (New York: Twayne, 1972), pp. 77–9; and George R. Price, *Thomas Dekker* (New York: Twayne, 1969), p. 142, who agrees with Brittin about the portions of the play written by each author. For the New Mermaids edition, see *The Roaring Girl*, ed. Andor Gomme (London: Ernest Benn, and New York: W.W. Norton, 1976); on Moll as "the moral force of the play," see p. xxxiv.
3. *Elizabethan Dramatists*, p. 89.

The tradition of the hermaphrodite that *The Roaring Girl* is indebted to goes back to Plato. In the *Symposium*, Aristophanes tells his famous tale in which originally there were three kinds of human beings: man, woman, and the hermaphrodite. Mankind, however, grew corrupt through his pride, and Zeus grew angry, dividing each kind in two. As a result, those beings previously male now seek a male mate, while those previously female seek a female mate, and those previously hermaphrodites seek the half they are missing. Aristophanes concludes:

> So you see, gentlemen, how far back we can trace our innate love for one another, and how this love is always trying to redintegrate our former nature, to make two into one, and to bridge the gulf between one human being and another.[4]

Importantly, the hermaphrodite represents the union of male and female, the union of contrary sexes.

In his commentary on Plato's *Symposium*, Marsilio Ficino interprets the fable as an allegory of love:

> Hence mutual love, the restorer of their original nature, is innate in all men, striving to make the two one again, and to heal the natures of men . . . This desire of restoring the whole—this force—has received the name of Love.[5]

For Ficino, as for Plato, man had an original identity that he lost and that he consequently attempts to regain through love.

According to Edgar Wind, an Orphic poet like Ficino

> could not doubt that the monstrousness of Aristophanes' fable was a sign that it concealed a sacred mystery; and in that he followed, perhaps more than he knew, the distant precedent of Alexandrian Platonism. The biblical passage: "and he divided them in the midst" (Genesis xv, 10) has been cited by Philo as crucial evidence for . . . the "Logos as cutter," who produces "creation by dichotomy" but is the "joiner of the universe" as well. In Aristophanes' fable the divided man longs to regain his original integrity; and . . . that benefit is conferred on him by the power of Love. . . . Instead of having to turn around to see the light . . . the Aristophanic man can attend to the upper and lower worlds simultaneously. . . . For Ficino the ridiculous monster . . . concealed a promise of celestial bliss.[6]

4. *Symposium*, 191d, trans. Michael Joyce, in *The Collected Dialogues of Plato*, eds. Edith Hamilton and Huntington Cairns (Princeton, N.J.: Princeton Univ. Press, 1961).
5. *Commentary on Plato's "Symposium,"* Speech 4, Chapter 1, trans. Sears R. Jayne (Columbia: Univ. of Missouri Press, 1944), pp. 154–5.
6. *Pagan Mysteries in the Renaissance* (1958; rev. and enl., New York: W.W. Norton, 1968), p. 202. Future citations will be included in the text.

Wind, noting that the hermaphrodite was treated both seriously and jocularly, suggests that if the hermaphrodite resembled a monster of abnormal portents, "it was not because of a willful preference for the grotesque. The unusual subject demanded an unusual tone". In fact, he says, the Platonic hermaphrodite "became . . . acceptable [as] an image for the universal man".

The figure of the hermaphrodite is widespread in Renaissance literature, Ben Jonson, for example, in *The New Inn* has Lord Beaufort refer directly to the Platonic myth (with perhaps the Christian overtones mentioned by Wind).

> Then I have read somewhere, that man and woman
> Were, in the first creation, both one piece,
> And being cleft asunder, euer since,
> Loue was an appetite to be reioyn'd.

In the same play, love is defined as "a spirituall coupling of two soules."[7] Although Jonson does not use the word "hermaphrodite" here, he does use the corresponding dramatic device, disguise, in which characters don the clothes of another—frequently, women donning men's clothes, and men donning women's clothes. The Host's "son" Frank, for example, is really his daughter Laetitia. Everyone, in fact, is masking his identity, and, as is revealed by the play's central episode, the "court of love," this identity is largely sexual in nature. In the end, everyone reveals who he really is, and all the appropriate couples reunite.

Perhaps a more memorable example of the theme occurs in Shakespeare's *Twelfth Night* (which Jonson evidently had in mind when he wrote *The New Inn*). Viola dons the disguise of a male page, and at the end, when her twin brother Sebastian appears, the Duke Orsino says, "One face, one voice, one habit, and two persons!"[8] The soldier Antonio asks Sebastian, perhaps referring to the Platonic myth in its Christianized form,

> How have you made division of yourself?
> An apple cleft in two is not more twin
> Than these two creatures. Which is Sebastian? (V.i.214–16)

And finally, Sebastian himself tells Olivia, the lover of the "page" Viola, "You are betroth'd both to a maid and a man" (255). The comi-

---

7. *The New Inn*, III.ii. 79–82 and 105, in *Ben Jonson*, eds. C. H. Herford and Percy and Evelyn Simpson (Oxford: The Clarendon Press, 1938), VI. That Jonson is referring directly to the Platonic myth, one of the characters, Lovell, lets us know: "It is a fable of Plato's, in his Banquet, / And vutter'd there, by Aristophanes" (86–7). In *Epicoene*, Jonson's parody of the Elizabethan notion of hermaphroditism becomes the subject for an entire play. On Jonson's use of the Platonic myth of the hermaphrodite, see Patrick Cheney, "Jonson's *The New Inn* and Plato's Myth of the Hermaphrodite," in *Renaissance Drama*, volume XIV.
8. *Twelfth Night*, V.i. 208, in *William Shakespeare: The Complete Works*, ed. Peter Alexander (London and Glasgow: Collins, 1951). Future citations will be included in the text.

cal confusion of sexual identity is resolved when Sebastian unites with Olivia, and Viola unites with the Duke. In Shakespeare, as in Jonson and other dramatists of the period, comedy is binary in form, beginning with a phase of confusion about sexual identity and ending with a recognition, in which separated lovers join to create a happy ending.

Underneath all the joking, of course, is a rather serious matter, as revealed, for example, in the more private love poetry of Donne. As many commentators have recognized, at the heart of Donne's love poetry is the idea of two souls becoming one, as such poems as "The Dissolution," "A Valedication: Forbidding Mourning," and "Epithalamion Made at Lincoln's Inn" reveal. As Donne puts it in "The Ecstacy," "we two [are] one anothers best":

> Our hands were firmely cimented
>   With a fast balme, which thence did spring,
> Our eye-beames twisted, and did thread
>   Our eyes, upon one double string;
>
> So to'entergraft our hands, as yet
>   was all our meanes to make us one.

In this "dialogue of one," Donne goes on to speak about love, which "these mixt soules doth mixe againe, / And makes both one, each this and that."[9] Man's true identity consists of his physical and spiritual union with a beloved of the opposite sex.

Perhaps the most significant Renaissance representation of the hermaphrodite and the principle of "two into one" occurs in Donne's great predecessor in love poetry, Edmund Spenser. In the original ending to Book III of The Faerie Queene, the heroine Amoret joins with the hero Scudamour in an embrace to form a "faire Hermaphrodite":

> Had ye them seene, ye would have surely thought,
>   That they had beene that faire Hermaphrodite,
> Which that rich Romane of white marble wrought,
>   And in his costly Bath causd to bee site:
> So seemd those two, as growne together quite.[1]

Amoret and Scudamour come together "like two senceles stocks in long embracement" thus participating in love's "sweet counteruayle." Although Spenser reveals that his figure derives from the Ovidian myth of Salmacis and Hermaphroditus, rather than Plato, he retains a symbolic meaning common to both myths during the period: the

9. The Poems of John Donne, ed. Sir Herbert Grierson (London: Oxford Univ. Press, 1933).
1. Faerie Queene, III. xii. 46 (original ending), in The Poetical Works of Edmund Spenser, eds. Ernest de Sélincourt and J.C. Smith (London: Oxford Univ. Press, 1909), I. Future citations will be included in the text. See Donald Cheney, "Spenser's Hermaphrodite and the 1590 Faerie Queene," PMLA, 87 (March 1972), 192–200.

hermaphrodite is a supreme symbol of two souls becoming one—
particularly, within the context of married love.

For Spenser, Amoret and Scudamour represent, in Edgar Wind's
terms, the "unfolding" of the great hermaphrodite, the goddess
Venus. In Book IV, canto x of *The Faerie Queene*, Venus is portrayed
as being both male and female:

> The cause why she was couered with a vele,
>   Was hard to know, for that her Priests the same
>   From peoples knowledge labour'd to concele.
>   But sooth it was not sure for womanish shame,
>   Nor any blemish, which the worke mote blame;
>   But for, they say, she hath both kinds in one,
>   Both male and female, both vnder one name;
>   She syre and mother is her selfe alone,
> Begets and eke conceiues, ne needeth other none. (IV.x. 41)

Covered in a veil, Venus is indeed a "pagan mystery," a great goddess
shrouding the principle of the union of contraries, *concordia discors*,
both male and female, to become a powerful self-contained creative
force in faeryland. Complete within herself, Venus takes as her task
the joining of other couples in love, as she does with Amoret and
Scudamour here in the Temple of Venus episode, so that they in
turn can participate in the mystery of love's creative union.

Traditionally, one of the forms of the hermaphroditic Venus is what
Wind calls the *Venus armata*. This figure represents the union of contraries by combining the feminine trait of amiability and the masculine
trait of fierceness. Although often the principle of *concordia discors* is
represented in the union of Venus and Mars, Venus can represent the
principle herself when "she adopts the martial weapons for her own".
"Dressed in armour, the . . . *Venus armata* signifies the warfare of love:
she is a compound of attraction and rejection, fostering her gracious
aims by cruel methods" (p. 91). Comparing pictures of the martial
Venus with the poetical self-portrait of the writer Navagero, Wind says:

> the roles of Mars and Venus, which would normally be divided
> between man and woman, both recur within man and woman
> as such. The principle of the "whole in the part" entails this
> rather baffling conclusion: that Venus is not only joined to
> Mars, but that his nature is an essential part of her own, and
> vice versa. True fierceness is thus conceived as potentially ami-
> able, and true amiability as potentially fierce. In the perfect
> lover they coincide because he—or she—is the perfect warrior.
> (p. 94)

Venus, in other words, dons armor primarily to overcome obstacles
standing between her and her object of desire—a symbol of her
power of love. But, as Wind is careful to note, "while appearing

armed, Venus may give to the armour a peaceable motive". The *Venus armata*, in short, comes to symbolize love's power to unite contraries peacefully as a means of happiness.[2]

In Spenser's *Faerie Queene*, Venus, though appearing as a hermaphrodite, does not actually appear in martial guise as *Venus armata*. In Book III, however, the heroine Britomart uses her powers to reunite Amoret and Scudamour (at least according to the original ending of Book III), thus serving as a forerunner to Venus and her similar reunion of the couple at the end of Book IV. Spenser portrays Britomart as a warrior maiden whose armor conceals her feminine beauty, often resulting in her being confused for one of her masculine counterparts. As the etymology of her name suggests ("Brito" = the female Britannia; "mart" = the male Mars), Britomart is a human (and British) form of the *Venus armata*:

> For she was full of amiable grace,
> And manly terrour mixed therewithall. (III.i.46)

Although a heroine of chastity, Britomart is destined to use her armor to unite with her lover, Artegall, so that they can fulfill their destiny of creating a long line of British kings and queens. Britomart is not sexually self-complete, like the hermaphroditic Venus, but she becomes a popular portrayal of a heroine who dons masculine attire, combines in her person both feminine and masculine traits, and uses her remarkable powers to unite other couples in love.

A decade after Spenser published the second part of *The Faerie Queene*, Thomas Dekker adapted the great romantic epic for the Jacobean stage in his *Whore of Babylon*, which borrows freely both themes and figures from the national epic.[3] Shortly after, Dekker collaborated with Middleton in writing *The Roaring Girl*, which in some respects can be seen as an adaptation of Spenser's great theme of the hermaphroditic nature of human love to Jacobean citizen comedy.[4]

---

2. Wind says that the "idea of Venus as a Goddess of moderation may be mythologically odd," but, he argues, Pico calls her "the goddess of concord and harmony," following Plutarch. In fact, the "concept of a beneficent, peaceable, guarded Venus was one of the more refreshing paradoxes of Neoplatonism" (p. 119). This duality, he adds, is not confined to Venus alone: "All the particular gods, in the Orphic theology as outlined by Pico, seem animated by a law of self-contrariety, which is also a law of self-transcendence" (p. 196). After providing examples of how this principle functions for all the major gods and goddesses (Venus is the goddess of concord but she loves strife), Wind concludes, "all the gods, without exception, appear in Orphic theology as inciters and moderators, they are *dei ambigui*" (p. 196).

3. See Price, *Thomas Dekker*, pp. 69–74.

4. I follow the definition of "citizen comedy" given by Alexander Leggatt in *Citizen Comedy in the Age of Shakespeare* (Toronto: Univ. of Toronto Press, 1973), p. 3: a comedy "set in a predominantly middle-class social milieu." Leggatt briefly but perceptively discusses *The Roaring Girl* as a citizen comedy treating the theme of "chaste maids and whores" (pp. 109–10), arguing that Moll is an embodiment of chastity. As such, Moll resembles Britomart, Spenser's heroine of chastity.

In *The Roaring Girl*, Moll, though by sex a female, appears in other ways as a male. Without much doubt, she is physically the strongest character in the play (much as Britomart is in *The Faerie Queene*). From the outset, Moll is described as

> a thing
> One knowes not how to name, her birth began
> Ere she was all made. Tis woman more than man,
> Man more than woman, and (which to none can hap)
> The sunne giues her two shadowes to one shape.[5]

One of the shopwives in the play, Mistress Gallipot, says of Moll, "Some will not sticke to say shees a man and some both man and woman" (II.i. 186–7), while in a more comic vein the bumbling henchman Trapdoor calls Moll "my braue Captaine male and female" (III.iii. 170) and "my . . . Maister and Mistresse"(V.i. 57), and refers to her "masculine womanhood" (II.i. 320) Moll says to Alexander Wengrave of herself:

> Me thinkes you should be proud of such a daughter,
> As good a man, as your sonne. (V.ii. 153–4)

She becomes, to Alexander, to Trapdoor, to others, a "Monster" (I.ii. 138) which in its unnaturalness must be avoided like a plague. Yet it is such an image of the hermaphrodite that the play treats sympathetically; it is such a hermaphrodite that Eliot praised so highly as embodying personal nobility. Like the hermaphrodite in the Neoplatonic tradition, Moll inspires both laughter and awe, jocularity and seriousness.

Moll's hermaphroditic nature helps explain her paradoxical personality—the fact that she is both benign and irascible. In the dialogue that follows the famous canting scene and the exposure of the real "cutpurses," Lord Noland inquires into Moll's history, wondering how she has acquired her knowledge of the lower world of London and how she came to be called Moll Cutpurse. Revealing her benign nature, Moll tells him,

> I must confesse,
> In younger dayes, when I was apt to stray,
> I haue sat amongst such adders; seene their stings,
> As any here might, and in full play-houses
> Watcht their quick-diuing hands, to bring to shame
> Such rogues, and in that streame met an ill name. (V.i. 285–90)

---

5. *The Roaring Girl*, I.ii. 131–35. All quotations are from *The Dramatic Works of Thomas Dekker*, ed. Fredson Bowers (Cambridge: Cambridge Univ. Press, 1958), III. Future citations will be included in the text.

She goes on to say that she is trying to bring with her to the higher world of society the knowledge of vice and folly which she has learned in the lower world, so that she can save her friends from "quicke danger" (311). Like the Neoplatonic hermaphrodite in a cosmic context, Moll in a social context can attend to the upper and lower worlds simultaneously. She unwittingly dramatizes her own innocence and virtue when she fails to be tempted by the watch and jewels that Alexander has set for her to steal (IV.i.). And she puts her benign wisdom to work when she advises Sebastian about marriage: "neuer while you liue sir take a wife running, many haue run out at heeles that haue don't" (II.ii. 54–6).

In contrast to this soft, benign part of her personality, Moll can also be irascible. When Mistress Openwork refuses Moll entrance to her shop, the Roaring Girl vents her fury by attacking the "fellow" who happens to be walking by at the time, and whom she accuses, probably with justice, of abusing her at a tavern the night before (II.i.). Her temper is quick, and she can take offense at a straw. In the scene in which Moll brings Mary Fitzallard (disguised as a page) to her lover Sebastian Wengrave, the following dialogue ensues:

SEB. I'le offer no worse play.
MOLL. Nay and you should sir,
       I should draw first and prooue the quicker man. (IV.i. 74–5)

In a successful attempt to appease her sudden "fury" (77), Sebastian offers Moll the viol, which, luckily for him, she plays contentedly.

At the heart of Moll's dual personality is her pride—a trait that can be expressed as being either benign or irascible. In the viol scene just referred to, Moll's pride becomes simultaneously both benign and irascible when she says to Sebastian,

well since you' l needes put vs [herself and the viol] together sir, I'le play my part as well as I can: it shall nere be said I came into a Gentlemans chamber, and let his instrument hang by the walls
 . . .
for though the world iudge impudently of mee, I nere came into that chamber yet, where I tooke downe the instrument my selfe. (IV.i. 81–91)

Aside from the comical sexual innuendoes here, Moll's language reveals both an inborn fierceness and a conscious attempt at amiability.

Moll's dual personality is reminiscent of Britomart's, and, more particularly, of the *Venus armata's*. In the preface to the printed edition of the play, Middleton perhaps hints that he is aware of this tradition (at the very least, as it appears in Spenser), when he says referring to Moll, "For Venus being a woman passes through the play in doublet and breeches." Like Venus in her "armed" form, Moll is a figure of both love and war, though, as we shall see, Moll shares the *Venus armata's* use of her "armour" for a "peaceable motive." Moll in essence becomes a civic *Venus armata*, and London's correlate of faeryland's Britomart. In fact, Moll manifests the Neoplatonic principle of *concordia discors* in a remarkably clear way. Throughout the play, we see her wielding her sword—in her wounding of the gallant Laxton (III.i), in her beating of the fellow outside the shop, and in her chasing away of the cutpurses (V.i). The threat of her martial weapon, to be sure, is always imminent, as Sebastian learns easily enough. But as a kind of counterpoint to her sword, Moll also plays the viol; she is, we are told, an accomplished, self-taught musician (IV.i. 80–1), and she can sing as well. In the scene in which she brings the disguised Mary together with Sebastian, which begins with her threats to Sebastian and ends with her music-making, the authors may be using the two symbols, the sword and the viol, to illustrate the principle of *concordia discors*, love's power to triumph over adversity to attain a peaceable end.

Moll's hermaphroditic nature also manifests itself in the plot. For, like *Venus armata*, she is both an inciter and a moderator, an exposer of vice and a reuniter of virtue. Although the plot is plagued by clumsy machinery and a general sense of disunity, it does have more unity than we may at first think. In fact, it is precisely Moll's hermaphroditic nature and personality that give the play the unity it does have.

Essentially, the play has two plots: a main plot and a subplot. In the main plot, the young hero, Sebastian Wengrave, loves the young heroine, Mary Fitzallard; but Sebastian's father, Alexander, adamantly opposes a match he once approved: Mary's dowry is not rich enough. The primary aim of the main plot, then, is to reunite the two lovers, despite the father's attempt to separate them. The secondary aim is to expose the father's folly and to reconcile him with the lovers.

In the subplot, the three shopkeeper couples, the Gallipots, the Openworks, and the Tiltyards (though the Tiltyards receive almost no attention), are all experiencing marital difficulties.[6] The gallants, Laxton, Goshawk, and Greenwit, try to seduce the three respective shopwives. But the gallants, especially the more developed Laxton and Goshawk, clearly have no genuine feeling for their mistresses. Hence, the primary aim of the subplot is to reunite the wives with

---

6. To simplify matters, I talk of the shopwives and their gallants as a single group. Holmes, in *The Art of Thomas Middleton*, pp. 104–5, points out that the authors may originally have intended to develop the relation between Greenwit and Mistress Tiltyard but then gave the idea up.

their husbands; and the secondary aim is to expose the gallants for men of lust, and then to reincorporate them as friends to the married couples.

The primary and secondary aims of the subplot thus correspond to the primary and secondary aims of the main plot: reunion and exposure-reintegration. From this, we might expect that the figure generally recognized as unifying the play, Moll, would be the reuniter and the exposer-reintegrator in *both* the main and the subplot. The issue, however, is not so simple, and consequently the plot as a whole seems not only complex but also disunified. The first problem arises over the primary aim, reunion; for, though Moll is directly responsible for the reunion of the young lovers in the main plot, she is not directly responsible for the reunion of the married couples in the subplot.

To add to this discrepancy between Moll's function within the two plots, there are two noteworthy episodes which seem to form plots of their own—but which, it can be argued, are really appendages to the main and subplot.[7] In the first of these (III.iii) bearing on the main plot, Jack Dapper is, like the hero Sebastian, called a "prodigal" by his own father. Unlike Sebastian, however, young Dapper spends his time gambling and running with a "thousand" women (III.iii. 57), and is consequently plotted against by his father, who tries to have him arrested and sent to prison. At the time of the arrest, however, Moll happens to enter, sees the plot, and warns Dapper, allowing him to escape while she battles the furious officers Curtleax and Hanger. This episode bears on the main plot in two important ways. First, it makes clear that Jack Dapper is the play's real prodigal son, thus enabling us to see Sebastian's integrity as a hero and his father's folly as a blocking force.[8] Second, the Dapper episode suggests that, though Moll in rescuing Dapper seems to be interrupting legal justice, she is really ensuring that Dapper avoid the fate of Malvolio in *Twelfth Night* or Shylock in *The Merchant of Venice*—expulsion from the comic society that she is helping to create.[9]

In the second of the appendage episodes (III.i) bearing on the subplot, the gallant Laxton, earlier the seducer of Mistress Gallipot, attempts to seduce Moll and offers to meet her in Gray's Inn Field,

---

7. Cf. Holmes, *The Art of Thomas Middleton*, pp. 102 ff.: "There is one structurally simple plot in *The Roaring Girl*, . . . and a more complex plot, or nexus of plots with a common motif." The play's plot structure corresponds most closely to Richard Levin's "three-level hierarchy" plot in *The Multiple Plot in English Renaissance Drama* (Chicago and London: The Univ. of Chicago Press, 1971), which features a main plot, a subplot, and "a third set of characters, usually of the clownish sort, who may be loosely attached to one of these major actions" (p. 55).

8. For the suggestion that Sebastian and Jack Dapper are meant to be compared, see III. iii. 53–7.

9. Although Jack Dapper is not brought on stage at the very end, he does appear in V.i reunited with both Moll and his friends.

where they will take a coach to Brainford to lie together. Moll agrees
to the meeting, but only to teach Laxton, with his "base thoughts"
(III.i.68), a lesson: she chastises his lust, wounds him with her
sword, and chases him away. Moll's exposure of Laxton, it can be
argued, bears indirectly on the shopwives' eventual exposure of the
gallants, hence on their reunion with their husbands. At first, for
example, Moll's behavior parallels that of the other women, when
she accepts Laxton's offer for a liaison: the wives, though with more
serious intent, allow themselves to be courted by their respective
gallants. Then Moll changes, exposing Laxton: and the shopwives
appropriately reject and expose the gallants, deciding that their husbands are better men. The fact that Laxton is the victim in both
cases seems significant. The authors may be suggesting that Moll's
exposure of a gallant, which is associated through imagery with a
shopwife's exposure of the same gallant, symbolizes the exposure of
gallants in general.[1] Moll tells Laxton:

> In thee I defye all men, their worst hates,
> And their best flatteries, all their golden witchcrafts,
> With which they intangle the poore spirits of fooles,
> Distressed needlewomen and trade-fallne wiues. (III.i.88–91)

The idea occurs two other times (III.i. 111–12 and 131–4). This jux-
taposition of plots to create unity is what David Holmes calls Middleton's "*montage* technique."[2] It is in this regard that Moll's relation
to the subplot becomes more coherent than we may have at first
thought.

Moll, then, in her hermaphroditic role, can be seen to unify the
plots. In the main plot, throught her role as reuniter, she helps
reunite Sebastian and Mary; she helps reunite Alexander with the
couple, in a group that includes Mary's father, Guy Fitzallard; and
she rescues Jack Dapper from the officers, thus ensuring that he
remain part of the comic society. Also in the main plot, through her
role as exposer, she helps expose Alexander for his folly; she exposes
Trapdoor, Alexander's unheroic henchman, and his equally shabby
compatriot, Tearcat, for the imposters and beggars that they are (V.i);
and she exposes the cutpurses who come to rob her and her friends.
In the subplot, through her role as reuniter, she indirectly helps
reunite the shopwives with their husbands. And also in the subplot,
through her role as exposer, she exposes Laxton for his lust and folly.

Moll's role in the plot, her dual personality, and her hermaphroditic nature all contribute to an understanding of what seems at first
sight a real hodge podge of imagery. In fact, much of this imagery

---

1. See II.i. 287 and IV.ii. 41, where the word "shallow" is attached to Laxton. Holmes, in
    The Art of Thomas Middleton, p. 108, makes this point also.
2. Holmes, *The Art of Thomas Middleton*, p. 109; see also p. 10.

becomes intelligible only in the light of Moll's hermaphroditism. She becomes, for example, an amphibian, like Jonson's Tom Otter in *Epicoene* ("a land and sea captain")—a creature of both the water and the land: a mermaid (I.ii.215), a duck (III.iii.4), and a swan (IV.i.78). Appropriately, she is associated with water (perhaps in accord with her link with Venus, who is traditionally born from the sea). Moll becomes, for example, an eel (II.i. 185–6). But she is also associated with the land; she is, according to Alexander, the dangerous "rocke" in the sea on which Sebastian will inevitably wreck himself (I.i.105–6). Near the end of the play, the motif of land and water comes together when a messenger arrives to tell Alexander that his son and Moll Cutpurse have eloped and are going out to sea; then Trapdoor appears and says that they are down at the Tower. Greenwit says: "One brings vs water-newes; then comes an other . . . And he reports the Tower" (V.ii.45–7). This kind of dramaturgy makes best sense if we see Moll being represented as a creature of two natures, an amphibian who is adaptable to both land and water, traditional symbols of reason and passion.[3] Similarly, Moll becomes, at various times, both the subject and the object of desire: she is both the fisherman and the fish (III.i.92–4 and I.ii.219–20); the rider and the horse (II.i. 294–5 and II.i. 256–7); the trapper and the trapped (particularly her trapping of Trapdoor and her being trapped by him—I.ii. 218 and 234–5); the player and the instrument (Moll as viol player at II.i. 191, and V.i. 212–3); and the tailor and the one who is fitted (V.i. 99–101).

Because Moll is a figure embodying both subject and object, balancing reason and passion, she has no real sexual desires herself: she is *asexual*. This is revealed more directly by her rejection of both Laxton and Sebastian (though Sebastian is merely playing a part here); by the prologue's reassurance that she is not the usual lusty roaring girl but rather one who "flies / With wings more lofty" (25–6); and by her remark to Sebastian that "I haue no humor to marry, I loue to lye aboth sides ath bed my selfe" (II.ii. 35–6).[4] As such, she bears resemblance to an eros figure Northrop Frye speaks of in *A Natural Perspective*:

> sexual identity is a more deep-seated theme in comedy than it looks. The center of the comic drive toward identity is an erotic drive, and the spirit of comedy is often represented by an Eros

3. The connection between water and passion requires little comment. The connection between land and reason ("continent" and "continence"), though perhaps less familiar, was still traditional. See Spenser's *Faerie Queene*, III.iv. 10 for the pun on "continent" and "continence", noticed by A.C. Hamilton in his edition of *The Faerie Queene* (New York and London: Longman's, 1977), p. 338. See also III.v. 25, where the severed head (reason) of the forester falls on the land, while his body (passion) falls in the water.

4. See IV.i. 123, where Moll sings a song about a dream she has had, in which she *does* become a lover; then she adds: "but being awake, I keepe my legges together."

figure who brings about the comic conclusion but is in himself
sexually self-contained, being in a sense both male and female,
and needing no expression of love beyond himself.[5]

Frye goes on to identify Shakespeare's Puck and Ariel as belonging
to this class of figure. Moll's asexual nature and her reconciling
function link her with the Eros figure as well; as Sebastian puts it:

> Twixt louers hearts, shee's a fit instrument,
> And has the art to help them to their owne,
> By her aduise, for in that craft shee's wise,
> My loue and I may meete. . . . (II.ii. 191–4)

The paradox involved in Moll being both Venus and Eros is not so
odd if we recall traditional portryals of Venus *herself* as an *eros* figure, as in Virgil's *Aeneid* or Spenser's *Faerie Queene*.

Strange as it may sound, Moll Cutpurse becomes a figure of love
representing the complete human identity, the union of male and
female, and the corresponding principle of *concordia discors*, insofar
as a drama of this nature will allow her to do so. The other couples
in the play—Sebastian and Mary, the Gallipots, the Openworks,
and the Tiltyards—all represent combinations of male and female
trying to attain the complete identity. Moll and her group of couples
thus correspond to Spenser's Venus and her couple, Amoret and
Scudamour. Moll is indeed the "spirit of comedy"—the spirit of love
as the shaping force of comedy.[6]

There remains a final consideration. When Dekker and Middleton
wrote *The Roaring Girl*, the age was in rapid transition. Elizabeth
had just died a few years before, and James had ascended the
throne. Compounding this fracture in social and political order, the
old cosmic order of geocentricity was being rendered inaccurate,
and a new cosmic order of heliocentricity was being offered in its
place, throwing into doubt man's role in the universe. Literary order

---

5. *A Natural Perspective: The Development of Shakespearean Comedy and Romance* (New
   York: Columbia Univ. Press, 1965), p. 82.
6. Throughout the play, the authors refer to Moll as a *spirit* or in some way connect her with
   the idea of *spirit*. Laxton, for example, calls Moll "the *spirit* of foure great parishes" (II.i.
   167). Trapdoor refers to her "heroicke *spirit*" (II.i. 320); Sebastian says of her: "She has a
   bold *spirit* that mingles with mankind" (II.ii. 169); Laxton says again, referring to Moll:
   "Heart I thinke I fight with a familiar [spirit], or the *Ghost* of a fencer" (III.i. 125); and
   Moll says of herself:

   > If I could meete my enemies one by one thus,
   > I might make pretty shift with 'em in time,
   > And make 'em know, she has wit, and *spirit*
   > May scorne to live beholding to her body for meate. (III.i. 131–4)

   And again: "Base is that Mindle, that kneels vnto her body. . . . My *spirit* shall be Mistresse of this house" (III.i. 137–9).

was also being threatened, for the great Elizabethan poet, Spenser, had just died, and his great artistic energy was splintering off in two principal directions: the lyric poetry of Donne, which rejected Spenser's style and form yet accepted his romantic vision; and the drama of Jonson, which rejected Spenser completely (at least for the while). The age was perhaps less in transition than in crisis.

This crisis seems to have been felt most intensely in the area of Jacobean drama—in comedy as well as in tragedy. An author like Dekker, for example, found himself in an age of Jonsonian satire with a Spenserian vision of romantic love. An author like Middleton, who shared Jonson's satiric habit of mind, found himself collaborating with a romantic like Dekker. Their creations—the characters within the plays—find themselves exchanging sexual identities. Amidst the confusion is born a hybrid form of comedy mixing romantic and satirical elements, such as we find in Dekker and Middleton's other collaboration, *The Honest Whore*, Part I, and in numerous other plays of the period. Indeed, the hybrid form becomes something of a norm.[7]

During this time, Dekker and Middleton combine their romantic and satirical sensibilities in *The Roaring Girl*. Yet what is innovative here is the authors' creation of a figure who combines them both. Moll Cutpurse becomes the true spirit of a new comedy, for in her hermaphroditism are contained, not merely her two natures (female and male), or her two personalities (benign and irascible), or even her two roles within the plot (moderator-reuniter and inciter-exposer), but also the two halves of her "creator's" mind. Moll thus can be seen as a symbol, not merely of a civic Venus, but of a new hermaphroditic form of comedy combining romance with satire. Dekker with Middleton, Spenser with Jonson. The hermaphrodite, conventionally a symbol of sexual identity, expands to become a symbol of artistic identity as well. Middleton himself may be suggesting a link between the hermaphroditic Moll and the hybrid form of play he and Dekker are writing when he says in the preface, "The fashion of play-making, I can properly compare to nothing, so naturally, as the alteration in apparell." "Our plaies follow the nicenes of our Garments," he adds: "mingled with diuerse colours, you shall linde this published Comedy." Like the play, Moll Cutpurse becomes "mingled with diverse colours." Moll becomes a symbol of hope for a

7. For this idea I am indebted to Price, *Thomas Dekker*, who is continually drawing attention to Dekker the romanticist and Middleton the satirist; and to Andor Gomme, in the New Mermaids edition of the play, who says, p. xxii: "Doubtless Dekker's influence is responsible for softening the characteristic acerbity of Middleton's satiric humour. The play seems deliberately to attempt a fusion of the two principal streams into which, as Miss Bradbrook points out, English comedy had divided in about 1600: 'On the one hand, the popular domestic themes handled in sanguine and traditional ways: on the other, themes equally traditional, but handled in ways which were melancholic and satiric.'"

regaining of artistic, as well as personal and social, identity—as the artistic energies of the period slowly transformed from the age of Spenser into the age of Jonson, and the serious dramatists tried to figure out, not merely who they were and where the world was going, but also what form their art should take.

MARY BETH ROSE

Women in Men's Clothing: Apparel and Social Stability in *The Roaring Girl*†

The central figure in Thomas Middleton and Thomas Dekker's city comedy *The Roaring Girl* (c. 1608–1611) is a woman named Moll Frith, whose distinguishing feature is that she walks around Jacobean London dressed in male clothing. It should be stressed that Moll is not in disguise: she is neither a disguised player, a man pretending to be a woman; nor is she a disguised character, whose role requires a woman pretending to be a man. Unlike the disguised heroines of romantic comedy, Moll seeks not to conceal her sexual identity, but rather to display it. Although certain of the *Dramatis Personae* in *The Roaring Girl* occasionally fail to recognize her immediately, the fact that Moll is a woman is well known to every character in the play. She simply presents herself in society as a woman wearing men's clothes. Demanding merely by her presence that people reconcile her apparent sexual contradictions, she arouses unspeakable social and sexual anxieties in the established society of the play. Indeed Middleton and Dekker create Moll as the fulcrum of *The Roaring Girl*, and the other characters' reactions to her tend to define them as social and moral beings. As a result, society's effort to assess the identity of this female figure in male attire becomes the central dramatic and symbolic issue of the play.

Recognizing the title figure's assumption of male attire as the symbolic focus of social and moral concern in *The Roaring Girl* allows us to connect the play with the intense, often bitterly funny debate about women wearing men's clothes that was taking place in contemporary moral and religious writing, and which came to a head in 1620 with a pair of pamphlets entitled, respectively, *Hic Mulier: Or,*

† From *English Literary Renaissance* 14.3 (Autumn 1984): 367–91 (John Wiley and Sons). Reprinted by permission.

The Man-Woman, and *Haec-Vir: Or The Womanish-Man*.[1] Indeed
the figure of the female in male apparel emerges from the documents of this controversy much as Moll Frith does from the text of
The Roaring Girl: an embodiment of female independence boldly
challenging established social and sexual values and, by the fact of
her existence, requiring evaluation and response. Although histori-
ans of Renaissance conduct literature as well as more recent literary
critics have discussed the *Hic Mulier / Haec-Vir* controversy,[2] no
attempt has been made to view *The Roaring Girl*, with its "man-
woman" heroine, in the context of this debate. Both because the
controversial issue involved has an ongoing importance in Renaissance England and because I am not seeking to establish a direct
influence between documents and play, the small chronological discrepancy between the performance and publication of *The Roaring
Girl* (c. 1608–1611) and the high point of the debate (1620) is not
relevant to my purposes here; rather I am interested in exploring the
fact that the figure of the female in male attire is portrayed in both
dramatic and social contexts with simultaneous admiration, desire,
abhorrence, and fear. The following essay attempts to demonstrate
the ways in which parallel treatments of women in men's clothing
in the drama and the debate illuminate this phenomenon of fashion
as the focus of considerable moral and social anxiety aroused by
changing sexual values in Jacobean England; and to show that,
taken together, artistic representation and social commentary suggest a deep cultural ambivalence in the British Renaissance about
female independence and equality between the sexes.

I

Elizabethan and Jacobean sermons and conduct books continually
castigate the fickleness of fashion and the vanity of sumptuous
apparel. To cite one very typical example, the writer of the sermon
"Against Excess of Apparel" in *Homilies Appointed to be Read in the*

---

1. The full names of these colorful pamphlets are as follows: *Hic Mulier: Or, The Man-
Woman: Being a Medicine to cure the Coltish Disease of the Staggers in the Masculine-
Feminines of our Times* and *Haec-Vir: Or The Womanish-Man: Being an Answer to a late
Booke intituled Hic-Mulier*. All citations from the pamphlets are taken from the edition
published by *The Rota* at the University of Exeter, 1973.
2. See Louis B. Wright, *Middle-Class Culture in Elizabethan England* (Chapel Hill, N.C.,
1935), pp. 494–97; Carroll Camden, *The Elizabethan Woman* (New York, 1952), pp.
263–67; Juliet Dusinberre, *Shakespeare and the Nature of Women* (London, 1975), pp.
231–71; Linda T. Fitz, "What Says the Married Woman: Marriage Theory and Feminism
in the English Renaissance," *Mosaic*, 13 (Winter, 1980), 1–22; and Linda Woodbridge,
Women and the English Renaissance: Literature and the Nature of Womankind, 1540–1620
(Urbana, 1984), pp. 139–51.

Time of Queen Elizabeth sees the English preoccupation with the novelties of fashion as a futile expenditure of energy, indicating an endlessly detrimental spiritual restlessness: "We are never contented, and therefore we prosper not."[3] Furthermore the conservative spirit frequently links propriety of dress with the coherence of society and views as a threat to social stability the tendency of the pretentious or the newly prosperous to dress so elegantly that it was becoming increasingly difficult to distinguish among social classes by the varied attire of their members.[4] Along with the upwardly mobile and the fop, women were singled out as creators of chaos for seeking to seduce men other than their husbands by wearing enticing clothes and for being generally disobedient, disrespectful, shallow, demonic, and extravagant in their preoccupation with fashion.[5]

From these characteristic themes the phenomenon of women dressing in male clothing begins gradually to assume a distinct identity as a separate issue; or, more accurately, as an issue that, in its symbolic significance, articulates a variety of social and moral concerns. The few available references to the phenomenon in the 1500s are largely parenthetical. In the early part of the sixteenth century, the idea of women wearing men's clothes apparently seemed too appalling even to be feared. Ever zealous of female virtue, John Louis Vives, for example, issues an ultimatum on the subject in *Instruction of a Christian Woman* (c. 1529) only as a last line in his chapter on feminine dress, a mere after-thought to the more important prohibitions against brazenness and extravagance in female attire. Citing Deuteronomy 22.5, he writes, "A woman shall use no mannes raymente, elles lette hir thinke she hath the mans stomacke, but take hede to the woordes of our Lorde: sayinge, a woman shall not put on mans apparell: for so to do is abhominable afore God. But I truste no woman will do it, excepte she be paste both honestee and shame."[6] Vives' confidence in womanly docility was, however, misplaced. In George Gascoigne's satire *The Steele Glas* (1576), complaints about women in male attire, although still

---

3. Quoted from *Certain Sermons or Homilies Appointed to be Read in Churches in the Time of Queen Elizabeth* (London: Society for Promoting Christian Knowledge, 1908), p. 327.
4. See, for example, "Against Excess of Apparel" in *Homilies*; Thomas Nashe, *Christs Teares over Jerusalem*, 1593, in John Dover Wilson, *Life in Shakespeare's England* (Cambridge, 1920), p. 125; and Phillip Stubbes. *Anatomy of Abuses*, 1583, ed. Frederick J. Furnivall, The New Shakespeare Society (London, 1877–1879), pp. 33–34.
5. See, for example, William Harrison, *Description of England, 1587* in Wilson, pp. 124–25. Cf. Wright, p. 493; Camden, pp. 257–67; and Fitz.
6. John Louis Vives, "Of raiments," in *Instruction of a Christian Woman*, trans. Richard Hyrde 1557), Book II, Chap. VIII. Deuteronomy 22.5 reads: "The Woman shall not wear that which pertaineth unto a man, neither shall a man put on a woman's garment: for all that do so *are* abomination unto the Lord thy God."

relegated to the status of an epilogue, are nevertheless becoming decidedly more pointed and vociferous:

> "What be they? women? masking in mens weedes?
> With dutchkin dublets, . . . and with Jerkins jaggde?
> With high copt hattes and fethers flaunt a flaunt?
> They be so sure even *Wo* to *Men* in dede."[7]

The astonished despair of female modesty expressed in Gascoigne's mournful pun takes the form of accusations of sexual and, by clear inference, social, moral, and cosmic perversion in the rhetoric of Phillip Stubbes. Writing in 1583, in the midst of a general denunciation of the apparel of both sexes, Stubbes mentions women with "dublets and Jerkins as men have heer, buttoned up the brest, and made with wings, welts, and pinions on the shoulder points, as mans apparel is."[8] Stubbes lucidly states his indignant alarm at the possibility of not being able to distinguish between the sexes: "Our Apparell was given us as a signe distinctive to discern betwixt sex and sex, and therefore one to weare the Apparel of another sex is to . . . adulterate the veritie of his owne kinde. Wherefore these Women may not improperly be called *Hermaphroditi*, that is, Monsters of bothe kindes, half women, half men."[9]

While Stubbes' rhetoric is always colorfully extravagant, the topic of women in male attire continued to elicit highly emotional reactions at a growing rate, particularly in the second decade of the seventeenth century when, amidst a marked increase in satiric attacks upon women in general, references to the "monstrous . . . *Woman* of the *Masculine Gender*" multiplied notably.[1] As Louis B. Wright has demonstrated, this expansion in both the volume and hostility of satire against women represented the misogynistic, ultra-conservative voice in the lively debate about woman's nature, behavior, and role that was taking place in the moral and religious writing of the early decades of the century.[2] According to Wright and other critics, the content of this conduct literature can be distinguished roughly

---

7. George Gascoigne, *The Steele Glas*, 1576, in ed. Edward Arber, *English Reprints*, V (London, 1868), pp. 82–83.
8. Stubbes, p. 73.
9. Stubbes, p. 73. Cf. Harrison, in Wilson, pp. 124–25.
1. Henry Fitzgeffrey, *Notes from Black-fryers*, 1617. Cited by Wright, p. 492. See Wright, pp. 483–94 for other references to the "man-woman," including Barnabe Rich, in *The Honestie of this Age* (1614); Alexander Niccoles, in *A Discourse of Marriage And Wiving* (ed. of 1620); and Thomas Adams, in *Mystical Bedlam* (1615).
2. Wright, p. 490. Anger against women reached its zenith in Joseph Swetnam's misogynistic tract, *The Araignment of Lewd, Idle, Froward, and unconstant Women* (1615), which had ten printings by 1634 and inspired several responses (see Wright, pp. 486–93), including a stage-play, *Swetnam, the Woman-hater, Arraigned by Women*, (1620).

along class lines: where "learned and courtly" works tended to discuss women in the abstract and spiritualized terms of neoplatonic
philosophy, middle-class tracts disputed more practical and social
issues, such as the appropriateness of female apparel.[3] While the
documents in the controversy surrounding women in male attire
indicate that both upper- and middle-class females followed the
fashion, they are much too partisan and factually imprecise to convey the actual extent to which the style was adopted.[4]

Nevertheless by 1620 the phenomenon of women in men's clothing had become prominent enough to evoke an outraged protest
from King James, recorded in a letter of J. Chamberlain to Sir D.
Carleton, dated January 15, 1620:

> Yesterday the bishop of London called together all his clergie
> about this towne, and told them he had expressed command-
> ment from the King to will them to inveigh vehemently against
> the insolencie of our women, and theyre wearing of brode
> brimed hats, pointed dublets, theyre haire cut short or shorne,
> and some of them stilettoes or poinards, and such other trinck-
> ets of like moment; adding that if pulpit admonitions will not
> reform them he would proceed by another course; the truth is
> the world is very much out of order.

On February 12, Chamberlain adds the following: "Our pulpits ring
continually of the insolence and impudence of women, and to helpe
the matter forward the players have likewise taken them to taske,
and so to the ballades and ballad-singers, so that they can come
nowhere but theyre eares tingle; and if all this will not serve, the
King threatens to fall upon theyre husbands, parents, or frends that
have or shold have power over them, and make them pay for it."[5]
The King's protest amounted to a declaration of war. While undoubt-
edly resulting in part from James' considerable misogyny,[6] the actions

---

3. Wright, p. 507 and Fitz, pp. 2–3.
4. Along with the numerous isolated references to the *Hic Mulier* phenomenon cited in
   Wright, these documents include the *Hic Mulier* and *Haec-Vir pamphlets*, noted above,
   and another pamphlet, *Mulde Sacke: Or The Apologie of Hic Mulier: To the late Declamation against her* (1620). By referring to the *Hic Mulier* phenomenon as a "transvestite
   movement," or even as a "rough-and-ready unisex movement" (p. 15), Fitz implies more
   coherence and range to the fashion than these pamphlets can document. Cf. Woodbridge, pp. 139–51.
5. Edward Phillips Statham, *A Jacobean Letter-Writer: The Life and Times of John Chamberlain* (London, 1920), pp. 182–83.
6. We should not, I think, take for granted that misogynistic and feminist attitudes can be
   aligned neatly with gender in the Renaissance. The relative paucity of literature in the
   early 1600s in which women are clearly speaking for themselves makes specifically female
   attitudes extremely difficult to distinguish and assess. Resolving the problem of the corre-
   lation between gender and attitude is not, however, prerequisite to the present analysis,
   which seeks to compare the sexual values clearly articulated in the *Hic Mulier/Haec-Vir*
   debate with the artistic conception of a *Hic Mulier* figure in *The Roaring Girl*.

following his protest also revealed that, among all the satiric targets on the subject of female fashion, women in men's clothing had assumed threatening enough proportions in the conservative mind to be singled out in a conscientious and thorough attempt to eliminate the style from social life. In February, 1620 the pamphlets *Hic Mulier*, which represented the conservative viewpoint, and *Haec-Vir*, which defended the practice of women wearing male attire, appeared. Because the pamphlets are anonymous, it is impossible to link their opinions to the gender of their author or authors. More importantly, the subject of the unconventional "man-woman" had evolved into a full-fledged debate, in which conservative and liberal positions are clearly and elaborately defined.

Wright believes the hostile conservative response to women in men's clothing was a defensive reaction against an increasingly successful demand both for moral and spiritual equality between the sexes and for greater social freedom for women: freedom, for example, from confinement to the home, from the double standard of sexual morality, from wife-beating and from forced marriage. "The average [i.e., middle-class] woman," Wright concludes, "was becoming articulate in her own defense and . . . was demanding social independence unknown in previous generations."[7] According to Wright, the female adoption of male apparel aggressively and visibly dramatized a bid for social independence, which comprised a largely successful and coherent challenge to existing sexual values that is reflected in *Haec-Vir*, a pamphlet Wright believes to be "the *Areopagitica* of the London woman, a woman who had attained greater freedom than any of her predecessors or than any of her European contemporaries."[8] It is true that the challenge that women in male attire presented to the existing imbalance of power between the sexes can be discerned in the vindictive bitterness of the opposition to the androgynous style. Yet Linda T. Fitz has recently provided a useful and fascinating corrective to the hopeful interpretation of the extent and coherence of Jacobean feminism advanced by Wright and critics like Juliet Dusinberre by stressing the restrictiveness, rather than the liberating potential, of middle-class conduct literature. In her discussion of the controversy surrounding women in men's clothing, Fitz points out some serious oversights in Wright's optimistic view of the *Hic Mulier/Haec-Vir* debate; nevertheless Fitz ends by conceding that "Wright is quite justified in his . . . assessment" of a resounding victory for female freedom articulated in this

7. Wright, p. 490.
8. Wright, p. 497.

controversy.[9] My own analysis of the debate suggests an attitude
toward the *Hic Mulier* phenomenon and the sexual freedom it represented which is more complex than either Wright perceives or Fitz
explores, an attitude that both acknowledges injustice and fears
change, that wants sexual freedom yet perceives its attainment as
conflicting with an equally desirable social stability.

II

After an introductory lament that "since the daies of *Adam* women
were never so Masculine" (sig. A3), the pamphlet *Hic Mulier* or *The
Man-Woman* begins by propounding a familiar Renaissance ideal of
woman as chaste, maternal, compassionate, discreet, and obedient,
a model of behavior and sentiment from which the notorious "man-
woman" is believed to depart "with a deformitie never before
dream'd of" (sig. A3v).[1] In contrast to this modestly attired paragon,
the *Hic Mulier* figure, sporting a "cloudy Ruffianly broad-brim'd
Hatte, and wanton Feather . . . the loose, lascivious civill embracement of a French doublet . . . most ruffianly short lockes . . . for
Needles, Swords . . . and for Prayer bookes, bawdy Jigs" is "not halfe
man, halfe woman . . . but all Odyous, all Divell" (sigs. A4–A4v). In
elaborating the polemical intention of this pamphlet—to eliminate
the heinous fashion by demonizing its proponents—the author
builds a case around two major arguments.

As might be expected, the first group of arguments centers on the
dangerous sexual chaos which the author assumes will result from
the breakdown of rigid gender distinctions symbolized by the "man-
woman's" attire. The writer perceives in *Hic Mulier's* choice of male
clothes unconventional sexual behavior; therefore she automatically
becomes a whore, who inspires by her lewd example a pernicious
illicit sexuality in others. As implied in the description of her "loose,
lascivious civill embracement of a French doublet, being all unbut-
ton'd to entice" (sig. A4v), she will allow, even invite, "a shameless
libertie to every loose passion" (sig. C2). Despite—indeed because
of—her mannishness, then, *Hic Mulier* displays and encourages a
free-floating sexuality, a possibility which the author views as
socially destabilizing and therefore disastrous, "most pernicious to

---

9. Fitz. pp. 16–17. Fitz, for example, sees as unfortunate the argument in *Haec-Vir* (sig. C2v)
that it is a law of nature that differences between the sexes be preserved by designated
dress and behavior. She also remarks that "Renaissance women so far accepted the masculine rules of the game that they felt they had to adopt the clothing and external attributes
of the male sex in order to be 'free.' This was true in drama as in life: witness the transvestite heroines of Shakespeare's romantic comedies." See also Woodbridge, pp. 148–49.
1. See Suzanne W. Hull, *Chaste Silent & Obedient: English Books for Women 1475–1640*
(San Marino, Cal, 1982). Hull provides an ample bibliography of documents that articulate the Renaissance ideal of womanhood.

the common-wealth" (sig. C2). As we will see, this interesting association between socially threatening female sexiness and the breakdown of polarized gender identities and sexual roles becomes very
important in *The Roaring Girl*. The fear seems to be that without
rigidly assigned, gender-linked roles and behavior, legitimate, faith-
ful erotic relations between the sexes will become impossible and
the integrity of the family will consequently disintegrate: "they [i.e.,
the "men-women"] are neither men, nor women, but just good for
nothing . . . they care not into what dangers they plunge either their
Fortunes or Reputations, the disgrace of the whole Sexe, or the blot
and obloquy of their private Families" (sigs. B2, C2).

However ominous, the unleashing of Eros and the breakdown of
sexual polarization do not preoccupy the author as much as do questions of social status and hierarchy. The implied norm behind the
satire in the pamphlet is a stable society which derives its coherence
from the strict preservation of such essential distinctions as class,
fortune, and rank. Not only do women in men's clothing come from
various classes in society; they also have the unfortunate habit of
dressing alike, obscuring not only the clarity of their gender, but the
badge of their social status as well, and thereby endangering criti-
cally the predictable orderliness of social relations. To convey the
seriousness of this offense, the author employs the rhetorical device
of associating the hated style by turns with decaying aristocrats and
gentry ("the adulterate branches of rich stocks" [sig. B1]), women of
base birth ("stinking vapours drawne from dunghils" [sig. B1]),
females of the upper classes "knowne great" ("no more shall their
greatness or wealth save them from one particle of disgrace"
[sigs. B1v, B2v]), and middle-class wives (tailors have "metamorphosed more modest old garments . . . for the use of Freemens wives
than hath been worne in Court, Suburbs, or Countrey" [sig. C1v]), all
of which leads to the indignant outburst: "It is an infection that emulates the plague, and throwes itselfe amongst women of all degrees . . .
Shall we all be co-heires of one honor, one estate, and one habit?"
(sigs. B1v, B4v), Like death and disease, then, the female in male
attire serves as a leveler; and, just as such issues as the inflated
sale of honors by the Crown seemed to the conservative mind to
be undermining social coherence by threatening the traditional
prestige of inherited nobility, so the phenomenon of women of different social positions dressing in similar male clothing appeared
intolerably chaotic. As Fitz has shown, English Renaissance women,
particularly in the middle classes, used their apparel as a showpiece
to advertise the prosperity of their fathers and husbands.[2] That
women should perversely refuse, by donning look-alike male

2. Fitz, pp. 9–10. Also see Wright, pp. 490–91. see also Dusinberre, pp. 234–35.

clothes, to serve their crucial function as bearers of social class status and distinction is the issue that arouses the author's most vindictive antipathy: "Let . . . the powerfull Statute of apparell but lift up
his Battle-Axe, so as every one may bee knowne by the true badge of
their bloud, or Fortune: and then these *Chymera's* of deformitie will
bee sent backe to hell, and there burne to Cynders in the flames of
their owne malice" (sig. C1v).

The pamphlet *Hic Mulier* ends with an invective against all social
change (sig. C3). Given the hectic violence of this author's conser-
vatism, it is not surprising that the rebuttal in the pamphlet *Haec-
Vir: Or The Womanish-Man*, which appeared seven days later, would
dwell on the folly of thoughtlessly adhering to social custom. Interestingly, the *Haec-Vir* pamphlet ignores the issue of whether women
of different social categories dressing alike as men disrupt the align-
ment of social classes; instead the second pamphlet argues solely in
terms of gender and sexual roles. Rather than appearing as the product of a single mind, *Haec-Vir* is presented as a dialogue between
two characters, the *Hic Mulier* and the *Haec-Vir* figures, suggesting
by its very form and by the introduction of a new figure, the womanish man, to whom I will return, a greater openness to discussion and
to cooperation between the sexes. The irrationality of the author of
the first pamphlet is also clarified and undercut at the beginning of
the second when the two figures conduct a witty exchange about
their mutual inability to identify one another's gender. Thus a tolerant and urbane tone is set in which *Hic Mulier* (now a sympathetic
figure) can defend her behavior.

Hic Mulier's defense elaborates in positive terms the fact that her
attire symbolizes a demand for recognition of spiritual and moral
equality between the sexes, a recognition which she regards as her
birthright: "We are free-borne as Men, have as free election, and as
free spirits, we are compounded of like parts, and may with like
liberty make benefit of our Creations" (sig. B3). Consequently she
counters *Haec-Vir's* charge that assuming male apparel makes her a
mere slave to the novelties of fashion both by defining her outfit as
symbolizing her freedom of choice and by redefining slavery as
Haec-Vir's mindless submission to the tryanny of pointless custom,
"for then custome, nothing is more absurd, nothing more foolish"
(sig. B2). The customs she resents as most false and destructive to
female freedom and equality are those gender-linked stereotypes
which constrain female behavior to compliance, subordination,
pathos, and passivity:

> But you say wee are barbarous and shameless and cast off all
> softness, to runne wilde through a wildenesse of opinions. In

this you expresse more cruelty then in all the rest, because I stand not with my hands on my belly like a baby at *Bartholomew Fayre* . . . that am not dumbe when wantons court mee, as if Asse-like I were ready for all burthens, or because I weepe not when injury gripes me, like a woorried Deere in the fangs of many Curres: am I therefore barbarous or shamelesse? (sig. B3)

"*I stand not with my hands on my belly like a baby at* Bartholomew Fayre . . . *as if Asse-like I were ready for all burthens*." *Hic Mulier* argues that to reduce woman to the position of static icon, allegedly "so much better in that she is something purer" (sig. B1v) than man, is actually to infantilize and dehumanize her by denying her full partici-pation in adult reality, which she optimistically defines as a world of creative movement and change, in which man can "alter, frame, and fashion, according as his will and delight shall rule him" (sig. B1v). This conception, which locates adult reality in the creative opportuni-ties provided by public life, recognizes that women are unjustly con-fined by tradition to perpetual fantasy and immaturity. It therefore forms the most strikingly modern of *Hic Mulier's* arguments.

The eloquence and clarity with which these convictions are expressed make the retrenchment that occurs in the pamphlet's con-clusion all the more startling. Having established herself as the rational contender in the debate, the "man-woman" suddenly with-draws before the irrational onslaught of *Haec-Vir*, the womanish man who ignores her arguments, rather than systematically rebutting them. Suddenly the focus shifts to the way that *Haec-Vir* (who, it has been suggested, represents the homosexuality of the Jacobean court)[3] has relinquished his manhood and become a fop, aberrant male behaviour which is now viewed as the sole reason for the existence of the notorious "man-woman." In an astonishing abandonment of her considerable powers of logic, *Hic Mulier* nostalgically evokes chivalric gallantry, recalling the bygone days when men were men:

> Hence we have preserved (though to our owne shames) those manly things which you have forsaken, which would you againe accept, and restore to us the Blushes we lay'd by, when first wee put on your Masculine garments; doubt not but chaste thoughts and bashfulnesse will againe dwell in us . . . then will we love and serve you; then will we heare and obey you; then will wee like rich Jewels hang at your cares to take our Instruc-tions. (sigs. C2v, C3v)

It is a bargain, an offer he can't refuse; the dialogue concludes with *Haec-Vir* having the last word, just as he had had the first, and the

3. Dusinberre, pp. 234–35, 239.

entire phenomenon of women in men's clothing is rationalized, not
as an attempt to achieve unrealized social freedom for women, but
rather to return society to the idealized sexual norm of gender polarization and male dominance. As in King James' protest and the end
of the *Hic Mulier* pamphlet, responsibility for the unconventional
style of female dress, now recognized by all as deformed, is seen to
rest with men because power does.[4]

Although the concluding section of the *Haec-Vir* pamphlet articulates this drastic shift in perspective, it is nevertheless short, and it
fails to cancel or even to qualify the dominant logic of *Hic Mulier's*
stirring defense of her freedom, a speech which remains the focus
of the second pamphlet. We are therefore left with a disjunction
between the stubbornly rebellious, salient content of the second pamphlet and the conservative structure of the debate as a whole. On the
one hand, the dominant content of the *Haec-Vir* pamphlet convinc-
ingly challenges the justice and reality of the existing sexual power
structure by enumerating the illusory, sentimental, and destructive
premises on which it is based. On the other, the form of the debate as
a whole perpetuates the status quo by attempting to absorb this
cogent demand for change into a larger movement of re-aligning the
established society into conformity with an old ideal, a rhetorical
endeavor that does not, however, entirely succeed in quelling the vigor
of the opposition. As a result of this disjunction between content and
form, female independence and equality between the sexes are depicted
in the debate as desirable and just, but also as impossible for a hierarchical society to absorb without unacceptable disruption.

III

A pronounced ambivalence toward sexual equality as represented by
the *Hic Mulier* figure is discernible in the *Hic Mulier/Haec-Vir*
debate, then, and this attitude can be viewed in aesthetic terms as a
disjunction between content and form. In *The Roaring Girl* a similar
dislocation between thematic content and dramatic form can be
perceived in the representation of the title character, Moll Frith, a
point to which I will return. Middleton and Dekker modeled their
unusual central figure after a real-life "roaring girl," popularly known
in Jacobean London as "Moll Cutpurse." As this name implies, the
real Moll was an underworld figure, notorious as a thief, whore,
brawler, and bawd. Much of the reliable evidence we have about her

---

4. See *Hic Mulier* (sig. C2v): "To you . . . that are Fathers, Husbands, or Sustainers of these
new *Hermaphrodites*, belongs the cure of this Impostume; it is you that give fuell to the
flames of their wilde indiscretion." Cf. J. Chamberlain, in Statham, pp. 182–183: "A tax
upon unruly female relatives! . . . the King threatens to fall upon theyre husbands, parents or frends that have or shold have power over them, and make them pay for it."

exists in the court records made after her several arrests for offenses that included a scandalous appearance at the Fortune Theater, where she "sat there upon the stage in the publique viewe of all the people there p[rese]nte in mans apparrell & playd upon her lute & sange a songe."[5] Most of the existing criticism of *The Roaring Girl* attempts to date the play with reference to this incident.[6]

Whatever the precise connections between the events in the life of the actual Mary Frith and the performance and publication of *The Roaring Girl*, the court records show that the playwrights drew heavily on the habits and physical appearance of the real-life Moll, with her brawling, singing, and smoking, her lute, her boots, her sword, and, above all, her breeches; as has been suggested, it is also probable that Middleton and Dekker were attempting to benefit from the *au courant* notoriety of the actual Moll in the timing of their play.[7] Nevertheless in his address to the reader attached to the 1611 quarto, Middleton takes pains to distinguish the created character from the real person, hinting that the play will present an idealized interpretation of this odd figure: "'Tis the excellency of a writer to leave things better than he finds 'em."[8] In fact the playwrights maintain an ambivalent attitude toward the outlaw status of their central character, in whom courageous moral and sexual principles combine with a marginal social identity, both of which are symbolized in the play by her male attire.

The address to the reader and ensuing prologue clarify the controversial nature of the title character and emphasize the importance of assessing her identity:

> Thus her character lies—
> Yet what need characters, when to give a guess
> Is better than the person to express?

5. Cited in P. A. Mulholland, *"The Date of The Roaring Girl," Review of English Studies*, 28 (1977), 22, 30–31. See also Andor Gomme, Introd., *The Roaring Girl*, by Thomas Middleton and Thomas Dekker, (London, 1976), pp. xiii–xix, and Margaret Dowling, "A Note on Moll Cutpurse—'The Roaring Girl,'" *Review of English Studies*, 10 (1934), 67–71. There is a pamphlet called *The Life and Death of Mrs. Mary Frith*, published in 1662, but it is not thought to be reliable. For a review of the play's dramatic and non-dramatic sources, as well as references to the real Moll Frith, see Gomme, pp. xiii–xix, and Mulholland, pp. 18–31.

6. Mulholland, pp. 18–31, is the most recent example. Gomme, pp. xiii–xix, also sums up the attempts to date the play.

7. Mulholland, 18–19. As Mulholland observes (pp. 20–21), the *Consistory of London Correction Book* record concerning Mary Frith, which he cites at length on pp. 30–31, provides an extraordinary account both of the actual Moll and of the vehement opposition in Jacobean society to women wearing male attire, which is one offense of hers that is reiterated in the *Correction Book* entry.

8. Thomas Middleton, "To the Comic Play-Readers, Venery and Laughter," in Thomas Dekker and Thomas Middleton, *The Roaring Girl*. All citations from the play are taken from *Drama of the English Renaissance*, eds. Russell A. Fraser and Norman Rabkin (New York, 1976), II, 334–38.

> But would you know who 'tis? Would you hear her name?
> She's called mad Moll; her life our acts proclaim.
>
> (Prologue, 26–30)

In their introduction of Moll Frith, the playwrights evoke themes
identical to those surrounding the *Hic Mulier* figure in the Hic
Mulier/Haec-Vir debate. First, they associate Moll's male apparel
with erotic appeal and illicit sexuality.

> For venery, you shall find enough for sixpence, but well couched
> and you mark it; for Venus being a woman passes through the play
> in doublet and breeches; a brave disguise and a safe one, if the
> statute untie not her codpiece point.
>
> ("To the Comic Play-Readers")

Secondly, as in the debate, erotic questions are less preoccupying
than social ones: the entire prologue attempts to assign Moll a specific class and rank, "to know what girl this roaring girl should be /
For of that tribe are many" (Prologue, 15–16). While the dramatists
assure us that their Moll is neither criminal, brawler, whore, nor city
wife, the question of her actual social status is left unanswered. As
the action unfolds, the playwrights' vision of the controversial "roaring girl's" exact position in the Jacobean social hierarchy gradually
assumes its distinct and complicated shape; and other characters
are defined as social and moral beings according to their responses
to her.

The play has a traditional New Comedy plot in which a young
man, Sebastian Wengrave, outwits his snobbish, greedy father, Sir
Alexander Wengrave, who has thereatened to disinherit Sebastian if
he marries the woman he loves, all because of her relatively meager
dowry. The subplot involves a theme equally characteristic of the
Jacobean dramatic satirist: the attempt of lazy, poor, arrogant,
upper-class "gallants" to cheat and seduce the wives of middle-class
shopkeepers. Like the prologue and the *Hic Mulier*/*Haec-Vir* debate,
the main plot stresses social issues while the secondary plot focuses
on erotic complications. The conservative faction in the play is most
strikingly represented by the father, Sir Alexander, and the lecherous, misogynistic gallant, Laxton, both of whose negative attitudes
toward Moll resemble those of the author of the *Hic Mulier* pamphlet toward women in men's clothing.

Moll enters the play for the first time during the subplot, as Laxton
and his cohorts are busily seeking to form illicit liaisons with shopkeepers' wives, chuckling privately over their erotic cunning and
prowess. In this Renaissance equivalent of the locker room, Moll, who
will smoke and swear, is greeted enthusiastically by the men, although
with considerably less relish by the women, one of whom screams,

"Get you from my shop!" (2.1.248). Both men and women, however, associate her mannishness with deformed and illicit sexuality:

MRS. G.   Some will not stick to say she is a man, and
          some, both man and woman.
LAX.   That were excellent: she might first cuckold
          the husband, and then make him do as much for the wife.
                                                  (2.1.219–22)

Like the author of the *Hic Mulier* pamphlet, Laxton finds this mannish woman sexy ("Heart, I would give but too much money to be nibbling with that wench") (2.1.193–94); he also automatically assumes from her unconventional sexual behavior that she is a whore: "I'll lay hard siege to her; money is that aqua fortis that eats into many a maidenhead; where the walls are flesh and blood, I'll ever pierce through with a golden augur" (2.1.203–05). Complacently, Laxton secures an assignation with Moll, to which he travels overcome with self-pleasure and a thrilling sense of his own power in arranging a forbidden encounter.

Laxton is unpleasantly surprised. In his confrontation with Moll, which takes the appropriate form of a duel, Moll emerges as a defiant champion of female freedom from male sexual dominion, a role symbolized by her male attire. When Laxton arrives on the scene searching for a woman in a "shag ruff, a frieze jerkin, a short sword, and a safeguard [i.e., a petticoat]" (3.1.34–35), Moll appears instead in male clothes, the significance of which she underscores: when Laxton, who takes a few moments to recognize her, remarks, "I'll swear I knew thee not," Moll replies meaningfully, "I'll swear you did not; but you shall know me now." Laxton, who is not at all clever, mistakes this response for an erotic overture: "No, not here; we shall be spied" (3.1.58–61). Discarding subtlety as hopeless, Moll beats up Laxton while delivering a stirring oration on the sexual injustices suffered by women at the hands of arrogant, slanderous men:

> Thou'rt one of those
> That thinks each woman thy fond flexible whore . . .
> How many of our sex, by such as thou,
> Have their good thoughts paid with a blasted name
> That never deserved loosely . . .
> There is no mercy in't.
>   (3.1.77–93)

Furthermore, Moll attributes female sexual vulnerability specifically to the superior social power of male seducers, which she defies:

> In thee I defy all men, their worst hates
> And their best flatteries, all their golden witchcrafts,
> With which they entangle the poor spirits of fools,

Distressed needle-women and tradefallen wives;
Fish that must needs bite, or themselves be bitten.
Such hungry things as these may soon be took
With a worm fastened on a golden hook.
Those are the lecher's food, his prey; he watches
For quarreling wedlocks and poor shifting sisters
(3.1.97–105)

Finally, she does not simply dwell on female victimization, but asserts positively the capacity of women for full sexual responsibility, authority, and independence:

I scorn to prostitute myself to a man,
I that can prostitute a man to me . . .
She that has wit and spirit,
May scorn to live beholding to her body for meat;
Or for apparel, like your common dame,
That makes shame get her clothes to cover shame.
(3.1.116–46)

Like the sympathetic *Hic Mulier* figure in the debate, Moll takes upon herself the defense of all women. Indeed Laxton's attempted violation of Moll's chastity connects her with, rather than distinguishes her from, the shopkeepers' wives, most of whom are willingly engaged in sexual collusion with the gallants when the play begins. As a result, we perceive that the "man-clothed" Moll,[1] the notorious roaring girl and *Hic Mulier*, is actually a sexual innocent compared to the conventional middle-class wives. More important than the wives' hypocrisy, however, is their eventual reform; at the end of the play they see through the schemes of their would-be seducers and choose to reject them in favor of their husbands, just as Moll's defeat of Laxton has portended that they would. The seducing gallants, who represent illicit sexuality, therefore turn out not to constitute a real threat to the social order at all. Moll herself recognizes this fact immediately: "Oh, the gallants of these times are shallow lechers . . . 'Tis impossible to know what woman is throughly honest, because she's ne'er throughly tried" (2.1.336–40).

As Moll's defeat of Laxton makes clear, free-floating, amoral eros is stripped of its socially destructive power when women decide to take responsibility for themselves. The aborted sexual encounter between Moll and Laxton also dramatizes the specious logic involved in connecting Moll's unconventional male attire automatically with whorish behavior. In their depiction of Laxton's complacence, the playwrights clearly associate lechery and misogyny with obtuse,

---

1. The phrase is from Fitz, p. 16.

unobservant social conformity.[1] As we have seen, the idea of mind-lessly adhering to social custom is the principal target of the sympa-thetic *Hic Mulier* figure when she defends her freedom in the debate. In *The Roaring Girl* this theme is amplified in the main plot through the representation of the censorious attitudes and actions which Sir Alexander Wengrave takes toward Moll Frith.

In his self-righteousness, self-deception, and self-pity, Sir Alexan-der is all self, incapable of distinguishing his emotional attachments from virtue. Proud of what he thinks is his shrewd observation of social life, trying to conform to a preconceived ideal, he continually misapprehends the realities which confront him. Sebastian recog-nizes that his father's vulnerability to the opinion of others exceeds even his greed, and he forms a plan to gain both his inheritance and his true love, Mary Fitzallard, by telling his father that he plans to marry Moll Frith, the outrageous roaring girl who fights, smokes, swears, and wears men's clothes. Like Laxton, Sir Alexander assumes from Moll's masculine attire that she is both a whore and a thief, who can be entrapped into stealing money, exposed, and safely removed from the proximity of his son. Like Laxton, he fails repeat-edly in his assaults on her integrity.

Sir Alexander inveighs against Moll as a monster (1.2.130–36; 2.2.81–83), a siren (2.1.219–20), a thief (1.2.175; 4.1.201–06; 2.2.139), and a whore (1.2.137; 2.2.160). One funny scene shows him spying on her, appalled, as her tailor fits her for breeches. Like the conservative author of the *Hic Mulier* pamphlet, Sir Alexander perceives in Moll's male clothing a symbol not only of perverse sexu-ality, but also of the inevitable disintegration of stable marital rela-tions: "Hoyda, breeches? What, will he marry a monster with two trinkets [i.e., testicles]? What age is this? If the wife go in breeches, the man must wear long coats, like a fool." (2.2.81-84). At the end of the play, before a nearly-reformed Sir Alexander has discovered his son's true marital intentions, Moll's urbane teasing exposes his desire to maintain rigid gender roles as a regressive anxiety:

> MOLL: (referring to herself) Methinks you should be
>   proud of such a daughter,
>   As good a man as your son . . .
>   You do not know what benefits I bring with me;
>   No cheat dares work upon you with thumb or knife,
>   While you've a roaring girl to your son's wife.
>   (5.2.153–62)

---

1. Laxton expresses his general view of women in 3.2.266–69: "That wile / By which the ser-pent did the first woman beguile / Did ever since all women's bosoms fill; / You're apple-eaters all, deceivers still."

More than any of the specific evils he attributes to her, Sir Alexander fears Moll's conspicuousness, her unconventionality, her social aberrance; the sheer embarrassment of having such a daughter-in-law is equivalent to ruin. "Why wouldst thou fain marry to be pointed at?" he asks his son. "Why, as good marry a beacon on a hill, / Which all the country fix their eyes upon, / As her thy folly dotes on" (2.2.142–46). It is Sir Alexander's shallow, malicious willingness to accept received opinion without observing for himself, his bourgeois horror of nonconformity, that moves Sebastian to a rousing defense of Moll, the clearest articulation of her honesty in the play:

> He hates unworthily that by rote contemns . . .
>   Here's her worst,
> Sh'as a bold spirit that mingles with mankind.
> But nothing else comes near it; and often times
> Through her apparel somewhat shames her birth;
> But she is loose in nothing but in mirth.
> Would all Molls were no worse!
>
>   (2.2.176–86)

And it is precisely this thoughtless social conformity, dramatized by his malignant intolerance of Moll, that Sir Alexander abjures at the end, thereby making possible the formation of a new comic society which will be both flexible and just:

> Forgive me; now I cast the world's eyes from me,
> And look upon thee [i.e., Moll] freely with mine own . . .
>   I'll never more
> Condemn by common voice, for that's the whore,
> That deceives man's opinion, mocks his trust,
> Cozens his love, and makes his heart unjust.
>
>   (5.2.244–51)

In "The Place of Laughter in Tudor and Stuart England," Keith Thomas analyzes the ways in which comedy conservatively affirms the status quo by revealing, mocking, and containing social tensions; yet, Thomas points out, "There was also a current of radical, critical laughter which, instead of reinforcing accepted norms, sought to give the world a nudge in a new direction."[2] Given the heavy emphasis which the majority of English Renaissance society placed on gender-polarized sexual decorum and subdued, modest female behavior, it is evident that, with their idealized comic portrait of the *Hic Mulier* figure Moll Frith, Dekker and Middleton were joining those who, like the author of the *Haec-Vir* pamphlet, were beginning to call for

---

2. Keith Thomas, "The Place of Laughter in Tudor and Stuart England," *Times Literary Supplement* (January 21, 1977), 78.

greater freedom for women and equality between the sexes. As we
have seen, serious opposition to Moll is represented in the play as
mindless conformity. Not only do the playwrights decline to link Moll's
freewheeling, immodest habits and appearance with perverse or dishonest behavior, but they also give her ample opportunity to acquit
herself from her reputation as a criminal (5.1.323–73). Furthermore,
Dekker and Middleton portray as noble Moll's integrity in refusing
Sebastian Wengrave's proposal of marriage, made before she knows it
is only a sham to deceive his father. Like the sympathetic, eloquent
Hic Mulier figure, Moll refuses the conventional subordination
required of a wife:

> I have no humor to marry . . . I have the head now of myself,
> and am man enough for a woman. Marriage is but a chopping
> and changing, where a maiden loses one head, and has a worse
> i' th' place.   (2.2.38–48)

Moll's virginity represents the particular condition of independence
which Carolyn Heilbrun defines as "that fierce autonomy which sep-
arates the individual from the literal history of his sexual acts":[3]
"Base is that mind that kneels unto her body . . . My spirit shall be
mistress of this house / As long as I have time in't" (3.1.149–52).

How far does *The Roaring Girl* go in its sympathetic imaginative
vision of sexual nonconformity, female independence, and equality
between the sexes, all conditions embodied in the title character?
Clearly Laxton's humorous stupidity and Sir Alexander's petty malice
are no match for Moll's integrity, vitality, intelligence, and courage. Yet
a more subtle counter-movement in the play resists the absorption of
Moll into the tolerant new society which forms in the final scene.

Far from direct disapproval, this strand of qualified feeling can be
discerned as an ambiguous undercurrent in the primarily positive
attitude with which Moll is regarded by Sebastian and his fiancée,
Mary Fitzallard, the couple whose relationship and opinions represent the desirable social norm in the play. For example, when Sebastian
reveals to Mary his scheme of pretending to court Moll, he describes
the roaring girl as "a creature / so strange in quality" (1.1.100–01)
that Mary could not possibly doubt his love. As noted, Sebastian provides the major defense of Moll in the play; but the defense, while eloquent and just, is delivered to his father in the course of a deception
and is couched entirely in terms of existing standards of sexual decorum, the basis of which Sebastian never questions: "and oftentimes /
Through her apparel [she] somewhat shames her birth; / But she is
loose in nothing but in mirth" (2.2.183–85). Is Sebastian referring to

---

3. Carolyn G. Heilbrun, *Toward a Recognition of Androgyny* (New York, 1973), p. 39.

Moll's gender, social status, or both in his reference to her birth? This point is never clarified, nor is the rather odd remark which Mary makes when Sebastian introduces her to Moll:

SEB. This is the roaring wench must do us good.
MARY. No poison, sir, but serves us for some use;
Which is confirmed in her.
(4.1.148–50)

Furthermore, Moll herself seems to acquiesce in the view which regards her as aberrant, thereby indirectly affirming existing sexual values: when Sebastian proposes to her she responds, "A wife you know ought to be obedient, but I fear me I am too headstrong to obey . . . You see sir, I speak against myself" (2.2.40–41,62). These and similar remarks are too infrequent and undeveloped to undercut the predominant theme of approval and admiration which surrounds Moll in the play; but they do qualify the potential for any radical change in sexual values implicit in the full social acceptance of Moll Frith.

The play makes clear that, if the stifling, malignant conformity which unjustly opposes Moll is one thing, incorporation of her into society is quite another. Full social acceptance is no more the destiny of the *Hic Mulier* figure in this play, no matter how benevolent, than it is the fate of the sympathetic *Hic Mulier* in the debate, no matter how reasonable, eloquent, or bold. Earlier I observed that the playwrights' ambivalence toward Moll can be discerned as a disjunction between thematic content and dramatic form. While the dominant content of *The Roaring Girl* elicits but does not clarify this issue, formal analysis makes its subtlety more readily perceptible. A brief discussion of the function of disguise in the play should help to clarify the point.

Although Moll Frith wears male clothing, she makes no attempt to conceal her identity and all the other characters know she is a woman: in short, she is not in disguise. When used simply to denote a costume, worn in a play or festival for example, "disguise" could be used as a morally neutral term in Jacobean England. But discussions of apparel in the moral and religious literature more often use "disguise" as an inclusive censorious term meaning, roughly, "deformity of nature" and comprehending in the range of disapproval not only the player, but the fop, dandy, overdressed woman and, of course, the *Hic Mulier*.[4] According to this conservative mentality, the roaring girl

4. See, for example, *Hic Mulier*, sig. C3: "Doe you make it the utter losse of your favour and bounty to have brought into your Family, any new fashion or disguise, that might either deforme Nature, or bee an injury to modestie." Cf. Harrison, in Wilson, p. 123: "You shall not see any so disguised as are my countrymen of England," and Nashe, in Wilson, p. 125: "England, the players' stage of gorgeous attire, the ape of all nations' superfluities, the continual masquer in outlandish habiliments, great plenty-scanting calamities art thou to await, for wanton disguising thyself against kind; and digressing from the plainness of thy ancestors."

would be in "disguise"; but, as we have seen, the play rejects precisely this negative interpretation of Moll's apparel. More illuminating for present purposes is a brief comparison between Moll and the disguised heroines of Shakespearean romantic comedy.

In contrast to Moll, who insists on being recognized as a woman, heroines like Rosalind and Viola seek to conceal their identities and to protect themselves by masquerading as men. Modern criticism has been particularly adept at recognizing the symbolic, structural, and psychological functions of these romantic disguises. On the psychological level, the male disguise allows the Shakespearean heroine the social freedom to extend her personality and expand her identity by exploring the possibilities inherent in male sexual roles.[5] This opportunity for heightened awareness and personal growth incorporates into the desirable comic society formed at the end of the play an androgynous vision, recently defined as "a psychic striving for an ideal state of personal wholeness, a microcosmic attempt to imitate a mythic macrocosm," in which "being a human being entails more than one's sex identification and attendant gender development"[6]

The romantic comic form, however, represents neither a mythical nor a revolutionary society, but a renewed traditional society, whose stability and coherence is symbolized by marriage and is based on the maintenance of traditional sexual roles.[7] It is the temporary nature of the heroine's male disguise which contains the formal solution to the potential psychological and social problems it raises: that is, the heroine gladly sheds her disguise with its accompanying freedoms at the end of the play, in order to accept the customary social role of wife, thereby allowing the play's androgynous vision to remain spiritual and symbolic without awakening the audience's dissatisfaction or desire for social change.[8] Northrop Frye has shown that the resolution of comedy, which is usually erotic, is often brought about by a bisexual Eros figure who, like Puck, "is in himself sexually self-contained, being in a sense both male and female, and

5. See Alexander Leggatt, *Shakespeare's Comedy of Love* (London, 1974), p. 202; Helen Gardner, "*As You Like It*," in *Modern Shakespearean Criticism*, ed. Alvin B. Kernan (New York, 1970), pp. 199, 202; Helene Moglen, "Disguise and Development: The Self and Society in *Twelfth Night*," *Literaure and Psychology*, 23 (1973), 13–19; and Dusinberre, p. 257.
6. Robert Kimbrough, "Androgyny Seen Through Shakespeare's Disguise," *Shakespeare Quarterly*, 33 (Spring, 1982), 20, 19. Cf. Margaret Boerner Beckman, "The Figure of Rosalind in *As You Like It*," *Shakespeare Quarterly*, 29 (Winter, 1978), 44–51.
7. Cf. Gardner, pp. 190–203 and Northrop Frye, "The Argument of Comedy," in ed. Kernan, pp. 165–73.
8. Cf. C.L. Barber, *Shakespeare's Festive Comedy: A Study of Dramatic Form and its Relation to Social Custom* (Princeton, N.J., 1959), pp. 245–47; Leggatt, p. 211; F. H. Mares, "Viola and other Transvestist Heroines in Shakespeare's Comedies," in ed. B. A. W. Jackson, *Stratford Papers on Shakespeare* (McMaster University Library Press, 1969 for 1965–1967), pp. 96–109; and Nancy K. Hayles, "Sexual Disguise in *As You Like It* and *Twelfth Night*," *Shakespeare Survey*, 32 (1979), 63–72.

needing no expression of love beyond himself." In Shakespeare's later comedies, this structural role is taken over by the disguised female; but when the Eros figure is no longer supernatural, "his" character must break down, as Viola's does into Viola and Sebastian in *Twelfth Night*, or be superseded, as Rosalind's is, by the figure of Hymen in *As You Like It*.[9] As another critic puts it, "The temporary nature of the male disguise is of course essential, since the very nature of Shakespearean comedy is to affirm that disruption is temporary, that what has been turned topsy-turvy will be restored."[1]

Like Shakespearean comedy, *The Roaring Girl* concludes festively with the re-formation of a flexible and tolerant society, whose stability and integration are symbolized in marriage. But in *The Roaring Girl* the functions performed by the disguised heroine in Shakespeare are structurally divided and displaced. Moll clearly answers to much of Frye's analysis of the comic Eros figure: first, with her self-imposed virginity, refusal to marry, and men's clothes, she is "in a sense both male and female" and needs "no expression of love beyond [her] self"; secondly, it is she who brings about the benevolent and satisfactory resolution of the action when she actively helps Sebastian to gain Mary. Sebastian recognizes her function as the play's Eros figure when he says, "Twixt lovers' hearts she's a fit instrument / And has the art to help them to their own" (2.2.204–05). In Frye's terms, Moll is a figure in whom Eros "is a condition, not a desire."[2] But unlike Puck, Moll is not supernatural; she is human and will not disappear from social life. She is neither on an odyssey toward sexual and social integration, as Rosalind and Viola are, nor can she be said to grow psychologically, happily internalizing the discovery of love and freedom in the way that they do. She has no intention of marrying, no intention of relinquishing either her outfit or the unconventional principles and behaviour it represents. She therefore assumes the social and psychological freedom of the traditional disguised heroine without providing the corresponding reassurance implicit in that heroine's eventual erotic transformation. These functions are instead displaced onto Mary Fitzallard, who, disguised as a page, joyously sheds the disguise to take her place as Sebastian's wife in the final scene. Moll, on the other hand, having served as the instrument who brings about the happy ending, is nevertheless excluded from the renewed comic society of married couples which forms on the stage at the end of the play. Sir Alexander makes this clear when he defines the new society by addressing "You kind

---

9. Northrop Frye, *A Natural Perspective* (New York, 1965), pp. 82–83.
1. Clara Claiborne Park, "As We Like It: How a Girl Can be Smart and Still Popular," in *The Woman's Part*, eds. Carolyn Ruth Swift Lenz, Gayle Greene, and Carol Thomas Neely (Urbana, Ill., 1980), p. 108.
2. Frye, p. 83.

gentlewomen, whose sparkling presence / Are glories set in marriage, beams of society / For all your loves give luster to my joys" (5.2.260–62). The playwrights conclude *The Roaring Girl* with an epilogue in which they emphasize the strangeness of the fictional, and the criminality of the real, Moll Frith.

In a sense the dramatists call attention to both a structural and social ambiguity in the world of the play by refusing to conflate Moll and Mary into a single figure.[3] By excluding Moll from the traditional, rejuvenated society demanded by the comic form, Middleton and Dekker never quite succeed in separating her from her outlaw status, despite the approval and admiration with which her integrity, courage, and freedom are depicted in the play. It is true that Moll herself displays nothing but a benign indifference toward acceptance by established society: "I pursue no pity / Follow the law and you can cuck me, spare not; / Hang up my viol by me, and I care not." (5.2.253–55). Moll's good-natured indifference allows the predominant tone of the ending of the play to remain festive. Yet her definition of herself as anti-social (5.1.362–63) and her exclusion by others combine to render unsettling the fact that her sexual independence has left her isolated from the very social structure which her courage and vitality have done so much to enliven and renew. The question of her social identity, raised at the beginning of the play, therefore remains unresolved at the end. It is because she has helped to create a society from which she is both excluded and excludes herself that Moll's status remains unclear; insofar as it is ambiguous, marginal, and problematic, Moll's social identity can be seen as a metaphor for the changing condition of women in early modern England.

IV

Both *The Roaring Girl* and the *Hic Mulier/Haec-Vir* debate represent the figure of the woman in men's clothing as the symbolic focus of concern about sexual freedom and equality in Jacobean society. Each text depicts this unconventional figure as attractive and virtuous, while those who regard her as socially and sexually disruptive are represented in contrast as hostile, anxious, and self-deceived. When confronting the irrationality of her enemies, the *Hic Mulier* figure emerges as the voice of reason and common sense. In both play and debate it is she who possesses imagination, insight, and courage; it is she who embodies the premise of freedom and even of happiness. Nevertheless this hopeful, likeable figure fails in each

3. See Gomme, p. xxiii, who points out that Mary and Moll have the same name, and that Moll "impersonates" Mary in the final scene "in order to complete the trick which secures Mary's happiness."

context to gain full social acceptance; not only is she excluded by others, but she herself acquiesces in her own defeat: in the debate she retreats completely, surrendering to the very values she had arisen to oppose; in the play she remains pleasantly isolated from society, a loveable outlaw whose eccentricity insures that she will not constitute a social threat. But while these formal resolutions of debate and play are both agreeably festive in tone, neither effort to adhere to the comic purpose of reconciling social tensions is entirely convincing. The powerfully rendered figure of *Hic Mulier* continues in each case to tower over the less compelling society that endeavors unsuccessfully to absorb her; viewed in terms of aesthetic logic, the *Hic Mulier* figure becomes content that cannot (illogically) be contained by form.

With their similarly ambivalent visions of *Hic Mulier* and Moll Frith as necessary but disruptive, benevolent but anti-social, both the debate and the play present an image of Jacobean society as unable to absorb one of its most vital and complex creations into the existing social and sexual hierarchies. The mixed approval and exclusion of the *Hic Mulier* figure evident in artistic representation and social commentary indicate a simultaneous search for and rejection of greater flexibility in sexual values. The parallel treatments of the controversy surrounding women in men's clothing in the dramatic and moral literature therefore combine to illuminate a particularly heightened time of groping for resolutions: in both *The Roaring Girl* and the *Hic Mulier/Haec-Vir* debate, the moral ambiguity and social challenge of sexual identity and equality as they were perceived in Renaissance England stand sharply before us.

JONATHAN DOLLIMORE

[Subjectivity, Sexuality, and Transgression in *The Roaring Girl*]†

Any study of transgression finds itself, of necessity, and soon, asking some searching questions—e.g.: does transgression primarily refer to an action, a social practice, or even more generally still, the struggle to produce alternative cultures and knowledges? How do we assess its success or failure? And who is "we"? Who decides whether transgression is regressive or progressive, revolutionary, or reactionary—or neither? Such a study raises questions which

† From "Subjectivity, Sexuality, and Transgression: The Jacobean Connection" from *Renaissance Drama n.s.* 17, edited by Mary Beth Rose (Evanston: Northwestern University Press, 1986), pp. 53–58, 60, 61–64, 65–72. Reprinted by permission.

invite—demand perhaps—a materialist analysis, by which I mean an analysis which seeks to be theoretically rigorous, historically aware, and politically involved.

Issues of transgression are inextricably bound up with those of subjectivity, and if poststructuralism enables us better to understand transgression in the Renaisance, this is perhaps because its conceptions of subjectivity are actually closer to those found in the Renaisance than is commonly reckoned. Often, essentialist conceptions of the self which only take effective hold in the Enlightenment and are then subsequently developed within Romanticism and Modernism, have been erroneously aligned with those in the Renaissance. Consider for example that great imperative of the Renaissance, *Nosce teipsum*, know thyself. Today, for poststructuralism, know thy discursive formations. But surely in the Renaissance also: terminology apart, did not *nosce teipsum* mean something like that? Though it has generally been appropriated by humanist criticism as a recognizable origin of itself, it may nevertheless have something crucial in common with the formulations of poststructuralism. Of the few central beliefs uniting the various poststructuralisms (and connecting them with postmodernism) this is one of the most important: human identity is more constituted than constitutive; constituted by, for example, the preexisting structures of language and ideology, and by the material conditions of human existence. Thus is the subject decentered, and subjectivity revealed as a kind of subjection—not the antithesis of social process but its focus.

In the Renaissance also the individual was seen as constituted by and in relation to—even the effect of—a preexisting order. To know oneself was to know that order. There is most obviously perhaps the tripartite division of the soul, a model inherited from classical culture and undergoing various further subdivisions in the intervening centuries. And as regards being an effect of a prior order we need only consider Richard Hooker's declaration: "God hath his influence into the very essence of all things, without which influence . . . their utter annihilation could not choose but follow" (2:26). Or the commonplace with which Sir John Davies begins his *Nosce Teipsum*: God wrote the law directly into the hearts of our first parents. Hooker concurs: the law of Reason, the universal law of mankind, is "imprinted" in men's souls and "written in their hearts" (1:166, 228). And when Montaigne and Bacon stress the determining power of social custom, they are developing the same idea of an order prior to and determining of the individual, though now of course with the crucial difference that it is a nonteleological order, historical rather than divine, material rather than metaphysical.[1]

---

1. For further analysis of custom in this respect, see Dollimore, esp. 9–19.

Obviously there are far-reaching differnces between Renaissance metaphysics and poststructuralism. For one thing the Renaissance veiw of identity as constituted (metaphysically) was also and quite explicitly a powerful metaphysic of social integration. In other words, to be metaphysically identified was simultaneously to be socially positioned—the subject in relation to the Prince, the woman in relation to the man, and so on. Metaphysics here underpins a discursive formation of the subject, of subjection. This link between subjectivity and subjection, which for poststructuralism has to be disclosed before it can be resisted, is, by comparison, both made explicit and endorsed in the Renaissance. Another difference: within Renaissance metaphysics a constituted identity might nevertheless be essentially fixed (e.g., the soul as divine creation) in a way that poststructuralism would also reject (identity is not only constructed but contingently so). Despite these differences, however, poststructuralism is helping us to see again what the Renaissance already knew: identity is in-formed by what it is not. It also helps us to see that if (as was apparent in the early seventeenth century) identity is clearly constituted by the structures of power, of position, allegiance, and service, any disturbance within or of identity could be as dangerous to that order as to the individual subject. Hooker, in a now famous passage, asked: "see we not plainly that obedience of creatures unto the law of nature is the stay of the whole world?" (1:157). Equally plain of course is that in this view disobedience is literally world shattering. The metaphysical construction of subjectivity is also an admission—and production—of its disruptive potential, a disruption in and of the very terms of its construction. A conception of the self as socially and/or metaphysically constituted produces one idea of transgression while a conception of the self as essentially (if not socially) unified and autonomous, quite another. That difference is addressed in what follows.

II

Lillian Faderman, in her book *Surpassing the Love of Men* (ch. 4), records two separate cases of women in France who in the sixteenth century were punished for using transvestite disguise and deploying dildos in their lesbian relations.[2] From one modern point of view these women's transgression is deeply suspect. I'm not referring to the conservative perspective which condemns sexual deviance per se, but to another perspective, one which might actually endorse deviance in principle, at least if it were seen as a quest for authentic selfhood. But

---

2. See also Crompton.

here, precisely, is the problem; even (or especially) from this radical perspective, the women's behaviour was inauthentic, not truly transgressive: in their use of men's clothing and the dildo they were trying to imitate precisely that masculine order which they should have been transcending. This, then, was regressive, not progressive, false, not true consciousness. Compare the heroine of *Rubyfruit Jungle* (1973) who articulates the perspective in question when confronted with a butch/femme lesbian bar: "That's the craziest, dumbass thing I ever heard tell of. What's the point of being a lesbian if a woman is going to look and act like an imitation man? Hell, if I want a man, I'll get the real thing not one of these chippies" (Brown 47–48). Or again, the anonymous interviewee cited by Esther Newton: "I hate games! I hate role playing! It's so ludicrous that certain lesbians, who despise men, become the exact replicas of them!" (7).

But the question remains: why were those two French women in the sixteenth century found so threatening? One of them was sentenced to be burned and the other hanged, punishments dictated, apparently, not by their lesbianism per se but their transvestism and use of the dildo—*at once*, I want to suggest, appropriations of masculinity, inversions of it, and substitutions for it.

The kind of transgression whose test they retrospectively failed, namely, transgression as a quest for authenticity, has been a powerful idea from romanticism through modernism and into the sexual revolution. Underpinning and endorsing the philosophy of individualism, it suggests that in defying a repressive social order we can discover (and so be *true* to) our *real* selves. Its view of human subjectivity is essentialist. Moreover it affirms that truth and reality are profoundly subjective, inextricably bound up with the essential self. For convenience and only provisionally I call this idea of transgression humanist. Clearly it is rooted in the essentialist humanism generated by the Enlightenment and undergoing various mutations ever since. And in our own century, it stems from what might fairly be called a radical humanism. Consider one of its classic expressions, André Gide's *The Immoralist* (1902). In that novel sexual transgression becomes a quest for the essential self. Its hero, Michel, throws off the culture and learning which up to that point have been his whole life, in order to find himself, "the authentic creature that had lain hidden beneath it . . . whom the Gospel had repudiated, who, everything about me—books, masters, parents, and I myself had begun by attempting to suppress. . . . Thenceforward I despised the secondary creature, the creature who was due to teaching, whom eduction had painted on the surface" (51). He composes a new series of lectures in which he shows "Culture, born of life, as the destroyer of life" (90). The true value of life is bound up with individual uniqueness: "the part in each of us that we feel is different from other people is just the part that is rare, the part that makes our special value" (100). Here, effectively, the self is understood in terms of a presocial, individuated essence, nature, and identity, and on that basis is invested with a quasi-spiritual autonomy. Culture has repressed this authentic self, and the individual embarks on a quest to recover it, a quest which is an escape from culture.

The significance for our culture of humanist transgression, this escape from repression into the affirmation of one's true self, can hardly be overestimated. Contrary to what has sometimes been implied, it didn't appear with existentialism; nor did it disappear when that movement ceased to be fashionable. And its prevalence has led us to misconceive both the significance and practice of transgression in earlier periods, especially the Renaissance, and even in some of our own contemporary subcultures. What intrigues me about that earlier period, especially its drama, is a mode of transgression which finds expression through the inversion[3] and perversion of just those preexisting categories and structures which humanist transgression seeks to transcend, to be liberated from; a mode of transgression which seeks not an escape from existing structures, but rather a subversive reinscription within them—and in the process a dis-location of them. I call this, again provisionally, transgressive reinscription. Examples preliminary to the main instances which follow might include the malcontent who haunts the very power structure which has alienated him, seeking reinscription within it but at the same time demystifying it, operating within and subverting it at the same time; the revengers whose actions constitute an even more violent bid for reinscription within the very society which has alienated and dispossessed them; the assertive woman, the woman on top,[4] who simultaneously appropriates, exploits, and undermines masculine discourse.

Humanist transgression in the name of authenticity has never been able to comprehend this other kind of transgression, that performed in the name of inversion, perversion, and reinscription. Moreover humanist transgression has proved wanting. Marked indelibly with the traces of idealist culture, it was perhaps inevitable that it should prove wanting. Inevitable, too, that in the wake of its failure we should become deeply skeptical about the very possibility of transgression. Because, in the words of Michel Foucault, "there is no single focus of great Refusal, no soul of revolt, source of

3. Anthropological and historical studies of inversion in the Renaissance have stressed both its ubiquity and its cultural significance. But what and how it signified—in particular whether it disrupted or ratified those dominant forms being inverted—depended crucially on context and cannot be decided independently of it. See especially Davis, and Kunzle, both in Babcock; and Stallybrass and White.
4. See Davis, and Kunzle.

all rebellions, or pure law of the revolutionary" (95–96)—because of that, there now seems to be only law itself, coercively or ideologically at work: coercively in the sense of being actively and increasingly repressive, ideologically in the sense of actively preempting resistance and subversion because somehow preceding and informing them. And so in recent years we have become preoccupied with the so-called containment of transgression—not merely its defeat by law, but its production and harnessing by law for law's own ends.

There is, for example, a functionalist argument to the effect that transgression may only be licensed, a kind of ritual safety valve which, far from undermining the existing order, actually reinforces it. Then there is the psychological version of this argument: paradoxically the sacred is most valued by the sacrilegious, and real faith lies in honest doubt. This argument includes Richard Sennett's notion of disobedent dependence, a defiance presupposing the very dependence it is trying to subvert, and in which "transgression is perhaps the most important element." This is a defiance based upon dependence, a rebellion not so much against authority as within it; the transgressor indeed disobeys but authority regulates the terms. As such this form of disobedience "has very little to do with genuine independence or autonomy . . . the world into which a person has entered through the desire to transgress is seldom however a real world of its own, a true alternative which blots out the past" (Sennett 33–34).[5] Sennett's argument might then be broadly supported by a structuralist or indeed poststructuralist argument to the effect that transgression, especially transgressive inversion, too often remains within—i.e., *merely* reverses—the binary opposition which structures both it and the law being contravened. (This would be the critique, in theoretical guise, of the "mannish" lesbian.) There are, then, at least three versions of this powerful argument whereby transgression is contained.

* * *

I want to suggest that what is overlooked, both in humanist transgression and in some recent arguments for the inexorable containment of transgression, is the part played by contradiction and dis-location in the mutually reactive process of transgression and its control. I'm using the term contradiction in its materialist sense to denote the way social process develops according to an inner logic which simultaneously, or subsequently, effects its negation. Three

5. Cf. Freud: "defiance signifies dependence *as much as obedience does,* though with a 'minus' instead of a 'plus' sign before it" (*Introductory Lectures on Psychoanalysis* 195; emphasis added).

paradigms of this derive from Hegel, Marx, and Freud—Hegel's theory of the master/slave dialectic, Marx's theory of the fundamental contradiction between the forces and relations of production, and the Freudian proposition just referred to, namely, the return of the repressed via the mode of its repression. In a revolutionary conjuncture contradictions may contribute to the disintegration of an existing order, though only (usually) through terrible suffering and struggle. That has to be said. In a nonrevolutionary conjuncture contradictions render social process the site of contest, struggle, and change. And, again, suffering. The contradictions which surface in times of crisis are especially revealing: they tell us that no matter how successful authority may be in its repressive strategies, there remains something potentially uncontrollable not only in authority's *objects* but in its *enterprise*, its rationale, and even its origin.

Deviancy, whether of Faustus's kind or that of the transvestite, plays a revealing part here, both as that which becomes especially visible in times of crisis, and that which focuses the inherent contingency of, and potential contradictions within, power. This is why we are mistaken if we think that deviancy exists outside of the dominant order. Though socially marginal the deviant remains discursively central: though an outcast of society s/he remains indispensable to it. For example: the process of identifying and demonizing deviance may be "necessary" to maintaining social order, either in the sense that deviance poses an actual threat, or that it is perceived as threatening, or that a prevailing authority is able to relegitimate itself through that process of identifying and demonizing deviance. In practice these three responses to deviance are rarely separable.

Taking the example of deviancy, consider another but quite different instance of transgressive reinscription. The late Gāmini Salgādo once described the vagabonds of the Elizabethan low-life pamphlets as follows:

> Seen through the disapproving eyes of respectable citizens they were nothing but a disorderly and disorganized rabble, dropouts from the social ladder. But seen from within, they appear to be like nothing so much as a mirror-image of the Elizabethan world picture: a little world, tightly organised into its own ranks and with its own rules, as rigid in its own way as the most elaborate protocol at court or ritual in church. (13)

From the respectable view, then, these rogues were merely the dregs of civilization—potentially dangerous, it's true, but in no way a part of the real social order. From another view they comprise a mirror-image of that order. But if the second view is accurate, do not the rogues become another clear instance of transgression contained, of a subculture which has internalized the structures and values of the dominant culture? Are they not paradoxically reproducing the laws which exclude and oppress them, even as they seem to be escaping and subverting those laws? Not exactly, because this very mimickry of the dominant involves a scandalous inversion. In the words of one contemporary observer: "these cheaters turned the cat in the pan, giving to diverse vile patching shifts an honest and godly title, calling it by the name of law . . . to the destruction of the good labouring people" (Salgādo 15). And feeding back through that inversion is an equally scandalous interrogation of the dominant order being mimicked; civil society is itself shown to be rooted in a like corruption. If this subculture imitates the dominant from below, it also employs a strategy whereby it undermines the dominant. Even as civil society endlessly displaces corruption from the social body as a whole onto its low-life (this in all likelihood corresponding to the first view above, that of the respectable citizens who see the low-life as society's waste product), the latter reveals both the origional source and full extent of corruption within the dominant itself (Salgādo 16, 174). Inversion becomes a kind of transgressive mimesis: the subculture, even as it imitates, reproducing itself in terms of its exclusion, also demystifies, producing a knowledge of the dominant which excludes it, this being a knowledge which the dominant has to suppress in order to dominate.

In summary, then: change, contest, and struggle in part are made possible by contradiction and focused internally through deviancy. For all their differences both Foucault and Derrida lend support to this argument. Foucault, in the *History of Sexuality*, speaks of resistance not as outside power but inscribed within it as its irreducible opposite (96). And Derrida has stressed in *Positions* the political effectiveness of inverting binary oppositions, of inversion as a stage in displacement.[6] The force of these arguments, both of which are complex and which I can only allude to here[7] but whose importance I want to stress, increases if we observe further the extent to which binarism produces an instability in the very process of categorically dividing the world. It both produces ambiguities which it can't contain and invites transgression in and of its own terms. Thus the opposition us/them produces the scandal of the internal dissident; the opposition masculine/feminine produces the scandal of the transvestite, not to mention the troubling ambiguity of the hermaphrodite.

For my purposes here, the most interesting and relevant senses of "inversion" and "perversion" are not primarily or specifically sexual.

---

6. Derrida 41–42. Derrida stresses the importance of inversion as a stage in the process of displacing the binary. Even with this formulation it is easy to overlook the extent to which, in actual practice, in historical reality, an inversion already achieves a degree of displacement.
7. I explore this further in a related article, "The Dominant and the Deviant."

Traditionally inversion could mean reversal of position and reversal of direction, both being inimical to effective government and social stability. This sense of *active* alteration is there even more strikingly in perversion. Especially interesting is the slippage in an OED definition from divergence to evil: "turned away from the right way or from what is right or good; perverted, wicked"; similarly with another definition: "not in accordance with the accepted practice; incorrect, wrong." It is in this sense of actively altering—a divergence which is also a turning back upon—that the female transvestite of the early seventeenth century could be described as an "invert" and not at all in the sense of that word coined and popularized by the nineteenth-century sexologists (e.g., Krafft-Ebing and Havelock Ellis).

III

The female transvestite was indeed a deeply disturbing figure in the early seventeenth century.[8] As Lisa Jardine has recently reminded us, nowhere was the tension and struggle between classes, between residual and emergent cultures, between the mercantile order and what it was actually, or seemed to be, replacing, between rank and wealth, more apparent than in the obsession with dress and what it signified socially (141–42, 150).[9] Hence the attacks on the dress violations of the emergent (middle) class and the insubordinate (female) sex. The ideology of gender difference was just as fundamental as that of class in securing the social order. In fact patriarchy, class, and hierarchy all presupposed a law of gender difference which was at once divinely, naturally, and socially laid down, the law descending from the first through the second to the third.

It is *against and (again) in terms of* this metaphysic that dress violation occurred. A significant focus for the controversy was, of course, the theater, which, like the transvestite, was seen both to epitomize and promote contemporary forces of disruption. There was, for example, the general cultural disturbance generated by the theatrical emphasis on artifice, disguise, and role playing. Its significance can be gauged in part by looking at the range of objections to the theater as a place which subverted metaphysical fixity.

To begin with, the players were seen to undermine the idea that one's identity and place were a function of what one essentially was—what God had made one. The idea of a God-given nature and destiny had the corollary that nothing so essentially predetermined could or

---

8. This section is indebted to and was inspired by a number of recent studies of the transvestite controversy, especially the following: Dusinberre, esp. 231–305; Shepherd, esp. ch. 6; Jardine, esp. ch. 5; Woodbridge, esp. part 2; Rose, 367–91; Clark 157–83.
9. See also Whigham 155–69.

should ever change. In the words of one satirist, it was not so much that the player disguised his real self in playing; rather he had no self apart from that which he was playing: "The Statute hath done wisely to acknowledge him a Rogue and errant, for his chiefe essence is, *A daily Counterfeit* . . . His {profession} is compounded of all Natures, all humours, all professions."[1] The association here of the player and the rogue is significant. Both were itinerants and masterless men, sometimes both subjected to the same vagrancy laws (alternatively the player might be a royal servant—an interesting opposition in itself). They transgressed fixity not only because they were without fixed abode, but also because they lacked the identity which, in a hierarchical society, was essentially conferred by one's place in that society. But there was a further link among rogues, masterless men, and the players; according to some observers the theaters quite literally brought them into association, being the place "for vagrant persons, Masterless men, thieves, . . . contrivers of treason, and other idle and dangerous persons to meet together"(Chambers 4:122). Again we see the same anxiety: social stability depended crucially on people staying just as they were (identity), where they were (location), and doing what they always had done (calling). When the rogue meets the player two lawless identites converge.

This concern with unfixed identity was not unique to the theater; society and politics more generally contained a theatrical dimension, what Greenblatt calls "the theatricalisation of culture." Renaissance courts involved theatricality "in the sense of both disguise and histrionic self-presentation," while court manuals and rhetorical handbooks offered "an integrated rhetoric of the self, a model for the formation of an artificial identity" (162). And dissimulation was of course essential for the practice of realpolitik. The theater, then, provided a model, indeed a sustained exploration, of the role playing which was so important for social mobility, the appropriation and successful deployment of power. It follows that the recurring emphasis within Elizabethan and Jacobean plays on life itself as a process of playing was not merely theatrical projection; the world as a stage, life as artifice: these were ideas which the theater derived from as well as conveyed to its culture. As Louis Montrose has pointed out, this has a fascinating consequence: "If the world is a theatre and the theatre is an image of the world, then by reflecting upon its own artifice, the drama is holding the mirror up to nature" (57).

* * *

1. "A Common Player," 1615, quoted from Montrose 51 and 57.

IV

In *The Roaring Girl* (1608–11), a play with a transvestite hero/ine and in the 1620 pamphlet controversy over cross-dressing, which treated issues similar to those in the play, the contemporary sexual metaphysic was turned inside out: gender division was recognized as central not to a divinely sanctioned natural order but to a contingent and oppressive social order. Correspondingly the representation of gender inversion generates an interrogation of both the sexual metaphysic and the social order. Moll Cutpurse, the transvestite hero/ine of *The Roaring Girl*, is variously described as one who "strays so from her kind / Nature repents she made her" (1.2.211–20); who some say "is a man / And some both man and woman" (2.1.190–91), and yet others that she is "a codpiece-daughter" (2.2.89):

> a thing
> One knows not how to name: her birth began
> Ere she was all made: 'tis woman more than man,
> Man more than woman, and (*which to none can hap*)
> The sun gives her two shadows to one shape
> (1.2.128–32; italics added)

And yet this creature who so violates the natural order and traditional gender divisions by dressing as a man also does things better than a man: "I should draw first and prove the quicker man," she says (4.1.76)—and she does. In the process she attacks masculinity as a charade, asserting its failure *in its own sexual terms* (2.9.290 ff.), something which the language of the play echoes elsewhere, facetiously, but defensively, too (cf. 2.1.326 ff.; 2.2.75 ff.; 3.1.142 ff.). Moll also offers the truly exceptional view of prostitution as a sexual exploitation rooted in economic exploitation and patriarchal power:

> In thee I defy all men, their worst hates,
> And their best flatteries, all their golden witchcrafts,
> With which they entangle the poor spirits of fools.
> Distressed needlewomen and trade-fallen wives,
> Fish that must needs bite or themselves be bitten,
> Such hungry things as these may soon be took
> With a worm fastened on a golden hook:
> Those are the lecher's food, his prey, he watches
> For quarrelling wedlocks, and poor shifting sisters.
> (3.1.90–98)[2]

2. See also Woodbridge 524–55.

Recognizing all this, and being shown, too, where the power lies in this social order, the politics of inversion become persuasive, perhaps irresistible; this is Moll, about to thrash the predatory Laxton: "I scorn to prostitute myself to a man, / I that can prostitute a man to me" (3.1.109–10). Moll's denunciation of Laxton before she beats him up shows that the thrashing is partly in revenge for his not untypical masculine blend of misogyny and promiscuity (cf. 2.2.252–55), to which of course the prostitute can indeed testify (and perhaps also confirm): if these things appear incompatible—isn't misogyny a kind of hatred, and promiscuity a kind of love, albeit a debased one?—in reality they go hand in hand.

It's in these ways that *The Roaring Girl* begins to disclose how, because of the complex connections between sexuality, gender, and class, between sexual and economic exploitation, economic and political anxieties can be displaced into the domain of the sexual and, conversely, the sexual comes to possess enormous signifying power. Indeed, the king himself intervened in 1620 to try to eliminate female transvestitism.[3] He, like many others at that time, felt female transvestites were usurping male authority. This is indeed exactly what Moll does throughout the play, and especially when she beats up Laxton. But perhaps more importantly the transvestite was contributing to a knowledge and a culture which undermined the discursive formations of authority itself, through her perverse reinscription within those formations. This can be further illustrated, briefly, from the pamphlet controversy.

Hic Mulier, the voice of female transvestites in the most interesting pamphlet, *Haec Vir* (1620), insists that gender difference is an effect of custom only. Custom becomes the cause where once it was only the effect. Again, inversion. This is also an instance of what was to become the classic move in ideological demystification: the metaphysical is first displaced by, and then collapsed into, the social. Shorn of its metaphysical sanction, law, especially in the Renaissance, is in danger of losing its prescriptive power. Nothing is more absurd, nothing more foolish, says Hic Mulier, than custom. In fact, it is "an idiot" (Sig.B2; spelling modernized). The radical implications of this assertion can be seen from an observation of Montaigne's: "We may easily discern, that only custom makes that seem impossible unto us, which is not so" (1:39). Throughout the pamphlet Hic Mulier seems to be in sympathy with this remark of Montaigne's, but nowhere is her appropriation of the idea more challenging than in the way she dissolves both law and ideological fixity into a celebration of change and transformation and, by

3. See Chamberlain 2: 286–89.

implication, a celebration of her potential rather than her fixed nature: "Nor do I in my delight of change otherwise than as the whole world does" (Sig.B). At a time when many thought of change as synonymous with evil, or at least decline and degeneracy, this was indeed provocative. Hic Mulier is not only shameless but, as Sandra Clark has recently pointed out, she suggests that shame itself "is a concept framed by men to subordinate women to the dictates of arbitrary custom" (175). Hic Mulier claims, too, that women are as reasonable as men. And then the crucial claim: "We are as free born as men, have as free election, and as free spirits; we are compounded of like parts, and may with like liberty make benefit of our creations" (Sig.B3). It's a claim whose force in *this* instance comes through a demystification generated across inversion.

But consider now a misgiving voiced by Linda Woodbridge and shared by many others: "To me the one unsatisfying feature of the otherwise stimulating transvestite movement is that it had to be transvestite: Renaissance women so far accepted the masculine rules of the game that they felt they had to look masculine to be free" (145). For understandable reasons Woodbridge seems to prefer the "hermaphroditic vision" (145 and cf.317). The transvestite and the hermaphrodite: both were disturbing images; perhaps they are less so now. Potentially the hermaphrodite dissolves gender difference and, at least in its associated idea of androgyny, has become acceptable. Even in the Renaissance the figure could "symbolise the essential oneness of the sexes" (Woodbridge 140), and, with reference back to Plato's *Symposium*, the recovery of an original lost unity (itself intrinsically sexual). The idea remains alive today, of course; Kaja Silverman reminds us that the notion of an original androgynous whole, similar to that projected by Aristophanes, is absolutely central to the psychoanalytic theories of Jacques Lacan, where the human subject is defined in terms of an essential, intrinsic lack, because it is believed to be a fragment of something larger and more primordial (152–53). But the transvestite? S/he is a strange and disturbing figure still, though for different reasons now than in the Renaissance. Isn't s/he a figure who has exchanged one kind of incompleteness for another? If misgivings persist they are not exactly moral; I mean we don't exactly or openly disapprove. Isn't it rather that, as Woodbridge implies, the transvestite seems to be a victim of false consciousness, and by switching gender roles rather than dissolving them, reinforces the very sexual division which s/he finds oppressive? In this view the transvestite fails the test of humanist transgression, a perspective which pervades literary criticism still. But if the hermaphrodite threatens the binarism of gender through ambiguous unity, the female transvestite of the early seventeenth century positively disrupts that same scheme by usurping the master side of the opposition. To invoke again the earlier distinction between different kinds of transgression, the transvestite represents a subversive reinscription within, rather than a transcendence of, an existing order, while the hermaphrodite is often appropriated as a symbol of just such a transcendence. Essentially the aggressive female cross-dresser inverted the metaphysics of difference: from being a divine law inscribed essentially in each of God's subjects, which knowledge of self would confirm, sexual identity (and difference) is shifted irretrievably into the domain of custom, of the social, of that which can be contested. Perhaps this is the mode of transgression denied to the hermaphrodite, at least when associated with the mythological, the presocial, the transcendent.

V

What I've just offered have been partial readings of the *Haec Vir* pamphlet and *The Roaring Girl*, partial not in the sense (at least this isn't what I'm confessing) of being distortions of the texts, but rather readings that focus upon textual elements which can be correlated with oppositional cultural elements within Jacobean society, and consequently possible audience positions and reading responses. But the representation of the transvestite in the pamphlet and the theater is part of a cultural process whose complexity is worth exploring further. The complexity I'm concerned with isn't that supposed intrinsic property of the text which politically motivated critics always distort (in biased readings) and impartial critics transparently represent (in long readings). It's the complexity which is first and foremost a social process, and within which the text was, and still is, implicated. Viewing the text as part of a social process raises, unavoidably, the question of the containment of transgression. Both play and pamphlet have been seen to move toward a closure which contains—even eradicates—their challenging elements.

The *Haec-Vir* pamphlet ends, notoriously, with Hic Mulier declaring that women like her have only become masculine because men have become effeminate. They have taken up men's cast-off garments in order to "support a difference" (Sig. C2V)—in effect to maintain a sexual difference being abandoned by men. And if men revert to being masculine, the Hic Mulier figure continues, women will once again become feminine *and* subordinate. Actually this conclusion barely constitutes containment. To see this argument as somehow cancelling what went before is probably to interpret the pamphlet according to inappropriate notions of authorial intention, character utterance, and textual unity (all three notions privileging what is said finally as being more truthful than what went before). The Hic Mulier figure (an abstraction) is a vehicle for a variety of

defenses of the transvestite, radical *and* conservative, and there is no
good reason, given the genre, to privilege the one over the others as
more truthful, more sincere, more representative, or to be dismayed
that some of these arguments are incompatible with each other. Pre-
sumbly, if the different defenses had been split between several Hic
Mulier figures the problem (for us) would disappear—again alerting
us to certain, not necessarily appropriate, interpretative assumptions. But it is also true that this culminating defense, conservative
as it is, still partakes of the same fundamental challenge to gender
division as the other defenses: to suggest that gender difference can
be maintained through cross-dressing and inversion is still to maintain or imply the crucial claim: it is difference working in terms of
custom and culture (and so contestable) rather than nature and
divine law (and so immutable). Even with this conservative (ironic?)
defense, then, sexual difference is sustained by the very inversion
which divine law forbids, and the fact that it can be so sustained is
simultaneously a repudiation of the claim that sexual difference is
itself dictated by divine or natural law.

  The Roaring Girl is a much more interesting instance of containment. Right at the outset we're alerted to the fact that Mary Frith, the
real-life cross-dresser on whom the play is based, is being given a
more virtuous image than she in fact possessed (Dedication 19 ff.;
Prologue 26–27). The play plays down Frith's criminality. She seems
to have been several times arrested and variously recorded as being a
bawd, thief, receiver, gang leader, and whore, all of which, as Andor
Gomme remarks, the character Moll Cutpurse definitely is not, and
is only falsely accused of being in the play.[4] Whereas the deviance of
Mary Frith remained in certain respects implacably immoral and
antisocial, in the figure of Moll Cutpurse she is remade as the moral
conscience of the selfsame society whose gender categories she
transgresses. More specifically, Frith/Moll is appropriated for a partial critique of patriarchal law, sexual exploitation, and aristocratic
culture. At the same time she remains "isolated from the very social
structure which her courage and vitality have done so much to
enliven and renew" (Rose 389–90). In this respect Frith/Moll is represented in the tradition of the warrior woman and the folk figure of
Long Meg of Westminster, both of whom distinguish true morality
from false, the proper man from the braggart, and finally submit to
the former (see Shepherd esp. 70–72). At the same time, Moll, a figure who epitomizes the abnormal and the degenerate, and who also
apparently incites lewdness in others, paradoxically helps regenerate
a degenerate society and especially its ailing patriarchal basis: "Moll:

---

4. Gomme, xiv; see also Shepherd 74–76.

Father and son, I ha' done you simple service here" (5.2.206). Thus the relationship between the dominant and the deviant is nothing if not complex: if the demonizing of the deviant other leads to suppression and even extermination, the colonizing of the (internal) deviant involves an assimilation which re-forms, ethically and literally, even as it re-presents. The play reconstitutes Mary Frith as Moll Cutpurse, who in turn is used to reconstitute a social order while remaining on its margins—reformed and reforming but not finally incorporated; hence Moll's parting injunction to the assembled "gentlemen" of the final scene, "I pursue no pity: / Follow the law" (252–55).

In this case containment isn't the reaction of power after, and in response to, the event of subversion. It's intrinsic to the process of literary representation, social contest, and social change. Perhaps, then, containment is best seen as always already in play, even before we can identify a dominant-subversive opposition, or indeed anything like a subversive event. But by the same token, containment can effect rather than defeat change (and this doesn't presuppose the desirability or otherwise of that change; it might be reaction or progress or, as in this play, complex elements of both with each differently appropriated for different audience positions). Rather than seeing containment as that which preempts and defeats transgression we need to see both as potentially productive processes. *The Roaring Girl* presents a process in which containment of the deviant forms the basis of one social faction offering a critique of, and taking power from, another.

* * *

WORKS CITED

Babcock, Barbara A. *The Reversible World: Symbolic Inversion in Art and Society*. Ithaca and London: Cornell UP, 1978.

Brown, Rita Mae. *Rubyfruit Jungle*. London: Corgi, 1973.

Chamberlain, John. *Letters*. Ed. Norman E. McClure. 2 vols. Philadelphia: American Philosophical Society, 1939.

Chambers, E. K. *The Elizabethan Stage*. 4 vols. Oxford: Clarendon, 1923.

Clark, Sandra. "Hic Mulier, Haec Vir, and the Controversy over Masculine Women." *Studies in Philology* 82 (Spring 1985): 157–83.

Crompton, Louis. "The Myth of Lesbian Impunity: Capital Laws from 1270–1791." *Journal of Homosexuality* 6 (1980–81): 11–25.

Davis, Natalie Zemon. "Women on Top: Symbolic Sexual Inversion and Political Disorder in Early Modern Europe." *The Reversible World: Symbolic Inversion in Art and Society*. Ithaca and London: Cornell UP, 1978.

Derrida, Jacques. *Positions*. London: Athlone, 1981.

Dollimore, Jonathan. "The Dominant and the Deviant: A Violent Dialectic." *Critical Quarterly* 28 (1986).

Dusinberre, Juliet. *Shakespeare and the Nature of Women*. London: Macmillan, 1975.

Faderman, Lillian. *Surpassing the Love of Men: Romantic Friendship and Love between Women from the Renaissance to the Present*. London: Dent, 1981.

Foucault, Michel. *The History of Sexuality.* Vol. 1: *An Introduction.* New York: Vintage, 1980.

Freud, Sigmund. *Introductory Lectures on Psychoanalysis.* The Pelican Freud Library 1. Harmondsworth: Pelican Books, 1976.

Gide, André. *The Immoralist.* Harmondsworth: Penguin, 1960.

Gomme, Andor. Introduction. *The Roaring Girl.* By Middleton and Dekker. London: Benn, 1976.

Greenblatt, Stephen. *Renaissance Self-Fashioning.* Chicago: U of Chicago P, 1980.

Hic Mulier: Or, the Man-Woman and *Haec-Vir: Or, the Womanish-Man.* 1620. The University of Essex: The Rota, 1973.

Jardine, Lisa. *Still Harping on Daughters: Women and Drama in the Age of Shakespeare.* Brighton: Harvester, 1983.

Kunzle, David. "World Turned Upside Down: The Iconography of a European Broadsheet Type." Babcock.

Middleton, Thomas, and Thomas Dekker, *The Roaring Girl.* The New Mermaid edition. Ed. A. Gomme. London: Benn, 1976.

Montaigne, Michel. *Essays.* Trans. John Florio. 3 vols. London: Dent, 1965.

Montrose, Louis. "The Purpose of Playing: Reflections on a Shakespearean Anthropology." *Helios* ns 7 (1980): 51–74.

Newton, Esther. "The Mythic Mannish Lesbian: Radclyffe Hall and the New Woman." *The Lesbian Issue: Essays from Signs.* Ed. Estelle B. Freeman et al. Chicago: U of Chicago P, 1985.

Rose, Mary Beth. "Women in Men's Clothing: Apparel and Social Stability in *The Roaring Girl.*" *English Literary Renaissance* 14 (1984): 367–91.

Salgādo, G., ed. *Cony-Catchers and Bawdy Baskets.* Penguin English Library. Harmondsworth, 1972.

Sennett, Richard. *Authority.* London: Secker, 1980.

Shepherd, Simon. *Amazons and Warrior Women: Varieties of Feminism in Seventeenth-Century Drama.* Brighton: Harvester, 1981.

Silverman, Kaja. *The Subject of Semiotics.* New York: Oxford UP, 1983.

Stallybrass, Peter, and Allon White. *The Politics and Poetics of Transgression.* London: Methuen, 1986.

Whigham, Frank. *Ambition and Privilege: The Social Tropes of Elizabethan Courtesy Theory.* Berkeley: U of California P, 1984.

Woodbridge, Linda. *Women and the English Renaissance: Literature and the Nature of Womankind, 1540–1620.* Brighton: Harvester, 1984; Urbana: U of Illinois P, 1984.

JEAN E. HOWARD

Sex and Social Conflict:
The Erotics of *The Roaring Girl*†

In the printed preface to *The Roaring Girl*, entitled 'To the Comic Play-Readers, Venery and Laughter', the play advertises an intention to address erotic matter in a comic fashion.[1] Venery, in its double meanings of (a) the practice or sport of hunting beasts of game, and (b) the practice or pursuit of sexual pleasure, dominates this text. Most of the venery is overtly sexual. Young men hunt maids, and gallants pursue city wives for sexual satisfaction inside or outside marriage. Yet not all of the venery of this text is so relentlessly heterosexual as this summary suggests, and the sexual hunt provokes other types of venery as well, as angry fathers hound, harass, and entrap their wayward sons, and angry husbands stalk cuckolding gallants. At the centre of this complex world stands Moll Cutpurse, Venus 'in doublet and breeches' (Gomme 1976: Preface, 1.14), a figure who not only provokes erotic desire and sexualized aggression in others, but who also remains an erotic subject in her own right. As such, she threatens her culture's conventions for managing female desire. By examining various aspects of 'venery' in this drama I hope to show several things: first, that this site of licensed 'play' affords glimpses of a landscape of erotic desire and practice whose contours cannot quite be mapped in twentieth-century terms; second, that the manifest contradictions surrounding the play's representations of sexuality, marriage, and gender roles suggest that these were contested cultural phenomena—the source of anxiety and conflict as much as of laughter; third, that homoerotic bonds between men subtend this textual world and are not always easily reconciled with cultural imperatives to marry and reproduce; and, finally, that female sexual desire remains the most intractable aspect of the play's sexual economy.

Recently, feminist, gay, lesbian, and queer critics (the four categories are not necessarily discrete) have emphasized the political necessity and the analytic utility of investigating sexuality as a relatively autonomous system of cultural meaning and site of social struggle, one that cannot simply be subsumed under an analysis of gender difference and hierarchy (Sedgwick 1990: 27–35; Traub

---

† From *Erotic Politics: Desire on the Renaissance Stage,* edited by Susan Zimmerman (New York: Routledge, 1992), pp. 170–90. Reprinted by permission.
1. All citations from *The Roaring Girl* refer to the New Mermaids edition edited by Andor Gomme (1976).

1992).[2] As Gayle Rubin has written, in revision of her own earlier conflation of sex and gender into one system, 'Gender affects the operation of the sexual system, and the sexual system has had gender-specific manifestations. But although sex and gender are related, they are not the same thing, and they form the basis of two distinct arenas of social practice' (Rubin 1984: 308). In this essay I will attend to the specificity of sexuality by looking at how sexual practices and desires are represented in this text and points of conflict within the sexual economy rendered visible. But at the same time I will try to show *interconnections* between sexuality and other systems through which social conflict was regulated and registered in early modern England, especially the effect on sexual practice of class antagonisms and of a gender ideology that sexualized the desiring, speaking, publicly visible woman and simultaneously made her a threat to man's gender dominance and to patriarchal constructions of 'the good wife'.

Like gender, sexuality has increasingly been revealed as less an essential biological given than a socially constructed, historically variable set of practices and ideologies.[3] As gay and lesbian scholars have made clear, homosexuality, for example, does not have one set of meanings through time. In discussing same-sex relationships in early modern England, Alan Bray argues that while there were certainly sodomitical acts committed in the Renaissance, they were not undertaken by 'homosexuals', that is, by people for whom same-sex sexual orientation constituted a primary category of identity or subjectivity.[4] Rather than a distinct identity, homosexuality constituted a potential within everyone, a point on a continuum of possible sexual practices (Bray 1988: 25). Consequently, there may have been more fluidity in the matter of object choice, especially for men, than is 'normal' today when homosexual and heterosexual are typically

2. The word *queer* is a hotly contested one in gay and lesbian scholarship. For discussion of the term and for examples of 'queer critical practice', see *Social Text* 29 and *Differences* 3, 2, especially the lead essays by Warner (1991) and de Lauretis (1991) respectively. I use the term *queer* to indicate alternatives to normative heterosexuality. The value of the word for me lies in its ability to draw attention to sexuality as a primary site of oppression, but also of collective possibility and resistance, in a way that sidesteps the usual gendering and division of marginalized sexualities into gay, lesbian, and bisexual categories.
3. In the last decade there has been an enormous amount of work done on historicizing sexuality. Michel Foucault's *The History of Sexuality: An Introduction* (1980) remains a key text for literary and historical scholars.
4. Since Bray's book, debate has continued on the question of whether, for men, non-heterosexual emotional investments and practices constituted the basis for identity formation or a lifestyle in early modern England. While both Smith (1991) and Bredbeck (1991) accept the view that only the nineteenth century saw the emergence of 'the homosexual' as a medical/legal category, both also seem to entertain the idea that in some writing of the period there was 'the possibility of a homosexual subjectivity' (Smith 1991: 223). For Bredbeck's (1991) argument that such a subjectivity arises only 'subjunctively', in the imagined difference from the sodomitical monster of legal discourse, see especially Chapter IV, 'Tradition and the individual sodomite', pp. 143–85.

taken to signal unitary and fixed sexual identities. In addition, Galenic biological models depicting both boys and women as unfinished men may have enabled adult males—to some as yet undefined extent—to treat boys and women as interchangeable sexual objects (Laqueur 1990: 63–148). As I hope to show, however, a greater fluidity for men, at least, in the matter of sexual object choice did not mean that early modern England was a polymorphous paradise in which conflicts never arose between different modalities of erotic desire and sexual practice. Boys and women were 'the same' in their hierarchical relationship to adult males, but they were also 'different', if only in the crucial matter of their respective roles in reproduction. In addition, sexuality was certainly not 'free' in some absolute sense, but was regulated by the state, by village custom, by changing ideological imperatives.

Sodomy, for example, was a crime for which a man could die. Of course, for a long while sodomy was a comprehensive term for many 'devilish' or stigmatized practices including witchcraft, atheism, etc. Only gradually in the course of the sixteenth and seventeenth centuries did the term come to stress, in legal and popular discourse, anal penetration of one man by another, an act that to be prosecuted usually had to involve force and be perpetuated on a young child.[5] However, even though the definition of sodomy became more particularized as a specific sexual crime during this period, few were prosecuted for it. Despite a handful of notorious sodomy cases involving children or enemies of the state, there seems to have been wide cultural acceptance of what we would now call homosexual practices among Renaissance men, especially but not exclusively between men of unequal status or in clear positions of dependency and control such as servants and masters, students and schoolmen.[6] None the less, this form of sexual practice—as opposed to heterosexuality undertaken within marriage—was always potentially susceptible to severe punishment.

In texts that have survived, early modern English writers say less about sexual encounters between women than between men, though there *are* passages such as the report in Jane Sharp's *The Midwives Book* of women whose clitorises were so enlarged they could be used as penis-substitutes in sexual relations with other women. Writing of the clitoris, Sharp says:

5. For a careful account of the legal discourses concerning sodomy in sixteenth- and seventeenth-century England see Smith (1991: esp. 42–55).
6. Alan Bray (1988: esp. 48–56) has called attention to the ways early modern hierarchies of status, age, and economic power underwrote homosexual practices in schools, universities, households, the theatre and other social sites. For discussions of forms of homoerotic bonding between men of the same age and status in early modern literature see Smith (1991: 31–77).

commonly it is but a small sprout, lying close hid under the
wings, and not easily felt, yet sometimes it grows so long that it
hangs forth at the slit like a Yard, and it will swell and stand stiff
if it be provoked, and some lewd women have endeavoured to
use it as men do theirs. In the Indies and Egypt they are frequent, but I never heard but of one in this Country, if there be
any they will do what they can for shame to keep it close.

(1671: 32)

Interestingly, the fear of what we would now call lesbian eroticism is
projected on to the dark women of India and Egypt, though as Harriette Andreadis has pointed out in regard to Katherine Philips, some
women were quite open about having intimate same-sex friendships
with other women. What we don't know is whether such intimate
relationships involved genital sexuality or if the erotic components
of such friendships found other avenues of expression.[7]

If same-sex erotic relations were understood *differently* in the
early modern period than they are today, the same is true for what
we now call 'heterosexuality'. While marriage, and hence some
degree of heterosexual activity, was the norm in Protestant England,
sexual relations with women were often constructed as dangerous to
men and compared, unfavourably, to the 'safer' and more ennobling
realm of male friendship (Orgel 1989: 26; Rackin 1992). Men who
displayed excessive passion for women were termed effeminate
because they became like women in allowing passion to override
their reason and self-control. Moreover, women themselves were
often viewed as creatures with such strong sexual appetites that it
was only with difficulty that men could retain proper control over
these libidinous creatures. It is hardly surprising, therefore, to find
misogyny and fear of women's sexual appetites informing a number
of cultural productions from the period. On the other hand, while
heterosexuality was often stigmatized as dangerous and demeaning
to men, the late sixteenth and early seventeenth centuries also saw
increased cultural emphasis upon marriage, especially among the
middling sort, as the affective focus of their lives and not simply as
an economic necessity (Belsey 1985: 192–221). Many texts from
the period celebrate marriage and present women as the proper and
'natural' objects of masculine erotic desire.

This being the case, it is not surprising to find what Bruce Smith
has termed a 'contest' in some literary works of the period between

---

7. For a good discussion of the difficulties of finding an appropriate language to talk about
same-sex female intimacy in the early modern period, see Andreadis (1989).

homoerotic male friendship and the claims of heterosexual marriage (Smith 1991: 64–7). Genre, of course, mattered a great deal in representing this contest. Read enough Renaissance romantic comedies and one might think the theatre was part of a vast bourgeois apparatus to make heterosexuality compulsory, though not necessarily in ways equally advantageous to both sexes. When a woman like Hermia in *Midsummer Night's Dream* gets to wed the man of her desires, this achievement is often coupled with the loss of the woman's voice, mobility, and independence. On the other hand, read enough Renaissance tragedy and one might think the Renaissance theatre was a vast aristocratic apparatus for weaning men away from heterosexuality since so many of these texts offer only representations of devouring, cuckolding, sexualized women and highlight the intense bonds and aggressions between men.

Yet to speak monolithically of the connection between sexuality and dramatic genre is of limited usefulness because it misses much of what was uniquely volatile and contradictory about the production of erotic desire at the site of the stage where, for example, even a heterosexual marriage plot was acted out, literally, by a man and a boy actor.[8] Moreover, not only did the stage mime the desire of fictitious persons, but commentators of the period remark upon it as a space where erotic desire flowed between spectators, as well. Some of that desire was provoked by happenings on the stage, but some by the conditions under which spectatorship occurred. Amphitheatre playing made spectators as visible to one another as were the players; and since those spectators were both men and women, antitheatricalists worried aloud about the sexual outrages that might be perpetuated by same-sex or by opposite-sex partners either at the theatre or in the taverns and inns to which theatre-goers and actors would subsequently repair (Howard 1989: 31–49). I suggest that this particular theatre—with its all-male acting troupes, its mixed audiences (mixed by both gender and class), its penchant for plots of transvestite disguise, and its daylight conditions of playing such that stage and audience were equally spectacles—created conditions of erotic volatility in which desire could flow in many and often contradictory directions and where sexuality could become a staging ground for many forms of social struggle.

---

8. There is now a considerable literature talking about the gender and sexual implications of cross-dressing on the Renaissance stage. I summarize much of that literature in my essay 'Crossdressing, the theatre, and gender struggle in early modern England' (1988). See also Orgel (1989).

The conflicted terrain of erotic possibility

As a city comedy, *The Roaring Girl* stages erotic desire in a complex and often highly contradictory fashion that bears little resemblance to the treatment of 'venery' in the often timeless, relatively unlocalized world of Shakespearean romantic comedy. Urban and suburban spaces are particularized in this play, as are the social groups—young gallants, petty merchants, cutpurses and canters—who struggle for pre-eminence, and sometimes just for survival, in a cityscape that seems to fuel the fires of desire and to invite the intermingling of venereal and economic pursuits. In this setting sexuality repeatedly comes under scrutiny, and under contest, revealing an erotic terrain fraught with conflict and contradiction.

Consider, for example, a provocative and—to modern readers—puzzling moment in Act 4 when the hero, Sebastian, secretly brings his beloved, Mary Fitz-Allard, to his father's chamber. In typical comedy fashion, these two lovers have been scheming from the first scene of the play to outwit the covetous father, Sir Alexander Wengrave, who is blocking their marriage because he is worried about 'what gold / This marriage would draw from him' (1.1.79–80) and scorns Mary's dowry of five thousand marks (1.1.84). In Act 4, Sebastian meets Mary in his father's chamber. Moll Cutpurse, dressed 'in man's clothes' (4.1.39), accompanies the two lovers and, somewhat surprisingly, Mary *also* wears men's clothing. She is suited 'like a page' (4.1.39) in apparel rigged up by Moll's tailor. It is not altogether clear why this disguise is necessary. Mary is not like the plucky heroines of Shakespeare's plays who use their male disguises to protect themselves from sexual aggression during long pursuits of the men they love and whose disguises often are accompanied by a temporary assumption of masculine prerogatives of freedom of speech and action. Mary is a tamer version of these women, probably donning male disguise to enter Sir Wengrave's chamber unnoted, but hardly, like Portia, to argue in a courtroom or, like Rosalind, to educate her beloved as to the proper way to love a woman. The disguise, far from giving Mary the upper hand by concealing her identity from the world in general and her lover in particular, instead makes her more fully the object of Sebastian's erotic fancies. For example, when Moll, watching the two of them kiss, comments: 'How strange this shows, one man to kiss another' (4.1.46), Sebastian replies: 'I'd kiss such men to choose, Moll, / Methinks a woman's lip tasts well in a doublet' (4.1.47–8), and further, 'As some have a conceit their drink tastes better / In an outlandish cup than in our own, / So methinks every kiss she gives me now / In this strange form, is worth a pair of two' (4.1.54–7). The exchange simultaneously calls attention to the 'strangeness' of a seemingly same-sex erotic embrace, and also to its desirability.

Why is kissing a mannishly-clad woman so thrilling? Several answers are possible. One would stress the general transgressiveness of the scene and the setting. Sebastian is rebelling against his father by pursuing Mary, and at this moment he is doing so in his father's very chamber and in the company of a notorious roaring girl, Moll Cutpurse, who is *also* dressed as a man. In such a context, kissing the bride-to-be while she is dressed as a boy, 'outlandishly' transformed, could simply offer an added dimension of transgression to this highly transgressive moment. But another possibility is that it is not the context that makes the kiss 'worth a pair of two', but the very fact that Sebastian is kissing what looks, on the outside, like a boy; in sum, that his most intense erotic pleasure is what we would now call homoerotic in nature or, framed in accordance with Galenic notions of biology, it is the potential man within the young woman that constitutes the true object of Sebastian's desire.[9] Indeed, the name Sebastian itself in some quarters carried homoerotic connotations in the Reaissance, largely because of the long iconographic tradition of representing the arrow-pierced saint and his intimate relationship with Christ as 'an indirect ideal of homoerotic love' (Saslow 1977: 63).[1] Moreover, dressed as a page, Mary enacts the role of a gentleman's servant, one of the social positions most often marked out as constituting a culturally sanctioned object for a master's erotic investments.

The multiple sexual valences of this scene are further complicated, of course, by the fact that on the Renaissance stage Mary and Moll were played by male actors, not by women. While in performance the fact of the boy beneath the woman's clothes could

9. Thomas Laqueur (1990: esp. 63–148) provides a stunning analysis of the one-sex Galenic model of human anatomy widely held in the early modern period. Literary scholars such as Stephen Greenblatt (1988: 66–93, especially 92) have referred to Laqueur's work in suggesting 'an apparent homoeroticism in all sexuality' in the early modern period. I would argue that there *are* many representations of homoeroticism in early modern texts, representations which a heterosexist criticism has often been unable to acknowledge. On the other hand, there are many cultural reasons for this besides the existence of Galenic biological models, including the relatively late age of most marriages and the existence of many exclusively male institutions such as universities, Inns of Court, etc. In addition, as Greenblatt also acknowledges, much effort was expended in early modern England to secure gender difference and to promote heterosexual passion and its institutionalization in marriage. I therefore find it more useful, rather than stressing that at some level all sexuality was homoerotic, to emphasize the mixture of erotic interpellations operating on individual subjects, especially male subjects. The drama at times represents the negotiation of these competing interpellations as untroubled and at times as vexed and contestatory.
1. I am indebted to Mario DiGangi for pointing out to me the homoerotic significance of Sebastian's name and for pointing me toward both the Saslow article (1977) and one by Cynthia Lewis (1989) in which she explores the late mediaeval and early Renaissance associations of St Anthony with St Sebastian as embodiments, among other things, of homoerotic attraction. Obviously, the existence of these visual traditions gives further weight to a homoerotic reading of the Antonio-Sebastian friendship in *Twelfth Night* and the relationship between Antonio and Bassanio in *The Merchant of Venice*, Bastiano being the Italian diminutive for the name Sebastian (Lewis 1989: 205).

usually have been ignored by playgoers, it could *also* at any time have been brought to consciousness by a self-reflexive gesture or comment. At those instances when audience attention is directed to the boy actor *as* boy, or when within the terms of a fiction such as *The Roaring Girl* a male stage character expresses delight at kissing a masculinely clad body—at such moments a multiplicity of sexual possibilities open before the male spectator, in particular, a multiplicity fostered by the gap between the heterosexual imperatives of the marriage plot and the homoerotic reality of the material conditions of stage production and/or the expressed desires of particular male characters such as Sebastian.

Such moments seem to me productively multiple and contradictory in their erotic valences, making it impossible, for example, simply to characterize Renaissance stage comedy as an apparatus for producing bourgeois heterosexuality and channelling erotic energy into the emerging cultural form of companionate marriage. The stage drew upon, produced, and reproduced more than a single sexual discourse. At the level of the plot, plays ending in multiple marriages often contain a submerged, and sometimes an overt, resistance to heterosexual coupling. In *The Roaring Girl* that resistance is complexly staged. In the main plot, while Sebastian overtly pursues a heterosexual marriage, I have already commented on the fact that in doing so he finds particular piquancy in kissing his beloved when he/she is dressed as a man. Moreover, the aristocratic world in which he moves is largely a homosocial world devoid of women. Sir Alexander's house in the plays's second scene is peopled entirely by men—Sir Adam Appleton, Sir Davy Dapper, Goshawk, Laxton, Greenwit, and other 'gentlemen'. Sebastian seems to have no mother. Among the gentlemen who at the play's end gather at Sir Alexander's are Sir Thomas Long and Sir Beauteous Ganymede, a pair whose names suggest, respectively, phallic endowment, and homoerotic beauty.[2] In Act 5 Sir Thomas asks Jack Dapper about his 'sweet-faced boy' (5.1.23), and earlier Jack's father accuses him of wasting his money on worthless companions, including 'ningles / (Beasts Adam ne'er gave name to) (3.3.62–3). Despite the fact the plot focuses on getting Sebastian married, the 'gentleman' class as a whole seems less interested in marriage than in various modalities of same-sex bonding.

Where marriage *does* get emphasized is in the middle-class subplot. Here issues of sexuality have their own complexity. Shakespearean comedy, of course, rarely moved beyond the portrayal of courtship to engage the actuality of marriage. City comedy frequently

2. For excellent work on the significance of the names in this play see Garber (1991).

does, and in *The Roaring Girl* we have not only an aristocratic courtship plot involving Sebastian and Mary, but also the depiction of three actually existing marriages involving the Openworks, the Tilt-yards, and the Gallipots. Women, in the form of wives, are very visible in this plot in contrast to their near absence in the aristocratic plot. However, even in this merchant world, homoerotic bonds cut across heterosexual ties between men and their wives; and, just as impor-tantly, class antagonisms and gender conflicts affect erotic desire and performance in complicated ways. 'Venery' becomes a site of pro-found contradiction, and in attempting to resolve these contradic-tions, the play often shunts aside or silences the women, leaving their sexual desires perpetually deferred or unfulfilled.

Class antagonisms play a large role in structuring sexual relations in this plot. Ted Leinwand has argued that many of the stereotypes of city comedy embody class ideologies. For example, 'the merchant is revealed as the personification of the gentry's fears, and the clever gallant represents the gentry's will to sexual mastery at a time when its social and financial potency was uncertain' (Leinwand 1986, 123). In *The Roaring Girl* Laxton's and Goshawk's attempts to seduce Mistress Gallipot and Mistress Openwork in part validate Leinwand's thesis. These gallants are poor, especially Laxton, and what he most seeks through a liaison with Gallipot's wife is access to her husband's money.

But while these merchants *have* money, there are strong sugges-tions they are not satisfying sexual partners for their wives. Gallipot embodies one type of Renaissance effeminacy in that he dotes on his wife to excess, excusing every fault, making no demands, but, it is implied, leaving her sexually unsatisfied. As she rails at her 'apron hus-band' (3.2.30–1), 'your love is all words; give me deeds, I cannot abide a man that's too fond over me, so cookish; thou dost not know how to handle a woman in her kind' (3.2.23–5). By contrast, Mistress Open-work complains that her husband spends himself sexually with other women, leaving her no source of pleasure. This seems to be the basis for her anger in Act 2 at Moll who has come to her shop to buy the shag ruff. When Master Openwork greets Moll cordially, Mistress Openwork cries, 'How now, greetings, love-terms with a pox between you, have I found out one of your haunts? I send you for hollands, and you're i' th' low countries with a mischief. I'm served with good ware by th' shift, that makes it lie dead so long upon my hands, I were as good shut up shop, for when I open it I take nothing' (2.1.204–9). These marriages of sexual lack seem to indict the merchant-class man for impotency and the merchant-class woman for insatiability. Neither heterosexuality nor marriage seems very attractive in this depiction.

On the other hand, the gallants who hang about these merchant wives are represented through yet another class-based stereotype, that of the profligate aristocrat who has sold his family lands and whose degeneracy can be sexually symbolized. None of these gallants actually sleeps with the merchant wives, and the pun in Laxton's name suggests one reason. At least symbolically, he lacks a testicle; he is, in Mistress Gallipot's disillusioned words, 'a lame gelding' (4.2.38). The decaying branches of the aristocracy are in no position to challenge or reform the merchant class. In the end the wives are driven back to their husbands, not because these husbands become more sexually satisfying, but simply because they at least have money: 'we shopkeepers, when all's done, are sure to have 'em [the gallants] in our purse-nets at length, and when they are in, Lord, what simple animals they are' (4.2.45–7). She goes on to say, further, that when the gallants then importune with the merchant wives for favour, these wives then must 'ingle with our husbands abed, and we must swear they [the gallants] are our cousins, and able to do us a pleasure at court' (4.2.53–5).

It is worth pausing at the verb. Exactly what is it to ingle with one's husband? The *OED* glosses this very passage as 'to fondle with' one's husband. But to me the verb also suggests to play the ingle, that is, the boy catamite, with one's husband, possibly meaning to engage in anal sex with him. While anal sex can certainly be part of eroticism between men and women, it seems important that the wives, as they describe giving special sexual pleasure to their husbands in order to wheedle something from them, use a word bringing to mind the specific sexual act connected with the boy partner, the ingle or Ganymede. In 1598 in his *A Worlde of Wordes*, John Florio translated the Italian word *zanzerare* as 'to ingle boies, to wantonly play with boyes against nature' (Florio 1598: 459), suggesting that the verb 'to ingle' *could* mean something more provocative and 'against nature' than mere fondling.

While the homoerotic implications of Mistress Gallipot's speech are indirect, they resonate in my mind with the stage moment in which Sebastian takes double delight in kissing Mary dressed as a page. Such moments raise the possibility that for some men in this text erotic desire and pleasure are most intense when directed at and satisfied by other men or by women, who assume the clothes or the 'positions' associated with the Ganymede.[3] In this play the cultural

---

3. What I find impossible to resolve is the degree to which, when a woman 'ingles', her partner's pleasure depends on her being 'like a boy' at that moment or on her being 'like a *submissive* woman'. I think we are dealing here with two complexly related variables: sex (male/female) of object choice and status (subordinate/superior) of object choice. Though Galenic biology, at least, did not provide a basis for establishing sexual difference in modern terms, the culture generated many other ways of thinking about male and female as different 'kinds'. I cannot accept, therefore, the absolute interchangeability of woman and boy as social and sexual categories, though there was obviously more slippage between them than we can easily imagine today. *Both* the sex and the relative power and status of the sexual object seem factors in the erotic economy of this text.

imperatives to marry seem strong, but it is not clear that erotic desire lines up neatly with cultural imperatives. Among the aristocracy the imperative to marry remains connected in this play to the consolidation and passage of land and property, but the Wengrave milieu contains no actual women except the women who will or might marry Sebastian and produce heirs and fortune for the Wengrave line.

For urban merchants the imperative to marry seems linked to economic realities of another sort. The merchant couples work together, keep economically afloat by dividing between them the labour of making their businesses profitable. The scenes involving these couples are studded with details reflecting the realities of a shopkeeper's life: getting cloth from Holland, preparing orders in a rush for valued customers, keeping abreast of the finery most sought after by the court gallants, as when Mistress Tiltyard tells Jack Dapper which feathers are most in fashion among 'the beaver gallants, the stone riders, / The private stage's audience, the twelvepennystool gentlemen' (2.1.133–4). But these unions are not depicted as erotically fulfilling. There is the unmistakable implication that, like female play-goers, the publicly visible, economically useful urban wives were experienced by men as threatening figures: sexually demanding, potentially unchaste, and probably more interested, as a daily matter, in riding the stone horse from on top than in submissively 'ingling' with their husbands. These women are sexually attractive only to such spouses as the effeminate 'apron husband', Gallipot, whose vapid doting only proves the point that such wives, if uncontrolled, emasculate men and cause them to lose their proper masculine dominance.

I will return to the issue of the relationship between female subordination and female sexual attractiveness to men when I discuss Moll, but the resolution of the citizen plot reveals the deep strand of misogyny running through the merchant plot. These clever, economically useful women who demand more sex, or different sex, than their husbands afford them, are shunted aside at the end of Act 4 so that an orgy of bonding can occur between the merchant husbands and the aristocratic gallants. Goshawk's machinations to achieve Mistress Openwork having been revealed, Master Openwork says: 'Come, come, a trick of youth, and 'tis forgiven. / This rub put by, our love shall run more even' (4.2.215–16). In short, no contest involving a woman can disrupt male friendship. Class aggression pales before gender solidarity. Similarly, after Laxton has been exposed, Master Gallipot proclaims himself 'beholden—not to you, wife— / But Master Laxton, to your want of doing ill, / Which it seems you have not' (4.2.320–2). And as Master Openwork and Gallipot lead the way offstage to a feast of reconciliation, Gallipot's final words are: 'wife, brag no more / Of holding out: who most brags is most whore' (4.2.325–6). In other words, a woman who opens her mouth is a prostitute, a commonplace of the period (Stallybrass 1986: 126), but one suggesting why these talkative women frighten their husbands with the spectre of a female sexual demand they cannot answer, an independent subjectivity they cannot master. As this plot suggests, satisfactory sex for adult men seems to involve more than the sex, male or female, of the desired partner. Equally important is that that person be properly subordinate, whether he/she is an ingle, a wife, or a whore.

The Roaring Girl and her viol

Moll's presence in the play both complicates and clarifies these issues. She is made up, textually, of competing idcological strands. The contradictions prevent her from being read as an entirely unified subjectivity, but they also function to show what is at stake in her representation, what nexus of gender, class, and sexual contests her textual presence mediates. Some parts of her representation answer to a patriarchal anxiety about how modernity—here represented by the market place, urbanization, the whirl of fashion—have turned gender and sexual relations on their head. Seen from this perspective, Moll's cross-dressing objectifies disorder in order to put it to rights. We therefore find her intervening in the Wengrave plot on the side of the young lovers, since the father's attempts to block that marriage are unnatural and unjust. But we also find her attacking unmanly men and braggarts: men who lack the 'stones' appropriate to their sex. Watching Jack Dapper buy a feather, she is moved to remark that 'the gallants of these times are shallow lechers, they put not their courtship home enough to a wench, 'tis impossible to know what woman is thoroughly honest, because she's ne'er thoroughly tried' (2.1.290–3). She ends by saying 'Women are courted but ne'er soundly tried. / As many walk in spurs that never ride' (2.1.298–9). The emphasis is on men's failure to be sexual 'riders'. And the failings of braggart men are what she seems to reprove both when she trips up Trapdoor (2.1.334) and when she bests Laxton at sword play in Lincoln's Inn Fields (3.1.115–29). It is also important that when she is written in the ideology of 'correction', there is animosity between her and the merchant wives. At one point Moll wishes Mistress Openwork were a man so Moll could give her a beating, presumably to silence her tongue and chasten her independence (2.1.215–21). If Moll's 'corrections' worked, women would again be docile and men manly, and happy marriages would thrive.

Fortunately—and I use the adverb from my contemporary position as a modern feminist—there is much more to Moll's representation. First, the *fact* of her cross-dressing destabilizes the very essentialist binarisms that the 'corrective' cross-dresser overtly wishes to uphold. Moll not only dresses like a man, she behaves with all the ferocity and strength she seems eager to instil in men. She can fight and cant and smoke and support herself. The very fact she can do these things suggests that women are not inherently weak, silent, and dependent, nor men the only ones gifted with the sword. Moreover, Moll's connections with the shops of London and the commodities available from them further underscores how malleable are identities in a market place in which a commercial transaction can alter the self, right down, as Marjorie Garber has suggested, to the hint that Moll has acquired an artificial penis (Garber 1991: 223–4). One way to appropriate Moll as a radical figure is to stress those aspects of her representation that deconstruct the gender binarisms that underwrite patriarchal domination and to stress the way the expanding market economy, while increasing alienation and class exploitation, can also lead to results subversive of some forms of oppression, here the tyranny of an ideology of fixed gender characteristics. One's ability to transform one's appearance by the sartorial possibilities afforded by the market place thus becomes a potentially liberating phenomenon.[4]

Another way to appropriate Moll for radical purposes, and the one I will pursue, is to show how she lodges a critique of the specific material institutions and circumstances which oppressed women in early modern England. While many of Moll's actions point to a utopian future where oppressive hierarchies and binarisms have been undone, she also functions in the here-and-now of the play's world as an opponent of actually existing conditions that exploit women and other disadvantaged figures. To understand this aspect of Moll's representation and how she appears when read in a Marxist-feminist rather than a deconstructive-psychoanalytic problematic, it is necessary to examine how she functions in this text as erotic object *and* subject.

Interestingly, Moll *does* seem to function as erotic object in this text. Laxton, seeing Moll buying goods in the shops, dressed at that

---

4. The numerous sartorial transformations of various characters in this play give strong support to the position that the market destabilizes various traditional means of marking identity, since appearance can be altered at will. Moll, of course, takes the lead in sartorial alterations of self. In her first stage appearance she attempts to purchase a shag ruff; later she discusses with a tailor's messenger the measurements for a new pair of Dutch slops. It is probably the same tailor she later employs to make up a suit of men's clothes for Mary Fitz-Allard to wear when going to the chamber of Sebastian's father. Moll, of course, sometimes appears in women's clothes—a frieze jerkin, safeguard and short dagger, and sometimes in men's—breeches, doublet and sword. Hers are the most startling transformations of self, but other characters also remake themselves: Trapdoor appears in Act 5 as a wounded soldier; Mary Fitz-Allard comes on stage dressed at various times as a seamstress, a lady, and a male page; Greenwit tries to use a wig to pass as a summoner; the citizens' wives don masks as they are contemplating setting off for Brainford; and foolish Jack Dapper tries to make himself a proper gallant by buying a feather at Tiltyard's shop.

point as a woman, exclaims that he would 'give but too much money to be nibbling with that wench: life, sh'as the spirit of four great parishes, and a voice that will drown all the city: methinks a brave captain might get all his soldiers upon her' (2.1.169–72). This outspoken woman who often openly dresses as a man, doesn't marry, and roves about London buying things and consorting with canting underworld figures, is the most highly eroticized figure in the play. While Laxton actually tries to get her in a coach to speed off to a rendezvous in the suburbs, other men constantly speculate about Moll's genitalia, her erotic performance, and the possibility of engaging in sex with her. Trapdoor brags that when Moll's 'breeches are off, she shall follow me' (1.2.223), implying that in sexual intercourse he will take the lead which she typically takes in their daily relations of mistress and servant; later he tells her he has an immovable part 'to stand when you have occasion to use me' (2.1.327–8), again eroticizing their relationship. Alexander Wengrave, terrified Moll will enthral his son, and eager to cast her as a monster, says she casts 'two shadows' (1.2.132) and later alleges she has 'two trinkets' (2.2.74–5) in her breeches. The fact that the female Moll is personated by a male actor of course gives this accusation a particular piquancy in performance. Laxton, commenting on the sexual confusion engendered by Moll's cross-dressing, says that she 'might first cuckold the husband' (by sleeping with his wife) and then 'make him do as much for the wife' (by sleeping with the husband) (2.1.192–3). The point is that however odd and hermaphroditical Moll appears to some, she is constantly being discussed in erotic terms: as a potential bedmate, as one whose unfathomable 'doubleness' provokes speculation about her genital organs and her potential for a variety of sexual performances.

I would argue, moreover, that despite the fact Moll occasionally dresses as a man, in the first instance—though probably not exclusively—it is the *woman* in Moll that men seek, rather than the man. After all, from Moll's self-description, she hardly seems to embody the androgynous allure of the compliant young page, the part Mary assumes and the part usually seen as sexually attractive to adult men. Moll, however, is a loud, roving pipe-smoker: a roarer. This text, in fact, makes one long to know more about Elizabethan casting practices than we presently do. Was Moll played by the same type and age of actor as played Mary? Or was a slightly older, more full-bodied performer required, so that the contrast between the charming androgynous boy/woman and the more frightening, but alluring, hermaphroditical adult female could be registered? Whatever the casting choices made, what Laxton explicitly stresses when he fantasizes 'nibbling' with Moll is her prodigious female reproductive capacity (able to provide a captain with a whole regiment of soldiers), her enormous spirit (capturing the energies of four parishes), and her enormous voice (able to drown out all the city). He may in part wish to mate with her to produce a homosocial world of soldiers, but to achieve that end he has to acknowledge Moll's special reproductive capacities. Moreover, he has this fantasy of 'nibbling' with her while Moll is dressed in female clothing. At this moment she figures in his imagination as female excess, words spewing from an upper orifice, babies from a lower. In fact, the openness of her body is prefigured in the play's very title. A roaring girl, a version of the more common stage type, the roaring boy, is a woman given to copious, quarrelsome speech. To *be* a roaring girl is to have one's mouth open. Moll does, for a great deal of the play; and sometimes when it is open she is quarrelling and sometimes canting and sometimes just talking. And, of course, any woman whose mouth is opened in public spaces, in particular, is read as whorish, as incontinent with other bodily orifices as much as with the mouth.

What makes Moll erotically alluring, I think, is exactly what keeps her from being an example of the construction of femininity suitable for wives. Rather than sewn up, locked up, and quiet (remember that Mary first came to Sebastian's house dressed as a seamstress), Moll is open, excessive, mobile. Wives who exhibit the same characteristics are terrifically threatening because their openness seems to challenge husbands' proprietary rights in wives' bodies. But Moll is not a wife. She is, in fact, unmarried, notorious, and also lower class—hardly wife material for a Laxton or, as old Wengrave's horrified response attests, for a Sebastian. By contrast, Mary first comes to Sebastian in Act 1 as the docile seamstress, later as the androgynous servant, the page. While she is insistent in her pursuit of Sebastian, she always presents herself in properly subservient guises. Crucially, both Laxton and old Wengrave try to control the subversiveness of Moll, to subordinate her to them, by economic means. Assuming that money can buy her, Old Wengrave tries to get her to steal precious objects from his chamber so he can subordinate her to the power of the law (4.1.1 39). Laxton gives her money as he arranges their rendezvous in the coach. In fact, he gives her the ten angels (2.1.262) he received earlier in the same scene from Mistress Gallipot (2.1.93). The woman *from* whom he takes the money he does his best to avoid sexually (2.1.116–28); the woman *to* whom he gives it he does pursue sexually. The difference, obviously, has to do with Laxton's relative power in the two circumstances. In the first, he 'lacks stones' in relation to the economically prosperous middle-class merchants. Mistress Gallipot, while seen by him as sexually available, is not erotically stimulating, perhaps because she is powerful, if only economically, in ways he cannot control. But Moll lacks the cultural and economic status of the married merchant wife, and

Laxton seems to feel that if he can further subordinate her by getting her to accept money for sexual favours, then he can enjoy the
physical pleasures her openness seems to invite. Consequently, he
tries to subordinate her with angels, a word whose punning associations with ingles (Rubenstein 1989: 12) raises the possibility, at
least, that in turning Moll into his paid paramour, Laxton may want
from her a variety of sexual pleasures, those associated with the
ingle as well as with the woman as vessel of reproduction. What is
clear, however, is that to act on his desires Laxton must symbolically
subordinate Moll by making her his paid bedmate.

Moll, however, does not comply. While she initially accepts the
ten angels from Laxton, when she meets him at Lincoln's Inn Fields
she throws down his money, to which she adds ten angels of her
own, and demands he fight her with swords for the lot. She then
launches into a withering critique of his behaviour, a critique that
reveals that in constructing the character of Moll, Middleton and
Dekker tapped into discourses of radical protest (Shepherd 1981:
67–92) that provide the basis for a critique of the sex and gender
systems that far exceeds the tamer demands for more manly men
and womanly women voiced by Moll when she is represented as corrective 'reformer'. Moll is both a reformer and a radical. The voice of
the latter is on display when she castigates Laxton for thinking 'each
woman thy fond flexible whore' (3.1.71), a critique which ends

> In thee I defy all men, their worst hates,
> And their best flatteries, all their golden witchcrafts,
> With which they entangle the poor spirits of fools.
> Distressed needlewomen and trade-fallen wives,
> Fish that must needs bite or themselves be bitten,
> Such hungry things as these may soon be took
> With a worm fastened on a golden hook:
> Those are the lecher's food, his prey, he watches
> For quarrelling wedlocks, and poor shifting sisters,
> 'Tis the best fish he takes: but why, good fisherman,
> Am I thought meat for you, that never yet
> Had angling rod cast towards me? 'cause, you'll say,
> I'm given to sport, I'm often merry, jest:
> Had mirth no kindred in the world but lust?
> Oh shame take all her friends then: but howe'er
> Thou and the baser world censure my life,
> I'll send 'em word by thee, and write so much
> Upon thy breast, 'cause thou shalt bear't in mind:
> Tell them 'twere base to yield, where I have conquered.
> I scorn to prostitute myself to a man
> I that can prostitute a man to me,
> And so I greet thee.   (3.1.90–111)

This is a refreshingly economic explanation for prostitution and a stunning declaration of Moll's own freedom from the economic necessity that drives some poor women into the flesh trade, i.e., that makes them prey to man's ingling/angling rod. In doing so, she reverses the power relations that have made Laxton assume he can safely use her as an erotic object, a fond flexible whore. Elsewhere, in explaining why she won't marry, Moll offers a critique of the whole institution for being premised on female subordination. For a woman, marriage means loss of control and freedom: 'marriage is but a chopping and changing, where a maiden loses one head and has a worse i 'th' place' (2.2.43–4). At such moments, Moll embodies a position much more radical than that she adopts when trying to 'adjust' men and women to the hierarchical positions society marks out for them. Rather than specifying the 'real' Moll (a task that assumes she is a self-consistent representation of a unified psyche), I wish to stress how thoroughly her representation is enmeshed in contradictions, a sure sign it is doing the work of mediating complex social tensions.

One thing Moll's representation foregrounds is the tension that exists in this text between the pressure of urgent female sexual desire and a patriarchal culture in which women's sexuality is in theory subject to masculine control and regulation. Consider, for a moment, a striking feature of this play: its insistent linkage of Moll with the playing of a particular musical instrument, the viol. The original Moll Frith gained some of her considerable notoriety from playing a lute on the stage of the Fortune Theatre. As Linda Austern has shown, women playing musical instruments—usually the small stringed instruments or the virginals—were considered to be erotically stimulating to men, the combination of feminine beauty and the beauty of harmonious sound acting together to arouse uncontrollable passion (Austern 1989: 427). Consequently, if women played, they were to do so in private, for their own recreation or the delight of family and husband, and never in public. Moll Frith was thus transgressive in playing her lute on the public stage.

Moll Cutpurse is even more transgressive in that her instrument is not the lute, able to be tucked decorously beneath the breast, but the viol, played with legs akimbo. Moreover, she seems to appropriate this instrument not so much to make herself an erotic object, as to express her own erotic subjectivity. In 2.2.18 she enters with a porter bearing a viol on his back, taking it to her chamber. In Act 4, when Mary and she, both dressed as men, go to old Wengrave's chamber to meet Sebastian, Moll actually plays upon a viol that is hanging on the wall. Her taking up of this instrument is the occasion for a great deal of bawdy banter concerning Moll's skills as a musician, whether or not she initiates the taking up of a gentleman's instrument, and whether or not, as some 'close' women say, it is unmannerly to play on such an instrument. At the climax of this jesting, Moll says she does not care what other women say. When they accuse her of lewdness she falls asleep and dreams. Then, in two songs, she recounts her dreams, which turn out to be about two 'loose' women, one of whom gads about London and 'lays out the money' (4.1.104) and comes home 'with never a penny' (4.1.109), the other of whom sleeps with a man from the navy while her husband is in prison. These 'dreams' seem to function, doubly, as angry indictments of the hypocritical 'dames' who would call Moll whore and yet seize sexual pleasure for themselves, and as wishful projections of a longed-for freedom for herself. Moll seems to acknowledge the latter reading when, the songs over, she says 'Hang up the viol now, sir; all this while I was in a dream, one shall lie rudely then; but being awake, I keep my legs together' (4.1.127–9).

This encounter is absolutely riveting in the way it acknowledges, insists upon, female erotic desire, while making clear the cultural imperatives that operate to shape, channel, and control that eroticism. Except in dreams, Moll cannot be an autonomous sexual subject and escape being called a whore. The men who obsessively comment on her sexuality speculate about her 'doubleness', her ability to play either the man or the woman's part in sexual encounters. Moll herself, when refusing Sebastian's marriage proposal, says: 'I love to lie o' both sides o'th' bed myself' (2.2.36–7) meaning, clearly, that she likes her independence, but perhaps also indicating she likes a certain unspecified variety in sexual partners and practices. My point, however, is not to define Moll's 'real' sexual orientation, since to do so is impossible. Instead, I want to emphasize that heterosexual marriage is the only 'legitimate' avenue open to Moll for acting on any of her sexual desires, whatever they might be. And marriage she rejects on political grounds as entailing an insupportable subordination and loss of independence. She is equally firm in refusing extramarital encounters with the braggarts Laxton and Trapdoor who would make her a bought woman or a sexual prize.

Yet Moll never denies her sexuality. She has and acknowledges her sexual dreams; she has and acknowledges her 'instrument', that viol with which she is so insistently linked, the fingering of which seems to symbolize her skill at clitoral masturbation, as well as her potential skill at manual stimulation of the male penis. When Sebastian describes Moll's skill as a musician to his father, he calls her a musician 'of excellent fingering' (4.1.168) with 'the most delicate stroke' (4.1.170). Sir Alexander immediately sees these as the skills of a whore servicing, and undoing, men (4.1.173). But on the stage when Moll actually plays her instrument what the spectator sees is a woman whose strokes and clever fingering occur in the space between her own legs.[5] Her viol suggests her own sexual instrument and her masturbatory playing of it a final defiance of patriarchal, phallus-oriented, sexuality. At the play's end, joking with Sir Alexander Wengrave, now her friend, Moll says: 'and you can cuck me, spare not: / Hang up my viol by me, and I care not' (5.2.253–4). She can imagine enduring public humiliation for female transgression as long as she can defiantly exhibit her viol, sign of the sexual being she is. Through her one realizes that the culturally sanctioned ways for women to express erotic desire may exact too high a price to be employed. For Moll there seems to be no way, outside of dream and solitary pricksong, to gratify eros without enduring an unendurable subordination and exploitation. Yet in her jaunty defiance she makes us feel she is no victim, that keeping her legs together, outside of dreams, and retaining her mighty voice, her outlandish dress and her mobility are preferable to any other bargain she might have struck with her culture.

5. I call attention to Moll's autoeroticism to in part affirm the possibility of female sexual pleasure in a textual world thoroughly dominated by concerns with men's erotic desires and fulfilments, and also to call in question the contemporary presumption that sexualities, whether heterosexual or homoerotic, involve primarily alloerotic relations. In this regard see Sedgwick (1991).
   When I had finished this essay Bruce Smith found and gave to me the following poem which he had discovered in a mid-seventeenth century (1655) miscellany entitled *Wits Interpreter, The English Parnassus* compiled by one J. C. (John Cotgrave?). Many of the poems in the volume date from the early seventeenth century. The poem in question, 'The Violin', quite explicitly eroticizes the virgin's playing of the viol in ways suggesting autoeroticism.

> The Violin
>
> To play upon a Viol, if
> A Virgin will begin,
> She first of all must know her cliff,
> And all the stops therein.
>
> Her prick she must hold long enough,
> Her backfals gently take;
> Her touch must gentle be, not rough,
> She at each stroak must shake.
>
> Her body must by no means bend,
>   But stick close to her fiddle:
> Her feet must hold the lower end,
>   Her knees must hold the middle.
>
> She boldly to the bowe must flie,
>   As if she'd make it crack;
> Two fingers on the hair must lie,
>   And two upon the back.
>
> And when she hath as she would have,
>   She must it gently thrust,
> Up, down, swift, slow, at any rate
>   As she herself doth list.
>
> And when she once begins to find
>   That she growes something cunning,
> She'll nere be quiet in her mind,
>   Untill she find it running.   (123–4)

The ending of the play, which leaves Moll defiantly outside the marriage fold and Mary submissively within, is a fine example of the significant contradictions of this text's handling of the 'comic' matter of venery. This drama doesn't tell a single or simple story about sexuality and its relationship to institutions such as marriage. In its inability to do so it reveals the pressure points in the culture's ways of making sense of its multivalent and changing practices. For example, while this text privileges marriage as the central fact of middle-class life and the necessary means for the aristocracy to reproduce itself and pass on its money, marriage *per se* is not depicted as an untroubled or attractive institution, and sexual desire does not lodge inside it easily. The play suggests that for some men this is because they find more compelling the erotic allure of the boy page, for whom the cross-dressed virgin stands as simulacrum, than the erotic allure of the woman in and of herself. While, at least for men, there seems to be more fluidity in object choice than our current ideology of fixed sexual identities allows, none the less there is an implicit contest between the pull of the homosocial world embodied in the Wengrave milieu and the male-female bond of marriage, a bond given actual depiction only in the offputting antagonisms visible in the citizens' marital alliances.

There is much evidence in the play, moreover, for the complex way in which erotic desire is intimately entwined with power relations. For adult males the subordination of the sexual partner seems necessary. In Mary's case, she assumes the clothes and the acquiescent manner of the young male servant, the page. In Moll's case, Laxton *tries* to subordinate her with the angels that turn a free woman into a whore. The most sexually shunned woman is, predictably, the outspoken, publicly visible, economically productive wife. She is legitimate, but not entirely subordinate, caught as she is in the nowhere land between the actualities of marriage as a functioning economic institution that demands her visibility and independence and the ideologies of acquiescent femininity associated with the concept of wife.

The play, moreover, while raising quite explicitly the problem of female sexual desire, provides schizophrenic solutions to its satisfaction. While Mary supposedly gets her desire satisfied by marriage, the absence of actual wives in the Wengrave milieu, coupled with Sebastian's pleasure in her page's disguise, makes one wonder whether Mary-as-woman will continue to exist in any real form after marriage, and whether *her* sexual desires will be fulfilled. Certainly the experience of the citizens' wives is not encouraging. Moll, by contrast, resists marriage, knowing that whatever pleasures the institution affords to women are fundamentally premised on her subordination. What remains, for Moll, are the eroticisms of solitary fantasy and self-pleasure. Importantly, no sustaining community of women, parallel to the male homosocial and homosexual networks visible behind the foregrounded heterosexual couplings of the text, exists to absorb Moll. The citizen wives gossip with one another, but are jealous of Moll, and while Moll is kind to Mary, their female friendship does not seem to embrace the degrees of intimacy implied by the presence of a Sir Beauteous Ganymede among the men.

In short, *The Roaring Girl*'s representations of venery are fraught with frustrations and antagonisms. Much more starkly than in Shakespeare's comedies, for example, the idealizations of the heterosexual romance plot clash with the competing investments of male homoeroticism and the negative, satirical conventions by which middle-class marriage was frequently represented in misogynist literature and city comedy. The result is no green world of laughter and fulfilled desire, but the rough inequalities of an urban landscape of friction and of difference, in which desire, especially woman's desire, finds no easy fulfilment.

REFERENCES

Andreadis, Harriette (1989) 'The Sapphic Platonics of Katherine Philips, 1632–1664', *Signs* 15, 1: 34–60.

Austern, Linda (1989) '"Sing Againe Syren": Female Musicians and Sexual Enchantment in Elizabethan Life and Literature', *Renaissance Quarterly* 42: 420–48.

Belsey, Catherine (1985) *The Subject of Tragedy: Identity and Difference in Renaissance Drama*. London and New York: Methuen.

Bray, Alan (1988) *Homosexuality in Renaissance England*, 2nd edn, London: Gay Men's Press.

Bredbeck, Gregory W. (1991) *Sodomy and Interpretation: Marlowe to Milton*, Ithaca: Cornell University Press.

de Lauretis, Teresa (1991) 'Queer Theory: Lesbian and Gay Sexualities, An Introduction', *Differences* 3, 2: iii–xviii.

Florio, John (1598) *A Worlde of Wordes or A Most copious and exact Dictionairie in Italian and English*, London.

Foucault, Michel (1978) *The History of Sexuality: An Introduction*, vol. I, trans. Robert Hurley, New York: Random House.

Garber, Marjorie (1991) 'The logic of the transvestite: *The Roaring Girl*', in David Scott Kastan and Peter Stallybrass (eds). *Staging the Renaissance: Reinterpretations of Elizabethan and Jacobean Drama*, New York and London: Routledge.

Gomme, Andor (ed.) (1976) *The Roaring Girl* by Thomas Middleton and Thomas Dekker, New York: W. W. Norton.

Greenblatt, Stephen (1988) *Shakespearean Negotiations*, Berkeley: University of California Press.

Howard, Jean E. (1988) 'Crossdressing, the theatre, and gender struggle in early modern England', *Shakespeare Quarterly* 39, 4: 418–40.

———(1989) 'Scripts and/versus Playhouses: Ideological Production and the Renaissance Public Stage', *Renaissance Drama* 20: 31–49.

Laqueur, Thomas (1990) *Making Sex: Body and Gender from the Greeks to Freud*, Cambridge, Mass.: Harvard University Press.

Leinwand, Theodore B. (1986) *The City Staged: Jacobean Comedy, 1603–13*, Madison: University of Wisconsin Press.

Lewis, Cynthia (1989) '"Wise Men, Folly'Fall'n": Characters Named Antonio in English Renaissance Drama', *Renaissance Drama* 20: 197–236.

Orgel, Stephen (1989), 'Nobody's perfect', *South Atlantic Quarterly* 88, 1: 7–29.

Rackin, Phyllis (1992) 'Historical Difference/Sexual Difference', in Jean Brink (ed.), *Privileging Gender in Early Modern Britain*, Kirksville, Missouri: Sixteenth Century Journal Publishers.

Rubenstein, Frankie (1989) *A Dictionary of Shakespeare's Sexual Puns and Their Significance*, 2nd edn, London: Macmillan.

Rubin, Gayle (1984) 'Thinking sex: notes for a radical theory of the politics of sexuality', in Carole S. Vance (ed.) *Pleasure and Danger*, Boston: Routledge & Kegan Paul, 267–319.

Saslow, James M. (1977) 'The Tenderest Lover: Saint Sebastian in Renaissance Painting: A Proposed Homoerotic Iconology for North Italian Art 1450–1550', *Gai Saber* 1: 58–66.

Sedgwick, Eve (1990) *Epistemology of the Closet*, Berkeley: University of California Press.

——(1991) 'Jane Austen and the Masturbating Girl', *Critical Inquiry* 17: 818–37.

Sharp, Jane (1671) *The Midwives Book*, London.

Shepherd, Simon (1981) *Amazons and Warrior Women: Varieties of Feminism in Seventeenth Century Drama*, New York: St Martin's.

Smith, Bruce R. (1991) *Homosexual Desire in Shakespeare's England: A Cultural Poetics*, Chicago: University of Chicago Press.

Stallybrass, Peter (1986) 'Patriarchal Territories: The Body Enclosed', in Margaret W. Ferguson, Maureen Quilligan and Nancy Vickers (eds), *Rewriting the Renaissance: The Discourses of Sexual Difference in Early Modern Europe*, Chicago: University of Chicago Press, 123–42.

Traub, Valerie (1992) *Desire and Anxiety: Circulations of Sexuality in Shakespearean Drama*, London and New York: Routledge.

Warner, Michael (1991) 'Introduction: Fear of a Queer Planet', *Social Text* 29: 3–17.

WILLIAM N. WEST

Talking the Talk: Cant on the Jacobean Stage[†]

In 1610 "S.R.," the author of *Martin Markall, Beadle of Bridewell*, curtly explained the function of cant in mainstream sixteenth- and seventeenth-century English society: "If you can cant, you will never work."[1] Cant, also called "pedlars' French" or misidentified as "Gypsy," was supposedly the argot of the criminal subculture of London's vagabonds and beggars, a patois that simultaneously distinguished this underclass and made them dangerously incomprehensible to the law-abiding citizens they preyed upon. According to S.R., cant is a language defined by its negation of other social practices—the use of standard English and work. It is opposed to work, work's alternative. But S.R.'s compressed formula reveals several different attitudes of mainstream London toward the supposed existence of a parallel canting underworld.

First, cant is a marker of distinction.[2] Once you are marked by cant, distinguished as a canter, you have revealed something about your position outside the social organization as conceived by its dominant elements, and therefore you will never hold a legitimate position within that hierarchy. The various texts that record cant

---

† From *English Literary Renaissance* 33.2 (John Wiley and Sons, 2003), pp. 228–51. Reprinted by permission.

1. This essay has benefited greatly from its prehistory as a talk before the Group for Early Modern Studies Annual Conference in 1999, the University of Nevada, Reno, and the University of Colorado at Boulder. I am also deeply grateful for the support of Audrey Lumsden-Kouvel and the Newberry Library and to the Folger Shakespeare Library.

   "S.R." was probably Samuel Rid (according to A. V. Judges, editor of *The Elizabethan Underworld* [New York, 1930], pp. 514–15; henceforth "Judges") or Samuel Rowlands (Paula Blank, *Broken English: Dialects and the Politics of Language in Renaissance Writings* [London, 1996], p. 52). *Martin Markall* comes near the end of a long series of pamphlets which claimed to reveal that language and practices of the London underworld. Such pamphlets had been written since early in the reign of Elizabeth by writers such as Robert Greene and Thomas Dekker, to whose *Bellman of London* (1608) *Martin Markall* particularly replics. Many of these texts, which run the gamut from discussions of cheating at dice or cards, con-games, to histories of notable criminals, are usefully gathered in *Rogues, Vagabonds and Sturdy Beggars*, ed. Arthur Kinney (Barre, Mass., 1973). Also indispensable is the collection of "rogues' literature" assembled in Judges. The desire to gather these texts together was not confined to twentieth century scholars: both Robert Greene and later Thomas Middleton mention a *Black Book*, a complete (although like much of the rogue literature, probably fictional) register of the members and practice of the London Underworld.

2. For a discussion of the theoretical background of the concept of distinction as I am using it here and an exhaustively detailed practical analysis, see Pierre Bourdieu's *Distinction: A Social Critique of the Judgement of Taste*, tr. Richard Nice (Cambridge, Mass., 1984), a case study of taste and class allegiance in France in the 1960s and 1970s. The point that linguistic form serves to distinguish social groups, and that it is deployed self-consciously and reflexively to do so, is argued by Blank with respect to linguistic innovation—including neologism and regional dialect as well as cant—more generally in the sixteenth century, in *Broken English*, pp. 38–40.

also insist on its centrality to criminal and vagabond life. In Ben Jonson's masque *The Gypsies Metamorphosed* (1621), a group of rustics challenges the authenticity of a band of feigned gypsies by asking, "can they cant or mill, are they masters in their arts?"[3] This places the ability to cant on a par with skill in stealing (*milling*, in cant terms) as an identifying mark of the vagabond. Cant is represented as a hidden knowledge not to be shared with law-abiding citizens. According to Thomas Dekker in his pamphlet *O per se O* (1612), one of the ten commandments of the criminal underworld is not to reveal the secrets of cant: "Thou shalt teach no householder to cant, neither confess anything to them, be it never so true, but deny the same with oaths."[4]

Second, S.R.'s aphorism places cant in a subordinate relation to the still-developing standard vernacular English that the Tudor dynasty from Henry VIII onward had consciously labored to produce.[5] S.R. goes on to observe that cant is not even really a language, but a confused *omnium gatherum*, a bastard combination like the dog Latin S.R. uses to describe it: "this their language they spun out of three other tongues, viz., Latin, English, and Dutch—these three especially, notwithstanding some few words they borrowed of the Spanish and the French."[6] Those who cant will never work, in part, because cant itself will never work. It is a kind of hopeless confusion, "without all order and reason."[7] Dekker concurs in *Lantern and Candlelight* (1608): "I see not that it is grounded upon any certain rules."[8] Unlike written languages such as Latin which have a grammar, and English, which was increasingly seen to have a grammar of some kind akin to that of Latin, cant was something changeable, hybrid,

---

3. *The Gypsies Metamorphosed: A Variorum Edition*, ed. George Watson Cole (New York, 1931, rpt. 1966), p. 157. I have modernized the spelling of this text throughout.

4. Dekker, in Judges, p. 378. See also fn. 6 p. 298 for similar warnings.

5. Thomas Harman's epistle to the reader in *A Caveat or Warening for Common Cursetors* (Judges, pp. 66–67) begins with a discussion of the difficulty of orthography and orthepeia in standard English, which is changing so rapidly that he cannot always determine whether to risk incomprehensibility with Latinate words or archaism with Anglo-Saxon ones. Blank, *Broken English*, pp. 22–40, discusses the production of " 'new' vernaculars" as markers of class distinction by educated writers in all genres in the sixteenth century.

6. S.R., in Judges, pp. 398, 421. This complaint is also frequently made about English itself; see Blank, *Broken English*, and John Florio, *Florio His First Fruits* (1578; reprinted as *Memoirs of the Faculty of Literature and Politics of Taihoku Imperial University*, III, 1; ed. Arundell del Re, [Formosa, Japan, 1936]), fol. 50v: "[English] is a language confused, bepieced with many tongues: it taketh many words of the Latin, and mo from the French, and mo from the Italian, and many mo from the Dutch, some also from the Greek, and from the Britain" (text modernized). Cant legitimizes standard English by serving as its still more abject counterpart.

7. William Harrison, quoted in Blank, *Broken English*, p. 54.

8. Thomas Dekker, in Kinney, pp. 214–17. On the supposed disorderliness of cant in comparison with vernaculars like English, see Blank, *Broken English*. Blank also suggests, and I agree, that cant as it is recorded is best seen as an imaginary production of professional writers (p. 58). For a different view of cant, see Bryan Reynolds, "Criminal Cant: Linguistic Innovation and Cultural Dissidence in Early Modern England," *Literature-Interpretation-Theory*, 9 (1999), 369–95.

and confusing: an unproductive and inexpressive "gibberish."[9] Thomas Harman from Kent and one of the earliest writers on cant, describes it in *A Caveat or Warening for Common Cursetors* (1566), as "being half mingled with English when it was familiarly talked" (Judges, p. 114). But this confusion in cant is intentional, and indeed fundamental to the way cant was supposed to function. In *A Manifest Detection of Dice-Play* (1552), one of the earliest books on the underworld and its language, Gilbert Walker declares that cant is a professional jargon like the ones used by many guilds to communicate their specialized crafts (Judges, pp. 35ff.). Harman goes further and claims that cant was devised expressly to conceal the conversations of members of the criminal underclass from their intended victims (Judges, p. 114). S.R. asserts the same: "first of all they think it fit to devise a certain kind of language, to the end their cozenings, knaveries, and villainies might not be so easily perceived and known in places where they come" (Judges, p. 421). Unlike other languages, cant did not develop from human interaction (nor, for that matter, did it decay from some original perfection): it was said by Harman to be the invention of one Cock Lorel, a King of the Beggars from around 1501, whose name also appears in Awdeley, Jonson, and S.R.'s works. From its imagined origins, then, cant is a language that both requires and resists translation into ordinary English. It fails to conform to either of the two most widespread sixteenth-century explanations of language, being neither Adamic, and thus a divine gift, nor the flexible product of human reason and convention. Instead, it combines features of both—it is a conscious act of creation, but an entirely human one—and so negates both indeterminately, as a second Babel (the divine retraction of Adam's gift) and a diabolical inversion of language that conceals rather than expresses meaning (an inversion of a conventional language that supplements a human lack). Cant is a kind of abject language, a mirror reflection that reveals language as something strange and alien.

Third, the antithetical relation of cant to work and society allows it to serve as a synecdoche or metonymy for professional playing. Cant could be represented as existing on a continuum with playing and cheating as forms of deceit: "For the first original ground of cheating is a counterfeit countenance in all things, a study to seem to be, and not to be indeed."[1] Professional players were, of course, legally at risk of falling into the same criminal category as beggars, thieves, and other users of cant throughout the sixteenth century. In particular, one of the arguments regularly raised against professional

---

9. Dekker, *O per se O*, (Judges, p. 367); see also S.R., Judges, p. 421. Blank discusses the topos of the incomprehensibility and disorderliness of cant in *Broken English*, pp. 52–54.
1. Gilbert Walker (?), *A Manifest Detection of Dice-Play* (1552), in Judges, p. 36.

playing was that, like cant, it was by definition not work and so could not be a legitimate investment of labor or source of value. William Prynne's *Histrio-mastix* (1633), a work which encyclopedically rehearses the antitheatrical arguments of the two previous generations, puts this problem neatly: "Stage-plays in their best acception are but vanities or idle creations, which have no price, no worth or value in them; they cannot therefore be vendible because they are not valuable."[2] *The Refutation of the Apology for Actors* (1612), a response to Thomas Heywood's *Apology for Actors* (1612), makes the connection between playing and working manifest; players play so as not to work, as canters cant so as not to have to: "And what difference is there between the one sort and the other, but even none at all? For both alike excheat money from the commonality, and for round sums of silver give them nothing but multitudes of vain and foolish words."[3] Those who cant declare by that gesture their rejection of gainful labor and their socially allotted position and tasks, and instead associate their efforts with parasitism—vagabondage, beggary, and theft. The beggars of Richard Brome's *A Jovial Crew* (1641) themselves enact some of their cant rituals for the entertainment and edification of a local landowner and his family (5. 1).[4] This shared parasitism of beggars, players, and others points toward a final translation of S.R.'s phrase: cant serves as a sign that its speakers will never *need* to work—as a sign of their outsiders' status and as a practical tool for deception, cant will open up other sources of income from preying on more lawful Londoners. Like the players, users of cant were suspiciously successful at supporting themselves in spite of their irregular relation to work.

If cant is not, or does not, work, what made cant so interesting? The same writers who critique cant as disordered do so even as they offer to educate their audiences in the vocabulary and usage of cant. Although Thomas Dekker prefaced his late and largely second-hand *Lantern and Candlelight* (1608) with a claim of novelty, "But I am now to speak of a *People* and of a *Language*, of both which (many thousands of years since that *Wonder* wrought at *Babel*) the world till now never made mention" (Kinney, p. 216), the seemingly unlikely topic of cants proved to be one of the most popular themes of sixteenth-, seventeenth-, and eighteenth-century printing in England, during which period dozens of glossaries, manuals, and cony-catching pamphlets were published, all purporting to reveal

---

2. Quoted by David Mann, *The Elizabethan Player: Contemporary Stage Representations* (London, 1991), p. 96.
3. I[ohn] G[reene], *A Refutation of the Apology for Actors* (1615), p. 37.
4. Richard Brome, *A Jovial Crew*, in *Jacobean and Caroline Comedies*, ed. Robert G. Lawrence (London, 1973).

the mysteries of cant to their readers.[5] Even in 1566, the year Harman published the first glossary of cant, cant could be described as "now being known, and spread abroad," and S.R. notes scornfully that "These volumes and papers now spread everywhere, so that every jack-boy now can say as well as the proudest of that fraternity: 'Will you wap for a win or trin for a make?'"[6]—this despite the dangers that were regularly claimed for those who would reveal the secrets of canting. However exaggerated Harman's and S.R.'s observations of the spread of cant were, they suggest an avid audience for works on canting, not only in print, but on stage. Cant was regularly displayed in the writings of the period not as the abject non-language that it was explicitly described to be, but as a working and potentially threatening project. Writers like S.R., Dekker, Robert Greene, Thomas Middleton, and many others exploited a popular interest in the imaginary field of canting to develop what might be regarded as the "real" working project of cant: the unproductive labor (and the production of delight) of writing and circulating cant in the cony-catching pamphlets, in glossaries, and on stage.

The use of cant on stage has received substantially less attention than the more explicit and fully developed accounts of the printed works. But because theatrical performances of cant generally lack a full explanation of how cant works, they have the advantage, paradoxically, of in part avoiding a recapitulation of the ideologies of cant as garbled, pedestrian, and inefficacious. Instead they represent cant working rather than as static. In addition, as imaginary auditors we ourselves are the objects of the work of cant they display, entranced or bewildered by it as it works on us as a strange tongue. In the early years of the seventeenth century, a standardized scene for the examination and dissemination of cant evolved on the Jacobean stage. In it a canting character glosses (or especially is compelled to gloss) his eccentric language so that its hidden meaning is revealed to onstage characters who ordinarily would not understand it, as well as to the audience.[7] This "canting scene," as I will call it, has analogues in earlier, non-dramatic forms. Glossaries and lexicons of cant appear as early as 1509 with the *Liber*

5. On the cultural significance of the interest in cant, see Reynolds, "Criminal Cant," and Jodi Mikalachki, "Gender, Cant, and Cross-Talking in *The Roaring Girl*," *Renaissance Drama* N.S. 25 (1994), 119–43. The Newberry Library General Catalog lists literally dozens of volumes that concern the vocabulary of canting or "flash," as a comparable language of the eighteenth century was called.

6. Harman, in Judges, p. 117; S.R., in Judges, p. 386.

7. I say "his" because in the (fictional) works I have looked at the primary canter is male. This is in contrast to the observation made by Mikalachki, "Gender, Cant, and Cross-Talking," that canting is explicitly a gendered activity, with all our historical (i.e., documentary rather than fictional) instances of cant coming from women who are interrogated by men. I agree with Mikalachki's astute point that canting is gendered, but disagree with her on the meaning of this gendering.

vagatorum and remain a staple in works on the underworld for the next century; later works on cant are often no more than extensive glossaries.[8] A virtual translation scene between an "upright man" and a "rogue" (cant names for two ranks of criminals), in which each character's utterances are given first in cant and then translated into authorial English, appears in Harman's *A Caveat or Warening for Common Cursetors* and is copied in Dekker's *Lantern and Candlelight*. The dialogue form for translating a conversational situation was also familiar from works like John Florio's *First Fruits* (1578), which offered readers brief scenarios in Italian and then provided facing translations. But the dramatic potential of such a scene, with one character speaking first in the strange tongue of cant and then another character, or even the same character, explaining it, is exploited and brought physically to the stage in scenes from Shakespeare's *Winter's Tale* (1610), Dekker and Middleton's *The Roaring Girl* (1611), Beaumont and Fletcher's *Beggar's Bush* (c. 1611) and Jonson's *The Gypsies Metamorphosed* (1621).

* * *

Dekker and Middleton's *The Roaring Girl* presents the longest of these canting scenes, but it is also fairly typical. Moll is a multiply transgressive figure: quasi-criminal, dressing indiscriminately in male or female clothing, erotically attractive to both sexes, loving to lie, as she says, "o' both sides o' th' bed" (2.2.37),[9] assertively celibate. She is nonetheless in the service of a very conventional comic plot, trying to pair a young man with his girl against the wishes of his father. The play's canting scene (5.1) does nothing to advance this plot, but it confirms Moll's marginal and liminal status at the fringes of both the moneyed class and the disenfranchised criminal underworld. In the company of the protagonist and several of his well-to-do friends, Moll encounters two ruffians in the street, Tearcat and Trapdoor, who are disguised as maimed soldiers in order to beg. Tearcat recognizes Moll and tries to escape her notice by speaking in Dutch (a kind of canting propaedeutic perhaps), but Moll exposes the two men as counterfeits and compels them by bribery and force to teach their cant to her upper-class companions:

MOLL: I hope then you can cant, for by your cudgels, you, sirrah, are an upright man. . . . Sirrah, where's your doxy?—Halt not with me.

8. A. L. Beier, *Masterless Men: The Vagrancy Problem in England,* 1560–1640 (London, 1985), pp. 125–26.
9. Thomas Dekker and Thomas Middleton, *The Roaring Girl,* ed. Paul Mulholland (Manchester, 1987).

ALL: Doxy, Moll? What's that?
MOLL: His wench.
TRAPDOOR: My doxy? I have, by the solomon, a doxy that carries
            a kinchin mort in her slate at her back, besides my
            dell and my dainty wild dell, with all whom I'll
            tumble this next darkman's in the strommel, and
            drink ben booze, and eat a fat gruntling-cheat, a
            cackling-cheat, and a quacking-cheat.
JACK: Here's old cheating! (5.1.158–67)

Moll's first remark alludes to the close link established between
canting and authentic vagabondage—if Trapdoor carries the "cudgels" that distinguish him as "an upright man," a high-ranking under
world member, he must also be able to cant or face punishment
from other beggars as a counterfeit. Moll then explains to her fasci-
nated onstage audience (and the crowd in the theater as well) what
Trapdoor means. To swear by the "solomon" is to swear by the mass;
a "dell" and a "wild dell" are two more kinds of wench that Trapdoor
has access to; "darkman's" is nighttime, "strommel" is straw, and so
on. Through this scene Moll decodes Trapdoor's canting and then
compels further canting from Trapdoor. The scene, then, is not only
an example of canting, but a device for the production of cant.[1]
Trapdoor's example of canting does not communicate any important content to Moll or her friends. It is simply an example of what
cant might sound like.[2] The textbookishness of Trapdoor's speech is
easily recognizable from, for instance, the unnecessary inclusion
of two different kinds of "dell," the parallelism of the three sorts
of "cheat" (meaning simply "thing"), and the repetitive sentence
structure. It is just like a passage from an elementary language textbook; compare, for example, one from Florio's First Fruits: "Loro
hanno vin Chiaretto, vin Rosso, vin Secco, Moscatello, e Malvasia /
They have claret wine, red wine, Sacke, Muscadel, and Malmesey"
(fol. 15). This means that, unlike discourse more typically staged
in Jacobean drama, the cant of this scene does not pretend to
express the desire of any particular individual. In this sense it is
not intended to appear subjective. The "dells" that Trapdoor mentions and his description of his planned activities do not represent
expressions that originate in his character and thus might serve to
define it. They are like the role-playing familiar from a language

1. Blank explores the convincing idea that much of the so-called "recording" of dialects and
   non-normative forms of speech in early modern English is more correctly viewed as the
   production, for their own social advantage, of such forms by their writers (Broken
   English, p. 58). By (re)producing those forms, writers gained a certain authority to speak
   on behalf of (albeit unsympathetically) a marginal social group.
2. Cf. Roland Barthes's dictum of the semiotics of a Latin textbook, which do not communicate what they claim to mean ("I love—you (s.) love—he/she/it loves"), but only the statement "I am a Latin textbook."

class, where we learn to ask for train tickets we do not want to places we are not going—recipes for language-making rather than the use of language as expression. In short, this is language that is *objective*—an object for study and mastery rather than a vehicle for expressing the interior state of a subject. As represented, then, cant is a form in which desire can be expressed rather than the expression of desire—hence the possibility of successful mediation by a translator, and hence the artificiality of the speech-acts that the canter produces.[3]

What the scene claims to teach is cant itself. As I have suggested, this explanation is inadequate, but the pretense of the scene is that the language of the underworld is here opened fictionally to the characters onstage and perhaps to members of the audience. More than that, it inspires in its listeners—or perhaps models for them—strong emotional responses to canting, both a desire to learn cant (*"Jack*: Zounds, I'll give a schoolmaster half a crown a week, and teach me this pedlar's French," [5. 1. 178–79]) and a corresponding revulsion from it, in the very same character (*"Jack*: The grating of ten new cartwheels, and the gruntling of five hundred hogs coming from Romford market, cannot make a worse noise than this canting language does in my ears," [5. 1. 229–32]).

The scene offers in condensed form not merely a lesson in certain cant words and phrases, but a pair of axioms for understanding the entire phenomenon of cant, conceived as a marker of social distinctions. The first key to understanding the phenomenon of cant is to see that, for all its supposed difference, it presents a parallel world to upright London. John Awdeley, for instance, divides his contribution to rogue literature, *The Fraternity of Vagabonds* (1561), into two parts, each of which describes a different, neatly ordered society of thieves with its own hierarchy. At the end of *Martin Markall*, S.R. goes further and provides what amounts to an alternative but parallel history of England, in which the genealogy of the kings of the beggars and thieves, including both popular rebels like Jack Cade and Perkin Warbeck and folkloric heroes like Cock Lorel and Giles Hather, King of the Gypsies, echoes the genealogy of the socially sanctioned monarchs. The prose tracts are also enamored of the rituals of the thieves and beggars that invert and mirror the baptisms, weddings, oaths of fealty, and similar activities of ordinary society. On stage as well, these scenes receive unusual attention, especially the beggars' wedding, solemnized by a patrico, the vagabond version of a priest, or "stalling to the rogue," a ritual admitting a person to

---

3. For the possibility of the statement without a subject, see Gilles Deleuze and Felix Guattari, *A Thousand Plateaus: Capitalism and Schizophrenia*, tr. Brian Massumi (Minneapolis, 1987), p. 265.

the fraternity of vagabonds and thus an official induction to the
world of canting.[4] Moll has this kind of parallel structure in mind
when she explains to the men with her that "I know they have their
orders, offices, / Circuits, and circles, unto which they are bound"
(5.1.330–31). But this parallel world is significant not for what it
suggests about the actual organization of the Elizabethan underworld (or the limitated imaginations of its middling-class writers, or
even the critical possibilities it might offer for the existing order),
but for what this parallel structure means to the translators of cant.[5]
Because it emerges from and responds to a world that mirrors the
world of the writer and audience, cant, the play insists, can be translated without a remainder into mainstream (or aristocratic) speech.
That is, any given passage of cant can be rendered *exactly* into standard English—there are no double meanings or nuances that get
lost in translation, no remainder that escapes translation. In the
prose tracts this assumption is clear from the use of word lists as the
primary device for translating cant; while Florio translates phrases
in his work (although even then the translation is almost word for
word), Harman offers primarily lexical entries, "first plac[ing] things
by their proper names, as an introduction to this peevish speech"
(Judges, p. 114). This in turn means that just as Moll converts
Tearcat's Dutch or Trapdoor's cant into English, or more precisely
converts the speakers of cant into speakers of English, a speaker of
English could potentially become a speaker of cant. Jack Dapper, as
we have seen, is willing to pay for tutoring in cant, and Moll assures
him that it is quite possible:

> When next, my lord, you spy any one of those—
> So he be in his art a scholar—question him;
> Tempt him with gold to open the large book
> Of his close villainies; and you yourself shall cant
> Better than poor Moll can, and know more laws
> Of cheaters, lifters, nips, foists, puggards, curbers,
> With all the devil's blackguard, than it is fit
> Should be discovered to a noble wit.   (5.2.322–29)

---

4. See especially the wedding in Brome's *Jovial Crew*, where the "rightness" of the upright
   wedding is systematically inverted, so that the matron of honor collapses drunk and the
   wedding is called off because the bride is found to be a virgin.
5. On how in rogue literature the organization of vagabonds and beggars was exaggerated
   and "the nightmares of the learned seemed to come true" (Beier, *Masterless Men*, p. 8),
   see Beier, ch. 8, "The underworld uncovered" (pp. 123–45); Joel Samaha, "Gleanings
   from Local Criminal-Court Records: Sedition Amongst the 'Inarticulate' in Elizabethan
   Essex," *Journal of Social History*, 8 (1975), 63; Paul A. Slack, "Vagrants and Vagrancy in
   England, 1598–1664," *Economic History Review*, 27 (1974), 377: "Their descriptions
   were the result of contemporary desires to define and perhaps romanticize the vagrant
   phenomenon, to provide stereotypes in order to make the reality more explicable and
   more palatable."

Harman, too, recognizes that his cant dictionary is only a beginning, but offers it to citizens as a first step toward mastering the language of their predators: "By this little ye may wholly and fully understand their untoward talk and pelting speech" (Judges, p. 117).

The second axiom that the scene from *The Roaring Girl* reveals is that cant relies on secrecy to prey on the legitimate world. Once Moll exposes them and their deceptive language, Trapdoor and Tearcat are rendered harmless; in fact, they reluctantly become implicit allies of the middle-class as they reveal their cant secrets to them. This claim to cant's secrecy is made explicit again in prose works beginning with Harman's, who finds his informants reluctant to reveal the secrets of cant to him, "For they would all say, if the upright men should understand thereof, they should not only be grievously beaten, but put into danger of their lives, by the said upright men" (p. 110).[6] In as much as cant, and indeed the entire apparatus of criminality, in this perspective, works by hiding, tricking, covering, and has no other power, exposing its hidden meanings, as Moll and Trapdoor do, diffuses its threat. As Walker notes, "a falsehood, once detected, can never compass the desired effect" (Judges, p. 36). Since cant expresses nothing truly strange or new—as its ready translation, given the proper key or translator, into English shows—all it is, is secret. With its secrets disclosed, it poses no threat to law-abiding citizens.[7] This is the reason offered by cony-catching pamphlets for their own existence as well: although they record criminal cons and cants, they do so in the service of the dominant culture. With their enemies' stratagems exposed, citizens were better equipped to guard against them. Because the canting scene presents itself as teaching non-criminals how to penetrate the previously secret communications of the criminal underworld, the translation of cant, then, is expansionist or imperialistic.[8] Playtexts and printed works alike repeatedly insist that it is forbidden to reveal cant and that users of cant must have been "stalled to the rogue." The "noble wit" of the audience, with the help of some liminal character, occupies the intellectual turf of the speaking "blackguard"—but in this representation only as a kind of safety precaution, because the blackguard is trying to move in on the citi-

6. Both Harman and Awdeley include introductory messages in which they emphasize the danger their informants undergo in revealing cant to outsiders (Judges, pp. 52, 62). This claim, which is repeated by virtually every cant writer, is part of the mystique of canting— that it is a forbidden knowledge to which its new learners are privileged to gain access.

7. See Cheryl Lynn Ross, "The Plague of *The Alchemist,*" *Renaissance Quarterly,* 41 (1988) on the alchemical and other jargons that Jonson calls "cant." While I do not agree with Ross's conclusions that cant is therefore meaningless, they seem to me to articulate aptly the presuppositions of the period about cant.

8. Stephen Greenblatt discusses both literal and figurative examples of linguistic colonialism in the period, in "Learning to Curse: Aspects of Linguistic Colonialism in the Sixteenth Century," in *Learning to Curse: Essays in Early Modern Culture* (London, 1990).

zen's property. By learning the underworld language of cant a citizen was only setting the scales right, reclaiming, even if proleptically, the belongings that are properly already his or hers. Armed with the knowledge of cant, he or she is in a position to avoid being deprived of his goods through fraud, violence, or theft. It is a kind of intellectual pre-emptive strike.

* * *

But why is cant reproduced at all? Under what circumstances might an upper-class speaker wish to master canting as a practice, rather than merely engage translators like Moll to do it for him? Although Hal's education in "dyeing scarlet" is not strictly cant, it suggests a partial explanation. What we see in *1* and *2 Henry IV* is not Hal's instrumental ability to "drink with any tinker in his own language" so as to be recognized as that man's "sworn brother" (*1 HIV* 2.5.16, 6), but his skill at mastering an erotics of language. While it is not clear what Hal can practically accomplish with his knowledge (his deceit of Falstaff in *2 HIV* seems gratuitous), it is equally clear that his homeliness gains him more than mere domination. It gains him love. People *like* Hal, and most especially the people whose culture Hal is busiest colonizing. The opening scenes of *Henry V* are likewise explicitly charged with language that both expresses and effects desire, not only the often-cited Prologue, but also the description of Henry's language given by the Bishops of Ely and Canterbury: "Hear him but reason in divinity / And, all-admiring, with an inward wish / You would desire the King were made a prelate" (1. 1. 39–41). When Hal's proletarian gestures fail him in his exchange with Williams and the other soldiers in *Henry V*, it may well be because Hal is so adept at speaking the other's language that he has lost the gracious *noblesse oblige* that distinguishes his appearances in Cheapside.

The rest of the canting scene of *The Roaring Girl* further explores this rhetorical erotics of language and its relations to other kinds of eroticism. Moll's translation continues, with Trapdoor producing ever wilder and more extensive examples of cant, until it ends abruptly with a remarkable exchange:

TEARCAT:	And then we'll couch a hogshead under the ruff-mans, and there you shall wap with me, and I'll niggle with you.
MOLL:	Out, you damned impudent rascal! [*Hits and kicks him.*] . . .
LORD NOLAND:	Nay, nay, Moll, why art thou angry? What was his gibberish? (5.1.188–95).

Moll duly restates and translates up to Tearcat's last phrase:

MOLL:	"And there you shall wap with me, and I'll niggle with you,"—and that's all.
BEAUTEOUS GANYMEDE:	Nay, nay, Moll, what's that wap?
JACK:	Nay, teach me what niggling is; I'd fain be niggling.
MOLL:	Wapping and niggling is all one, the rogue my man can tell you.
TRAPDOOR:	'Tis fadoodling, if it please you. (5.1.204–11)

Beauteous Ganymede's question is obviously not a real attempt to find out what wapping is, as Jack's expression of desire to stop talking and start niggling presently reveals; Jack knows just as well as the listener without Moll's telling him what "that wap" is, and Trapdoor's apparently unhelpful glossing seems just as transparent. What is represented here is a moment when Moll's control of the situation is challenged and Moll herself is wrong-footed. Her mastery over the form of canting dissolves before the crudity of the particular content of Trapdoor's utterance. We can recognize that Trapdoor's invitation is sexual without translation, although we are not likely to know exactly how or why. Nor, apparently, is the precise meaning important, or even whether wapping, niggling, and fadoodling all describe the same activity or different ones. This again points to the textbookishness of the example: we have no real propositions for Moll here, just an assertion of some form of power over her by Trapdoor, Beauteous Ganymede, and Jack, on the basis of her unwillingness to translate and their ability to keep using the terms she avoids.[9] The translation of the statement—the province of the prose works—does not express its real meaning in context. Moll, it seems, is reluctant to translate Trapdoor's proposition to her because it is sexual and she is in the company of men. The exchange with the men reinscribes her challenging gender identity back into a simple binary system of dominant men and weaker women. This also clarifies why Beauteous Ganymede is the first to take up Trapdoor's challenge to Moll. Like Moll, Ganymede, as his name implies, does not fit easily into a binary system of gendered erotics divided between women who passively receive sexual attention and men who actively offer it. By embarrassing Moll sexually, Ganymede at once puts her in her place as a woman and asserts his own belonging to the active male group. Earlier in the drama, in much more physically enacted sexual play, the similarly gender-disruptive

9. See Freud, *Jokes and Their Relation to the Unconscious*, tr. James Strachey (New York, 1960), on the aggressive form jokes assume because of their (sexual) content.

Laxton (i.e., Lack-stone, a man missing a testicle) is drawn on and thrashed by Moll when he presumes on her sexual availability (3.1). The give-and-take of language, apparently, offers other challenges and opportunities than that of physical struggle.

Interestingly, this power embedded in cant extends past the gendered form it assumes in this scene to other users of the language in contexts that are not gendered. Discussing the word "niggling" in the glossary of *Martin Markall*, S.R. sniffs that "Niggling . . . is not now used, but wapping" (Judges, p. 408). The real distinction between wapping and niggling, according to S.R., is not sexual or practical at all, but linguistic and cultural; those who mistakenly use the word niggling are revealing their own lack of familiarity with the criminal culture they purport to understand. S.R.'s book presents itself as a *Defense and Answers* to Dekker's *Bellman of London* and *Lantern and Candlelight*, and it argues that Dekker's work is a mere fiction derived from Harman. S.R's own book, in contrast, is accurate and up-to-date: it "enlarge[s Dekker's] dictionary (and Master Harman's) with such words as I think he never heard of, and yet in use, too" (Judges, p. 406), and finds in sexual vocabulary a touchstone to distinguish the true from the false.

But there is yet another play of power in *The Roaring Girl*'s representation of this lesson in cant. So obvious seems the sexual meaning of the terms wapping, niggling, and fadoodling that it is startling to learn that it is illusory. Wapping is not in fact fadoodling, since fadoodling means "nothing," and so the scene's content again changes.[1] In this light Trapdoor would seem to be Moll's ally, attempting to defuse the challenge of Ganymede and Jack by restoring privileged knowledge and the power of authenticity to himself and Moll. The theatrical audience is not likely to see this represented alliance, for they also are marked by it as informed or uninformed insiders like Moll and Trapdoor who recognize this distinction of knowledge or mere pretenders to understanding like Jack or Ganymede. You cannot even recognize the joke as a joke unless you get it. Even this mark of distinction offers no stable ground of meaning, however, as the joke is also immediately resexualized: fadoodling is nothing—or it is *nothing*, Elizabethan slang for female genitals.

My point is not to determine exactly what fadoodling means—or how a particular audience would have interpreted it—but to look at how it means, or more precisely the work it does on stage. The use of

---

1. According to Russell Fraser and Norman Rabkin's note, *Drama of the English Renaissance II: The Stuart Period* (New York, 1976). The *OED* glosses "fadoodle" as "something foolish," citing only a single example from 1670. The word apparently is not even cant. It does not appear in any of the contemporary canting dictionaries.

cant serves as a mark of distinction, a touchstone to divide its listeners, both the represented ones on stage and the real ones in the audience, into groups based on how they understand it. In this case, the mark works without everyone being aware of its working. Those who do not see that wapping is not fadoodling see one scene, while those who do see it see a different scene performed, as well as seeing that the rest of the audience does not understand the scene they see. But in addition to the social distinction provided by this play and echoed in many others, we can see that the mysterious language of cant is sexualized, eroticized, simply because it is alien. The operative principle is that when you can not understand what people are saying, it must be because they're saying something dirty. This principle is still in evidence in some productions and even commentaries on Shakespeare's plays, where one notices a sometimes desperate faith in the "bawdiness" of any phrase not immediately clear from context. For example, in a note to *The Taming of the Shrew*, the editors of the Norton edition gloss a reference to Petruchio's *ropetricks* as "rhetorical or sexual feats" (1.2.107) for no apparent reason— Shakespeare was not the only early modern writer to pun this way on "rhetoric."[2] In many productions innocent or even sexually intended lines have one leg of a *double entendre* kicked out from under them by the nudging and winking of the actors. Instead of concealing the content of criminal conversations, cant begins to look like the determined production of some area of secrecy or mystification, which can then become a locus of erotic (either explicitly sexual, or more generalized) fascination. The "secret" content is not as important as the eroticism of the form of secrecy.

* * *

We could call this the principle of fadoodling, a different way of conceiving the relationship of desire and language. Typically, we see rhetoric as expressing or shaping the desire of some subject. Eros and rhetoric can thus be represented as allied in classical and classicizing language, with rhetoric figured as the purely instrumental instigator or director of desire. But as these examples of cant show, rather than

2. This word has a long history in the commentary tradition, where it has flirted with a sexual meaning; see Brian Morris' Arden 2 edition of *The Taming of The Shrew* (London, 1981) for a full recapitulation (1.2.111). Morris withholds judgment, but seems inclined to think that no sexual meaning is necessary. See also Richard Levin, "Grumio's 'Rope-Tricks' and the Nurse's 'Ropery,'" *Shakespeare Quarterly*, 22 (1971), especially interesting because although Levin's evidence is entirely non-sexual, he concludes somewhat defensively that "this meaning does not contradict the sexual interpretation . . . but provides another, complementary level of humor" (p. 86). If one were inclined to take this passage as an allegory of interpretation, one could argue that rope-tricks are more about rhetoric than about sex.

shaping or intensifying already existent bodily erotics, rhetoric can also become narcissistic, self-directed, and thus come to oppose carnal erotics with its own self-contained circuits of desire, fulfilling them and provoking them anew. What these examples of cant on stage reveal is a discourse in which language itself is recognized as an object of desire. Gender is simply the most widely used frame within which desire is expressed in the culture of early modern Europe, as well as in our own.[3] For instance, Jonson's *Volpone* examines the desire of an absolute miser but quickly translates Volpone's desire for money into merely an instrumental one; it becomes a simple screen that hides his desire for Celia, which in turn is recognized as real and natural. But against this representation of monetary greed as a displacement or perversion of a natural sexual desire, we should place the figure of Epicure Mammon from *The Alchemist*, whose similar financial avarice is reduced, like Volpone's, to a sexual one for Dol Common, but is finally realized, as he describes the culinary and other pleasures that await him and his lover, in an orgasmic effusion of exotic language—the pleasures of which language were, of course, the only real currency that the stage could offer.[4]

* * *

The work of cant on the Jacobean stage, then, is to produce affect free from any immediately discernible content—to reveal the work that words do, purified of reference to things. Cant explores an economics not based merely on materialism as ordinarily defined, but based on the materialism and productivity of language. Because cant is, apparently, nonsensical or non-transparent, it shows only the perlocutionary force of its words, apart from any descriptive meaning.[5] But the force of cant is neither exhausted in referring nor in some form of act. Cant is language, ultimately, that produces effects—affect—by itself. More precisely, cant shows that words have a perlocutionary force aside from having a meaning. Their

3. Michael D. Bristol makes a similar point in "Vernacular Criticism and the Scenes Shakespeare Never Wrote," *Shakespeare Survey*, 53 (2000), where he reads non-scholarly remembrances and accounts of Shakespeare's texts and notes how they marshal "one's own background knowledge about how the world works" (p. 90), which is not always reducible to equations of "sex" and "power" (p. 102).

4. It consistently promised, or threatened, depending on its critic's point of view, a more literally sexual erotics as well. For a meditation on the exciting constructedness of gender and its importance on the early modern stage, see Greenblatt's "Fiction and Friction," in *Shakespearean Negotiations*, pp. 66–94.

5. I borrow the term "perlocutionary" from the work of J. L. Austin, where it stands for one of the three modes of effectivity an utterance may have. Austin distinguishes it from both the grammatical locution or diction of a statement and an "illocutionary" force that categorizes it as some particular type of verbal performance—christening, promising, warning. *How to Do Things with Words*, ed. J. O. Urmson and Marina Sbisà; 2nd ed. (Cambridge, Mass., 1972), esp. pp. 95–102, 110, 115.

force is erotic, producing self-subsisting desire that is regularly figured as sexual, although it is produced and sustained by language
and is lodged in the material fact of language itself. The erotics of
cant are not an expression of desire—cant attracts desire rather than
expressing it. Contrary to the ideology offered by the more fully
worked-out (and hence more fully controlled?) prose tracts, representations of cant on the stage are not a cover for a content that
must remain secret. The work of cant is to be an object, or better, a
practice, that through its unintelligibility lures desire.

JONATHAN GIL HARRIS

[From Terminal to Medicinal Consumption: *The Roaring Girl*][†]

In the city comedies that Middleton wrote before 1610, the accumu-
lation and loss of wealth is a recurrent theme; so it is no surprise that
the wasteful, pathological sense of "consume" features strongly in
their vocabularies.[1] *Michaelmas Term* (1606), for example, associates
the word with the wasting of fortunes: Shortyard prays that the
"mealy moth consume" the goods that Quomodo has offered him
(2.3.180), and Rearage complains that "consumption of the patri-
mony" is an affliction far worse than "consumption of the liver"
(2.1.117–18). The play also associates consumption with a syphilitically coded recklessness of appetite: Salewood, for example, complains that "I'll be damned, an these be not the bones of some quean
that cozened me in her life and now consumes me after death"
(2.1.125–26). Related to such destructive visions of consumption are
a string of metaphors that, as Gail Kern Paster has observed, identify
London and its commercial practices with a devouring, gastronomic
consumption verging on the cannibalistic.[2] The Courtesan's Father,

---

† From "Consumption and Consumption: Thomas Mun, *The Roaring Girl*," chapter 7 of
   Sick Economies: Drama, Mercantilism, and Disease in Shakespeare's England (Philadelphia: University of Pennsylvania Press, 2004). Reprinted with permission of the University of Pennsylvania Press.
1. Margot Heinemann observes that in Middleton's city comedies, "society has ceased to be
   based on inherited status; it is now a trading, venturing society based on exchange and
   credit," *Puritanism and Theatre: Thomas Middleton and Opposition Drama Under the
   Early Stuarts* (Cambridge: Cambridge University Press, 1980), chap. 6, "Money and
   Morals in Middleton's City Comedies," 88–106, esp. 95. See also Brian Gibbons,
   Jacobean City Comedy: A Study of Satiric Plays by Jonson, Marston, and Middleton, 2nd ed.
   (London: Methuen, 1980).
2. Gail Kern Paster, *The Idea of the City in the Age of Shakespeare* (Athens: University of
   Georgia Press, 1985), chap. 6, "Parasites and Sub-Parasites: The City as Predator in Jon-
   son and Middleton," 150–77.

for example, dubs London "This man-devouring city" (2.2.21); and Shortyard, talking to Easy about Quomodo, observes that "you have fell into the hands of a most merciless devourer, the very gull o'the city" (3.4.73–74). Consumption is associated in all these instances not with the removal of luxury goods from circulation, therefore, but with a pathological wasting of wealth and health alike.

In *A Trick to Catch the Old One* (1606), Middleton develops this wasteful vision of consumption in particularly pathological detail. As in *Michaelmas Term*, the dual depletion of wealth and health by the excessive appetite is syphilitically coded. Hence Witgood asks: "Why should a gallant pay but two shillings for his ordinary that nourishes him, and twenty times two for his brothel that consumes him?" (1.1.3–5). The association of consumption with venereal illness is implicitly reinforced by a string of references to Witgood's dealings with the Courtesan. Witgood bitterly asks her, "Hast thou been the secret consumption of my purse, and now com'st thou to undo my last means, my wits?" (1.1.27–28); the Courtesan refers to herself as "the secret consumption of your purse" (1.1.41), and Onesiphorus wonders of Witgood: "I wonder how he breathes: h'as consumed all upon that courtesan!" (1.1.103–4).

Consumption's status as a species of both corporeal and economic sickness is elaborated with most force in *A Trick to Catch the Old One*'s subplot involving the lawyer-cum-usurer Harry Dampit. His is, at least initially, a seeming rags-to-riches story: Witgood says of Dampit that "his own boast is that he came to town but with ten shillings in his purse and now is credibly worth ten thousand pound!" (1.4.24–25). Yet we never see Dampit at the height of his powers. By act 3, he is renting a lodging in a seedy part of London, and his health has degenerated: he is permanently drunk and "very weak, truly; I have not eaten so much as the bulk of an egg these three days" (3.4.16–17). Indeed, for all his usurious consumption of others' money, he has avoided consuming food: "I eat not one penn'ort' of bread these two years. Give me a glass of fresh beer. I am not sick, nor am I not well" (3.4.27–28). As he physically wastes away, Dampit is also economically consumed. When Lamprey visits him in hopes of borrowing a hundred pounds, he replies, with a pun that conjoins the economic and the pathological, "Alas, you come at an ill time; I cannot spare it i'faith" (4.5.23). Dampit's consumptive illness, figured as it is in the familiar language of devouring and wasting, underscores what the play insists on—that consumption is a specifically *endogenous* disorder, arising from internal venal sins rather than trade between nations.

Michaelmas Term and *A Trick to Catch the Old One* are a world apart from Middleton's later collaboration with Thomas Dekker, *The Roaring Girl*, which dramatizes consumption very differently. This shift is partly the result of an interesting generic experiment: the play yokes Middleton's trademark brand of city comedy, brimful with crafty upper-class scoundrels and wasteful consumers of inherited fortunes, with Dekker's distinctive version of citizen comedy, populated by colorful artisans and shopkeepers. The marriage of the two genres results in a recognizably modern treatment of conspicuous luxury consumption. As I shall also argue, though, *The Roaring Girl*'s new vision of consumption is equally enabled by two crucial reworkings of pathological discourse, both of which parallel the gambits employed by Thomas Mun in his defense of the East India Company: first, the association of consumption with foreign agents; second, the recuperation of consumption as a medicinal practice that has both individual and national benefits.

In *The Roaring Girl*, first performed at the Fortune Theater by Prince Henry's Men in 1611,[3] Middleton and Dekker stage practices of consumption that are more familiar to modern eyes. Indeed, the play might be interpreted as an early modern paean to the universal powers of retail therapy. Nearly all *The Roaring Girl*'s characters— gallants and lowlife, men and women, villains and hero(in)es—spend a considerable portion of their time shopping for the ideal luxury commodity. "What d'ye lack?" asks the shopkeeper Mistress Gallipot (2.1.1), and it is a question that seems to possess a corporeal dimension: as many readers have noticed, the line glances slyly at the testicularly challenged Laxton (or "Lacks Stone").[4] But his anatomical lack is emblematic of a more wide-spread insufficiency shared by virtually all the characters, a lack for which material goods provide the fetishistic stopgap throughout *The Roaring Girl*. As a result, the play seems to offer a full-fledged depiction of a consumer society in which luxury items are the engines of both desire and identity.

One of the play's most daring pieces of theatrical business involves the on-stage presentation of three shops—an apothecary's, a feather seller's, and a seamstress's. All three are examples of what was a relatively new phenomenon at the time the play was written: the luxury commodity outlet store. Of course, there were shops in London long before 1611; but the term "shop" was somewhat ambiguous and could also refer to an artisan's workplace, a stall in a market, or even a tray worn round the neck of a hawker. What we now regard as a shop, an indoor space catering primarily to consumers

---

3. I am persuaded by the evidence mustered by Elizabeth Cook for a date of 1611, which makes the play a later one than some earlier editors have adduced. See Thomas Middleton and Thomas Dekker, *The Roaring Girl*, ed. Elizabeth Cook (New York: Norton, 1997), xix. All references to the play are from this edition and are cited in the text.
4. See, for example, Marjorie Garber, "The Logic of the Transvestite," in David Scott Kastan and Peter Stallybrass, eds., *Staging the Renaissance: Reinterpretations of Elizabethan and Jacobean Drama* (London: Routledge, 1991), 221–34, esp. 224–27.

of luxury items, really only began to emerge in the late sixteenth century. The conjunction of three factors—substantial growth in the city's population, greater wealth amongst the middling sort, and increased availability of exotic luxury goods—had resulted in the proliferation throughout London of new retail outlets for foreign spices, drugs, clothes, and other fine items. Strolling shoppers in the early seventeenth century congregated in new fashionable areas dominated by such outlets: Cheapside, the Royal Exchange, and Britain's Burse in the Strand.[5]

The shops of *The Roaring Girl* respond to this new social phenomenon. Just as importantly, they also represent a new *theatrical* phenomenon. Plays from the 1580s and 1590s such as *Arden of Faversham* staged shop fronts but showed little interest in the goods inside them.[6] The most common interior "shop" location in plays from the 1590s was the cobblers' workshop, whose staging foregrounds artisanal labor rather than commodities for consumption. Hence *Locrine* (1591) depicts Strumbo, Dorothie, and Trompart "cobling shooes and singing"; *George a Greene* (1593) shows a shoemaker at work; Robert Wilson's *Cobbler's Prophecy* (1594) depicts Raph Cobler "with his stoole, his implements and shooes"; and Ben Jonson's *Case is Altered* (1597) displays the cobbler Juniper at work in his shop.[7] All of these scenes may depict goods destined to be retailed, but they do not represent processes of consumption; instead, they valorize the mystery of artisanal skill and the bonds of male fellowship. The props called for in these scenes are presented not as magical luxury items, then, but as material embodiments of relations of production.

By contrast, the Jacobean stage tended to parenthesize artisanal labor, reveling instead in the display of luxury commodities in their retail state. The transitional play was arguably Dekker's *Shoemaker's Holiday*, produced by the Admiral's Men in 1599. Like earlier cobbler plays, this citizen comedy depicts a cordwainers' workshop in which the property of male skill is celebrated over and above the

---

5. Dorothy Davis, *A History of Shopping* (London: Routledge and Kegan Paul, 1966), 101, 55. James Knowles describes Britain's Burse as "a commercial Utopia of wonders," including exotic luxury items such as wax fruit, parrots, porcelain, sundials, and gold chains: see "Cecil's Shopping Centre: The Rediscovery of a Ben Jonson Masque in Praise of Trade," *Times Literary Supplement*, February 7,1997, 14–15.
6. *Arden of Faversham*, ed. Hugh Macdonald (London: Malone Society Reprints, 1949), 3.51.1.
7. W. S., *Locrine*, ed. R. B. McKerrow (London: Malone Society Reprints, 1908), ll. 569–70; *George a Greene*, ed. F. W. Clarke (London: Malone Society Reprints, 1911), ll. 971–72; Robert Wilson, *The Cobblers Prophecy* (London, 1594), sigs. A3v–A4; Ben Jonson, *The Case is Altered* (London, 1609 [1597]), sig. A2. For these and all subsequent references to shop scenes, I am profoundly grateful for the generous assistance of Leslie Thomson. The value to the researcher of Alan C. Dessens and Thomson's *Dictionary of Stage Directions from Early Modern English Drama* (Cambridge: Cambridge University Press, 2000) is immeasurable.

physical items that the shoemakers produce. Yet the play also presents a shop retailing fine cloths, in which Jane the shopkeeper asks,
"What is it you lack?"[8] This question is the mantra of subsequent
plays that depict shops selling luxury goods: Mistress Gallipot's
"What d'ye lack?" in *The Roaring Girl* is echoed by a veritable chorus
of shopkeeper characters from Thomas Heywood's *Fayre Mayde of
the Exchange* (1602) to Philip Massinger's *Renegado* (1623).[9]

Contrary to the myth of the bare Shakespearean stage, plays with
shop scenes necessitated a myriad of expensive props. The playing
companies may have been able to furnish from their own stock many
of the scenes requiring the sale of clothes; as Peter Stallybrass has
noted, the early modern theater was in crucial respects an extension
of the English textile industry.[1] But certain other expensive goods
required in shop scenes would have had to be specially procured or
borrowed. This raises the distinct possibility that something resem-
bling modern practices of product placement was a feature of the
early modern theater.[2] The numerous goldsmith shop scenes from
the 1590s to the 1630s, for example, would have necessitated the
conspicuous display of items not normally found in theater companies' playing stock. In light of recent scholarship that has begun to
illuminate the extensive business connections between the theater

8. Thomas Dekker, *The Shoemaker's Holiday*, ed. Anthony Parr, 2nd ed. (New York: Norton,
   1990), 12.22. For an enlargement of the points I make in this paragraph, see also
   Jonathan Gil Harris, "Properties of Skill: Product Placement in Early Artisanal Drama,"
   in Jonathan Gil Harris and Natasha Korda, eds., *Staged Properties in Early Modern
   English Drama* (Cambridge: Cambridge University Press, 2002), 35–66, in which I discuss *The Shoemaker's Holiday's* conflicted attitudes toward property in relation to
   medieval mystery drama's presentation of artisanal skill.
9. Thomas Heywood, *The Fayre Mayde of the Exchange, With the Pleasant Humours of the
   Cripple of Fanchurch* (London, 1607 [1602]), sig. F1; Middleton and Dekker, *The Honest
   Whore, With the Humours of the Patient Man and the Longing Wife* (London, 1604),
   sig. B4; Dekker, *The Honest Whore, Part Two* (London, 1630 [1605]), sig. F2; George Chap-
   man, Ben Jonson, and John Webster, *Eastward Hoe* (London, 1605), sig. A2v; Edward
   Sharpham, *The Fleire* (London, 1607), sig. G2v; Dekker, *A Tragi-Comedy: Called, Match
   Mee in London* (London, 1631 [1611]), sig. C3v; John Cooke, *Greene's Tu Quoque, or
   The Citie Gallant* (London, 1614 [1611]), sig. B1; Middleton and John Webster, *Any
   Thing for a Quiet Life* (London, 1664 [1621]), sig. C3; Philip Massinger *The Renegado*
   (1623), in Daniel J. Vitkus, ed., *Three Turk Plays from Early Modern England: "Sclimas,"
   "A Christian Turned Turk," "The Renegado"* (New York: Columbia University Press, 2000),
   1.3.1.
1. Peter Stallybrass, "Worn Worlds: Clothes and Identity on the Renaissance Stage," in Mar-
   greta de Grazia, Maureen Quilligan, and Peter Stallybrass, eds., *Subject and Object in
   Renaissance Culture* (Cambridge: Cambridge University Press, 1996), 289–320. Seamstress's shops are explicitly called for in the stage directions of not only *The Roaring Girl*
   (2.1.0) but also *The Shoemaker's Holiday*, 12.0, and Thomas Heywood, *The Wise-Woman
   of Hogsdon* (London, 1638 [1604]), sig. A4V. The shop in John Cooke's *Greene's Tu
   Quoque* is explicitly "A Mercers Shop" (sig. B1), and the anonymous play *Knave in the
   Grain* (London, 1625) involves a transaction with a Mercer who retails "Boults of Sattin"
   (sig. l1).
2. See William Ingram, "Robert Keysar, Playhouse Speculator," *Shakespeare Quarterly* 37
   (1986): 476–88; and John H. Astington, "The Career of Andrew Cane, Citizen, Goldsmith, and Player," *MARDIE* (2003): I am grateful to Professor Astington for sharing a
   copy of his paper in advance of its publication.

companies and the London goldsmiths,[3] it is fair to speculate that the theatrical display of expensive goldsmith's wares—for example, the gold plate displayed by apprentices in Heywood's *Edward IV*, the fine wares of the "Goldsmiths shoppe" in Chapman, Jonson, and Webster's *Eastward Hoe*, or the ornate drinking mugs of Jonson's *Epicoene*—may have been part of a commercial quid pro quo: the playing companies obtained goods with which to dazzle their audiences, and the goldsmiths secured an opportunity to advertise their handiwork for free.[4] A similar relationship with London glassmakers may have been required to stage the Tunisian market scene of Massinger's *Renegado*, in which Gazet and Vitelli retail luxury Venetian items, including crystal glasses and a dazzling mirror.[5]

The shops called for in *The Roaring Girl* are likewise brimful with fashionable exotic luxury items that may have required the temporary loan of properties to Prince Henry's Men from private artisans or merchants. The goods retailed by Mistress Overwork in her seamstress's shop are finished cloths imported from the Continent, including "holland linens" and other luxury textiles from the Low Countries—"fine bands and ruffs, fine lawns, fine cambrics" (2.1.2–3).[6] Mistress Tiltyard's feather store retails even more conspicuous luxury items: highly fashionable "spangled" plumage, possibly from Oriental and New World parakeets.[7] But while the company may have possessed sufficient cloth, costumes, and feathers to stock these two shops, it is most likely that the actors would have had to obtain new outlandish properties for Mistress Gallipot's apothecary shop. As we saw in Chapter 5, apothecaries tended to retail exotic commodities; Nathanael Carpenter asserted that "Apothecaries . . . owe most of the medicinable drugges to India."[8] But the apothecary's store also conventionally boasted *wunderkammers* of spectacular goods that were not necessarily for sale, yet

---

3. Thomas Heywood, *Edward IV* (London, 1599), sig. Hiv; Chapman, Jonson, and Webster, *Eastward Hoe*, sig. A2. Juana Green has speculated that the mugs of *Epicoene* may have been provided by Robert Keysar, a master goldsmith who was an organizer of the Children of the Queen's Revels—the company that first performed the play. See her "Properties of Marriage: Proprietary Conflict and the Calculus of Gender in *Epicoene*," in Harris and Korda, eds., *Staged Properties*, 261–87, esp. 269.

4. See Harris, "Properties of Skill," esp. 41–7.

5. Philip Massinger, *The Renegado*, 1.3.2–3.

6. For a discussion of the fashionability of Low Country clothes in early seventeenth-century London, see Ann Rosalind Jones and Peter Stallybrass, *Renaissance Clothing and the Materials of Memory* (Cambridge: Cambridge University Press, 2000), chap. 3, "Yellow Starch: Fabrications of the Jacobean Court," 59–85.

7. See Margaret W. Ferguson, "Feathers and Flies: Aphra Behn and the Seventeenth-Century Trade in Exotica," in de Grazia, Quilligan, and Stallybrass, eds., *Subject and Object in Renaissance Culture*, 235–59; and Jones and Stallybrass, *Renaissance Clothing*, 53.

8. Nathanael Carpenter, *Geography Delineated Forth in Two Bookes, Containing the Spaericall and Topicall Parts Thereof* (Oxford, 1625), sig. G3.

added to the luster of their medicinal wares.[9] In *Romeo and Juliet*, Shakespeare describes "an apothecary" in whose "needy shop a tortoise hung / An alligator stuff'd and other skins" (5.1.37, 42–43); and Thomas Nashe refers to "an Apothecaries Crocodile, or dride *Alligatur*."[1] The staging of apothecaries' shops in the London playhouses may have likewise demanded the display of such trademark properties. In Edward Sharpham's play *The Fleire* (1607), for example, the apothecary Signor Aluno enters "*his shop with wares about him.*"[2] It is quite possible that Mistress Gallipot's shop would have been similarly decorated.

Confronted with the spectacle of the three shops, members of the play's original audiences were given the opportunity to mimic the characters in their perusal of fashionable, eye-catching foreign goods. Such window shopping would not have been confined to the shopkeeper scenes. In addition to the exotic items on display in the apothecary's, seamstress's, and feather seller's shops, the play flaunts a veritable procession of foreign luxury items: the presumably Dutch "falling bands" (1.1.16) that the disguised Mary Fitzallard carries in the first scene; the "cup of rich orleans," a French plum drink, that Neatfoot offers her (1.1.23–24); the "German watch" with which Sir Alexander attempts to bait Moll (4.1.11). Nor should we forget the audience's vicarious, olfactory consumption of the play's omnipresent North American tobacco (or, as it is also called, the "Indian potherbs" [2.1.10–11]), clouds of which are conspicuously exhaled by Laxton, Goshawk, and Moll in several scenes. Thus was the aptly named Fortune Theater turned into an early-seventeenth-century predecessor of the modern shopping mall, and its audiences cast as potential consumers of synesthetic exotica. As Margaret Ferguson has astutely noted of both the *Wunderkammer* and the early modern stage, "Those relatively new European institutions were coming to function as showcases for New World luxury objects."[3] What Ferguson does not spell out, however, are the ways in which such display implicated the theaters in the *interpellation* of consumer desire—desire both for the foreign goods they displayed and for drama itself as a new species of luxury commodity.

The playwrights were all too aware of this latter function. Middleton's opening letter "to the comic play-readers" literally sells the play

9. Some London apothecaries, like James Petiver, earned reputations as collectors of foreign goods; but such goods seem to have been part of the apothecary's traditional paraphernalia. On Petiver, see Marjorie Swann, *Curiosities and Texts: The Culture of Collecting in Early Modern England* (Philadelphia: University of Pennsylvania Press, 2001), 3.
1. Thomas Nashe, *Have With You to Saffron-walden; or, Gabriel Harueys Hunt is vp* (London, 1596), sig. F2.
2. These include boxes of "*Arringus*," bottles of "ciuet," and "spirit of roses"; Sharpham, *The Fleire*, sigs. G2v–G3.
3. Ferguson, "Feathers and Flies," 247.

as a luxury commodity available for consumption, whether in Thomas Archer's "shop in Popes head-pallace, neere the Royall Exchange" (as the 1611 title page says) or in the Fortune Theater. In his letter, Middleton compares the play to new fashions in clothes: "the fashion of play-making I can properly compare to nothing so naturally as the alteration in apparel" (1–3). The "epilogus" likewise compares its version of Moll to "the picture of a woman (every part / Limned to the life) hung out . . . to sell" (2–3). Other references to playgoing in *The Roaring Girl* draw attention to the commodification of the theater as a new luxury consumer item. Mistress Tiltyard refers to the "twelvepenny-stool gentlemen" (2.1.137), who paid what was then a substantial fee for the privilege of sitting onstage during the performances of plays by the children's companies. And Sir Alexander Wengrave, speaking to his party guests, turns *The Roaring Girl's* theatrical consumers into his own expensive tchotchkes: under the pretext of showing the other characters his favorite "parlor," he instead displays the well-dressed audience: "when you look into my galleries, / How bravely they are trimmed up" (1.2.14–15). This is a reminder that early modern audience members paid to see not only the play but also each other. As the actors remark of the "goods" in Sir Alexander's parlor, "these sights are excellent!" (1.2.33).

Consumption, in other words, is not only *The Roaring Girl's* theme; at least in performance, it is also the play's very ontological condition. Yet it is so only catachrestically, for the consumer practices that *The Roaring Girl* foregrounds—the purchase of luxury goods, including the watching of theater's commodified "sights"—do not ever go by the name "consumption" in the play itself. How does *The Roaring Girl's* abiding fascination with what we recognize as practices of consumption square with the pathological discourses of consumption that I have sketched in *Michaelmas Term* and *A Trick to Catch the Old One*? And how might the play look forward to Thomas Mun's conflicted discourses of consumption as both foreign scourge and domestic panacea?

The play's two explicit usages of the term "consumption" and its cognates hark back to Middleton's earlier city comedies. The predatory Laxton, seeking to bleed the Mistress Gallipot of her husband's wealth under the pretext of seducing her, remarks: "She has wit enough to rob her husband, and I ways enough to consume the money" (2.1.93–5). And Master Gallipot fears that his wealth, including "my barns and houses / Yonder at Hockley-hole" are "consumed with fire" (3.2.96–97). These wasteful codings of consumption are implicitly supported by a rash of similar remarks with a pathological edge. Sebastian Wengrave, complaining that his father, Sir Alexander, has refused to allow him to marry Mary Fitzallard, the poor gentlewoman he loves, remarks: "He reckoned up what gold /

This marriage would draw from him, at which he swore, / To lose so much blood could not grieve him more" (1.1.84–86). Sebastian's familiar equation of money with blood is hinted at also in Sir Davy Dapper's complaint about his son Jack's profligate habits. Sir Davy believes these to pathologically consume not only Jack's wealth but also his body:

> A noise of fiddlers, tobacco, wine, and a whore,
> A mercer that will let him take up more,
> Dice, and a water-spaniel with a duck,—oh,
> Bring him abed with these: when his purse jingles,
> Roaring boys follow at's tail, fencers and ningles,
> Beasts Adam ne'er gave name to; these horse-leeches suck
> My son; he being drawn dry, they all live on smoke. (3.3.64–70)

Sir Davy's critique here sounds remarkably like Thomas Mun's blast against "piping and potting." Mun, we remember, asserts that tobacco sends wealth up "in too much Smoake"; he also sees it as robbing the nation of its virility. His remark that tobacco "hath made us effeminate in our Bodies, weak in our Knowledge, poor in our Treasure, declined in our Valour, unfortunate in our Enterprises" (sig. L2)[4] describes to a tee Sir Davy's foppish son: Jack Dapper's jingling "purse" attracts "roaring boys" and "ningles" who [. . .] "suck" him "dry." But Mun's description applies just as well to Laxton, whose dubious virility sees him robbed not only of stones but also of intelligence, money, swordsmanship, and entrepreneurial skill.

Yet even as *The Roaring Girl* anticipates Mun's critiques of the effeminating and enfeebling effects of foreign luxury goods like tobacco, the play also manifests his aversion to restrictions on consumption. Despite Sir Jack Dapper's wasteful behaviors, Moll protects him from his father's mean-spirited attempts to control his spending and punish his profligacy. Instead, the play seems to endorse the voluntarist self-restraint championed by Mun. When Sir Alexander tries to tempt Moll into stealing a golden chain, a ruff, and a German watch, he fails miserably; for she knows how to control herself and her desires. And it is this self-control that distinguishes her consumption from that of the other consumers. Laxton

---

4. Thomas Mun, *A Discourse of Trade, From England Vnto the East-Indies: Answering to Diuerse Obiections Which Are Usually Made Against the Same* (London, 1621). In the chapter from which this piece is excerpted, the section on *The Roaring Girl* is preceded by a discussion of this text. (*Editor's note*).

and Dapper compulsively consume luxury goods to fill a lack that is metaleptically refashioned as their desire's effect as well as its cause. The more they get, the more they lose; witness Laxton, whose testicular "cutting" drives him to crave Moll as a kind of surrogate dildo, a "fat eel between a Dutchman's fingers" (2.1.191–92). But after obtaining money from Mistress Gallipot with which to woo Moll, he is "cut" yet more: "Here's blood would have served me this seven year in broken heads and cut fingers" (3.1.127–28), he exclaims after Moll has roundly beaten and scarred him with her sword, thereby forcing a metaphorical reenactment of his castration: "I yield both purse and body" (3.1.121).

Moll, by contrast, is the sublime object of consumer ideology.[5] An impossibly complete being, she is the one character who cannot answer Mistress Gallipot's question, "what d'ye lack?" because she is represented throughout the play as utterly self-sufficient. Her nickname is Cutpurse, but her own testicular "purse" is not cut. If the play's other characters, by consuming, are castrated as they try to remedy a lack within themselves, Moll's consumption is the mark of a unique hermaphroditic plenitude: her fashionable clothes mark her as "both man and woman" (2.1.220), possessed, in Sir Alexander's words, of "two trinkets" (2.2.82). Sir Alexander's term recalls the mercantilist disdain for luxury "trifles," but it simultaneously images a testicular wholeness that renders Moll's consumption "consummate" rather than "consumptive." Moll is less consumer, perhaps, than phantasmatic consumer icon, immaculate in her trendsetting power: as the tailor tells her, "You change the fashion" (2.2.87–88).[6]

Moll's consummate consumption is evident also in *The Roaring Girl's* treatment of another fashionable commodity: language. Neatfoot the servingman and Jack Dapper are ardent, if awkward, collectors and spenders of the choice term. Likewise, Mistress Overwork says that before she met her husband, she had "my Latin tongue, and a spice of the French" (2.1.356–57). This commodification of fashionable language as foreign "spice" extends also to canting, the lowlife argot that Dapper refers to as "peddlar's French" (5.1.185). In the play's penultimate scene, Jack Dapper tells Lord Noland that

---

5. I am, of course, referring to Slavoj Žižek, *The Sublime Object of Ideology* (London: Verso, 1989).

6. There is a significant body of critical literature on the meanings of Moll's hermaphroditic cross-dressing: see Garber, "Logic of the Transvestite"; Jean E. Howard, "Cross-Dressing, the Theatre, and Gender Struggle in Early Modern England," *Shakespeare Quarterly* 39 (1988), 417–39; and Mary-Beth Rose, "Women in Men's Clothing: Apparel and Social Stability in *The Roaring Girl*," *English Literary Renaissance* 14 (1984): 367–91. All these essays, however, understand Moll's transvestism largely in terms of gender and sexuality. I wish to suggest that if Middleton and Dekker invoke the old Platonic ideal of the "consummate" hermaphrodite, they do so equally in the (no less gendered) economic context of consumption.

"we are making a boon voyage to that nappy land of spice-cakes" (5.1.57–58)—not Cockaigne, let alone the Spice Islands, but Pimlico, a clearinghouse for exotic wares.[7] But the upper-class luxury consumers' planned day trip is interrupted by a chance encounter with the equally exotic commodity of "peddlar's French." Moll apprehends the cony-catchers Trapdoor and Tearcat, and together with them offers a crash course in canting to Jack Dapper's band of voyagers. Defending her possession of such knowledge from charges of moral turpitude, Moll tells Sir Noland:

> Suppose, my lord, you were in Venice—
> LORD NOLAND
> Well.
> MOLL
> If some Italian pander there would tell
> All the close tricks of courtesans, would not you
> Hearken to such a fellow?
> LORD NOLAND
> Yes.
> MOLL
> And here,
> Being come from Venice, to a friend most dear
> That were to travel thither, you would proclaim
> Your knowledge in these villainies, to save
> Your friend from their quick danger. Must you have
> A black ill name, because ill things you know? (5.1.349–57)

Moll presents her skill as a high-minded, nationalistic anthropology, whereby consumption of luxurious (and lecherous) Venetian commodities no longer causes damage but returns wealth to England in the form of protective knowledge. As in Mun's writing, this controlled luxury consumption is presented as a nationalist form of venture capital, according to which an initial loss is the occasion for future revenue—like the profligate Bassanio's shooting of a second arrow as a means of recovering the first and thereby acquiring a fortune (*The Merchant of Venice*, 1.1.140–43).

The healthy consumption of lowlife terms involves an altogether different discourse of consumption from that of *Michaelmas Term* or

---

7. Pimlico, in Hogsdon, seems to have become stereotypically associated with the exotica of other lands. In the anonymous pamphlet *Pimlyco, or Runne Red-Cap: Tis A Mad World at Hogsdon* (London, 1609), the author states: "You that weare out your liues and weary your bodies, in *Discouery of strange Countries*, (been for pleasure or profite) rig out a *Fleet*, and make a *Voiage* to an *Iland* which could neuer be found out by the *Portugals, Spaniards, or Hollanders*, but only (and that now of late) by *Englishmen*. The name of its *Pymlico*" (sig.A2). Interestingly, the pamphlet also presents Pimlico as a competitor with the Fortune Theater (where *The Roaring Girl* was first performed) and the Bull Theater in the display of exotic pleasures: "each afternoone thy *house* being fill / Makes *Fortune* blind, or *Gelds the Bull*" (sig. D2).

A Trick to Catch the Old One. And although the word "consumption" does not figure explicitly in this discourse, we can glimpse its presence in the swarm of eating metaphors that dominates the canting scene. Trapdoor tells Lord Noland: "half a harvest with us, sir, and you shall gabble your bellyful" (5.1.195–96). The harvest of canting terms promised by Trapdoor offers a wholesome repast that safeguards rather than wastes the health of the English body politic. Trapdoor's images of nutritious eating, which resonate also with Dapper's pursuit of "nappy spicecakes," work also to recode "consumption" as a mode of dietary health—just as Mun suggests in *A Discourse of Trade* that "the moderate vse of wholesome Druggs and comfortable Spices" serves not "to surfeit, or to please a lickorish tast (as it often happeneth, with many other fruites and wines) but rather as things most necessarie to preserue their health, and to cure their diseases" (sig. B3v).[8]

   The Roaring Girl's conflicting attitudes toward consumption as both wasteful and nutritive are shadowed by its conflicting attitudes toward the ingestion of poison. On the one hand, Mistress Overwork insists that gustatory consumption can easily become poisonous: berating the predatory Goshawk, she asks him: "hast not thou / Sucked nourishment even underneath this roof, / And turn'd it all to poison?" (4.2.204–6). Yet in the previous scene, speaking of their dependence on Moll Cutpurse, Mary remarks to Sebastian, "No poison, sir, but serves us for some use" (4.1.148). Mary's maxim evokes Paracelsus's theory of the medicinal value of poisons, a version of which also haunts Mun's *Englands Treasure by Forraign Trade.* Something of this attitude also applies to the play's justification for the consumption of "peddlar's French." Valerie Forman has shown how *The Roaring Girl* is preoccupied with issues of commodity exchange and the fungibility of money and goods.[9] But in the play's recuperation of consumption, what is at stake is not straightforward monetary exchange; in the manner of Mun, the play instead invests in the future yield of venture capital. The moral for *The Roaring Girl's* audiences and for Mun's readers is thus the same—nothing ventured, nothing gained; but equally, nothing consumed, nothing ventured. In the process, Middleton and Dekker make a case for the Fortune Theater as a purveyor of luxury commodities that increase the nation's wealth, in the form of knowledge if not of treasure.

* * *

8. For a useful discussion of the links between economic and gastronomic consumption in early modern drama, see Margaret Healy, *Fictions of Disease in Early Modern England: Bodies, Plagues, and Politics* (New York: Palgrave, 2001), 202–28.
9. Valerie Forman, "Marked Angels: Counterfeits, Commodities, and *The Roaring Girl*," *Renaissance Quarterly* 54 (2001): 1531–60.

Selected Bibliography

• Indicates works included or excerpted in this Norton Critical Edition

Texts and Textual Criticism

Bowers, Fredson, ed. *The Dramatic Works of Thomas Dekker*. Vol. 3. Cambridge: Cambridge University Press, 1958.

• Bullen, A. H, ed. *The Works of Thomas Middleton*. Vol. 4. Boston: Houghton, 1885. Rpt. New York: AMS Press, 1964.

Cook, Elizabeth, ed. *The Roaring Girl*. 2nd ed. New Mermaids. London: A. & C. Black, 1997.

• Ellis, Havelock, ed. *Thomas Middleton*. Vol. 2. London: T. Fisher Unwin, 1904.

Gomme, Andor, ed. *The Roaring Girl*. New Mermaids. London: A. & C. Black, 1976.

Kahn, Coppélia, ed. *The Roaring Girl, or Moll Cutpurse. Thomas Middleton: The Collected Works*. Gen. eds. Gary Taylor and John Lavagnino. Oxford: Oxford University Press, 2007. 721–78.

Knowles, James, ed. *The Roaring Girl and Other City Comedies*. Oxford: Oxford University Press, 2001.

McLuskie, Kathleen E., and David Bevington, eds. *Plays on Women*. Based on the Revels Plays edition. Manchester: Manchester University Press, 1999.

Mulholland, Paul, ed. *The Roaring Girl*. Revels edition. Manchester: Manchester University Press, 1987.

———. "Some Textual Notes on *The Roaring Girl*." *Library* 32, 5th series (1977): 333–43.

———. "The Date of *The Roaring Girl*." *The Review of English Studies* n.s. 28 (Feb. 1977): 18–31.

———. "*The Roaring Girl*: New Readings and Further Notes." *Studies in Bibliography* 37 (1984): 159–70.

Price, George R. "The Manuscript and the Quarto of *The Roaring Girl*." *Library* 11, 5th series (1956): 180–86.

Mary Frith and the Moll Cutpurse Legend

Bunker, Nancy Mohrlock. "Feminine and Fashionable: Regendering the Iconologies of Mary Frith's 'Notorious Reputation'." *Explorations in Renaissance Culture* 31.2 (Winter 2005): 210–57.

- Caulfield, James. "Moll Cut-Purse." *Portraits, Memoirs, and Characters of Remarkable Persons, From the Reign of Edward the Third, to the Revolution.* London, 1794.
- Chamberlain, John. *The Letters of John Chamberlain.* 2 vols. Ed. Norman Egbert McClure. Philadelphia: American Philosophical Society, 1939. Rpt. Westport, CT: Greenwood Press, 1979.

Chandler, Frank Wadleigh. *The Literature of Roguery.* Vol. 1. Boston: Houghton Mifflin, 1907. Rpt. New York: Burt Franklin, 1958.

Dowling, Margaret. "A Note on Moll Cutpurse, 'The Roaring Girl.'" *Review of English Studies* 10, old series (1934): 67–71.

Eccles, Mark. "Mary Frith, The Roaring Girl." *Notes and Queries* 32.1 (March 1985): 65–66.

Fincham, Francis W. X. "Notes from the Ecclesiastical Court Records at Somerset House." *Transactions of the Royal Historical Society* 4, 4th series (1921): 103–39.

Freeman, Arthur. "The Roaring Girl." *Elizabeth's Misfits: Brief Lives of English Eccentrics, Exploiters, Rogues, and Failures, 1580–1660.* New York: Garland, 1978. 189–214.

Frith, Valerie. "'Never was any woman like her': Mary Frith, Commonly Called Mal Cutpurse." *Women & History: Voices of Early Modern England.* Ed. Valerie Frith. Toronto: Coach House Press, 1995. 239–57.

Hutchings, Mark. "Mary Frith at the Fortune." *Early Theatre* 10.1 (2007): 89–108.
- Johnson, Charles. "The Life of Mol Cutpurse, a Pickpocket and Highwaywoman." *A General History of the Lives and Adventures of the Most Famous Highwaymen, Murderers, Street-robbers, etc.* London, 1734.

Korda, Natasha. "The Case of Moll Frith: Women's Work and the 'All-Male Stage'." *Women Players in England, 1500–1660: Beyond the All-Male Stage.* Ed. Peter Parolin and Pamela Allen Brown. Burlington, VT: Ashgate, 2005. 71–87.
- "Moll Cutpurse." *Macmillan's Magazine* 72 (May/Oct. 1895): 407–13.

Meadows, George Denis. "Mary Frith, The Roaring Girl." *Elizabethan Quintet.* New York: Macmillan, 1956. 238–63.

Mowry, Melissa. "Thieves, Bawds, and Counterrevolutionary Fantasies: *The Life and Death of Mrs. Mary Frith.*" *Journal for Early Modern Cultural Studies* 5.1 (Spring/Summer 2005): 26–48.
- Nakayama, Randall S., ed. *The Life and Death of Mrs. Mary Frith, Commonly Called Moll Cutpurse.* 1662. New York: Garland, 1993.

Seligmann, Raphael. "With a Sword by Her Side and a Lute in Her Lap: Moll Cutpurse at the Fortune." *Musical Voices of Early Modern Women: Many Headed Melodies.* Ed. Thomasin LaMay. Burlington, VT: Ashgate, 2005. 187–209.

Todd, Janet, and Elizabeth Spearing, eds. *Counterfeit Ladies: The Life and Death of Mal Cutpurse, The Case of Mary Carleton.* New York: New York University Press, 1994.

Ungerer, Gustav. "Mary Frith, Alias Moll Cutpurse, in Life and Literature." *Shakespeare Studies* 28 (2000): 42–84.

The Woman's Champion; or the Strange Wonder Being a true Relation of the mad Pranks, merry Conceits, Politick Figaries, and most unheard Stratagems of Mrs. Mary Frith, commonly called Mall Cutpurse. London, 1662. (a chapbook version of *The Life and Death,* listed above under Nakayama, ed.)

Critical Studies of The Roaring Girl

Baston, Jane. "Rehabilitating Moll's Subversion in *The Roaring Girl.*" *SEL* 37.2 (1997): 317–35.

• Bradbrook, M. C. *The Growth and Structure of Elizabethan Comedy.* 1955. Rpt. London: Chatto and Windus, 1973.

Chakravorty, Swapan. "'Cheaters Booted': A Note on *The Roaring Girl,* V.ii 221." *Notes & Queries* 44.1 (Mar. 1997): 72–75.

———. *Society and Politics in the Plays of Thomas Middleton.* Oxford: Clarendon, 1996.

Champion, Larry S. *Thomas Dekker and the Traditions of English Drama.* New York: Peter Lang, 1985.

• Cheney, Patrick. "Moll Cutpurse as Hermaphrodite in Dekker and Middleton's *The Roaring Girl.*" *Renaissance and Reformation* 7.2 (May 1983): 120–34.

Comensoli, Viviana. "Play-making, Domestic Conduct, and the Multiple Plot in *The Roaring Girl.*" *SEL* 27.2 (1987): 249–66.

Cressy, David. "Gender Trouble and Cross-Dressing in Early Modern England." *Journal of British Studies* 35.4 (1996): 438–65.

Dawson, Anthony B. "Mistris Hic & Haec: Representations of Moll Frith." *SEL* 33.2 (1993): 385–404.

DiGangi, Mario. "Sexual Slander and Working Women in *The Roaring Girl.*" *Renaissance Drama* 32 (2003): 147–76.

Dollimore, Jonathan. *Sexual Dissidence: Augustine to Wilde, Freud to Foucault.* Oxford: Clarendon, 1991.

• ——— "Subjectivity, Sexuality, and Transgression: The Jacobean Connection." *Renaissance Drama* 17 (1986): 53–81.

Dynes, William R. "The Trickster-Figure in Jacobean City Comedy." *SEL* 33.2 (1993): 365–84.

Easterling, Heather C. *Parsing the City: Jonson, Middleton, Dekker, and City Comedy's London as Language.* New York: Routledge, 2007.

Eastwood, Adrienne L. "Controversy and the Single Woman in *The Maid's Tragedy* and *The Roaring Girl.*" *Rocky Mountain Review of Language and Literature* 58.2 (2004): 7–27.

• Eliot, T. S. *Elizabethan Essays.* 1934. Rpt. New York: Haskell House, 1964.

Findlay, Alison. *A Feminist Perspective on Renaissance Drama.* Oxford: Blackwell, 1999.

Forman, Valerie. "Marked Angels: Counterfeits, Commodities, and *The Roaring Girl.*" *Renaissance Quarterly* 54.4 (2001): 1531–60.

Garber, Marjorie. "The Logic of the Transvestite: *The Roaring Girl.*" *Staging the Renaissance: Reinterpretations of Elizabethan and Jacobean Drama.* Ed. David Scott Kastan and Peter Stallybrass. New York: Routledge, 1991. 221–34.

Gilbert, Ruth. *Early Modern Hermaphrodites: Sex and Other Stories.* New York: Palgrave, 2002.

• Harris, Jonathan Gil. *Sick Economies: Drama, Mercantilism, and Disease in Shakespeare's England.* Philadelphia: University of Pennsylvania Press, 2004.

Heller, Herbert Jack. *Penitent Brothellers: Grace, Sexuality, and Genre in Thomas Middleton's City Comedies.* Newark: University of Delaware Press, 2000.

Helms, Lorraine. "Roaring Girls and Silent Women: The Politics of Androgyny on the Jacobean Stage." *Women in Theatre.* Themes in Drama vol. 11. Ed. James Redmond. Cambridge: Cambridge University Press, 1989. 59–73.

Hendricks, Margo. "A Painter's Eye: Gender and Middleton and Dekker's *The Roaring Girl.*" *Women's Studies* 18 (1990): 191–203.

Hirschfeld, Heather. "What Do Women Know? *The Roaring Girl* and the Wisdom of Tiresias." *Renaissance Drama* 32 (2003): 123–46.

Howard, Jean E. "Crossdressing, the Theatre, and Gender Struggle in Early Modern England." *Shakespeare Quarterly* 39.4 (1988): 418–40.

• ———. "Sex and Social Conflict: The Erotics of *The Roaring Girl.*" Zimmerman 170–90.

———. *The Stage and Social Struggle in Early Modern England.* New York: Routledge, 1994.

Jacobs, Deborah. "Critical Imperialism and Renaissance Drama: The Case of *The Roaring Girl.*" *Feminism, Bakhtin, and the Dialogic.* Ed. Dale M. Bauer and Susan Jaret McKinstry. Albany: State University of New York Press, 1991. 73–84.

Jankowski, Theodora A. *Pure Resistance: Queer Virginity in Early Modern English Drama.* Philadelphia: University of Pennsylvania Press, 2000.

Jardine, Lisa. *Still Harping on Daughters: Women and Drama in the Age of Shakespeare.* 1983. Rpt. New York: Columbia University Press, 1989.

Kermode, Lloyd Edward. "Destination Doomsday: Desires for Change and Changeable Desires in *The Roaring Girl.*" *English Literary Renaissance* 27.3 (1997): 421–42.

Kitch, Aaron. "The Character of Credit and the Problem of Belief in Middleton's City Comedies." *SEL* 47.2 (2007): 403–26.

Krantz, Susan E. "The Sexual Identities of Moll Cutpurse in Dekker and Middleton's *The Roaring Girl* and in London." *Renaissance and Reformation* 19.1 (1995): 5–20.

• Leggatt, Alexander. *Citizen Comedy in the Age of Shakespeare.* Toronto: University of Toronto Press, 1973.

• Leinwand, Theodore B. *The City Staged: Jacobean Comedy, 1603–1613.* Madison: University of Wisconsin Press, 1986.

McLuskie, Kathleen E. *Dekker and Heywood: Professional Dramatists.* New York: St. Martin's Press, 1994.

McManus, Clare. "*The Roaring Girl* and the London Underworld." *Early Modern English Drama: A Critical Companion.* Ed. Garrett A. Sullivan, Jr., Patrick Cheney, and Andrew Hadfield. Oxford: Oxford University Press, 2006. 213–24.

McNeill, Fiona. "Gynocentric London Spaces: (Re)Locating Masterless Women in Early Stuart Drama." *Renaissance Drama* 28(1997): 195–244.

Menon, Madhavi. *Wanton Words: Rhetoric and Sexuality in English Renaissance Drama.* Toronto: University of Toronto Press, 2004.

Mikalachki, Jodi. "Gender, Cant, and Cross-Talking in *The Roaring Girl.*" *Renaissance Drama* 25 (1994): 119–43.

Miller, Jo E. "Women and the Market in *The Roaring Girl.*" *Renaissance and Reformation* 14.1 (1990): 11–23.

Mousley, Andy. *Renaissance Drama and Contemporary Literary Theory.* New York: St. Martin's Press, 2000.

Mulholland, Paul. "Let Her Roar Again: *The Roaring Girl* Revived." *Research Opportunities in Renaissance Drama* 18 (1985): 15–27.

———. "A Source for the Painter Analogue in the Epilogue of *The Roaring Girl.*" *Modern Language Review* 86.4 (1991): 817–20.

O'Callaghan, Michelle. *Thomas Middleton, Renaissance Dramatist.* Edinburgh: Edinburgh University Press, 2009.

Orgel, Stephen. *Impersonations: The Performance of Gender in Shakespeare's England.* Cambridge: Cambridge University Press, 1996.

———. "The Subtexts of *The Roaring Girl.*" Zimmerman 12–26.

Reynolds, Bryan, and Janna Segal. "The Reckoning of Moll Cutpurse: A Transversal Enterprise." *Rogues and Early Modern English Culture.* Ed. Craig Dionne and Steve Mentz. Ann Arbor: University of Michigan, 2004. 62–97.

• Rose, Mary Beth. "Women in Men's Clothing: Apparel and Social Stability in *The Roaring Girl.*" *English Literary Renaissance* 14.3 (1984): 367–91.

Rustici, Craig. "The Smoking Girl: Tobacco and the Representation of Mary Frith." *Studies in Philology* 96.2 (1999): 159–79.

Sedinger, Tracey. "'If Sight and Shape be True': The Epistemology of Crossdressing on the London Stage." *Shakespeare Quarterly* 48.1 (1997): 63–79.

• Shepherd, Simon. *Amazons and Warrior Women: Varieties of Feminism in Seventeenth-Century Drama.* New York: St. Martin's Press, 1981.

Stage, Kelly J. "*The Roaring Girl*'s London Spaces." *SEL* 49.2 (2009): 417–36.

Stuart, Roxana. "Dueling en Travestie: Cross-Dressed Sword Fighters in Three Jacobean Comedies." *Theatre Studies* 38 (1993): 29–43.

• Swinburne, Algernon Charles. *The Age of Shakespeare.* 1908. Rpt. New York: AMS Press, 1965.

Taylor, Miles. "'Teach Me This Pedlar's French': The Allure of Cant in *The Roaring Girl* and Dekker's Rogue Pamphlets." *Renaissance and Reformation* 29.4 (2005): 107–24.

Thomson, Leslie. "'As Proper a Woman as Any in Cheap': Women in Shops on the Early Modern Stage." *Medieval and Renaissance Drama in England* 16 (2003): 145–61.

Tomasian, Alicia. "Moll's Law: *The Roaring Girl*, Moll Frith, and Corrupt Justice from the Streets to the Star Chamber." *Ben Jonson Journal* 15.2 (2008): 205–31.

Twyning, John. *London Dispossessed: Literature and Social Space in the Early Modern City*. New York: St. Martin's Press, 1998.

• West, William N. "Talking the Talk: Cant on the Jacobean Stage." *English Literary Renaissance* 33.2 (2003): 228–51.

Woodbridge, Linda. *Women and the English Renaissance: Literature and the Nature of Womankind, 1540–1620*. Urbana: University of Illinois Press, 1984.

Zimmerman, Susan, ed. *Erotic Politics: Desire on the Renaissance Stage*. New York: Routledge, 1992.